The Transformation of American Air Power

A volume in the series

<small>CORNELL STUDIES IN SECURITY AFFAIRS</small>

edited by Robert J. Art, Robert Jervis, *and* Stephen M. Walt

A full list of titles in the series appears at the end of the book.

The *Transformation* of *American Air Power*

BENJAMIN S. LAMBETH

A RAND RESEARCH STUDY

Cornell University Press

ITHACA AND LONDON

First Published 2000 by Cornell University Press

Printed in the United States of America

Library of Congress Cataloging-in-Publication Data

Lambeth, Benjamin S.
    The transformation of American air power / Benjamin S. Lambeth.
        p. cm. — (Cornell studies in security affairs) (A RAND research study)
    Includes bibliographical references and index.
    ISBN 0-8014-3816-0 (cloth : alk. paper)
        1. United States. Air Force. 2. Air power—United States. 3. United States—History,
    Military—20th century. I. Title. II. Series. III. Series: A RAND research study
        UG633 .L26 2000
        358.4'00973—dc21   00-009529

Cloth printing   10   9   8   7   6   5   4   3   2   1

To my mother and the memory of my father

Contents

Preface

This book describes the evolution of American air power from the time of U.S. involvement in Southeast Asia a generation ago to the dawning of the 21st century. More specifically, it reviews the deficiencies of American air power that were unmasked during the failed Vietnam experience, explores the many initiatives that were subsequently undertaken to correct those shortcomings, explains the reasons for air power's spectacular performance during the 1991 Persian Gulf war, and considers the growing role of space in U.S. and allied military operations of all types. In addition, the book examines the continuing controversy over air power and its combat potential relative to that of other force elements, an issue that has dominated the U.S. defense debate ever since the successful conclusion of Operation Desert Storm. Its aim is to cast light on a basic question: Should air and space assets continue to be viewed as support for surface forces, or can they now, at least in some circumstances, achieve strategic effects directly and thereby set the conditions for victory in joint warfare?

Many people are due special note for having helped to energize and guide this work during its four-year evolution. First and foremost, I express my thanks to General Ronald Fogleman, USAF (Ret.), who blessed this endeavor in 1996 during his tenure as U.S. Air Force chief of staff and, in so doing, was principally responsible for making my writing of the book possible. I am also grateful for the help I received toward fine-tuning the book's outline during a two-day air power conference in London sponsored by the Royal Air Force in September 1996. Among those attending who offered valuable feedback were Air Chief Marshal Sir Michael Graydon, RAF, chief of the air staff; Air Chief Marshal Sir Patrick Hine, RAF (Ret.); Air Vice Marshal Tony Mason, RAF (Ret.); Group Captain Andrew Lambert, director of defense studies, RAF; and Lawrence Freedman, professor of war studies, University of London. Others to whom I owe acknowledgment for their suggestions include General Michael Dugan, USAF (Ret.); Lieutenant General Ervin Rokke, USAF, Colonel Jamie Gough, USAF, and Alan Gropman of National Defense University; Fred Frostic, deputy assistant secretary of defense for plans and requirements; Andrew Marshall, director of net assessment, office of the secretary of defense; Rebecca Grant, IRIS Corporation; and my RAND colleague David Ochmanek.

For having provided helpful reactions to all or parts of an earlier draft, I thank General Richard Hawley, commander, Air Combat Command; General Thomas Moorman, vice chief of staff, Headquarters USAF; General Merrill McPeak, USAF (Ret.); General Joseph Ashy, USAF (Ret.); General Charles Horner, USAF (Ret.); Lieutenant General Buster Glosson, USAF (Ret.); Lieutenant General Stephen Croker, USAF (Ret.); Lieutenant General Joseph Moore, USAF (Ret.); Major General Marvin Esmond, USAF, commander, Air Warfare Center; Major General Perry Smith, USAF (Ret.); Major General Jasper Welch, Jr., USAF (Ret.); Major Generals Gregory Martin and Bruce Carlson, successive directors of operational requirements, Headquarters USAF; Major General Donald Shepperd, director, Air National Guard; and Brigadier General John Barry, USAF, commander, 56th Fighter Wing.

I am also grateful for the many suggestions for improving the book that I received from Brigadier General David Deptula, Colonel Charles Westenhoff, and Lieutenant Colonel Steve McNamara, office of the deputy chief of staff for air and space operations, Headquarters USAF; Colonels Doug Fraser and Mike Worden, successive staff group heads in the office of the chief of staff, Headquarters USAF; Lieutenant Colonel Gregg Billman, Majors Mitchell Ackerman, Mark Alred, Jeff Gruner, and Mark Moore, and Captains Rob Evans and Mike Smith, USAF Weapons School; Lieutenant Colonel Randy Roebuck and Major J. J. Hernandez, 184th Bomb Wing, Kansas Air National Guard; Colonel Richard Skinner, office of the principal deputy assistant secretary of the Air Force for acquisition; George Bradley III, director of history, Air Force Space Command; Lieutenant Colonel Forrest Morgan, strategy and policy division, Headquarters USAF; Alan Gropman, National Defense University; Price Bingham, Robert Haffa, Gordon Jenkins, Chip Pickett, and Barry Watts, Northrop Grumman Corporation; Karl Mueller, School of Advanced Airpower Studies (SAAS), Air University; Colonel Robert Owen, former dean of SAAS; Lieutenant Colonel Evan Hoapili and Major Cynthia McKinley, Headquarters Air Force Space Command; Colonel Don Sexton, directorate of operational requirements, Headquarters USAF; Lieutenant Colonel Steve Chabolla, 1998 Air Force fellow at RAND; Colonel Roseanne Bailey, USAF, deputy commander for maintenance, 354th Fighter Wing; Lieutenant Colonel Larry Weaver, USAF, office of the under secretary of defense for policy; David MacIsaac, former professor of history, U.S. Air Force Academy; Colonel Joel Martel, French Air Force research associate at RAND for 1998; and my RAND colleagues Nora Bensahel, Russ Glenn, Jon Grossman, Stephen Hosmer, Jeff Huff, Bill Naslund, David Ochmanek, Bill O'Malley, Jed Peters, Bob Preston, John Stillion, Jack Stockfisch, Alan Vick, and Skip Williams.

In addition, I acknowledge the support I received from Colonel Dennis Drew, USAF (Ret.), associate dean of SAAS, who organized a faculty seminar for me to discuss my research when I visited Maxwell Air Force Base (AFB) in January 1997, and Professor David Mets and the students in his SAAS air power theory course, the latter of whom were invited to critique an earlier version of this book as a final exam exercise and who shared with me their reactions during an often pointedly critical roundtable discussion at Maxwell in May 1998.

Beyond that, I am indebted to the Council on Foreign Relations for having convened a day-long author's review panel on behalf of my manuscript at its Washington office in November 1997. Members of that panel who read and commented on the draft included General Charles Boyd, USAF (Ret.), former deputy commander in chief, U.S. European Command; Robert Ellsworth, former deputy secretary of defense; Alton Frye, John Hillen, and Colonel Frank Klotz, USAF, Council on Foreign Relations; Andrew Marshall, director of net assessment, office of the secretary of defense; General Edward Meyer, USA (Ret.), former Army chief of staff; Admiral Stansfield Turner, USN (Ret.), former director of the Central Intelligence Agency; and General Larry Welch, USAF (Ret.), former Air Force chief of staff. General Welch, in particular, provided me with a searching written response that proved uniquely helpful in sharpening the book's focus.

I am similarly indebted to Major General Eitan Ben-Eliahu, commanding officer of the Israeli Air Force (IAF), who invited me to brief the highlights of my research to the entire IAF leadership at a roundtable session during his weekly staff meeting at IAF headquarters in Tel Aviv in October 1999, just after I had completed the initial draft of my chapter on NATO's air war for Kosovo. Finally, I owe thanks to Thomas Henriksen, associate director of the Hoover Institution at Stanford University, who kindly extended to me an opportunity to be a visiting scholar at Hoover in 1997 while I was writing the first draft of this book and who later organized a seminar for me at Hoover in April 2000, attended by Hoover's military fellows and former Secretary of Defense William Perry, to offer me critical feedback on my Kosovo chapter.

In addition to the many reactions from various Air Force readers noted already, I sought a cross section of responses from people of other backgrounds who might not so readily share all of my beliefs and assumptions. Although this book is about air power, not land or sea power or, in the first instance at least, joint-force employment, I nonetheless wanted critical feedback from credible professionals of different service outlooks. Toward that end, I received helpful reactions from General John Tilelli, USA, commander in chief, U.S. Forces in Korea; General Terrence Dake, USMC, assistant Marine Corps commandant; General Wayne Downing, USA (Ret.), former commander in chief, U.S. Special Operations Command; Vice Admiral Michael Bowman, USN, Commander, Naval Air Forces, U.S. Pacific Fleet; Colonel Alan Stolberg, USA, Headquarters U.S. European Command; Captain Gerald Mittendorff, USN (Ret.); and Commander Glenn Krumel, USN, RAND's Navy Executive Fellow in 1994. Not all of these individuals (or, for that matter, any of the others noted) would agree with every point in the pages that follow. Indeed, some would disagree strenuously with parts of the book's argument. All the same, they were uniformly helpful in ensuring that I bend every effort to be fair to their service's positions in the roles and resources debate and that I characterize U.S. air power in a manner that captured not only its recently acquired strengths but also its continued limitations. How well I succeeded in that effort will be for them and others to judge.

Last, I express my appreciation to RAND management for having granted me a year's leave of absence in 1997 to write the first draft of this book, as well as for having provided me with generous additional support over the ensuing three years that enabled me to complete it. I thank Robert Jervis of Columbia University, Roger Haydon, my editor at Cornell University Press, and Mary Babcock for their help in putting the final touches on the manuscript. I also thank Guy Aceto, art director at *Air Force Magazine*, who kindly allowed me free rein of his uncommonly rich file of military aviation photography to assemble the photo gallery included herein.

Although primarily a result of research, this book has been informed as well by a RAND career's worth of firsthand exposure to the cutting edge of military aviation in all combat air arms of the U.S. Air Force, Navy, and Marine Corps, as well as with the Royal Air Force, the Canadian Forces, the German Luftwaffe, the Royal Australian Air Force, the Royal Netherlands Air Force, and the Israeli Air Force. That exposure has included, since 1976, the opportunity to fly on some 280 operational training missions, including missile firings and live weapons drops on tactical targets, in more than 35 different types of fighter, attack, and jet trainer aircraft worldwide. In addition, it has included front-seat or left-seat experience in the T-37, T-38, F-111, F-5, F-104, and F/A-18 with the U.S. Air Force, Canadian Forces, and Royal Australian Air Force and in the MiG-21 and MiG-23 with the Mikoyan Design Bureau in Russia. It also has included time in the fighter academic environment, notably attendance at the U.S. Air Force's Tactical Fighter Weapons and Tactics Course, the Aerospace Defense Command's Senior Officers' Course, and portions of Navy Fighter Weapons School (Topgun) and the Weapons and Tactics Instructor (WTI) course offered by Marine Aviation Weapons and Tactics Squadron One (MAWTS-1).

While researching and writing this book, I had the good fortune to fly on F-15 air-to-air training missions with the 33rd Fighter Wing at Eglin AFB, Florida, and the 154th Composite Wing at Hickam AFB, Hawaii; multiple day and night F-16 air-to-ground sorties with the 150th Fighter Group, Kirtland AFB, New Mexico; an F-16 Aggressor sortie in support of a Red Flag exercise and F-15E, F-16CJ, and E-3 AWACS (airborne warning and control system) syllabus sorties with the USAF Weapons School at Nellis AFB, Nevada; an AT-38 basic fighter maneuvers sortie with the 560th Flying Training Squadron at Randolph AFB, Texas; an F-16 close air support training mission immediately below the demilitarized zone with the 51st Fighter Wing, Osan Air Base, South Korea; a medium-altitude F-16 laser-guided bomb delivery training mission with the 31st Fighter Wing, Aviano Air Base, Italy; a combat insertion training mission in the left seat of a C-17 with the 437th Airlift Wing at Charleston AFB, South Carolina; and a six-hour orientation mission in the aircraft commander's seat of a B-1B bomber operated by the 184th Bomb Wing at McConnell AFB, Kansas. Finally, in October 1999 I flew on AH-1 attack helicopter and F/A-18D all-weather strike fighter sorties in connection with the final exercise of WTI course 1-00 at MAWTS-1, which entailed a realistic five-day program aimed at planning and executing integrated air operations involving all functions of Marine aviation. These hands-on flying opportunities brought me up-to-date with virtually the entire spectrum of current Air Force and Marine Corps mission employment activity. I need hardly say that I am greatly beholden to the leaders of all the U.S. and allied air forces with which I have been privileged to fly over the past two decades. I hope that at least some of this rare experience for a civilian defense analyst is reflected to useful effect in the pages that follow.

BENJAMIN S. LAMBETH

Santa Monica, California

[1]

Air Power Comes of Age

American air power underwent a quantum leap in credibility after the opening days of Operation Desert Storm in 1991. The convergence of high technology with intensive training and determined strategy, to which the allied coalition's successful air campaign against Saddam Hussein's Iraq attested, bespoke a breakthrough in the strategic effectiveness of American air power after a promising start in World War II and more than three years of misuse in the Rolling Thunder bombing campaign against North Vietnam from 1965 to 1968.[1] The speedy attainment of allied air control over Iraq, and what that allowed American air and space assets to accomplish afterward by way of enabling the prompt achievement of the coalition's objectives on the ground, marked, in the view of many, the final coming of age of air power.

It has not always been that way. Throughout most of the cold war, "strategic" air power tended to be associated exclusively with long-range bombers and nuclear weapons and was treated as an instrument whose sole reason for being was not to be used. Everything else short of "strategic" air power, so defined and understood, was regarded as "tactical" or "theater" air power, whose sole purpose was to support U.S. ground forces in combined-arms *land* warfare. Virtually no consideration was given in U.S. defense planning to the potential ability of conventional air power to achieve strategic effects independently of ground action that might, in and of themselves,

---

[1] On the first count, see Stephen L. McFarland, *America's Pursuit of Precision Bombing, 1910–1945*, Washington, D.C., Smithsonian Institution Press, 1995, and Geoffrey Perret, *Winged Victory: The Army Air Forces in World War II*, New York, Random House, 1993. On the second, see Mark Clodfelter, *The Limits of Air Power: The American Bombing of North Vietnam*, New York, Free Press, 1989.

determine the course and outcome of a campaign or war. To be sure, Western observers marveled at Israel's bold use of its fighters during the opening hours of the Six-Day War in June 1967, destroying Egypt's and Syria's air forces on the ground by surprise and thus ensuring that the remainder of Israel's preemptive attack would be unmolested by enemy air action.[2] By and large, however, despite that remarkable and arguably outcome-determining role, "strategic" air power was thought of almost entirely in nuclear terms. The rest of American combat aviation was relegated to little more than a supporting role in a combined-arms approach to warfare in which infantry and armor constituted the cutting edge of American nonnuclear power.

It was only as the 1991 Gulf war approached that at least some American airmen began to realize that technology trends during the preceding decade may have imparted to American air power a qualitative improvement in its ability to achieve theater joint-force objectives directly.[3] Some in the Air Force even saw the emerging air campaign against Iraq as promising to win the war for the coalition almost single-handedly.[4] For the most part, however, there was rampant uncertainty among Americans as to whether air power could swing the outcome without the need for a major ground campaign and whether the coalition would emerge from the gathering showdown without sustaining substantial losses in both men and materiel. Computer models based on traditional assumptions about attrition warfare predicted allied casualties in the thousands.[5] The final authorizing order endorsed by President George Bush to the allied coalition commander, General H. Norman Schwarzkopf, the day before the war began acknowledged that friendly casualties could run as high as 10 percent of the coalition's fielded ground troops.[6]

[2] For more on this, see Edward Luttwak and Dan Horowitz, *The Israeli Army*, New York, Harper and Row, 1975, pp. 209–298.

[3] Prominent among them was Colonel John A. Warden III, USAF, who was the first to codify this new idea systematically in *The Air Campaign: Planning for Combat*, Washington, D.C., National Defense University Press, 1988.

[4] Most notably, the Air Force chief of staff, General Michael Dugan, told reporters on the record early on during the Desert Shield buildup that the looming air campaign then being planned in the Pentagon would so shatter Iraq's ability to resist that allied land forces could "walk in and not have to fight." Quoted in Rick Atkinson, *Crusade: The Untold Story of the Persian Gulf War*, Boston, Houghton Mifflin, 1993, p. 292. Shortly thereafter, Dugan was relieved by Secretary of Defense Dick Cheney for usurping the prerogatives of the president and other senior civilian leaders in disclosing U.S. contingency plans.

[5] Jerry Seper, "Deadly Vigil in Iraqi Bunkers," *Washington Times*, January 24, 1991.

[6] John H. Cushman, Jr., "Pentagon Report on Persian Gulf War: A Few Surprises and Some Silences," *New York Times*, April 11, 1992. According to the chairman of the Joint Chiefs of Staff, Army General Colin Powell, Schwarzkopf's personal estimate to Cheney was 5,000 casualties. Powell said that his own personal estimate was 3,000 killed, wounded, or missing. Colin Powell, *My American Journey*, New York, Random House, 1995, pp. 498–499.

Despite this concern, there was no denying the effect that initial air operations had in shaping the subsequent course of the war. The opening coalition attacks against Iraq's command and control facilities and integrated air defenses proved uniformly successful, with some 800 combat sorties launched in the blackness of night in radio silence against Iraq's most militarily critical targets and only one coalition aircraft lost—a Navy F/A-18, presumably to a lucky infrared missile shot from an Iraqi MiG-25.[7] Over the next three days, the air campaign systematically struck at the entire spectrum of Iraq's strategic and operational assets, gaining unchallenged control of the air for the coalition and the freedom to operate with near impunity against Iraq's airfields, fielded ground forces, and other targets of military interest.

After the cease-fire was declared five weeks later, most observers acknowledged the important role played by *all* allied force elements in producing Iraq's military defeat, albeit with often widely differing interpretations, typically forming along service lines, regarding the relative weight carried by those various force elements. Nevertheless, the predominant view was summed up in a comment by retired Royal Air Force (RAF) Air Vice Marshal Tony Mason that "the Gulf war marked the apotheosis of twentieth-century air power."[8] The only unsettled question, then as now, was whether, in the words of a U.S. Air Force air power theorist, Desert Storm symbolized not only a transformation of American air power but also "the domination of air power and a new paradigm of warfare" presaging "a fundamental shift in the way many wars will be conducted and the need for a new way of thinking about military operations."[9]

In the early aftermath of the Gulf war, there seemed ground for guarded hope that the American defense community might have taken due note of that experience and seen in it the value of a seamless integration of *all* combat elements—in the right mix and at the right time—to produce an outcome such as the world witnessed against Iraq. Yet if air power had acquired a new mystique in the public's eye, and perhaps in the perceptions of future troublemakers around the world as well, things all too soon reverted to form within the Washington policy community. Because of air power's much-expanded lethality and effectiveness, as demonstrated repeatedly

[7] Although the exact cause of the downing of this aircraft remains one of the unsolved mysteries of the Gulf war, those who have studied the event tend to suspect that it most likely was shot down by a long-range infrared AA-6 air-to-air missile cued by the MiG's infrared search and tracking system. The absence of active radar illumination and the infrared missile's passive homing system would have accounted for the lack of any warning of the imminent attack.

[8] Air Vice Marshal R. A. Mason, RAF (Ret.), "The Air War in the Gulf," *Survival*, May/June 1991, p. 225.

[9] Colonel Dennis Drew, USAF (Ret.), "Desert Storm as a Symbol," *Airpower Journal*, Fall 1992, pp. 6, 13.

throughout the Gulf war, claims asserting its heightened relevance and importance triggered intense infighting among the services as post–cold war defense spending began to decline and as each service sought to protect its perceived share of the credit for the war's outcome—and, in some cases, its increasingly threatened program equities and budget shares.

In one of the first rounds fired in the post–Gulf war interservice debate over who did what in Desert Storm, the Air Force chief of staff, General Merrill McPeak, gave a widely publicized briefing extolling the accomplishments of air power in which he spoke, perhaps unconsciously, of the air "campaign" but only of a ground "operation." [10] That distinction may have seemed fair enough under the circumstances, considering that the air war lasted 37 days while the combined-arms ground offensive took only 4 days. Nevertheless, it was bound to push Army hot buttons. His comment that most directly touched Army sensitivities, however, came in reply to a query from a reporter as to whether, had the air campaign been allowed to continue, Iraq's forces could have been defeated without an allied ground offensive. McPeak replied that his "private conviction" was that Desert Storm had been "the first time in history that a field army has been defeated by air power." [11] His words were chosen carefully so as not to appear to suggest that air power had won the war single-handedly. McPeak further hastened to stipulate that "there are some things air power can do and does very well and some things it can't do, and we should never expect it to do very well, and that is to move in on the terrain and dictate terms to the enemy. Our ground forces did that," he conceded, and "they did a remarkable job."

Nevertheless, the fight was on. Those in the Army who saw their own image of warfare threatened by McPeak's outspoken claims responded that the air campaign had been little more than a sideshow to the main event and that the Air Force had, in effect, been off fighting its own private war while allied ground units did the work that mattered most. They further countered that organic Army assets such as tanks and attack helicopters, rather than the coalition's fixed-wing aircraft, were principally responsible for routing and destroying Saddam Hussein's ground forces.

Later, McPeak put down an even more provocative marker when he declared that air power in Desert Storm "came of age as a decisive element in combined-arms warfare" and showed its capability of "dominating warfare to achieve major international objectives." Again, the Air Force chief made a point to stress that he had said "in combined-arms warfare," and he praised both the "magnificent ground attack through Kuwait and Iraq" by

[10] General Merrill A. McPeak, USAF (Ret.), *Selected Works 1990–1994*, Maxwell AFB, Ala., Air University Press, August 1995, p. 18.

[11] Ibid., p. 47.

U.S. Army and Marine forces and "the absolutely leakproof blockade imposed by our sailors." He further granted that "there will be other contingencies in which we airmen play only a supporting role."[12] Such attempts at appearing to be evenhanded, however, were soon lost in the noise. What was heard loudest and remembered most from McPeak's self-described "mother of all briefings" was his assertion that "this time our number was called, we carried the ball, and we scored."

Predictably, the bitter enmity aroused by such contentious claims as to what allied air power had accomplished in Desert Storm was starkly reflected in the internecine jockeying that accompanied the preparation of the Defense Department's report on the war ordered by Congress through Title V of the 1991 National Defense Authorization Act. The drafting of that so-called Title V report, entitled *Conduct of the Persian Gulf Conflict*, was dogged throughout by interagency and interservice infighting. Typical of the many instances of such friction was an early effort by Navy and Marine participants to downgrade the role played by the joint-force air component commander (JFACC), Air Force Lieutenant General Charles Horner, from "commander" to that of a mere "coordinator."[13] In another such example, one account spoke of an Army demand that the coalition's bombing of Iraq only be classed as an "operation" rather than an "air campaign," since in Army parlance no less than in that of the Air Force a *campaign* is the main event, whereas an *operation* merely serves the campaign's objectives.[14]

The release of the Title V report, a committee product cobbled together by no fewer than three dozen military drafters under the direction of the office of the secretary of defense, was delayed nearly three months beyond its January 15, 1992 deadline levied by Congress because of "hundreds" of such alleged disputes over how the war had been fought and what was to be learned from it. In characteristic bureaucratic fashion, most such disputes resulted either in neutral compromise language or in the elimination of any reference to the contested subject.[15] In his overview of the report, Secretary of Defense Dick Cheney declared as his personal belief that the decisiveness of the coalition's win had been "attributable in large measure to the extraordinary effectiveness of air power."[16] That notwithstanding, against 135 pages on the air war, the report devoted 100 pages to the ground war and 85 to naval operations, suggesting that the final Title V product was

---

[12] Ibid., p. 51.

[13] Barbara Opall, "Pentagon Gulf War Report May Ease Service Discord," *Defense News*, January 13, 1992, p. 3.

[14] See Barton Gellman, "Disputes Delay Gulf War History," *Washington Post*, January 28, 1992.

[15] Barton Gellman, "Gulf War Failures Cited," *Washington Post*, April 11, 1992.

[16] Cushman, "Pentagon Report on Persian Gulf War: A Few Surprises and Some Silences."

more a compromise document than a conclusive U.S. government statement of what had actually happened in the war and what it suggested for future U.S. defense planning.

Since then, a high-stakes controversy has emerged in the United States centering on how best to apportion operational roles and budget shares among the four services at a time of uncertain challenges and near-unprecedented fiscal constraints. Naturally, given the predominant role played by the allied air campaign in Desert Storm and the far-reaching claims made on behalf of air power as a result of its performance, the roles and resources controversy has gravitated toward air power as the principal lightning rod for debate. At its core, this debate has come to concern the extent to which the United States can now rely on accurate air-delivered standoff attack weapons in lieu of ground forces to achieve theater combat objectives and minimize the incidence of American casualties.

Against that background, this study seeks to offer a perspective on the nature and meaning of the qualitative improvements that have taken place in American air power since the mid-1970s, with a view toward explaining air power's newly acquired strengths and continued limitations in joint warfare. Its goal is to provide a basis for better understanding of what has increasingly become *the* central issue in American defense planning, namely, the implications of recent and impending improvements in U.S. capabilities to acquire, process, and transmit information about an enemy's forces and to attack those forces with accurate long-range weapons that can only be delivered by air. The study concentrates on air power's combat potential in major theater wars, as opposed to smaller-scale operations and irregular conflicts such as urban combat, since it is the former situations in which the transformation of American air power has registered its greatest effects and is most likely to prove pivotal in determining combat outcomes.[17]

The central argument of the study is that over the past two decades American air power has experienced a nonlinear growth in its ability to contribute to the outcome of joint operations at the higher end of the conflict spectrum, owing to a convergence of low observability to enemy sensors (more commonly known as "stealth"), the ability to attack fixed targets consistently with high accuracy from relatively safe standoff ranges, and the expanded battlespace awareness (sometimes called "information dominance") that has been made possible by recent developments in command,

---

[17] For discussion of these latter topics, see Alan Vick, David T. Orletsky, John Bordeaux, and David A. Shlapak, *Enhancing Air Power's Contribution Against Light Infantry Targets*, Santa Monica, Cal., RAND, MR-697–AF, 1996, and Alan Vick, John Stillion, David Frelinger, Joel S. Kvitky, Benjamin S. Lambeth, Jefferson P. Marquis, and Matthew C. Waxman, *Air Operations in Urban Environments: Exploring New Concepts*, Santa Monica, Calif., RAND, MR-1187–AF, 2000.

control, communications, and computers and in information, surveillance, and reconnaissance (C4ISR for short). As a result of these developments, American air power has finally acquired many of the capabilities needed to make good on the long-standing promise of its pioneers of being able to set the conditions of victory in joint warfare.

In this respect, the study builds on Robert Pape's argument that modern American air power has, among other things, "made it possible to conduct a sustained independent air attrition offensive against a stationary, dug-in ground force and substantially destroy it."[18] Although it takes issue with Pape's treating that capability overly narrowly as "theater" or "tactical" air power rather than as what it really is, namely, air power without qualification, the study concurs wholeheartedly with his broader insistence that such air power "can do most of the work" in joint warfare against organized enemy armored and mechanized forces. Indeed, it is what the air weapon now offers theater commanders by way of combat potential in such situations compared to other forces that involves the highest budgetary stakes and has provoked the greatest controversy in the interservice roles and missions face-off. In essence, American air power now possesses the wherewithal for neutralizing an enemy's military means not through the classic imposition of brute force, but rather through the functional effects achievable by targeting his key vulnerabilities and taking away his capacity for organized military action.

The study further argues that the long-simmering dispute between airmen and land warriors over the efficacy of "strategic bombing," usually defined as air attacks against an enemy's population and urban-industrial infrastructure, has been rendered largely moot as a result of the lately acquired ability of American air power, properly applied, to achieve prompt strategic effects by neutralizing an opponent's military capability. This attribute of air power is a matter of the *objective* being pursued rather than of the targets being attacked. As Colin Gray expressed it, "There is no such beast as 'strategic' air power and there are no such things as 'strategic' targets." It follows, at least in principle, that "all weapons are tactical in their immediate effect and strategic in the consequences of their actions."[19] It is only a question of how successful air power application may be in achieving those effects and consequences from case to case.

Indeed, the study maintains, the age-old claims on behalf of air power's putative effectiveness against so-called strategic *targets* rather than in pursuit of desired strategic *results* has needlessly led airmen into losing posi-

[18] Robert A. Pape, *Bombing to Win: Air Power and Coercion in War*, Ithaca, N.Y., Cornell University Press, 1995, p. 326.
[19] Colin S. Gray, *Explorations in Strategy*, Westport, Conn., Praeger, 1996, p. 61.

[7]

tions in the controversy over the merits of the air weapon compared to other force elements. To take Desert Storm as a case in point, there is no question that the air campaign achieved strategic effects against Iraq's force capabilities. There is also no question that allied attacks against so-called strategic targets (such as electrical power plants, leadership, and transportation nodes in and around Baghdad) had little strategic effect in determining the campaign's ultimately successful outcome.

Finally, the study maintains that the recurrent controversy between some Air Force and Army partisans over the issue of whether air power should be regarded as "supported by" or "supporting of" the land commander has been both misguided and a source of needless friction in the interservice debate. From the vantage point of the theater joint-force commander, the employment of air power, land power, and sea power must *all* be focused, as appropriate in each situation, on the strategic goal of rendering an opponent unable to fight and on the tactical goal of doing so with minimum cost to friendly forces. When viewed this way, there is no such thing as an "air war," a "land war," or a "maritime war," strictly speaking. Rather, there is a single *theater* war in which all force elements have the opportunity, at the joint-force commander's discretion, to achieve the effects of massing forces without having to mass by making the most of new technologies and concepts of operations. What is distinctive about contemporary American air power, this study maintains, is that it has pulled well ahead of surface force elements, both land and maritime, in its *relative* capacity to do this, owing not only to its lately acquired advantages in stealth, precision, and information dominance, but also to its abiding characteristics of speed, range, and flexibility.

The study's focus solely on American air power is deliberate for two reasons. First, despite much ongoing activity in air power enhancement among the developed countries around the world, the United States unquestionably is home to most of the cutting-edge work that is now being done in this regard. To note one example, only the United States can afford to pursue such high-end stealth applications as those currently embodied in the F-117, B-2, and F-22 combat aircraft. Second, the study's concentration on American air power reflects what Air Vice Marshal Mason called the emergent "differential" between the air forces of the United States and those of all other countries in terms of overall size, technical capability, extent of reach and sustainability, and breadth of operational and support services provided.[20] Among all the world's air forces, only the United States currently maintains a full spectrum of land- and sea-based strike assets, inter-

---

[20] For more on this reality and its implications, see the chapter entitled "The Era of Differential Air Power" in Air Vice Marshal Tony Mason, RAF (Ret.), *Air Power: A Centennial Appraisal*, London, Brassey's, 1994, pp. 234–278.

continental-range bombers, and a supporting panoply of tanker, airlift, and space surveillance and targeting adjuncts offering the ability to engage in global power projection and all-weather precision attack. This is in no way meant to denigrate the many strengths in both equipment and personnel that distinguish the air arms of the United States's principal allies around the world. It is merely to acknowledge the central truth of the uniqueness of American air power and its range of offerings to a theater commander, as was borne out by the shortfalls in the delivery capability of precision munitions and in their interoperability with U.S. forces that afflicted most of the non-U.S. air forces that participated in NATO's air campaign against Yugoslavia in 1999.

Three bounding rules need stipulating to clarify what is meant here by *air power*, which is really a shorthand way of saying air and space power. First, *air power* does not refer merely to combat aircraft or to the combined hardware assets of an air arm, even though these may seem at times to be the predominant images of it held by both laymen and professionals alike. Rather, in its totality, air power is a complex amalgam of hardware and less tangible but equally important ingredients bearing on its effectiveness, such as employment doctrine, concepts of operations, training, tactics, proficiency, leadership, adaptability, and practical experience. These and related "soft" factors vary enormously among air arms around the world operating superficially similar kinds, and often even identical types, of equipment. Yet more often than not, they are given little heed in what typically passes for "air capability" analysis. Only through their combined effects can one ultimately determine the extent to which raw hardware will succeed in producing desired combat results.

Second, air power is inseparable from battlespace information and intelligence. Owing to the dramatic growth in the lethality and effectiveness of American air power in recent years, it has become both correct and fashionable to speak increasingly not of numbers of sorties per target killed, but rather of number of kills achieved per combat sortie. Yet air power involves far more than merely attacking and destroying enemy targets. It also involves knowing what to hit and where to find it. It is now almost a cliche that air power can kill anything it can see, identify, and engage. It is less widely appreciated that it can kill *only* what it can see, identify, and engage. Air power and intelligence are thus opposite sides of the same coin. If the latter fails, the former is likely to fail also. For that reason, accurate, timely, and comprehensive information about an enemy and his military assets is not only a crucial enabler for allowing air power to produce pivotal results in joint warfare, but also an indispensable precondition for ensuring such results.

On this point, Air Force Colonel Phillip Meilinger has noted that "in essence, air power is targeting, targeting is intelligence, and intelligence is analyzing the effects of air operations."[21] In so doing, he spotlighted the indivisibility among the hardware adjuncts of air power, awareness of an enemy's most important vulnerabilities, and the ability to do prompt and accurate damage assessment and feed the results directly back into operations planning in pursuit of strategic effectiveness. Some might object that the latter two of these factors are only enablers rather than inherent components of the air weapon. Yet without them, air power can be reduced to a point of irrelevance in its ability to work to its fullest potential. A good example was the failure of the allied air campaign to eliminate Iraq's nuclear weapons development capability during the 1991 Gulf war despite the most determined efforts of the campaign's planners to do so. As Meilinger insisted, "It is an evasion for airmen to claim that this was a failure of intelligence and not of air power, because the two are integrally intertwined and have always been so."[22] This means that tomorrow's air campaign planners will have an ever more powerful need for accurate and reliable real-time intelligence as a precondition for making good on their most far-reaching promises.

Third, air power, properly understood, knows no color of uniform. It embraces not only Air Force aircraft, munitions, sensors, and other capabilities, but also the aviation assets of the Navy and Marine Corps, along with Army attack helicopters and battlefield missiles. In this regard, it is worth recalling that the first allied weapon impact in Operation Desert Storm on the night of January 17, 1991, was not a laser-guided bomb delivered by an Air Force F-117 stealth fighter, but a Hellfire missile launched against an Iraqi forward air defense warning site by an Army AH-64 Apache attack helicopter. As was well attested by that example, air power entails a creative harnessing of *all* of the diverse combat and combat-support elements of the U.S. armed forces, including space and information warfare adjuncts, that exploit the medium of air and space to visit fire and steel (or, as it may be in the case of information operations, ones and zeros) on enemy targets. Recognition and acceptance of the fact that air warfare is an activity in which all four U.S. services have important roles to play is a necessary first step toward a proper understanding and assimilation of air power's changed role in modern war.

That said, the present study's predominant focus on air power as a weapon in the direct service of a joint-force commander necessarily dictates greater attention to Air Force and Navy contributions and relatively less to the air assets of the Army and Marine Corps, since the latter are regarded by their parent services not, in the first instance at least, as a part of a larger "air

---

[21] Colonel Phillip S. Meilinger, usaf, *Ten Propositions Regarding Air Power*, Paper No. 36, Fairbairn, Australia, raaf Air Power Studies Center, September 1995, p. 13.
[22] Ibid., p. 14.

power equation," but rather as niche equities fielded mainly to support the maneuver objectives of a ground commander. Marine aviation is normally employed in the single-battle setting of a Marine Air-Ground Task Force (MAGTF), a combined-arms entity with a distinctively land or amphibious warfare focus. For its part, Army aviation is likewise deemed a maneuver element organically coupled to an Army division or corps and employed principally in direct support of a ground commander's scheme of maneuver. For these reasons, Army and Marine generals have typically resisted the release of their aviation elements to the operational control of a JFACC, usually an Air Force general, even though those air elements in many circumstances, as was repeatedly seen in Desert Storm, have every potential for being used to great effect independently of the ground or MAGTF commander's more immediate land warfare objectives. Because of the study's focus on the strategic uses of American air power, however, the chapters that follow address Army and Marine aviation only insofar as those assets contribute directly to the pursuit of a theater commander's overarching campaign objectives.

Granted, one cannot venture generalizations about the air power offerings of the four services that apply with equal validity for all occasions. Nevertheless, current and emerging air employment options now offer theater commanders in principle the promise of engaging and neutralizing an enemy's military forces from standoff ranges with virtual impunity, thus reducing the threat to U.S. troops who might otherwise have to engage undegraded enemy forces directly and risk sustaining high casualties. They also offer the potential for achieving strategic effects from the earliest moments of a joint campaign through their ability to attack an enemy's core vulnerabilities with both shock and simultaneity. That transformation in capability, as the following chapters explore in detail, is the essence of American air power's recent coming of age.

[2]

The Legacy of Vietnam

The Vietnam war remains a dark memory for most Americans. With respect to the use of air power, it is often cited as an object lesson in the mismatching of means and ends. Even today, more than two decades after the fall of Saigon, there persists a widespread belief that the war's outcome represented not just a failure of U.S. strategy, "but of air power in particular," in the words of an Australian scholar who has long studied the subject.[1] In a similar vein, a U.S. Air Force air power historian pronounced without qualification in 1986 that "when considered from the standpoint of air power theory and doctrine, the U.S. efforts in Indochina between 1965 and 1971 must be adjudged a failure verging on a fiasco."[2] That belief was reinforced among many in the wake of the Desert Storm success in 1991 when President Bush said of the latter campaign, "By God, we've kicked the Vietnam syndrome once and for all."[3]

Criticism of air power's performance in Vietnam is not without merit by any means. The recurring American air attacks against North Vietnam between 1965 and 1972 made for the longest bombing campaign in U.S. history. At the war's height, the United States had fully half its fighter and attack aircraft committed to Southeast Asia. By 1968, more than 3,000 U.S. aircraft were operating within the borders of South Vietnam, with still others based in Thailand, the Philippines, and Guam. In all, American aircrews

---

[1] C. D. Coulthard-Clark, "The Air War in Vietnam: Re-evaluating Failure," in Alan B. Stephens, ed., *The War in the Air, 1914–1994*, Canberra, Australia, RAAF Air Power Studies Center, 1994, p. 163.
[2] David MacIsaac, "The Evolution of Air Power since 1945: The American Experience," in Air Vice Marshal R. A. Mason, RAF, ed., *War in the Third Dimension: Essays in Contemporary Air Power*, London, Brassey's, 1986, p. 19.
[3] Quoted in Stanley W. Cloud, "Exorcising an Old Demon," *Newsweek*, March 11, 1991, p. 52.

flew more than 1,248,000 fixed-wing sorties throughout the war. These sorties also expended a record-setting abundance of ordnance. As a baseline for appreciating the extent of that effort, the six-week Desert Storm air campaign in 1991 saw fewer than 2,800 coalition aircraft deliver 85,000 tons of munitions in a clear war-winning endeavor. That was scarcely more than two-thirds of what the allies dropped on Germany in March 1945 alone. In contrast, between 1962 and 1972, the United States dropped eight *million* tons of bombs in Southeast Asia, twice the tonnage dropped by all the warring nations in World War II.[4]

Finally, the war's cost was exorbitant in terms of equipment, to say nothing of its longer-term impact on American politics and society. The United States lost 2,561 fixed-wing aircraft and 3,587 helicopters to enemy fire in Southeast Asia. Adding noncombat accidents and other operational losses, the respective totals topped out at 3,720 fixed-wing aircraft and 4,869 helicopters. Of 833 Air Force F-105s produced, 383 were lost in combat.[5] Only half the aircrews in all services downed were eventually recovered. In all, 58,000 Americans lost their lives, 300,000 came home wounded, and $150 billion in national treasure was expended, all for a crushing setback for the United States.

Because air power played such a prominent part in the American involvement in Southeast Asia, it has often been tarred by the brush of America's defeat in that tragic chapter of its history. In air power's defense, some argue that the American defeat was solely a consequence of failed leadership and strategy, which was allowed by association to tarnish the reputation of the air weapon and what it could accomplish. In league with many students of the subject, Richard Hallion, for example, suggested that "air power was misused in Vietnam, with that misuse often clouding results attributed to the limits *of* air power when they really stemmed from limits *on* air power."[6]

Yet a retrospective look at Vietnam reveals that although this observation is fair enough as far as it goes, it accounts for only a part of air power's overall failure to deliver. There is no denying that the American defeat in Southeast Asia was, first and foremost, a product of flawed strategy and a lack of abiding national commitment and purpose. That said, however, a review of U.S. air operations throughout most of the war also leaves little room for doubt that there were significant deficiencies in the character of the American air weapon, in the appropriateness of its use in many cases, and in the

---

[4] Earl Tilford, *Setup: What the Air Force Did in Vietnam and Why*, Maxwell AFB, Ala., Air University Press, 1991, p. 293.

[5] J. C. Scutts, *F-105 Thunderchief*, New York, Charles Scribner's Sons, 1981, p. 64.

[6] Richard P. Hallion, *Storm over Iraq: Air Power and the Gulf War*, Washington, D.C., Smithsonian Institution Press, 1992, p. 19, italics in the original.

organization and ability of its wielders to make the most effective use of it. During the first phase of the war in particular, from the Tonkin Gulf incident in August 1964 to the Tet offensive in 1968, the application of air power was hampered by a combination of restrictive rules of engagement and short-comings in equipment and operator proficiency that undermined its effec-tiveness, as well as by the predominance of a proxy-fed war of insurgency in South Vietnam for which the American air weapon was, for the most part, ill-suited and of limited use. The later, and far more effective, U.S. air oper-ations in 1972, by way of contrast, applied to a more amenable kind of war involving North Vietnamese regular forces in large numbers. They also ex-ploited new systems, such as laser-guided bombs (LGBs) and improved means of electronic warfare, that would form the basis for air power's sub-sequent gains in capability.

HIGHLIGHTS OF THE AIR WAR

America's interest in Vietnam predated its combat involvement there by a decade or more. The Eisenhower administration had closely followed France's colonial tribulations in Indochina during the early 1950s. It ulti-mately turned down a French plea in the spring of 1954 for air support to save beleaguered Dien Bien Phu, which was soon thereafter overrun by Vietminh forces, with only 73 of the 15,000 French soldiers in the garrison managing to escape. Ten years later, that interest deepened as an increasing American presence in Vietnam again led the U.S. leadership to consider air strikes against North Vietnam, this time as part of a widening program of U.S. military assistance to South Vietnam, which was beset by a thriving in-surgency supported by Hanoi.

Already by the summer of 1963, the United States had 16,500 military ad-visers in South Vietnam. In March 1964, a National Security Action Memo-randum issued by the White House directed the Joint Chiefs of Staff (JCS) to develop options for putting increased military pressure on Hanoi, to in-clude joint American and South Vietnamese air attacks against industrial and military targets. The plan that resulted called for retaliatory raids in re-sponse to Viet Cong acts of aggression and a bombing campaign of increas-ing intensity against North Vietnam's airfields; bridges; supply and ammu-nition depots; petroleum, oil, and lubricants (POL) storage facilities; and other targets. The JCS thought that such a campaign, properly executed, would "accomplish destruction of the North Vietnamese will and capabili-ties as necessary" to compel Hanoi to desist from supporting insurgency operations in South Vietnam and Laos. By mid-August 1964, Air Force plan-ners had developed a list of 94 targets for a 16-day air campaign aimed at undermining Hanoi's ability to "take direct action" in support of the Viet

Cong insurgency. The JCS chairman, Army General Earle Wheeler, backed the idea and kept the Air Force's plan under continual revision throughout the fall of 1964, a year of prelude to full-scale American combat involvement and one that saw 149 U.S. soldiers killed in action and 19 declared either missing or captured.[7]

The Roots of American Involvement

The first U.S. air attacks against North Vietnam took place in August 1964. They were unlike anything envisioned in the JCS plans. In response to an alleged firing by North Vietnamese patrol torpedo (PT) boats on two U.S. destroyers operating offshore in international waters, President Lyndon Johnson obtained from Congress the Tonkin Gulf resolution, which gave him a green light in principle to wage aerial war against North Vietnam. Johnson declined at that point, however, to authorize the JCS plan, opting instead for a more measured response code-named Operation Pierce Arrow, in which 64 U.S. Navy aircraft attacked targets directly associated with North Vietnam's alleged provocation, notably the POL stocks and other port facilities at Vinh that were said to have been used by the offending PT boats. An estimated 25 North Vietnamese vessels were destroyed or damaged in a strike launched from the carriers USS *Ticonderoga* and USS *Constellation* at 1100 local time, at a cost of two Navy aircraft downed by enemy antiaircraft artillery (AAA) fire. That event, with the first bombs hitting their targets an hour and a half *after* Johnson announced the attack to the world, marked the beginning of what would become a policy of deliberate but incremental U.S. action against Hanoi. Instead of a concerted effort, as the JCS had recommended, the administration opted for tit-for-tat retaliatory attacks against North Vietnam as deemed appropriate, along with military assistance and direct intervention to help South Vietnam deal with the mounting Viet Cong insurgency.

The next provocation came on November 1, 1964, when the Viet Cong attacked the American air base at Bien Hoa with sappers and mortar fire, killing four Americans, destroying five B-57 bombers, and badly damaging eight others. As a retaliatory measure, the JCS proposed a counterattack by B-52s against North Vietnam's fighter base at Phuc Yen, followed by attacks on other airfields and POL storage areas in the Hanoi-Haiphong area. Johnson rejected those proposals out of legitimate and understandable concern over the possibility of provoking the Soviet Union and China into responses that might lead to escalation beyond the effort's worth. As he graphically

---

[7] Mark Clodfelter, *The Limits of Air Power: The American Bombing of Vietnam*, New York, Free Press, 1989, pp. 45–47; JCS Memorandum 471-64, June 2, 1964, cited in Senator Mike Gravel, ed., *The Pentagon Papers*, Vol. III, Boston, Beacon Press, 1971, pp. 144, 172.

put it, "We don't want a wider war [because the North Vietnamese] have two big brothers that have more weight and people than I have."[8] Instead, Johnson created a National Security Council working group to assess U.S. options.[9]

Not long afterward came two more Viet Cong provocations in the form of the bombing of a Saigon hotel quartering U.S. junior officers on Christmas eve, 1964, killing 2 and wounding 38, and a more damaging mortar attack on the American air base at Pleiku on February 7, 1965, which caused extensive materiel destruction and some casualties. The latter affront prompted Johnson to retaliate by initiating Operation Flaming Dart, which entailed four air strikes into the southern part of North Vietnam on February 8–9.[10] In the wake of the attack on Pleiku, the JCS advocated an eight-week air campaign against North Vietnam that would require the movement of 325 aircraft, including B-52 bombers, from the Western Pacific to Southeast Asia. Johnson consented to redeploying the aircraft but refused to approve the proposed bombing campaign.[11]

Operation Rolling Thunder

After yet another Viet Cong attack, this time on American military personnel at Qui Nhon, Johnson authorized a strike on March 2, 1965, by 104 U.S. aircraft and 19 South Vietnamese aircraft against an ammunition dump and small naval base at Quang Khe in the southern portion of North Vietnam. Shortly thereafter, on March 13, he finally approved the commencement of the sustained bombing that later came to be known as Operation Rolling Thunder.[12] The code name chosen for that effort was anything but coincidental, for it described an intentional gradualist strategy that remained studiously limited to targets well south of the Hanoi and Haiphong industrial complex. The avowed premise of the effort was that "if air strikes could destroy enough supplies to impede the flow of men and weapons coming south, [they] could help save American and South Vietnamese lives."[13]

---

[8] Quoted in Clodfelter, *The Limits of Air Power*, pp. 43–44. Johnson was particularly concerned to avoid any actions that might risk provoking a Chinese intervention. As he told one visitor, "If one little general in shirt sleeves can take Saigon, think about two hundred million Chinese coming down those trails. No sir! I don't want to fight them." Quoted in Stanley Karnow, *Vietnam: A History*, New York, Viking Press, 1983, p. 406.
[9] Clodfelter, *The Limits of Air Power*, p. 53.
[10] Lon O. Nordeen, Jr., *Air Warfare in the Missile Age*, Washington, D.C., Smithsonian Institution Press, 1985, p. 11.
[11] Clodfelter, *The Limits of Air Power*, p. 79.
[12] Ibid., p. 53.
[13] Ibid., pp. 54–58, 60.

Rolling Thunder, officially described as "a program of measured and limited air action . . . against selected targets in the DRV [Democratic Republic of Vietnam]," consisted primarily of interdiction missions against North Vietnamese highways and railways below the 20th parallel.[14] In the collective view of the JCS, this limited bombing effort promised to do little to weaken either the Viet Cong or Hanoi's ability to support it. Short of a major change in the character and operational intent of Rolling Thunder, the JCS maintained, the United States would not succeed in achieving its declared goals of stopping the flow of Hanoi's logistical support to the Viet Cong and inducing North Vietnam's leaders to accept a free and independent South Vietnam.[15] Although Secretary of Defense Robert McNamara rejected most of the JCS proposals, he did approve an increase in the monthly sortie rate from 2,500 to 4,000. At the same time, he placed sharp restrictions on approved targets for these sorties, using the rationale that Rolling Thunder should present only a "credible threat of *future* destruction [while making] it politically easy for the DRV to enter negotiations."[16]

The gradualist strategy of the Johnson-McNamara leadership, with its slow-motion release of approved targets, gave Hanoi a priceless opportunity to build up its defenses. In August 1964, North Vietnamese air defenses were limited to some 1,400 AAA guns, 22 acquisition radars, and 4 fire control radars. By March 1965, those numbers had increased to 31 acquisition radars, 9 AAA control radars, and 30 MiG-15 and MiG-17 fighters. By mid-June, the number of North Vietnamese fighters was up to 70, with the MiG-21 making its first appearance in December. The first SA-2 surface-to-air missile (SAM) was observed by a U-2 in April 1965.[17] Afterward, SA-2 sites proliferated rapidly throughout North Vietnam, and enemy AAA grew to be more lethal than anything ever encountered by allied aircrews over Germany in World War II. By the beginning of 1967, Hanoi was credited with possessing between 7,000 and 10,000 AAA guns and more than 200 identified SA-2 sites.[18] Indeed, North Vietnam became so well endowed with SA-2s that it could afford the inefficient luxury of salvoing them against attacking U.S. aircraft. By August 1967, it was estimated that at least 3,500 SAMs had been launched for the destruction of 80 U.S. aircraft.[19]

Owing to massive Soviet military assistance, the provision of early-warning and height-finding radars gave Hanoi coverage of all of North Vietnam

---

[14] Gravel, ed., *The Pentagon Papers*, Vol. III, p. 271.

[15] Ibid., pp. 88–91.

[16] Memorandum, McNamara for the President, July 30, 1965, cited in Gravel, ed., *The Pentagon Papers*, Vol. III, p. 388, italics in the original.

[17] Scutts, *F-105 Thunderchief*, p. 51.

[18] Ibid., p. 83.

[19] Ibid., pp. 72–73.

and much of the Tonkin Gulf. It also gave North Vietnam the ability to provide its pilots and gunners with the range, altitude, speed, and azimuth of attacking U.S. aircraft and the beginnings of a fully operational Soviet-style integrated air defense system (IADS). On paper, the SA-2 had a poor effectiveness rate against American fighters, as attested by the hundreds fired for each U.S. aircraft the Soviet-built missile actually downed. Nevertheless, consistent with Soviet IADS doctrine, it had the intended effect of forcing U.S. fighters down to altitudes below 3,000 ft to escape its lethal parameters and into the heart of what an Air Force study later called "the heaviest AAA environment in all aerial warfare."[20] Air Force and Navy aircrews recognized a minimum altitude of about 3,000 ft above the ground as the base altitude "below which small arms and light automatic weapons were king."[21] More than 80 percent of all U.S. aircraft shot down were lost in that forbidding environment. The lethal blend of AAA, radar-guided SAMs, and MiGs in creating an envelope of overlapping fire from near–ground level to the higher-altitude regime above 25,000 ft made operating in the skies over North Vietnam an enterprise in which *no* altitude was safe.

Meanwhile, North Vietnam's MiGs enjoyed a sanctuary at their five main operating bases of Kep, Phuc Yen, Gia Lan, Hien An, and Hoa Loc—all secure from attack inside the 25-mile Hanoi circle. For U.S. aircrews, it was a constant source of frustration to fly past these bases, knowing that they were being used by the North Vietnamese Air Force (NVAF) with impunity. Repeatedly, orders for attacks into the most heavily defended areas were appended with a firm injunction stating, "Not, repeat, not authorized to attack North Vietnamese air bases from which attacking aircraft may be operating."[22]

The U.S. military all along had wanted to destroy North Vietnam's SAM sites while they were still under construction and before they had acquired an operational capability. However, Johnson and McNamara refused permission for that out of concern over the possible presence of Soviet or Chinese advisers in those areas.[23] The rules of engagement throughout Rolling Thunder stipulated that American aircraft could only attack SAM sites that were actually firing at them. Political restrictions further proscribed the free hunting of SAMs by dedicated F-105F Wild Weasel SAM killers. Instead, the Weasels were directed to accompany the strike force and suppress any radars en route to the target. Only if a SAM site directly threatened Ameri-

---

[20] U.S. Air Force, *Air War—Vietnam*, New York, Bobbs-Merrill, 1978, p. 57.

[21] Rear Admiral Paul T. Gillcrist, USN (Ret.), *Feet Wet: Reflections of a Carrier Pilot*, New York, Simon and Schuster, 1990, p. 266.

[22] U.S. Air Force, *Air War—Vietnam*, p. 214.

[23] Clodfelter, *The Limits of Air Power*, pp. 79–85; David C. Humphrey, "Tuesday Lunch at the Johnson White House: A Preliminary Assessment," *Diplomatic History*, Winter 1984, p. 90.

can aircraft could it be attacked. McNamara's assistant secretary for international security affairs, John McNaughton, viewed the installation of the SAMS as "just a political ploy by the Russians to appease Hanoi." In a memorandum to McNamara, he wrote in earnest, "We won't bomb the sites, and that will be a signal to North Vietnam not to use them."[24] McNaughton further counseled against determined U.S. bombing of North Vietnamese military targets in general and stipulated that any such strikes would be approved "only as frequently as is required to keep alive Hanoi's fear of the future."[25]

Such restraints imposed by Washington, however well intentioned and even legitimate in some cases, had the effect of asking American airmen to fight with one hand tied behind their back. Throughout much of Rolling Thunder, the Air Force leadership had sought, without avail, to engage multiple targets whose destruction could have crippled North Vietnam's supply network. Haiphong harbor, for example, could have been all but closed by a simple attack on the dredge that kept its shipping channel clear. Such an attack would have disrupted up to 85 percent of North Vietnam's military imports for a long time.[26] Yet it was repeatedly disapproved by the Johnson-McNamara team in favor of attempts to send "signals" to Hanoi through studied restraints in the use of force. Over time, these attempts became predictable and put the lives of U.S. aircrews at added risk.

The self-defeating nature of many of these restrictions was graphically shown by the results produced once North Vietnam's MiG bases were finally cleared for attack. In the initial airfield attacks in May 1967, U.S. Air Force fighters destroyed 26 MiGs on the ground. In a later three-day effort in October, 20 more MiGs were destroyed in bombing raids against Phuc Yen and Cat Bi airfields.[27] After these attacks, Hanoi moved many of its fighters to sanctuary bases in China, from which they operated only sporadically until four years later.

Operation Rolling Thunder ended in 1968 just as it had begun three years earlier, in reaction to steps taken by the North Vietnamese. The Tet offensive, a wave of simultaneous attacks launched by enemy troops against almost 40 towns and cities throughout South Vietnam at the beginning of 1968, resulted in a resounding defeat for the Viet Cong and North Vietnam's regulars. However, public opinion in the United States interpreted Tet as a disaster for American strategy. In its wake, President Johnson on March 31

---

[24] Colonel Alan Gropman, USAF, "The Air War in Vietnam, 1961–73," in Mason, ed., *War in the Third Dimension*, p. 39.

[25] Ibid., p. 40.

[26] General T. R. Milton, USAF (Ret.), "USAF and the Vietnam Experience," *Air Force Magazine*, June 1975, pp. 108–109.

[27] U.S. Air Force, *Air War—Vietnam*, p. 247.

declared a halt to all U.S. bombing of North Vietnam north of the 20th parallel. He further announced his decision not to run for a second term as president. Seven months later, Johnson halted all U.S. bombing of North Vietnam, bringing Rolling Thunder to a close after almost a million sorties were flown and nearly 1,000 U.S. aircraft were lost to enemy fire.

As far as any lasting effect on North Vietnam's contribution to the insurgency in the south was concerned, the three years of sporadic bombing had scored scant results. As early as April 1965, barely a month into Rolling Thunder, the director of the Central Intelligence Agency, John McCone, argued in a memorandum to McNamara and other administration principals that the bombing had not been "sufficiently heavy and damaging really to hurt the North Vietnamese" and had only "hardened their attitude." McCone added that the recent decision by the administration to commit large numbers of U.S. troops on the ground in South Vietnam made sense only if the United States was prepared to "hit North Vietnam harder, more frequently, and inflict greater damage." Like that proffered by the JCS, McCone's counsel was ignored by those in a position to act on it. Three weeks after submitting his memorandum, he resigned in frustration.[28]

A little more than a year later, an assessment of Rolling Thunder by a panel of scientists commissioned by McNamara concluded that rather than weakening North Vietnam, the bombing campaign had actually *improved* Hanoi's war fighting capacity by compelling North Vietnam to create redundant supply networks and eliminate choke points, making it that much harder for future U.S. attacks to achieve results.[29] The lead sentence of the panel's report stated categorically that the bombing had shown "no measurable effect on Hanoi's ability to mount and support military operations in the south."[30] By 1969, less than a year after the halt of the bombing campaign, the transportation system that had fed the Ho Chi Minh Trail was fully repaired, and traffic flowing through it was unprecedentedly heavy. Many bridges that had been repeatedly attacked were also back in operation. Apart from periodic reconnaissance overflights and so-called protective reaction strikes, the bombing hiatus put American aircrews out of action over North Vietnam until mid-1972. Rather than sending a "message" to Hanoi and enforcing the latter's compliance with U.S. wishes, the low-intensity Rolling Thunder campaign, which ultimately visited 643,000 tons of bombs on North Vietnam, merely gave Hanoi's leaders the time they needed to continue the buildup of their air defenses.

---

[28] Quoted in H. R. McMaster, *Dereliction of Duty: Lyndon Johnson, Robert McNamara, the Joint Chiefs of Staff, and the Lies That Led to Vietnam*, New York, HarperCollins, 1997, pp. 256–257.

[29] Jason Summer Study Report, December 1967, cited in Gravel, ed., *The Pentagon Papers*, Vol. V, pp. 222–225.

[30] Zalin Grant, *Over the Beach: The Air War in Vietnam*, New York, Simon and Schuster, 1986, p. 276.

The "In-Country" War

In contrast to the total ineffectiveness of Rolling Thunder, U.S. air power performed marginally better in South Vietnam, at least in attacking targets against which it could make a perceptible difference. Largely unfettered by the constraints that had limited its utility over the north, its employment in support of the ground war in South Vietnam was hindered only by weather and equipment limitations and by recurrent parochial disputes among the services over command and control. Unlike Rolling Thunder, U.S. air operations in support of the ground war in South Vietnam were controlled not by civilian policymakers in Washington, but by uniformed officers in the Military Assistance Command, Vietnam (MACV).

Close air support (CAS) was a major mission for U.S. aircraft in the "in-country" war. No fire zone in South Vietnam was more than a 15-minute flight away from a major Air Force or Marine operating base, and the ground war's demand for air support sorties was prodigious. There was accordingly a profusion of on-call CAS missions, with O-1, O-2, and OV-10 forward air controller (FAC) aircraft directing literally thousands of Air Force and Marine fighter sorties in dedicated fire support to beleaguered U.S. ground units around the clock, often in the face of withering enemy AAA fire and prohibitive weather.

In a powerful reflection of the extent to which many U.S. ground commanders came to rely on air power's presumed ability to answer their prayers in situations of dire need, a former Air Force FAC who had served with an Army battalion during the bloody Ia Drang Valley campaign of November 1965 recalled an instance in which an F-100 on an emergency CAS mission had pressed the attack too closely and inadvertently dropped napalm on U.S. forces, causing friendly fatalities. Of his Army battalion commander, the stunned FAC later reminisced, "After the napalm strike, Colonel Moore looked at me and said something that I never forgot: 'Don't worry about that one, Charlie. Just keep them coming.'"[31] Although more than 300 Americans died in the battle, nearly 2,000 enemy troops were killed.

On many occasions, CAS proved longer on promise than on delivery. For example, in Operation Masher beginning in January 1966, the Air Force flew 600 sorties involving A-1s, F-4s, and B-52s, many of which were dedicated to clearing foliage for helicopter landing areas. Two-thirds of these sorties were planned 24 hours in advance, which meant that ground commanders had to nominate targets and request ordnance so far ahead of time that enemy positions often changed before the scheduled strikes could register their effects. The remaining third of the sorties were diverted from

---

[31] Lieutenant General Harold G. Moore, USA (Ret.) and Joseph L. Galloway, *We Were Soldiers Once . . . and Young*, New York, HarperPerennial, 1992, p. 191.

other missions or scrambled on call. Diverted aircraft generally arrived over their assigned targets within 20 minutes, while scrambled missions often took twice as long. In both cases, moreover, the ordnance delivered was rarely optimal.[32] Firefights with enemy troops on the ground were typically brief, meaning that CAS coordination mechanisms had to work fast to achieve the desired results. Difficulties in this regard often led, some times fairly and others not, to an image of air power as nonresponsive to ground commanders.

Perhaps the best-remembered testament to air power's potential for affecting the outcome of ground operations was its defense of the U.S. Marine base at Khe Sanh on the eve of the Tet offensive in 1968. On January 20, a North Vietnamese defector revealed that a major attack was imminent as part of a larger planned offensive to capture the entire Quang Tri province. Sure enough, in the early hours of January 21, two divisions of North Vietnamese regulars attacked in strength, destroying 98 percent of the base's ammunition stocks and damaging its runway and parking ramp. The next day, U.S. air power entered the equation in force with B-52 strikes on four enemy positions and sustained attacks by Air Force, Navy, and Marine fighters. Because enemy forces occupied the high ground overlooking the only land approach, the base's ammunition supply had to be replenished by air. For a time, more than half the aircraft that attempted to service Khe Sanh sustained battle damage, prompting a command decision that the mission was too dangerous for the twin-engine C-7 and the C-123 without auxiliary jet engines. Most of the deliveries subsequent to that decision were accomplished by the more capable C-130. Eventually, landing at Khe Sanh became so hazardous because of enemy fire that supplies had to be air-dropped.[33]

Three of the classic missions of air power—interdiction, close support, and airlift—were exercised extensively in the defense of Khe Sanh, with Air Force, Navy, and Marine fighters providing CAS, supplemented at night by AC-47 gunships that provided continuous gunfire and illumination of enemy forces.[34] At the height of the battle, the commander of U.S. forces in Vietnam, General William Westmoreland, designated the Seventh Air Force commander, General William Momyer, the sole manager for these operations as well as for all other tactical air operations in South Vietnam. The Air Force had long sought approval for such a unified air commander, given the high concentration of air assets operating in the area. At first, the Marine Corps balked at placing aircraft of the 1st Marine Aircraft Wing in the hands

[32] John Schlight, *The War in South Vietnam: The Years of the Offensive, 1965–68*, Washington, D.C., Office of Air Force History, 1988, p. 197.
[33] Bernard Nalty, *Air Power and the Fight for Khe Sanh*, Washington, D.C., Office of Air Force History, 1973, pp. 42–67.
[34] For further details, see Gropman, "The Air War in Vietnam, 1961–73," pp. 44–45.

of an Air Force commander 400 miles away at Tan Son Nhut, understandably fearing that they would be stripped of their ability to respond quickly to requests for air strikes from their own ground units. Nevertheless, Westmoreland dug in and directed Momyer to coordinate all air attacks using all available assets, including Marine fighter units and Strategic Air Command (SAC) B-52s. Westmoreland later wrote that he felt so strongly about the issue that it was the only occasion during his entire service in Vietnam that prompted him to consider resigning.[35]

Notably, although Westmoreland's "single manager for air" concept was to have been implemented on March 10, it did not go into effect until April 1, after the threat to Khe Sanh had been eliminated. Nevertheless, U.S. air power earned full credit for having broken the siege. Whereas the French in 1954 had had only 200 predominantly light observation aircraft to rely on at Dien Bien Phu, the United States had at its disposal nearly 2,000 fixed-wing aircraft and 3,300 helicopters. Overall, the defense of Khe Sanh was ensured by some 10,000 Air Force fighter sorties, 5,000 Navy sorties, 7,000 Marine sorties, and 2,500 B-52 sorties. Owing to this nonstop aerial bombardment, appropriately code-named Operation Niagara, an estimated 10,000 troops of the forces of North Vietnam's military commander, General Vo Nguyen Giap, were killed. In contrast, U.S. casualties at Khe Sanh totaled 205 killed and 852 wounded.[36]

After the war, 60 percent of polled U.S. Army generals found Army–Air Force cooperation to have been excellent, with only 2 percent rating it unsatisfactory.[37] One senior Army general was reported to have called Khe Sanh the first major ground battle won almost entirely by air power.[38] Such generosity on the Army's part is not surprising in hindsight, since more than 124,000 B-52 sorties had already been flown in the war, with 94 percent of those so-called Arc Light raids conducted in direct support of U.S. troops in South Vietnam and each aircraft dropping 30 tons of bombs per sortie. A long-term result was that this much-appreciated help—even though much of the tonnage dropped was merely destroying empty jungle—had a powerful effect in defining and cementing an Army perception that air power's greatest and most appropriate use was in direct, often close, support of the ground commander.

The final phase of American air employment in South Vietnam focused on turning the war over to the South Vietnamese, an effort that had begun

---

[35] Cited in Phillip B. Davidson, *Vietnam at War: The History, 1946–1975*, New York, Oxford University Press, 1988, p. 559.

[36] Ibid., p. 552.

[37] Hallion, *Storm over Iraq*, p. 22.

[38] Cited in Major General Robert N. Ginsburgh, USAF, "Strategy and Air Power: The Lessons of Southeast Asia," *Strategic Review*, Summer 1973, p. 21.

[23]

under Johnson and increased in intensity under President Richard Nixon, who succeeded him in 1969. Senior planners in the Nixon administration envisioned air power as a shield behind which Army of the Republic of Vietnam (ARVN) forces might develop the ability to fight on their own, using American weapons. In the first test of this Vietnamization strategy, called Operation Commando Hunt, Seventh Air Force continued its attacks on the Ho Chi Minh Trail to prevent enemy forces from accumulating enough supplies to launch an offensive. In November 1968, bombing missions into southern Laos had increased 300 percent, from 4,700 sorties flown the previous month to 12,800 sorties.[39] Some of the later estimates on the effectiveness of Commando Hunt were clearly exaggerated. Nevertheless, in conjunction with the secret bombing of North Vietnamese bases in Cambodia in 1969 and 1970, the operation did help disrupt some of the supply lines running from North Vietnam.

In December 1971, North Vietnamese regular forces shelled the South Vietnamese capital of Saigon, in gross violation of the agreement that had led to Johnson's bombing halt three years earlier. Nixon responded, beginning on December 26, with Operation Proud Deep Alpha, a five-day bombing campaign in which Seventh Air Force fighters flew more than 1,000 sorties against North Vietnamese supply targets south of the 20th parallel, with the intent to dissuade Hanoi from launching the offensive that U.S. military leaders were predicting for February 1972.[40] By one later Air Force account, the operation was "beset with problems and disappointments from initial planning through final execution," starting with monsoon weather so severe that most of the attacking aircraft were forced to drop their bombs in the blind.[41] The attacks did little to halt the continuing buildup of North Vietnamese supplies opposite the demilitarized zone (DMZ), which U.S. intelligence by that time had assessed as a prelude to a full-scale invasion.

Operations Linebacker I and II

On March 30, 1972, North Vietnam launched the Easter offensive, a full-fledged conventional assault against the south by some 125,000 troops in 14 infantry divisions and 26 separate regiments, supported by hundreds of tanks and artillery pieces. To man this force, Giap drew on every North Vietnamese Army (NVA) division and separate regiment in North and South Vietnam. Hanoi also moved a number of SA-2 missile batteries into the DMZ, along with SA-7 shoulder-fired infrared SAMs and a profusion of AAA to in-

---

[39] Tilford, *Setup: What the Air Force Did in Vietnam and Why*, p. 173.
[40] Clodfelter, *The Limits of Air Power*, pp. 151–154.
[41] Quoted in Marshall Michel, *Clashes: Air Combat over North Vietnam, 1965–1972*, Annapolis, Md., Naval Institute Press, 1997, pp. 195–196.

tensify its air defenses. This massive push, in which the Viet Cong played almost no role, came after the United States had completed extensive withdrawals of ground forces in connection with Nixon's policy of Vietnamization, which had left U.S. force levels at only around a fifth of their former strength. South Vietnam now provided the bulk of ground units to meet the enemy invasion.

The Nixon administration's response to the Easter offensive contrasted sharply with the slow buildup of ground and air forces that had taken place under Johnson and McNamara during the mid-1960s. Air power and naval gunfire became the primary instruments for helping prevent the collapse of South Vietnam and to counter Hanoi's attempt to force unification by military means. Within a week, the commander in chief of U.S. Pacific Command (CINCPAC) recommended mining North Vietnam's harbors, training naval gunfire on coastal targets, and striking forcefully against North Vietnamese air bases and air defenses.[42]

In light of the sharply escalated ground fighting, augmenting the number of American aircraft in Southeast Asia became a top priority. On March 30, the day the Easter offensive began, the United States had 495 combat aircraft in the theater. By the end of July, that number had grown to 1,380 as Fifth Air Force reinforced Seventh Air Force and the Marine Corps, which had no fixed-wing aircraft in the theater, redeployed two squadrons of ground attack jets to South Vietnam. By the end of July, the Navy had deployed six carrier battle groups to the Tonkin Gulf, making for the greatest concentration of naval power opposite Southeast Asia at any time during the war.

This renewed buildup of U.S. air power was first committed to action in a response called Operation Freedom Train, which involved strikes against targets in North Vietnam and in support of ARVN troops and their American allies who were in direct contact with North Vietnamese heavy units rolling into the south. For the first time in ground fighting, there was a direct correlation between the weather and the progress of North Vietnamese operations, with NVA units advancing whenever poor flying weather prevented U.S. fighters and helicopter gunships from supporting ARVN units.[43] Partly as a result, air operations over North Vietnam and the DMZ were unburdened of many of the restrictive rules of engagement that had so badly undermined Rolling Thunder. The initial objectives in Freedom Train included North Vietnamese SAM and ground-controlled intercept (GCI) sites, artillery, tanks, troops, and logistic areas. Air Force and Navy aircraft flew almost 3,000 sorties, and B-52s struck the Haiphong area for the first time.[44]

---

[42] Eduard Mark, *Aerial Interdiction in Three Wars*, Washington, D.C., Center for Air Force History, 1994, p. 374.
[43] Davidson, *Vietnam at War*, p. 688.
[44] Ibid., p. 376.

On May 9, over the objections of both the secretary of defense and secretary of state, President Nixon implemented Operation Linebacker, a massive air campaign aimed at destroying North Vietnam's warmaking potential. The declared goals of Linebacker were to isolate Hanoi as a logistics center and to disrupt and destroy its logistics infrastructure, land lines of communications, and command and control assets deemed crucial to supporting its offensive against the south.[45] In what seems in hindsight to have been a preview of the approach that characterized air operations two decades later in Operation Desert Storm, the attack plan developed by Pacific Air Forces (PACAF) featured four phases—against railroad bridges, storage and marshalling areas, other storage and transshipment points, and command and control and counterair targets. These phases were planned to be executed simultaneously rather than sequentially, with Phase IV targets attacked at the outset so as to facilitate achieving rapid success in the other phases.

The opening attack of Operation Linebacker, which included the mining of North Vietnam's harbors for the first time, was carried out by 32 F-4s and a support package of 58 SAM suppressors, strike escorts, and electronic countermeasures (ECM) and reconnaissance aircraft against the Paul Doumer bridge and the Yen Vien railroad yard in downtown Hanoi. This attack package and target set typified many of the early Linebacker missions, with relaxed rules of engagement giving American air power an unprecedented chance to show greater effectiveness. By the second week of May, the JCS, now fully empowered by President Nixon to be bold, had re-extended the bomb line from just 25 miles north of the DMZ to a full 238 miles north.

LGBs were used to good effect by the Air Force for the first time on a routine basis during the Linebacker attacks. On May 13, four flights of F-4s armed with precision-guided Mk 84s and M-118s dropped the Thanh Hoa bridge with dispatch. What had taken hundreds of sorties with inconclusive results during Rolling Thunder was accomplished in this instance in a single day. Throughout the month of May, F-4s attacked 14 other bridges along the rail lines to China and essentially shut down all North Vietnamese rail traffic. The availability of precision-guided munitions (PGMs) further allowed strike planners, for the first time, to attack with smaller force packages, in some cases consisting only of two or three four-ship flights, and to employ release at altitudes above the reach of most AAA.[46]

---

[45] Ibid., p. 381.

[46] A "flight" (referred to as a "division" in Navy terminology) is Air Force parlance for a formation of four fighters or attack aircraft operating together as an integral fighting unit. It is composed of two two-aircraft "elements" (called "sections" in Navy parlance), with the flight leader and his subordinate element leader occuping positions 1 and 3 in the formation and the two element wingmen occupying positions 2 and 4, respectively.

Linebacker air operations also supported U.S. Army and ARVN troops by making the most of the accurate LGBs for attacks against enemy armor. In a prelude to the systematic "tank plinking" that was conducted by Air Force F-111Fs and F-15Es in Desert Storm a generation later, LGBs played a prominent role in the defense of Hue during the North Vietnamese offensive from April 1 through mid-August 1972. More than 70 percent of the enemy tanks destroyed or damaged in the U.S. counteroffensive through the end of May were the result of precision attacks by tactical aircraft or gunships. By the middle of August, American and Vietnamese air power had destroyed 285 North Vietnamese tanks.[47]

Friendly forces in contact with advancing North Vietnamese units relied heavily on airborne FACs, just as they had during the late 1960s. Air Force and Marine pilots flying OV-10 spotter aircraft marked targets in the dense foliage and then directed fighters in to bomb them. During the siege of An Loc that began on April 12 and climaxed with a repulsion of a North Vietnamese attack on May 19, such air support was both heavy and successful. At the siege's peak, close to 7,000 shells a day had fallen on An Loc's defenders. By late June, only 300 rounds a day were incoming as the enemy threat to the position had subsided.[48] Air power had inflicted enough losses on North Vietnam's forces to eliminate their ability to sustain the offensive.

Still, MACV's inability to devote many attack sorties to the most vulnerable portions of the enemy's lines of communication while the battle raged in the south made for a serious limitation on the combat effectiveness of Linebacker. Heavy air defenses continued to require numerous strike support aircraft to accommodate the MiGs, SAMs, and AAA, thus reducing the number of dedicated bomb droppers. Armed reconnaissance against trucks was virtually impossible in the most heavily defended northern portion of North Vietnam. In May and June, American air power destroyed an estimated 489 vehicles near the DMZ versus only 38 in areas farther north.[49] Even when unburdened of most restrictions, American air power of that era faced limits on its breadth of effective target coverage.

After gaining important concessions in the Paris peace talks, President Nixon halted the Linebacker bombing of North Vietnam on October 22. In all, U.S. aircraft dropped 155,548 tons of bombs during the six months of Linebacker, about a quarter of the tonnage that was dropped during all three years of Rolling Thunder. The campaign inflicted more damage on North Vietnam than did all previous U.S. bombing efforts. When the attacks ended, U.S. aircraft had destroyed nearly all of the fixed oil storage facilities

---

[47] Major A. J. C. Lavalle, ed., *Air Power and the 1972 Spring Invasion*, Washington, D.C., USAF Southeast Asian Monograph Series, 1985, p. 57.

[48] Mark, *Aerial Interdiction in Three Wars*, pp. 393–394.

[49] Davidson, *Vietnam at War*, p. 391.

in North Vietnam and 70 percent of the country's electric power–generating capacity.[50]

Despite the bombing halt, Hanoi grew intransigent in the Paris peace talks and again attacked in force in December 1972. This time, following a 72-hour ultimatum to no avail, Nixon lifted all restraints and unleashed Operation Linebacker II. No longer was the intent to "send messages" or to "ratchet up the pain." It was now to impose *force majeure* and brutally coerce Hanoi to the negotiating table to agree to a permanent end to the war. The campaign lasted from December 18 to December 29 and included more than 700 B-52 sorties against the heart of the Hanoi-Haiphong military-industrial complex. The concept of operations centered on night, high-altitude radar bombing of all targets in the Hanoi-Haiphong area by B-52s, with each raid launched in successive waves, hitting its assigned targets at 4- to 5-hour intervals. The first night involved 129 B-52s, with the lead group of aircraft from U-Tapao, Thailand, committed against the MiG-21 bases at Hoa Loc, Kep, and Phuc Yen. Plans also called for Navy ground attack aircraft to suppress coastal AAA sites, while F-4s laid down chaff corridors to blanket Hanoi's SAM acquisition and tracking radars.

At the same time, EB-66, EA-3, and EA-6 jammers were employed to generate additional clutter on the enemy's radar screens. Enemy airfields and SAM sites along the B-52 entry and departure routes were attacked by F-4s, A-7s, and F-111s, with F-105 Wild Weasels providing active SAM suppression and additional F-4s accompanying the B-52s to provide MiG cover. A Navy radar picket ship, assigned the call sign Red Crown, stood by some 25 miles off the coast of Haiphong to provide MiG threat advisories and to vector Air Force and Navy fighters toward any MiGs that got airborne. Finally, C-130s and HH-53 helicopters were readied to provide support for any downed aircrews who might be assessed as worth attempting to rescue in light of the perceived risk. The operation was the first integrated air offensive of the entire war that sought to achieve the shock effect that later was the hallmark of opening night in Desert Storm.

Linebacker II was hardly a pushover for the attacking American aircrews. In particular, SAC's B-52s entered the campaign using highly stereotyped penetration tactics that helped substantially to account for the 15 that were ultimately brought down by North Vietnamese SAMs. B-52 attack tactics for the first three nights of Linebacker II were identical to those that had been previously used over less heavily defended areas of Southeast Asia. As such, they were entirely predictable to the North Vietnamese. Moreover, they were developed not in consultation with any of the U.S. fighter aircrews who were familiar with the density and effectiveness of Hanoi's de-

---

[50] Clodfelter, *The Limits of Air Power*, pp. 166–167.

fenses, but by staff planners sitting at SAC headquarters in the United States, half a globe away. In the words of one well-documented account, "SAC headquarters sent the B-52s into the target in a string, all flying about the same heading and the same altitude; then, after the B-52s dropped their bombs, they performed a maneuver—'the post-target turn'—that blocked their ECM equipment and left them vulnerable to SA-2 attack."[51] It was only after the first three nights of the campaign, when so many B-52s were shot down owing to their rote repetition of the same attack routes, that SAC's planners finally desisted from these stereotyped tactics, listened to their aircrews, and allowed the B-52 units to develop and employ their own preferred tactics.

Nevertheless, the effect of the 11-day bombing campaign on Hanoi's ability to resist was crushing. In what now stands as another preview of the functional effects achieved by allied air power two decades later in Desert Storm, the rail system around Hanoi was attacked with such persistence and intensity that poststrike reconnaissance showed that repair crews were making no effort to restore even token rail traffic.[52] Two days before the conclusion of Linebacker II, all organized enemy air defense efforts ceased, as North Vietnam had exhausted its supply of SA-2s. In the words of Alan Gropman, the country was "laid open for terminal destruction."[53] The American air attacks finally drove Hanoi to the negotiating table a week later. It also put down a place marker with respect to what air power could accomplish if properly applied.

Remarkably, given the intensity of the bombing, relatively few North Vietnamese civilians were killed, owing in large measure to the use of accurate LGBs against targets in the densest urban concentrations and to strict rules of engagement regarding targeting and weapon-release criteria to minimize collateral damage. Although the most outspoken American antiwar critics were quick to castigate the campaign as another Hiroshima, the official North Vietnamese tally for civilian fatalities resulting from Linebacker II was 1,318 in Hanoi and 305 in Haiphong, hardly the equivalent, as Stanley Karnow later noted, "of the Americans' incendiary bombing of Tokyo in March 1945, for example, when nearly 84,000 people were killed in a single night."[54] Taken together, the two Linebacker campaigns entailed 6,700 B-52 sorties and 56,000 fixed-wing attack sorties.[55] Years later, Giap conceded that the time had been right for seeking the greatest possible con-

[51] Michel, *Clashes*, pp. 273–274.
[52] General George J. Eade, USAF, "Reflections on Air Power in the Vietnam War," *Air University Review*, May 1974, p. 8.
[53] Gropman, "The Air War in Vietnam, 1961–73," p. 57.
[54] Karnow, *Vietnam: A History*, p. 653.
[55] Hallion, *Storm over Iraq*, p. 57.

cessions from the United States. Linebacker II convinced the North Vietnamese not to hold out any longer in the negotiations.[56]

Although the cease-fire ultimately agreed on began on January 18, 1973, the war would not be fully over for the United States until the last of the American prisoners of war held by North Vietnam were repatriated. Since the beginning of American involvement in air operations over Southeast Asia in 1961, some 2,000 pilots and aircrew members had been killed, more than 1,000 had been declared missing in action, and nearly 600 were known to be held captive in North Vietnam. Definitive closure on this unsettled account was bound to be needed for the United States to make final peace with its abortive combat experience in Southeast Asia. "As the last Americans left Hanoi in March," in Karnow's quiet coda on the bitter American involvement, "the prevailing sentiments in the United States were relief that the war had ended and revulsion toward the very subject of Vietnam."[57]

Problems with Strategy and Implementation

Much of the frustration the United States experienced over the application of air power during the ineffectual Rolling Thunder campaign had to do with fundamental failings of leadership at the national level. Those failings manifested themselves in an enduring absence of any constancy of goals, a misguided strategy from the start, self-deceiving measures of effectiveness, and needlessly self-imposed operational restrictions. The majority of the service chiefs under McNamara saw the problem as emanating from North Vietnam rather than the Viet Cong. They also, rightly or wrongly, eventually came to see air power as the trump card for American success in Vietnam. Yet the civilian leaders, for their part, never made up their mind whether they were fighting a counterinsurgency war or dealing with a foreign invasion.

The ambivalence of the civilian leadership about what the war represented and what the stakes entailed naturally occasioned many of the missteps in the way in which it was conducted. At bottom, the Johnson administration's approach represented a classic instance of the fallacy of mirror-imaging. As Mark Clodfelter put it, Johnson and McNamara "subconsciously assigned the enemy Western values and translated a guerrilla war into a conventional conflict that they could better understand."[58] Reduced to basics, the American goal was to punish, to persuade, and to co-

---

[56] Peter MacDonald, *Giap*, New York, W. W. Norton, 1993, p. 314.

[57] Karnow, *Vietnam: A History*, p. 656.

[58] Major Mark Clodfelter, USAF, "Of Demons, Storms, and Thunder: A Preliminary Look at Vietnam's Impact on the Persian Gulf Air Campaign," *Airpower Journal*, Winter 1991, p. 19.

erce, but not to win. The intent of the bombing of North Vietnam was not to achieve strategic objectives so much as to send "signals" in a vain effort to convince Hanoi's leaders that continued fighting was futile. In a compelling indictment of the Johnson administration's approach to the emerging situation in 1965, H. R. McMaster noted that the aim of using force against Hanoi "was not to impose one's will on the enemy but to communicate with him." The result was an approach calculated to produce "a fundamentally flawed strategy that permitted deepening American involvement in the war without consideration of its long-term costs and consequences."[59]

Pentagon civilians under McNamara insinuated themselves directly into all manner of operational details regarding the planning and execution of U.S. air strikes, to include matters of target selection, weapons loads, and even approach routes and final target attack profiles. During the early days of Rolling Thunder, attacks were directed by these civilian planners to take place on a particular day, with no consideration given to such operationally critical matters as prevailing weather in the target area.[60] Targets approved for attack were released in small packages over which Johnson and Mc-Namara retained total control, making their selections during their Tuesday lunch meetings without even an invited military presence until 1967. At first, Johnson and McNamara reserved for themselves final approval authority over all targets, going so far, on occasion, as to decide personally the dates and times of scheduled attacks. Later, they yielded the day-to-day scheduling to the JCS, while retaining veto power, which they freely exercised as they thought necessary.

In keeping with McNamara's tendency to treat the war against Hanoi essentially as a management problem, a recurrent practice was to evaluate the bombing campaign's progress by statistical measures rather than by the actual operational effects achieved. For the air war against the north, the equivalent of McNamara's "body count" metric used in South Vietnam was the combat sortie rate. That measure was accepted all too readily without challenge by many in uniform. Criteria employed for assessing operational performance were driven by McNamara's obsession with quantifiables, which often led to lapses of integrity at lower levels of the chain of command in order to live within this system of accountability. By one informed account, "there was constant pressure to show results in the numbers of targets hit, so that anyone listening to the Saigon briefing might have concluded that North Vietnam possessed more trucks per capita than any country in the world."[61]

McNamara's fixation on the sortie rate and other such measurables rather

---

[59] McMaster, *Dereliction of Duty*, pp. 62–63.
[60] Grant, *Over the Beach*, p. 26.
[61] Ibid., p. 112.

than on actual combat results not only occasioned a misleading sense of how the air war was unfolding, but also frequently led to ill-considered decisions on force commitments. For example, during the time of an alleged munitions shortage early in the war, U.S. aircraft were frequently launched into high-threat areas with only one or two bombs on their racks in the interest of keeping the sortie rate up. Moreover, because of the emphasis placed on the sortie rate irrespective of operational effectiveness, many missions were needlessly risky for the dubious value to be gained. Typical of these were road reconnaissance forays looking for vehicles and other secondary targets of opportunity in the face of lethal fire from unobserved AAA and infrared SAMs. Such wasteful employment of expensive aircraft and valuable aircrews resulted in numerous losses of both.

FRAGMENTED COMMAND AND CONTROL

Restrictive rules of engagement were not the only factors that hampered the application of U.S. air power during Rolling Thunder. The fragmentation of air power by commanders intent on preserving their organic capabilities further diminished the efficiency of air power's employment, owing to a jury-rigged arrangement that MACV's former chief of intelligence later said "exemplified *disunity* of command."[62] As early as 1965, Rolling Thunder's mounting daily sortie rate indicated that better control was needed over the diverse U.S. assets operating over North Vietnam. Up to that point, CINCPAC and his subordinate commander in chief of the U.S. Pacific Fleet (CINCPACFLT) had delegated authority for day-to-day Rolling Thunder planning to the commanders of the Air Force's Seventh Air Force in Saigon and the Navy's Carrier Task Force 77 deployed on Yankee Station in the Tonkin Gulf off the coast of North Vietnam. When that arrangement proved unsatisfactory, the joint Air Force and Navy Rolling Thunder Armed Reconnaissance Coordinating Committee developed the so-called Route Package system, in which North Vietnam was divided up into geographical areas numbered in sequence, starting at the DMZ and working northward. Planners broke North Vietnam into seven regions. The Navy's Task Force 77 got four of these, Route Packages II, III, IV, and VI-B adjacent to the coastline, since the carrier deck cycle and aircraft range limitations made it easier for the Navy to operate on direct lines to the littoral. The Air Force's 2nd Air Division (later Seventh Air Force) drew Route Packages I, V, and VI-A.[63]

[62] Davidson, *Vietnam at War*, p. 397; italics in the original.
[63] Lieutenant Colonel Stephen J. McNamara, USAF, *Air Power's Gordian Knot: Centralized versus Organic Control*, Maxwell AFB, Ala., Air University Press, 1994, pp. 105–106.

These "Route Packs," as they came to be called for short by aircrews and target planners, were conceived as a part of McNamara's graduated strategy, with successively more important and more heavily defended targets being those in the higher categories. Route Pack VI, embracing the northernmost part of the country, included the Hanoi-Haiphong complex, the enemy's MiG bases, and the greatest concentration of infrastructure targets. Because of its target density, it was divided into western and eastern halves as indicated earlier, with the interior Route Package VI-A going to the Air Force and the littoral Route Package VI-B to the Navy.[64]

This fragmented approach stood in stark contrast to the most basic beliefs about the employment of air power going back to World War II and before. Ever since the early admonishments of U.S. Army air power advocate Brigadier General William "Billy" Mitchell, airmen had argued for the centralized integration of all air assets under the control of one commander. Basic Air Force doctrine forged in World War II called for a single manager to orchestrate the use of air power most efficiently across the theater. Yet in Vietnam, complex command arrangements made it impossible to establish a single manager for air operations. Because of the many differences between Air Force and Navy operating procedures, a formal system of joint command and control was not established. Efforts to coordinate Air Force strikes out of Thailand with operations from Navy carriers in the Tonkin Gulf were rare. This denied the fighter forces of the two services any opportunity to combine their capabilities to greatest effect.

To his credit, MACV's commander, General Westmoreland, noted in his memoirs that "creating a unified command for all of Southeast Asia would have gone a long way toward mitigating the unprecedented centralization of authority in Washington and the preoccupation with minutiae at the Washington level."[65] In most respects, however, the Air Force's concept of a single manager for air operations lost considerable ground during the Vietnam war. CINCPAC, as the local theater commander, decided which interdiction missions would fall to the Navy's Task Force 77 and which to the Air Force's Seventh Air Force. The Navy retained control of Task Force 77 air operations throughout the war, filling requests for air support to ground operations on a temporary basis only.[66] The Marines kept de facto control of their air assets, even though Seventh Air Force had formal control. The Army fought for and won permanent control of its helicopters. For its part, MACV maintained that air operations in Route Package I, just north of the

---

[64] Ibid., p. 45.
[65] General William C. Westmoreland, *A Soldier Reports*, Garden City, N.J., Doubleday, 1976, p. 411.
[66] See McNamara, *Air Power's Gordian Knot*, p. 104, for a detailed discussion of these complex arrangements.

DMZ, were an extension of the land war in South Vietnam. On the strength of that argument, it gained control over that Route Package.[67]

Even the Air Force split control of its assets. Because of their primary nuclear tasking, SAC maintained an iron control over its B-52s, managing their role in the war through an echelon attached to MACV headquarters. For his part, the Seventh Air Force commander had two roles. He was in charge of Rolling Thunder interdiction missions in his assigned Route Packages in North Vietnam and also coordinated air support to ground forces as the deputy commander for air operations to MACV. As an Air Force airman concluded years later in a postmortem on these arrangements, the fact that the Air Force allowed SAC to retain control of its B-52s and that PACAF maneuvered to keep its own Thirteenth Air Force away from any jurisdiction in Vietnam "did not help to convince the other services that the Air Force was serious" when it espoused the centralization of air power in Southeast Asia.[68]

AIR POWER RIDES A LEARNING CURVE

When it came, however, to correcting problems highlighted by the war that were fixable at the operator level, airmen rode a steep learning curve and responded, more often than not, with both determination and success. At times, the use of air power was ineffective for no other reason than equipment limitations. A case in point involved the so-called Sky Spot missions, in which Air Force F-105s or F-4s would be led by an EB-66 pathfinder at medium altitude to conduct level radar bombing through cloud cover, using formations and target approach tactics not unlike those employed by U.S. Army Air Force B-17s in World War II. The purpose of these missions was to deny the enemy a weather sanctuary and to disrupt the movement of supplies in conditions when interdiction operations could not be flown visually. The accuracy of such bombing was poor, however, since the fighters were limited to dropping their weapons in unison on a radio voice command from the EB-66.

The same held with respect to early efforts to use the F-105 for all-weather, round-the-clock bombing of suspected North Vietnamese supply columns along the Ho Chi Minh Trail. The radar bombing system fitted to the F-105 was designed to deliver a nuclear weapon against an area target, for which a miss by 1,500 to 2,000 ft was acceptable. Against point targets using conventional weapons, however, such inaccuracy offered little assur-

---

[67] Grant, *Over the Beach*, p. 111.
[68] McNamara, *Air Power's Gordian Knot*, p. 97.

ance that the intended target would be hit. It further risked causing considerable unintended damage. On top of that, target choices for these missions often entailed a case of the tail wagging the dog, in that the target was selected more for its topographical features and distinctive radar signature than for any intrinsic military importance. Since the physical nature of the target was crucial to the predicted outcome of the attack, the menu of targets available for such missions was limited. Perhaps most debilitating of all, the hardware available at the time to apply air power lacked the needed intelligence, surveillance, and reconnaissance (ISR) wherewithal to locate worthwhile targets, attack those targets with consistent accuracy, and assess the impact of individual sorties or even weeks' worth of sorties.

Many, though by no means all, such equipment problems encountered by U.S. air power during its initial combat exposure in Vietnam were a result of the predominant cold-war strategy orientation that had so heavily influenced U.S. fighter development during the latter half of the 1950s. Nuclear missions were stressed and conventional weapons training minimized, to a point where it was commonly said that the "theater air forces were trying to be little SACs, with the primary and only mission being the nuclear one."[69] This emphasis was prompted by the massive retaliation strategy enunciated by the Eisenhower administration in the early 1950s, which stipulated that any global conflict could assume nuclear proportions almost from the outset and that American forces must be configured accordingly. It was an emphasis, moreover, that persisted well into the 1960s, despite the new stress the Kennedy administration had come to place on general-purpose forces and nonnuclear preparedness. "As late as 1964," an official Air Force history of the early Vietnam war pointed out, "the Air Force continued to maintain that strategic nuclear forces provided the best instrument to prevent wars at all levels. While conceding the need for some forces to be ready to fight limited and conventional wars, it remained wedded to the primacy of the nuclear arsenal as a deterrent to all kinds of wars."[70]

As a result, Republic Aviation's F-105—which ended up being the workhorse of the air war against North Vietnam—was designed from pitot tube to afterburner petals to be a nuclear bomber. Although it had some built-in conventional capability, the only way Tactical Air Command (TAC) could get the SAC-dominated Air Force to procure it was to give it a primary nuclear delivery capability and mission. One of the reasons why the F-105 won out over the rival North American F-107 in a design competition was because the former came equipped with an internal weapons bay in the

[69] Milton, "USAF and the Vietnam Experience," p. 109.
[70] Schlight, *The War in South Vietnam*, p. 309.

fuselage capable of accommodating a nuclear store.[71] Because of its primary nuclear strike mission, the F-105 was not designed with the expectation that it would need to be able to sustain hits from AAA fire. As a result, hydraulic lines for the dual flight control system ran side by side, making it possible for a single round to take out both systems simultaneously and render the aircraft uncontrollable.[72]

The Air Force also had an undertrained pool of fighter pilots for the novel challenges of Vietnam, owing to its stress on the nuclear strike role and its commensurate de-emphasis of nonnuclear operations. This is not to say that the pilots assigned in the initial cadre were less than technically competent. According to the Air Force's Red Baron study of air combat engagements conducted shortly after the war, before June 1966 more than 50 percent of Air Force fighter pilots in the theater had more than 2,000 hours of total flying time, with an average of 510 hours in the type of aircraft they were flying in combat.[73]

The question had to do not with overall quality of airmanship, but rather with the unbalanced *mix* of skills that had been imparted to Air Force aircrews by their training for cold-war contingencies. Powerful evidence of this skewed fixation was apparent in the commander's directive published in the PACAF F-100 pilot training manual for 1961: "Nuclear training will in every instance take precedence over non-nuclear familiarization and qualification. It is emphasized that conventional training will not be accomplished at the expense of the higher-priority nuclear training required by this manual. Non-MSF [mobile strike force] units will restrict conventional familiarization to the accomplishment of only one event per aircrew per year."[74] Indeed, nuclear weapons delivery remained a part of the mission qualification syllabus for the F-105, even for pilots checking out in the airplane for the first time en route to a combat assignment in Southeast Asia.[75]

Nevertheless, Air Force and Navy aircrews and their commanders were quick to rise to the challenges posed by the evolving war that related to identifiable shortcomings in their equipment and training. Their actions in this respect produced the most notable improvements in the areas of deal-

---

[71] Other reasons had to do with some undesirable design characteristics of the F-107 that had no direct bearing on its nuclear delivery applications.

[72] Once this problem became known, a fix was approved in which a third hydraulic system was installed with its lines routed away from the other two.

[73] U.S. Air Force, *Air War—Vietnam*, p. 222.

[74] *Aircrew Training Manual for F-100D/F*, PACAF Manual 51-6, Vol. 1, Hickam AFB, Hawaii, PACAF, March 1961.

[75] A windfall benefit of this, however, was that with the nuclear phase put first in the surface-attack segment of the conversion course, student pilots were able to gain an additional 20–30 hours of experience in the aircraft by the time they got to the conventional phase.

ing with North Vietnam's sAMs, gaining greater bombing effectiveness, and doing better in the recurrent air engagements against Hanoi's MiGs.

Countering the SAM Threat

The struggle by the Air Force and Navy to adapt to North Vietnam's ever-challenging air defense environment focused mainly on seeking ways of negating or minimizing the SA-2 threat. That missile, which had been responsible for bringing down the U-2 flown by Francis Gary Powers over the Soviet Union in May 1961, had a range of 17 nautical miles and was effective from 3,000 ft to well above 50,000 ft. A typical launch site included a tracking radar, several longer-range acquisition radars to detect incoming aircraft beyond the tracking radar's range, and a battery of six missile launchers, with six more missiles available in ready reserve. An SA-2 attack could be defeated if the engaged pilot saw the missile's exhaust plume during the burn phase and was able to make a timely determination that the missile was guiding on him. The tactical response in such a situation required both exquisite timing and nerves of steel. In effect, it involved outmaneuvering the missile by making a hard turn down and into it, followed by an abrupt pull-up and change of heading at just the right moment to cause the missile's tracking system to reach its gimbal limit and cease guiding. Although this tactic generally worked against a single SA-2, it could result in disaster if more than one missile was guiding on the same aircraft, by solving the second missile's guidance problem while negating the tracking solution of the first. Even when effective, moreover, this maneuver often forced the defending aircraft down into the lower-altitude AAA environment, making "the cure worse than the disease," in the later recollection of one Air Force pilot.[76]

Since this tactic was only marginally effective in reducing the rate of American aircraft losses to North Vietnam's SA-2s and AAA, a better fix was sought in the realm of ECM. An early development in this respect was the QRC-160 jamming pod, which was eventually developed to be carried by all strike aircraft. The tactical application of this device involved a standard spread formation, with up to 2,500 ft of separation between two-plane elements horizontally and 1,500 ft vertically. That arrangement allowed some fluidity within the flight so long as all four aircraft remained together in the same basic formation. In theory, the idea was that electronic emissions from the pods would envelop an attacking formation in overlapping jamming coverage, making a flight of four fighters look to enemy acquisition and tracking radars like a square mile of airborne reflected energy. No doubt any

---

[76] Michel, *Clashes*, p. 33.

such blob moving at 600 nautical miles per hour on an enemy's radar screen would be a dead giveaway that a strike formation was inside it. The challenge for the defenders was to locate and lock onto the individual fighters within that massive return.

This "pod formation" generally seemed to work to good effect. Air Force pilots flying out of Thailand reported that the tactic appeared to degrade enemy SAM radar performance to a point where Hanoi had to increase its MiG activity to compensate for it. Indeed, as one fighter wing commander reported, "Seldom has a technological advance of this nature so degraded the enemy's defensive posture. It has literally transformed the hostile defense environment we once faced to one where we can now operate with a latitude of permissibility."[77] In 1965, one Air Force aircraft was downed for every 16 SAMs fired. By 1966, the exchange ratio had dropped to one for 33, then in 1967 to one for 50 as the pods came into general use, and finally to one for 100 before Rolling Thunder came to an end in 1968.

One drawback of the pod formation was that its relative rigidity and the need to maintain precisely its intraflight spacing of aircraft made it difficult for pilots in the single-seat F-105 to maintain the visual lookout required to detect MiGs converging on the formation's dead-astern (or six-o'clock) position. Another drawback stemmed from the pod's limited jamming coverage, which restricted turns by a flight of attacking fighters to 15 degrees of bank inside SAM/AAA areas and 20 degrees of bank outside them. This restriction allowed for only small heading corrections, thus precluding any chance to make a last-minute feint toward a target. That, in turn, made the incoming strike formation predictable and enabled Hanoi's GCI controllers to get an early start on vectoring MiGs to engage it.[78]

Other notable SAM-suppression measures that came on line in time for Operation Linebacker included the introduction of the F-105G, an improved version of the earlier two-seat F-105F that mounted better SAM detection systems and self-protection jamming equipment. It also now carried *two* types of antiradiation missiles (ARMs), not only the familiar Shrike used in Rolling Thunder but also the new Standard ARM, a much larger missile with a heavy warhead and a guidance system that included a memory which allowed the missile to continue homing on a targeted SAM radar even if the radar ceased emitting. A shortcoming of the older Shrike was that the missile would go aimless if an enemy radar operator detected an incoming attack soon enough to turn his radar off or place it in standby mode.

Finally, the laying of chaff corridors ahead of attacking strike formations to spoof enemy SAM and AAA radars between the commencement of a bombing run and the moment of weapon release over the target made for another

[77] Quoted in ibid., p. 72.
[78] Ibid., p. 124.

important defense-suppression innovation during the second phase of the air war. It complemented the active jamming provided by the ECM pods and helped notably to allow U.S. aircraft to operate more safely in the medium-altitude environment over the most heavily defended targets around Hanoi and Haiphong. Owing in part to such improved electronic warfare equipment and techniques, the Air Force's loss rate over North Vietnam by 1967 had fallen to 1.6 aircraft per 1,000 combat sorties, down from 2.7 per 1,000 in 1966 and 3.2 per 1,000 in 1965.

Toward Better Bombing Effectiveness

Typical of the most demanding targets sought out by Rolling Thunder strike pilots was the infamous Thanh Hoa bridge. Called the Ham Rung, or Dragon's Jaw, by the North Vietnamese, this prestressed and heavily defended link in the Ho Chi Minh Trail complex spanned the Son Ma River. The first attempt against it less than a month into Rolling Thunder involved 46 F-105s, 16 of which carried the Bullpup missile, a visually tracked air-to-ground weapon that was command-guided by the pilot through a radio data link. The operation put multiple bombs and missiles on target, yet resulted in no discernible damage, confirming that any bridge-busting attempts in the future would have to be the province of accurately delivered 2,000- and 3,000-lb bombs. As an Air Force analysis commented later, this initial encounter proved that "firing Bullpups at the Dragon was about as effective as shooting B-B pellets at a Sherman tank."[79]

The repeated difficulty of taking out the Thanh Hoa and Paul Doumer bridges during Rolling Thunder led to concentrated efforts to develop and employ PGMs, starting with the Navy's AGM-62 Walleye, an electro-optically steered free-fall glide bomb with a 1,000-lb warhead, a television tracking camera in the nose to direct the weapon to impact, and a standoff range of nearly 8 miles. In the final mission against the Dragon's Jaw prior to the 1968 bombing halt, the Walleye succeeded in putting the bridge out of commission. Out of 68 other Walleye drops against barracks, power stations, and bridges, 65 were reported to have scored direct hits.[80] This represented the beginning of the precision munitions revolution whose payoff was fully realized a generation later in Desert Storm. A severe problem with Walleye, however, was its requirement for a target with a high-contrast aiming point, which meant that its effectiveness could be negated by weather obscurations or by North Vietnamese countermeasures, such as the use of camouflage or smoke generators near critical targets.

Later during Linebacker, as noted earlier, and for the first time in the his-

---

[79] U.S. Air Force, *Air War—Vietnam*, p. 36.
[80] Ibid., p. 59.

tory of air warfare, the more effective Paveway I LGBs were used to telling effect by the Air Force against the Paul Doumer bridge in the heart of the Hanoi complex. That mile-long bridge, named after the French governor general who had conceived the Indochina rail system at the turn of the 20th century, was the longest in North Vietnam. Dropped earlier in 1967 by M-118 3,000-lb bombs, it had been repaired during the four-year bombing hiatus and ended up back on the target list for Linebacker. On May 11, 1972, it was attacked by a flight of four F-4s carrying two M-118s and six Mk 84 2,000-lb LGBs. Two days later, both the Paul Doumer and Thanh Hoa bridges were confirmed down, in a testament to the newly emergent power of precision weapons. Before their advent, all that multiple U.S. air attacks against demanding targets like the Thanh Hoa bridge could show for their effort was the charring and bending of metal and only a temporary disruption of traffic flow.

In a precursor to Desert Storm's later proof of air power's ability to achieve the effects of mass with relatively few sorties, the use of laser-guided weapons during Linebacker enabled U.S. planners to achieve lethal effects against once-indestructible targets. The way the weapon worked was for an F-4 carrying a Pave Knife laser designator to illuminate the target with a gyro-stabilized laser beam. The laser spot would then create an imaginary cone-shaped envelope in the sky called the "basket," defined by the bomb's steering limits, into which an accompanying LGB-armed F-4 would release the weapon from a safe distance outside enemy AAA range. Once the bomb was in the basket, its seeker head and moveable steering fins did the rest of the work, more often than not with lethal accuracy.[81] During combat trials of the Paveway I, more than 50 percent of the bombs dropped scored direct hits, and the reported circular error average (CEA) for all bombs dropped was 8 ft.[82]

In yet another demonstration of the capability of these weapons, F-4s using Paveway LGBs destroyed the generator at a North Vietnamese hydroelectric plant while leaving the dam itself only 50 ft away untouched. With that improvement in achievable accuracy, destroying hard structures such as bridges with consistency and minimal effort became a new hallmark of American conventional air power. Other improvements in air-to-ground munitions prompted by the challenges of Vietnam included the CBU-24 cluster bomb, which proved highly effective against enemy AAA emplacements and troop concentrations in both North and South Vietnam, and the Snakeye folding-fin retardation attachment to standard Mk 82 general-purpose

---

[81] A drawback of this approach was that the designator aircraft could not designate for itself, so it did not carry laser-guided weapons. This reduced the number of bombs a four-ship flight of aircraft could deliver.

[82] Michel, *Clashes*, pp. 203–204.

bombs, which enabled attacking aircraft to release their bombs at low altitudes in level laydown attacks without getting caught in their own fragmentation pattern when the bombs exploded.

One problem with respect to ground-attack operations that remained unresolved to the very end of the Vietnam war was that American air power was never reliably effective at night. Despite steady progress in the development and application of night-capable systems, North Vietnam and the Viet Cong, rather than U.S. forces, owned the night to all intents and purposes. True enough, Air Force and Marine F-4s frequently employed flares for night attacks against identified targets at known positions in the "in-country" war, and Lamplighter C-130s were capable of dropping flares in support of F-4 night operations in the more benign AAA environments. That, however, made for inefficient use of air power at best, and night operations were not routinely conducted over North Vietnam until the very end. The Navy's A-6 was night-capable but was used only rarely in night operations. For its part, the Air Force's night-capable F-111, with its automatic terrain-following radar, entered the war in meaningful numbers only during the buildup to Linebacker II as the air war was coming to a close.[83]

Improving the Odds in Aerial Combat

During the initial abortive attempt against the Thanh Hoa bridge within the first month of Operation Rolling Thunder, which cost the Air Force five aircraft altogether, North Vietnamese MiGs downed U.S. fighters for the first time. In a textbook Soviet-style GCI-directed attack, two MiG-17s emerged from the haze below and behind a flight of F-105s orbiting at medium altitude 10 miles south of the bridge. Despite a last-minute radio call from the second F-105 element warning the first of an imminent attack, the engaged pilots did not react and were evidently taken by surprise. The MiGs closed to 1,500 ft and opened fire, downing both aircraft and disengaging before they could be counterattacked. This mission underscored, for the first time, the reality of the MiG threat. Time and again throughout Rolling Thunder, even if a MiG attack was detected early enough to be successfully negated, the attack forced U.S. strike aircraft to jettison their bombs in order to countermaneuver more effectively. Thus, as one account noted, "The MiGs could often thwart an American mission simply by taking off."[84]

Because of the nuclear emphasis of U.S. defense strategy throughout the 1950s and an associated conviction among many that the days of aerial dogfighting were over, neither the Air Force's nor the Navy's fighters devel-

[83] Clodfelter, *The Limits of Air Power*, pp. 158–163.
[84] Grant, *Over the Beach*, p. 10.

oped during that period were designed to prevail in the close-in air combat arena that predominated over North Vietnam. The F-105's high wing loading (the ratio of its gross weight to total wing area), intended to permit the hauling of a nuclear weapon to target at treetop level and near-sonic speed, made the aircraft an impossible match for the MiG-17 and MiG-21 in turn performance. For its part, the F-4 had been designed as a two-place fleet air defense interceptor. Visibility out of the cockpit to the rear was severely limited, and the twin J-79 engines produced a heavy smoke trail when their afterburners were not engaged, making it easy for MiG pilots and AAA gunners to visually acquire, identify, and track it. It was not unusual for an F-4 to be visually detectable by its black smoke trail from as far away as 30 miles, depending on the look angle. The F-4's greater thrust margin and lower wing loading gave it better maneuvering performance than that of the F-105, yet a sustained turn rate only on a par with that of the MiG-21 and considerably less than that of the more agile MiG-17. According to an unclassified performance comparison of the F-4C and MiG-21 at the time, "only in range and first-shot capability does the F-4C enjoy a substantial advantage over the MiG-21 throughout the envelope."[85]

Equally troublesome, the F-4's original mission of intercepting standoff threats to Navy carriers with long-range missiles occasioned it to be designed without an internal cannon. The shortsightedness of that omission with respect to the air combat arena soon became apparent. As it turned out, the F-105, with its internal 20-mm cannon, was highly effective in snapshot engagements inside 2,000 ft, which represented the minimum range for the AIM-9B Sidewinder infrared missile. That realization led to the Air Force's acquiring the F-4E with an internal gun toward the end of U.S. involvement in Vietnam.

In the interim, some F-4s were fitted with SUU-16 20-mm cannon pods mounted on the aircraft's centerline station. That development offered only a temporary fix, however, because of the increased fuel consumption and decreased maneuverability caused by the gun pod's high aerodynamic drag. Also, the early F-4C was not outfitted with a lead-computing gunsight, which required pilots to lead their target by putting the pipper well in front of the engaged MiG, in an air combat variant of "Kentucky windage," before pulling the trigger.[86] Nevertheless, although not optimized for air-to-air combat, the gun pod was credited with 10 MiG kills between 1965 and

[85] Major Robert Goertz, USAF, "An Analysis of Air-to-Air Missile Capability in Southeast Asia," *Air Command and Staff College Papers*, June 1968, p. 14. It should be added that the F-4C's first-shot advantage came from the beyond visual range capability of its AIM-7 Sparrow missile, which was proscribed from combat use in Vietnam by the visual identification rules of engagement.
[86] This shortcoming was soon corrected in the later-model F-4D, which was given a lead-computing sight to accompany the improved SUU-23 gun pod. Michel, *Clashes*, pp. 102, 111.

1968.[87] The Air Force further moved to install wing leading-edge slats on the F-4E to increase the aircraft's stability and turn performance in maneuvering engagements. Its appreciation that neither the F-105 nor the F-4 could turn with the more maneuverable MiGs ultimately contributed to a later requirement for the far-more agile F-15 as a pure air superiority fighter.

Nor was the AIM-7E semiactive radar missile carried by the F-4 optimized for maneuvering air combat. From the beginning of the Vietnam air war in 1965 until March 1968, Air Force aircrews fired 224 AIM-7s for 20 kills, yielding an overall success rate of only 8.9 percent. Part of the reason for this low rate of effectiveness was that aircrews failed to keep their target illuminated by radar throughout the missile's time of flight as a consequence of being forced to break off their own attack to negate an attack by an enemy aircraft. Another part of the explanation was that F-4 aircrews, as a matter of practice, would often fire missiles in ripple fashion or out of lethal parameters, with little expectation of a hit as a result. Such aircrew actions caused an estimated 33 percent of the AIM-7 missile's failures. Even the earlier-generation AIM-4 Falcon missile carried by combat air patrol (CAP) fighters performed better for a brief time, with 4 kills out of 43 firings for a success rate of 10.7 percent. During the same period, Air Force crews fired 175 AIM-9B Sidewinder heat-seeking missiles for 25 kills, yielding a slightly higher success rate of 16 percent.

This overall poor performance was a sobering testament to the fact that *all* of the U.S. air-to-air missiles employed in Vietnam had been designed in the first place not to engage hard-maneuvering fighters, but rather to shoot down nonmaneuvering bombers at high altitudes. Partly because of that, they suffered a pronounced problem with respect to realistic testing and aircrew familiarization. Against predictable bomber-type targets, it was relatively easy to satisfy the displayed firing parameters of the AIM-7E and to get a good infrared seeker tone with the AIM-9B. Once these missiles were taken to war against countermaneuvering enemy fighters, however, U.S. aircrews quickly learned that the advertised performance envelopes that they had been taught before being sent into combat bore little relation to such far more difficult and demanding targets.

Finally, the ability to gather and communicate real-time information on the air-to-air situation left a great deal to be desired. The EC-121 Rivet Top airborne radar system, a progenitor of the E-3 airborne warning and control system (AWACS), which was fielded a decade later, offered only cautionary and warning indications of North Vietnamese MiG activity. Its radar was badly degraded by ground return in the look-down mode, making it only marginally useful in the environment below 5,000 ft, where many of the

---

[87] Nordeen, *Air Warfare in the Missile Age*, p. 45.

most deadly air-to-air engagements occurred. Also, the EC-121, later better known by its call sign Disco, at best was able to transmit locational information on North Vietnamese MiGs, first by reference to grid areas on a map and later in range and bearing from Hanoi, which was code-named Bullseye. Since Disco was unable to provide terminal warning of a MiG intercept, most of the American fighters downed by MiGs over North Vietnam were caught by surprise.

On the positive side, all EC-121s by May 1967 were equipped with the QRC-248 enemy IFF (identification, friend or foe) transponder interrogator, which could read the SRO-2 transponder mounted on Soviet-exported MiGs. Although this highly classified system, code-named Teaball, was restricted to use in the passive mode to avoid alerting Hanoi to the system's existence, it helped to ease the IFF problem by ensuring that any Bullseye calls to U.S. fighters were reporting the presence of MiGs and not friendly aircraft. The price exacted by the security restriction to avoid compromising the system was that it could not be used offensively to vector U.S. fighters to attack the detected MiGs.[88]

As a harbinger of major gains yet to come in U.S. air power's capability, the EC-121 also was used to monitor the so-called McNamara wall, a series of acoustic and seismic sensors that were strewn along the Ho Chih Minh Trail to detect enemy personnel and vehicular movement. This system, code-named Igloo White, exploited a primitive phenomenology in comparison to later sensor improvements. Nevertheless, its operational intent of cueing an airborne platform to locate moving ground targets electronically for follow-up attacks by strike aircraft represented a significant first step in ISR fusion to make the most of parallel improvements in U.S. strike capability. This fusion process eventually led to the later E-8 joint surveillance target attack radar system (JSTARS) aircraft that played a pivotal role in the 1991 Gulf war.

In addition, a visual-identification (VID) rule of engagement for air-to-air missile employment, imposed to prevent inadvertent kills of friendly fighters, placed limits on the usable envelope of the AIM-7 missile, which had a range of about 12 miles in a head-on attack, by depriving Air Force and Navy aircrews of any opportunity to take advantage of the missile's beyond-visual-range (BVR) capability, along with the element of tactical surprise that went with it. The later development of novel techniques of electronic identification allowed CAP and strike escort aircraft, for the first time, to be relieved of their former VID restriction, thus enabling them to take fuller advantage of the BVR capability of the AIM-7 missile. Among other things, this reduced considerably the likelihood of a surprise attack by the

---

[88] Ibid., p. 100.

more nimble MiGs.[89] Those techniques included a scaled-down version of the QRC-248 enemy IFF interrogator called the APX-80, code-named Combat Tree, which was first added to a few F-4Ds and later to the F-4E. They also included a wing-mounted sight unit called TISEO (target identification system, electro-optical), essentially a long-range telescope slaved to the radar that could allow an F-4 crew to identify visually a radar target far enough out, at least in theory, to permit the BVR use of the AIM-7. Although the operational impact of TISEO was less than revolutionary, on at least one occasion it did prevent an F-4 from inadvertently downing another F-4.[90]

In the meantime, while these developments were percolating, there was no dearth of imagination on the part of U.S. aircrews when it came to coming to better terms with the MiG threat. One notable example was a clever ruse executed on January 2, 1967, which later became immortalized in the annals of air-to-air combat as Operation Bolo. Masterminded by then–Colonel Robin Olds, the commander of the 8th Tactical Fighter Wing based at Ubon, Thailand, the mission aimed to conduct a massive MiG sweep by tricking Hanoi into believing that the approaching aircraft represented a standard attack package. This subterfuge committed 48 F-4s configured for air-to-air combat but mimicking F-105 formations, attack tactics, and radio call signs and carrying the QRC-160 jamming pod to emulate F-105 ECM tactics. Sure enough, the ruse flushed the MiGs in force and resulted in seven downed and two probably downed MiGs, with no U.S. losses, eliminating an estimated half of North Vietnam's MiG-21 inventory at the time. More important, it typified the determination of U.S. aircrews and their commanders to apply stratagems wherever possible to operate effectively within the many politically dictated constraints they had been forced to endure.

Such initiative was further reflected on the Navy's part by a determined training response to the disconcerting performance of U.S. aircrews in aerial engagements against Hanoi's MiGs. The overall American kill ratio over the course of the eight-year war was 2.4 to 1. That was appallingly low in comparison to the Air Force's kill ratio during the Korean war (4.7 to 1 in 1950–1952 and 13.9 to 1 in 1952–1953). At times, notably between August 1967 and February 1968, U.S. fighters suffered an *adverse* kill ratio against the MiG-21, with 18 U.S. aircraft lost for only 5 MiG-21s downed. This was all the more disconcerting considering that, as one knowledgeable account later observed, "combat reports gave little evidence that the MiG pilots ever developed real air combat maneuvering skills beyond attacking from behind and executing hard turns for both offensive and defensive maneuvers."[91]

[89] Ibid., p. 259.
[90] Ibid., p. 267.
[91] Michel, *Clashes*, p. 162.

Although these discomfiting numbers were partly a consequence of equipment limitations, they also reflected weaknesses in the air-to-air maneuvering skills of both Navy and, even more so, Air Force pilots. Shortly after the war started, the Air Force had initiated a program called Feather Duster, using Air National Guard F-86Hs to simulate the MiG-17, with a view toward determining the best tactics for its F-4Cs and F-105s against that obsolescent but highly agile Soviet-made fighter. This two-part operational evaluation, which pitted the F-86H in several hundred mostly one-on-one engagements against the F-4C and F-105 at both high and low altitudes, clearly established that "big [U.S.] fighters have a definite fighting region and have problems if they move out of it."[92] In particular, it determined that U.S. pilots should not slow down and try to turn with a MiG-17, but instead should maintain their energy and conduct slashing attacks to make the most of their superior performance in the vertical plane.

The problem with these Feather Duster sorties was that they were all flown by highly experienced fighter pilots, which the Air Force generally lacked in the theater after its initial cycle of aircrew deployments to Southeast Asia. As noted earlier, those in the first cadre of F-105 pilots sent to Thailand in 1965 were uniformly high-time aviators with an average of 500 hours or more of flight experience in the aircraft. By 1966, however, the Air Force's policy of rotating aircrew members home after 100 missions over North Vietnam or a year of combat in South Vietnam placed a heightened demand on pilot production, with the result that by 1966 the Air Force was sending to Southeast Asia many combat pilots without a tactical fighter background. Newly minted F-4 pilots were assigned to the aircraft's back-seat, where their flying skills were irrelevant. More experienced and senior pilots flying in the F-4 as the aircraft commander were drawn increasingly from air defense units, the Air Training Command, and even bomber and transport units, all offering no preparation whatever for the highly stressful and fast-changing arena of aerial combat. By June 1968, the average time spent in the type of aircraft Air Force fighter pilots were to fly in combat in Southeast Asia had dropped from more than 500 hours to only 240 hours.[93]

There were also significant differences between Navy and Air Force tactics that accounted for the better performance of Navy pilots, especially those flying the F-8, which was operated as a dedicated air combat fighter. The basic fighting unit for a Navy MiG-CAP package was a two-ship element of aircraft, called a "section" in Navy parlance, with the two aircraft flying line abreast and separated by roughly the equivalent of a combat turn radius (typically 6,000 to 9,000 ft), such that either the pilot or the backseater (in the case of the F-4) could check and clear the other's six-o'clock position with-

[92] Ibid., pp. 17–19.
[93] Ibid., pp. 118–119.

out difficulty. This formation provided the section with mutual support, which enabled either fighter to turn promptly to protect the other upon detecting a MiG attack. As a former Air Force fighter pilot, Marshall Michel, described it, "The idea was for one fighter to engage the enemy—the 'engaged' fighter—while the non-engaged, or 'free,' fighter stayed close enough to see the engagement, but not so close that he could not look for other enemy aircraft without worrying about the other aircraft in his section."[94] From the very beginning of Rolling Thunder, Navy F-8 pilots accepted as a tactical given that it was "essential for the leader to pass the lead to the member of his flight who has the bogies [enemy aircraft] in sight."[95]

In contrast, the Air Force approach, dating back to World War II, was based on the four-ship flight as the basic fighting unit, with paired elements of two aircraft flying together in a formation called "fluid four." The element wingmen, in positions 2 and 4 in the formation, flew 1,500 to 2,000 ft behind their respective leaders and offset some 45 degrees, in an element formation called "fighting wing." As Michel explained it, "In theory, the wingmen's roles were to provide protection for their element leaders, who were designated as the attackers. In reality, the wingman was so close to the leader that he had to spend most of his time keeping in formation, giving him little time to look at the overall battle."[96] In practice, the only shooter in Air Force fluid-four tactics was the flight leader. Significantly, the main difference in combat leverage between the Air Force and Navy approaches to aerial combat was that a four-ship flight of F-4s in a fluid-four formation was able to use only 25 percent of its potential firepower (that of the flight leader), with the result that *two* Navy F-4s flying "fluid-two" tactics had twice the usable firepower of *four* Air Force F-4s flying fluid four.

Not surprisingly, Air Force fighter aircrews at the unit level were keenly sensitive to this deficiency of the fluid-four approach. As one flight leader who went on to become a multiple MiG killer openly complained after a botched engagement in June 1972, "The wingman was always just another airplane in the air. I would have preferred to have gone into Route Package VI, under the conditions [in which] we were operating, with two highly qualified crews [flying Navy fluid two] rather than four. . . . I had to spend 90 percent of my time keeping somebody in the flight from getting shot down [and] could not go about the business of MiG-CAP."[97] Nevertheless, the Air Force leadership adhered to fluid four and fighting wing tactics until the very end of the Vietnam war.

The Navy, having remained more faithful all along to the classic air-to-air mission in its fleet fighter squadrons, was the first to act on its disconcerting

---

[94] Ibid., p. 169.
[95] Gillcrist, *Feet Wet*, p. 299.
[96] Michel, *Clashes*, p. 169.
[97] Quoted in ibid., pp. 232–233.

losses to Hanoi's MiGs. Prompted by the poor U.S. showing in air-to-air combat over North Vietnam, indeed the worst in the history of U.S. aerial warfare, the Naval Air Systems Command shortly after the bombing halt in 1968 commissioned an extensive review of those engagements and what had occasioned their outcomes. Led by an experienced fighter pilot, Captain Frank Ault, the 480-page study issued a year later recommended 242 improvements in Navy systems and procedures, including increases in missile reliability, more comprehensive air combat maneuvering (ACM) training for fleet fighter squadrons, and the development of a core of air-to-air experts to train fleet fighter aircrews.[98] The Ault report led to the establishment of what began as the U.S. Navy Postgraduate Course in Fighter Weapons, Tactics and Doctrine, initially a department of VF-121, the Pacific Fleet's F-4 replacement training squadron at Naval Air Station (NAS) Miramar. Later to become better known by its informal name Topgun, it soon evolved into a separate Navy Fighter Weapons School, which offered a five-week course in advanced air combat tactics and took only the best pilots of the fleet's air-to-air squadrons.[99]

In contrast, seemingly in counterflow to the teachings of the Vietnam experience, the Air Force all but discontinued dissimilar air combat training (DACT) after the end of Rolling Thunder in 1968, just as the Navy was activating its Topgun effort. Not surprisingly, when the air war over North Vietnam resumed in 1972, the Navy's kill ratio rose dramatically, while that of the Air Force declined.[100] Before the establishment of the Topgun program, the overall Navy kill ratio was 3.7 to 1. Afterwards, it shot up for a time to 13 to 1, leading naval aviators to speak of the Vietnam air war as having been conducted in two phases—"before Topgun and after Topgun." Many Navy pilots, upon returning from their second combat tour, reported that their MiG encounters were "like Topgun, only these guys weren't half as good." The effect was to spawn an important and lasting realization among fighter pilots in both services that you fight like you train.

In Retrospect

The Vietnam war was a defining experience for American air power. Among other things, it revealed the consequences of the nation's previous

---

[98] The formal title of the study was "Air Warfare Missile Systems Capability Review." For a detailed firsthand review of the genesis and nature of that effort, see Captain Frank W. Ault, USN (Ret.), "The Ault Report Revisited," *The Hook*, Spring 1989, pp. 35–39.

[99] Lou Drendel, *. . . and Kill MiGs*, Warren, Mich., Squadron/Signal Publications, 1974, p. 30.

[100] From 1965 through 1968, the Air Force and Navy had a roughly equal kill ratio (2.25 to 1 for the Air Force and 2.42 to 1 for the Navy). In 1970–1973, the Navy's ratio rose to 13 to 1, while that of the Air Force declined to 1.92 to 1.

fixation on nuclear strategy at the expense of adequate preparations for conventional war. It further showed the costs of having goals with less than abiding clarity on the policy front, as well as the foolhardiness of committing air power in piecemeal fashion rather than with determination. Still other lessons had to do with the imposition of a strategy by civilian leaders that was divorced from the most elementary rules of military common sense and the divided manner in which air power was controlled and applied by those ultimately responsible for its performance. In particular, the air war over North Vietnam highlighted a number of emerging problems associated with conducting modern conventional war against a well-equipped and sophisticated opponent. In so doing, it provided a wake-up call regarding the kinds of defenses the United States and members of the North Atlantic Treaty Organization (NATO) would have to contend with in configuring themselves for a possible future counteroffensive against Soviet and Warsaw Pact forces in Central Europe.

Ultimately, the roots of the U.S. defeat in Southeast Asia went to the failure of the Johnson-McNamara team to assess correctly the nature of the war and to take military actions most appropriate to it. Instead of recognizing the essence of Hanoi's goals and the depth of Ho Chi Minh's commitment to them, McNamara sold President Johnson on a strategy of gradualism, on the premise that North Vietnam was of similar mind and would "get the message" intended by the "signals" being sent by Rolling Thunder, as though, in H. R. McMaster's formulation, the war was just "another business management problem that . . . would ultimately succumb to his reasoned judgment and others' rational calculations."[101]

This critique of Johnson and McNamara is not to suggest that the JCS, for their part, were entirely blameless for the creation of the Vietnam debacle. True enough, as McMaster well chronicled, the chiefs were adamant in their insistence on pursuing a war-winning strategy instead of the half-hearted "signaling" approach of Johnson and McNamara. Yet they remained badly divided on the details of implementation, with each typically advocating his own service's wherewithal as the preferred answer to the challenge. The Air Force chief, General Curtis LeMay, argued that a strategic air campaign against the north might obviate altogether the need to commit U.S. troops to combat on the ground in the south. The chief of naval operations saw the solution instead in mining North Vietnam's ports and conducting riverine patrols in the Mekong Delta. The Army chief argued for inserting large numbers of ground troops into South Vietnam *before* any commencement of bombing against North Vietnam. And the Marine Corps commandant repeatedly advocated a strategy that would ensure a large Marine share of the action in combating the Viet Cong insurgency. As McMaster concluded, this

---

[101] McMaster, *Dereliction of Duty*, p. 327.

desire by each chief "to further his own service's agenda hampered their collective ability to provide military advice." As a result, he added, "The intellectual foundation for deepening American involvement in Vietnam had been laid without the participation of the Joint Chiefs of Staff."[102]

Another factor that contributed to the American defeat in Vietnam was the asymmetry in stakes between the two sides, a problem that had plagued the French as well. For Hanoi, it was a total war for total objectives. At the outset of the Indochina conflict, Ho Chih Minh warned a French visitor, "You can kill ten of my men for every one I kill of yours. But even at those odds, you will lose and I will win."[103] Clearly, Rolling Thunder saddled North Vietnam with indirect costs that were far higher than its purely destructive effects. By the estimate of Admiral U. S. Grant Sharp, who was CINCPAC at the time, the bombing drove Hanoi to divert 500,000 to 600,000 civilians to the work of air defense and bomb damage repair and caused extensive economic deterioration and dislocation.[104] However, North Vietnam was quintessentially a labor-intensive society, and these costs had little effect on Ho's determination not to flinch from his abiding goal of unifying the two Vietnams.

Without question, the restrictive rules of engagement imposed by Washington and the various equipment and training shortcomings that afflicted Rolling Thunder contributed to an unsatisfactory performance by American air power. Just as the overall war effort was hamstrung by its indeterminate objectives, U.S. air power also suffered the effects of a strategy that could not help but limit its effectiveness. That said, it bears stressing that insofar as war is, by definition, an instrument of policy, politically imposed rules of engagement will *always*, in some form or another, be a handmaiden of force employment decisions to ensure that the manner in which force is applied conforms to political objectives and perceived risks. The right lesson to be drawn from the Vietnam experience on this account is not that political control and restrictive rules of engagement are improper constraints on the use of air power (or any other force element, for that matter), but rather that once reasonable political objectives, strategies, and rules of engagement are decided on, political leaders should stay out of the operational details of force employment in due deference to the trained professionals who know their business best.

Furthermore, it is fair to say in hindsight that the prevailing American air power assets of the day could not have engaged targets across North Vietnam in a consistently productive manner even in the best of circumstances. North Vietnamese SAMS, AAA, and MiGs made operating at every altitude

---

[102] Ibid., p. 83.
[103] Quoted in Karnow, *Vietnam: A History*, p. 183.
[104] Cited in Davidson, *Vietnam at War*, p. 437.

dangerous. As a result, the Air Force and Navy attack formations that became commonplace during the course of Rolling Thunder relied on ever-larger numbers of support aircraft to jam and attack enemy defenses so that a few fighters might succeed in actually putting bombs on target.[105] In addition, until North Vietnamese actions on the ground presented sufficiently massed aggregations of enemy troop strength to give U.S. air power a serious target to shoot at, the use of air power, regardless of the sortie count or bomb tonnage dropped, was bound to be ineffective against the low-volume supply lines in both North and South Vietnam that ran through heavily overgrown terrain.

Beyond that, it remains unclear whether a more classic "strategic" air campaign unburdened of all the Washington-imposed restrictions would have made a notable difference in affecting Hanoi's ability to continue supporting the war in the south. Unlike Germany in World War II, North Vietnam was a nonindustrialized state that presented few infrastructure targets worthy of the name, and virtually none whose elimination would have fundamentally altered Hanoi's determination to regain control of the south. Agriculture accounted for nearly half the country's gross domestic product, and 80 percent of its laborers were farmers.

True enough, as Kenneth Werrell pointed out, the dramatic display of air power over the 11 days of Linebacker II led many airmen to believe that "they might have won the war had they been allowed to run it."[106] Yet the undeniable effect that Linebacker II had in driving Hanoi to the negotiating table did not negate the facts that it neither resulted in North Vietnam's defeat nor reflected an application of air power appropriate to the U.S. government's ultimately failed effort to conduct a successful counterinsurgency campaign in the south, which is what the fighting in Southeast Asia was fundamentally all about. As the panel of scientists convened by McNamara to assess the effectiveness of Rolling Thunder concluded as early as August 1966, North Vietnam was "basically a subsistence agricultural economy" that presented an "unrewarding target" for U.S. air power, at least so long as the war remained predominantly an insurgency in the south rather than a clash of regular forces on both sides.[107]

As for the war in the south, the limited ISR assets available to MACV all too often were incapable of generating meaningful targets for U.S. air power. Naturally as a result, nonexistent ISR in the jungle typically meant a failure

---

[105] In a typical Air Force Linebacker strike into Route Package VI, to note just one example, it took some 48 Weasel, chaff bomber, chaff escort, strike escort, and MiG-CAP aircraft to get a dozen LGB-carrying strikers to target, making for a support-to-striker ratio of 4 to 1.

[106] Kenneth P. Werrell, "Air War Victorious: The Gulf War vs. Vietnam," *Parameters*, Summer 1992, p. 45.

[107] Karnow, *Vietnam: A History*, p. 499.

on air power's part. Even in the best case when U.S. bombing finally broke the enemy siege at Khe Sanh, it took 2.5 combat aircraft sorties, each with a heavy ordnance load, to kill just one of General Giap's soldiers. Although air power eventually overwhelmed the enemy through brute force at Khe Sanh, its performance scarcely warranted accolades either for the hardware employed or for the force effectiveness achieved.

At best, then, the performance of U.S. air power in Vietnam was mixed. Its uneven record, while predominantly a result of shortcomings in equipment and aircrew proficiency, could also be attributed, at least in part, to swings in Hanoi's strategy for prosecuting its operations in the south. As Robert Jervis recalled on this point, "The American conventional offensives that worked well when the North Vietnamese thought they could win by large-scale battles failed when the latter reverted to guerrilla warfare; the weakness of the American effort against unconventional warfare led the north to seek more decisive conventional battles in 1972, which in turn made their forces vulnerable to the kind of American air strikes that had yielded so few results previously; the return to unconventional war forced the south to disperse its army and thus facilitated the success of the North Vietnamese offensive in 1975." [108]

This suggests that if the Vietnam experience offers any worthwhile teaching with respect to the uses and limitations of air power today, it should be that the air weapon can be potent indeed when employed against a conventional opponent but is likely to be relatively less effective, all other things equal, against an adversary who uses low-intensity and unconventional tactics, such as the Viet Cong did in South Vietnam until the war escalated to conventional operations in 1968. U.S. air operations over both North and South Vietnam produced telling results against the sort of massed, logistics-intensive conventional assaults that characterized Khe Sanh and the 1972 Easter offensive. Yet they had little measurable effect on the more slack and low-volume North Vietnamese supply lines that fed the Viet Cong insurgency before 1968.

With respect to the rationale underlying U.S. air attacks against North Vietnam, it also bears noting that the responsibility for Washington's failure to apply a viable strategy did not fall solely on the shoulders of Johnson and McNamara. As Barry Watts pointed out, there was "a fundamental disconnect between the Air Force's strategic bombing and the limited nature of the insurgency that the U.S. faced in Vietnam," a disconnect which prevailed at least throughout the Rolling Thunder phase of the air war between 1965 and 1968. Part and parcel of that disconnect was "an illusion that the efficient application of firepower could substitute for strategy," an illusion that kept Air

---

[108] Robert Jervis, *System Effects: Complexity in Political and Social Life*, Princeton, Princeton University Press, 1997, p. 45.

Force leaders "from developing any strategy for Southeast Asia other than the application of increasing doses of air-delivered firepower on traditional 'strategic' targets."[109]

All the same, the U.S. air assets employed over North Vietnam in 1972 were considerably advanced in capability over those that were available between 1965 and 1968. Notable among their improved capabilities was the routine availability of LGBs, whose use against bridges and other point targets offered a telling preview of future possibilities. Still, until the Linebacker II attacks ultimately beat down North Vietnam's air defenses decisively, enemy SAMs and AAA posed a considerable threat to American air power. Night and all-weather operations remained extremely difficult throughout the war, and the costs of attacking heavily defended targets in the northernmost Route Packages remained high enough to prevent the decisive use of air power. Yet Air Force and Navy aircrews finally did learn over North Vietnam by 1972 how to operate effectively in the sort of heavy air defense environment that they might expect to encounter elsewhere in the future. Armed with that experience, they embarked on a slow process of improving the capabilities of U.S. air power in all dimensions, not only with respect to its hardware ingredients, but also in the no less important areas of training and tactics. That legacy of an otherwise lamentable chapter in the history of American air power put all four services on a vector to perfect their air assets during the two decades that spanned Vietnam and Desert Storm.

[109] Barry D. Watts, "Review of Earl Tilford, *Crosswinds: The Air Force's Setup in Vietnam*," in *Air Power History*, Winter 1993, p. 56.

[3]

Building a Mature Air Posture

If the Vietnam experience highlighted disturbing shortcomings in American air power, the concurrent Soviet military buildup provided more than the needed incentive for it to acquire a sharper edge. While the United States was bogged down in Southeast Asia between 1965 and 1972, the Soviet Union, encouraged and abetted by Washington's embroilment in Vietnam, carried out a massive expansion of its nuclear and general-purpose forces. In the crucial realm of intercontinental and submarine-launched ballistic missiles, Moscow achieved acknowledged parity with the United States in both numbers and overall force quality. During the same period, the Soviets also upgraded their forward-deployed conventional forces into a daunting juggernaut overshadowing Western Europe. That development, in turn, confronted U.S. defense planners with a rapidly growing threat and brought with it both new and uniquely imposing challenges for American air power.

It was not, to be sure, only American *air* power that underwent a major refurbishment under the influence of this resurgent Soviet challenge. On the contrary, although the U.S. defeat in Vietnam was primarily a failure of national strategy, it revealed deep deficiencies in all four services. In response, each drew the appropriate lessons from Vietnam and reacted with determined and, in some cases, quite far-reaching reforms. At the heart of the reforms was a new stress on incorporating leading-edge technology and a major focus on acquiring increased combat proficiency.

In the case of the Army, a series of training and doctrine reforms initiated during the early 1970s helped lift that service out of its early post-Vietnam trauma and transform it into an all-volunteer force guided by fundamentally new concepts of warfare. Its National Training Center located at Fort Irwin in the California desert became an active battle laboratory for providing realistic unit-level training in armored combat in a combined-arms setting. A concurrent push by the Army to modernize its equipment inventory was dominated by the introduction of the M1 Abrams tank, the M2 Bradley armored fighting vehicle, the AH-64 Apache attack helicopter, the UH-60 Blackhawk utility helicopter, and the Patriot advanced surface-to-air missile (SAM). These post-Vietnam acquisitions provided the Army with an impressive array of new weapons for conducting land warfare. At the same time, new developments on the doctrine front, explored in more detail later in this chapter, focused on configuring the Army to counter a surprise Warsaw Pact armored assault against NATO by supplanting its defensive orientation and attrition mentality with a new concept of maneuver warfare aimed at engaging attacking enemy forces both close and deep simultaneously, and with heavy reliance on Air Force support. By the late 1980s, the Army's 16 active divisions had fully recovered from their post-Vietnam demoralization and were at peak readiness for maneuver warfare against a peer opponent.

For its part, the Navy likewise registered significant gains during the early years after Vietnam. Those gains aggregated under the aegis of the Navy's newly articulated Maritime Strategy, which aimed at hunting down Soviet ballistic missile submarines from their northernmost bastions to the open ocean, protecting the Atlantic sea lanes for reinforcements from the United States to Europe in the event of a NATO–Warsaw Pact showdown, and neutralizing any Soviet air or naval forces that might contest American control of the high seas worldwide. The U.S. Marine Corps also made moves to carry out plans for providing amphibious assaults on the flanks of any possible NATO–Warsaw Pact battleground, rediscovering along the way its classic traditions of maneuver warfare while retaining its unique status as the sole U.S. service equipped and trained to conduct combat operations in all three mediums of warfare. Among the most notable hardware developments associated with this bolstering of the naval establishment in the early post-Vietnam years were new nuclear-powered aircraft carriers, a new generation of Los Angeles–class fast-attack nuclear submarines, the long-range Tomahawk land-attack cruise missile, and new ship and air defense weapons, all pointed toward a 600-ship fleet designed to support the Maritime Strategy.

The United States and its NATO allies got an arresting preview of what an all-out showdown with the newly expanded Soviet conventional force posture might entail when they witnessed the 1973 Yom Kippur war between Israel and its Arab adversaries. Caught with little warning and unprepared to incur the political costs of a second preemption in six years, Israel was overwhelmed by the combined Arab attack and lost 97 aircraft—more than a third of its entire air force—to enemy surface-to-air fire in the course of recovering to eventual victory. The 1973 war also involved armored battles of an intensity that had not been experienced since World War II, with Israeli and Arab forces sustaining materiel losses of 50 percent in less than two weeks of ground fighting. The war revealed, for the first time, the lethality of the Soviet SAM and antiaircraft artillery AAA threat. It further underscored for the West the absolute necessity of being prepared to fight and win outnumbered, both in the air and on the ground, through force multipliers in the form of better equipment, tactics, and training.

As the U.S. military began organizing itself to accommodate to this new situation, the last thought in anyone's mind was that the payoff would be tested two decades later not out of such familiar bases as Bitburg, Spangdahlem, and Hahn in West Germany, but instead out of far-flung places in the Arabian desert with little-known names like Al Kharj and Khamis Mushait. In response to this more immediate challenge, numerous efforts were set in train that gave the United States an unmatched air posture by the time of Iraq's invasion of Kuwait in 1990. These improvements left no facet of U.S. air power untouched. Among other things, they included such seemingly mundane developments as an extended service life and increased reach for the Air Force's airlifter fleet through the rewinging of the C-141 and C-5 and the provision of an inflight refueling capability in both; the reengining of the KC-135 tanker and introduction of new KC-10s to further extend the reach and sustainability of U.S. conventional striking power; and a streamlining and consolidation of the Air Force's maintenance and logistics infrastructure to increase the efficiency and sortie generation capacity of its combat air arm.

A full accounting of these and other measures undertaken to maximize the leverage of the American air weapon during the two decades that separated Vietnam and Desert Storm would add up to a major study in its own right. The most dynamic and consequential changes in the U.S. air posture since Vietnam, however, occurred at the sharp end—in the air superiority and ground-attack mission areas where American air power faced its most demanding challenges. Among the many areas in which major gains were made after Vietnam, the three most notable were aircrew proficiency, equipment performance, and concepts of operations. Improvements in these three areas ranged from greatly enhanced training and tactics through new and better platforms, munitions, and other hardware to more effective employment techniques and joint-service strategies. The resulting transformation of American air power occasioned by these developments was roundly validated by the success of the allied air campaign in Desert Storm. To understand what largely prompted and guided it, however, we must first recall at least the basics of the threat which American air power was organizing itself to address.

[56]

THE OPERATIONAL CHALLENGE FACING NATO

The core problem for U.S. defense planners in the wake of Vietnam was the growing presence of Soviet armored and mechanized infantry forces deployed in large numbers in the Warsaw Pact forward area. Those forces were configured in accordance with an unmistakable offensive conventional warfare doctrine. By 1986, the Warsaw Pact was poised to mobilize some 60 divisions—including non-Soviet Warsaw Pact forces—already pre-positioned in the forward area. With reinforcements from the Soviet Union, that number could be increased to between 90 and 120 divisions, along with up to 3,600 supporting combat aircraft. For their part, the United States and its NATO allies could marshal only 45 divisions even after several weeks of prior mobilization time. The number of Soviet tanks opposite NATO in the first echelon alone all but ensured that any war in Europe would be a "come as you are" war, dominated by quick and violent Soviet armored thrusts that could potentially decide the outcome even before American reinforcements would have a chance to come into play.

Lending further teeth to that imposing capability was the Soviet military's resurrection of the Operational Maneuver Group (OMG), an idea first developed by the Soviet High Command in World War II. That concept, first observed during the Warsaw Pact's *Zapad* 1981 summer training exercise, entailed the use of large, tank-heavy formations to exploit breakthroughs aimed at quickly seizing key command centers, nuclear weapons facilities, bridges and choke points, and other high-value objectives in NATO's rear. The best evidence at the time suggested that the reborn OMG would be a division- or corps-sized combat unit assembled from existing order of battle and composed mainly of heavy armored forces reinforced with artillery and aviation, with the intent to be both highly mobile and more survivable and self-sustainable than typical line units. Its operational function was believed to be early commitment immediately behind the first attacking echelon, with a view toward penetrating quickly to NATO's rear and capturing important predesignated objectives.[1] The concept faced serious problems with respect to resupply, and it had other vulnerabilities as well, against which NATO was eventually to develop a counter-strategy for leveraging in the form of its Follow-On Forces Attack (FOFA) plan. Soviet doctrine sought to avoid any extended exposure of those vulnerabilities, however, by a rapid exploitation of shock and surprise. The likelihood of such exploitation was further enhanced by the concurrent establishment of a theater command

---

[1] A particularly authoritative treatment at the time was C. N. Donnelly, "The Soviet Operational Maneuver Group: A New Challenge for NATO," *International Defense Review*, September 1982, pp. 1177–1186.

apparatus capable of supporting an immediate transition of Soviet ground forces from peacetime to a combat footing.

In addition to their formidable ground posture, the Soviets registered important gains in theater air forces during the late 1970s and early 1980s. The introduction of the MiG-23 with improved radar range and a forward-hemisphere missile capability gradually supplanted the emphasis of Vietnam-era air combat on countering sneak attacks from the rear with a new Western awareness of the looming all-aspect air-to-air missile threat. At the same time, the once largely defensive Soviet fighter force was fundamentally changed by the deployment of new multimission aircraft like the Su-24 tactical bomber, an F-111 counterpart with respectable all-weather ground-attack capabilities. By 1982, the USSR was producing some 1,300 new fighters a year, about three to four times the fighter replacement rate of the U.S. Air Force. That translated into a production rate on the average of more than three new combat aircraft a day, or a squadron a week and a wing a month —a rate, moreover, that was sustained by the Soviet defense industry without significant interruption throughout the late 1970s.

The subsequent appearance, by the mid-1980s, of the fourth-generation MiG-29 and Su-27 gave Soviet Frontal Aviation, for the first time, air-to-air performance capabilities comparable to those of the U.S. F-14/15/16/18 class of fighters. In addition to their high acceleration and maneuverability, these new aircraft featured look-down/shoot-down avionics and weapons that rendered Warsaw Pact air forces capable of head-on attacks against NATO aircraft, both within and beyond visual range. Soviet and Warsaw Pact air power appeared poised, through a sustained air operation conducted over several days in successive waves, to neutralize NATO's air power by concentrated conventional attacks against NATO airfields, ground-based air defenses, nuclear weapons storage facilities, and command and control systems.[2] Its imposing numbers were undergirded by an operational philosophy that was indifferent to attrition so long as the forward momentum of a combined-arms theater campaign was being maintained.[3]

In all, by the mid-1980s, the Soviet Air Force and its Warsaw Pact adjuncts could outnumber a reinforced U.S. Air Forces in Europe (USAFE) by as much as three to one if it brought forward assets based within the USSR and in-

[2] For one of the most informed assessments of the so-called Warsaw Pact "air operation plan" at the time, see Philip A. Peterson and Major John R. Clark, "Soviet Air and Anti-Air Operations," *Air University Review*, March–April 1985, pp. 36–54.

[3] The good-news aspect of this otherwise imposing threat picture was that Soviet pilot proficiency was rightly assessed to have been considerably lower than that of the United States and that Moscow's concept of air operations was both inflexible and dependent on ground control, two vulnerabilities that could be exploited by NATO. For a fuller treatment of the evidence bearing on this, see Benjamin S. Lambeth, *Russia's Air Power in Crisis*, Washington, D.C., Smithsonian Institution Press, 1999, especially pp. 71–116.

cluded earlier-generation aircraft like the MiG-21 and Su-7. If NATO European fighters were introduced into the equation, the balance would look more like two to one, or possibly less. Either way, this added up to a clear NATO inability to match the Warsaw Pact weapon for weapon and a consequent need to pursue force multipliers aimed at denying the Warsaw Pact any advantage from its numerical edge and offensive doctrine.

A REVOLUTION IN TRAINING

Doubly motivated by the lessons of Vietnam and the need to redress the growing military imbalance in Europe, American airmen worked on multiple fronts from the early 1970s through the mid-1980s to forge an unprecedentedly capable air weapon. At the forefront of this effort was a dramatic growth in the intensity and realism of aircrew training in all services. The effect of Topgun in driving up the Navy's kill ratio against Hanoi's MiGs during the "second" air war over North Vietnam in 1972 bore ample witness to the fact that pilot proficiency was no less important than systems capability in determining combat outcomes. Further confirmation of this was offered by the Air Force's later Red Baron study, which attributed the low U.S. kill ratio in Vietnam primarily to poor or inappropriate training.[4] Prompted by that awareness, post-Vietnam fighter training became firmly grounded on the premise that first-class hardware, in and of itself, could not guarantee air combat success. Both quality equipment and adequate numbers afforded great combat *potential*, but the extent to which that potential might be leveraged to good effect in practice depended on the way those advantages were employed.

The multifront effort pursued by the Air Force and its fellow air combat arms in the Navy and Marine Corps beginning around 1973 to make the most of their existing hardware while a successor generation of aircraft and munitions was nearing deployment was dominated by an emphasis on dissimilar air combat maneuvering and other measures to introduce greater realism and intensity into day-to-day training. Those initiatives were concentrated, for the most part, at the services' main training centers located throughout the American Southwest, because of the unique airspace offerings, threat arrays, and range instrumentation those complexes were able to provide. Nevertheless, the underlying intent, ultimately realized in spades a decade later, was to offer war as a daily training diet to Air Force, Navy, and Marine combat units not only at those training centers but also at their home stations worldwide.

---

[4] *Project Red Baron III: Air-to-Air Encounters in Southeast Asia*, Vol. I, Executive Summary, Cameron Station, Va., Defense Documentation Center, June 1974.

Dissimilar Air Combat Training and the Aggressor Program

The first major post-Vietnam training initiative pursued by the Air Force was the establishment of a serious program of dissimilar air combat training (DACT). That long-overdue move was grounded in the fact that air combat maneuvering between fighters of the same type not only was unrealistic but also, because the opposed aircraft had the same performance capabilities, mainly showed who the more capable pilots were—or, in the case of pilots of roughly equal skill, which ones could better exploit the aircraft's handling features at slower airspeeds, where any turning engagement among matched opponents was bound to degenerate were it allowed to progress to that stage. In contrast, training against fighters of different sizes and with different performance in such key areas as acceleration, instantaneous and sustained turn rate, corner velocity (the lowest speed at which maximum allowable gravity force, or g, can be attained), and airspeed bleed-off rate during hard turns promised to give Air Force aircrews not only better preparation for the real world of air combat, but also needed skills at comparative performance assessment and at leveraging their own aircraft's advantages against an enemy's known weaknesses, in a way that could never be acquired solely through training between similar aircraft types—which had generally been the norm in Air Force practice up to that point.[5]

Toward that end, in the face of rampant nervousness throughout the Air Force's middle and upper leadership levels and owing entirely to the strong support of General William Momyer, the commander of Tactical Air Command (TAC) at the time, the 64th Fighter Weapons Squadron, the Air Force's inaugural Aggressor squadron, was activated at Nellis AFB in October 1972 and became operational in June 1973. Shortly thereafter, it was followed by a sister unit in the 65th Fighter Weapons Squadron at Nellis and by similar units in Europe and the Pacific.[6] This development followed in the tradition of Topgun but was informed by a different approach. Instead of exposing Air Force aircrews to dissimilar fighter types flown to their performance limits, the Aggressor program consciously sought to emulate known or suspected *Soviet* operating practices, which were more rigid and stylized than those typical of U.S. fighter practice. That had the advantage of giving

[5] Although DACT did not become commonplace in Air Force practice until after Vietnam, it was approved in principle by TAC as early as February 1966 in TAC Manual 51–6. See "Dissimilar Aircraft Engagements," *USAF Fighter Weapons Review*, Summer 1976, pp. 14–20 (reprinted from the March 1968 issue).

[6] For a firsthand account of this history by one of the charter members of the Aggressor program, see Colonel Dawson R. O'Neill, USAF (Ret.), "How the Aggressors Began—I Think," *Daedalus Flyer*, Spring 1998, pp. 12–17.

U.S. aircrews a reasonable approximation of what they could expect to encounter in air-to-air combat against their Soviet (or Soviet-trained) counterparts, along with the confidence that such exposure naturally inspired.

The Aggressor program clearly reflected the Air Force's belated acceptance of the criticality of DACT in preparing its aircrews for a showdown with their Soviet counterparts or with any Soviet client state operating the latest in Soviet-made fighters. Initial Aggressor training at Nellis employed the T-38 supersonic trainer, which was later replaced by the radar-equipped and more maneuverable F-5E to provide a slightly faster and more realistic MiG-21 threat simulator. The DACT scenarios progressed in sequence from one-on-one to progressively more complex multiaircraft engagements. As one indicator of the demanding nature of the training syllabus, upgrading Aggressor instructors, much like the select students attending the advanced courses offered by the separate USAF Fighter Weapons School and the Navy's Topgun program, were taught to know precisely their aircraft's energy state and maneuvering performance purely by feel. For example, they would fly a sustained six-g level turn first by monitoring the g meter. Then they would perform the same maneuver without looking inside the cockpit. Finally, they would perform it in a realistic defensive air combat situation by looking back hard over their right shoulder while flying the aircraft unnaturally with their left hand on the control stick. Only after they could determine their g loading by feel alone to within half a g were they cleared to move on to the next syllabus block. Upgrading Aggressor pilots were also taught to assess an opposed aircraft's energy state at any moment by observing its nose position and other telltale indicators.

Each Aggressor squadron employed six ground-controlled intercept (GCI) controllers to simulate the Soviet style of close control, and an Aggressor GCI site was established within the Nellis range complex. The Aggressor mission was to support the USAF Fighter Weapons School and the large-force Red Flag training exercise (see below), as well as to conduct field visitations to fighter units throughout the tactical air forces to provide both flying and academic training in Soviet weapons and tactics. A typical Aggressor deployment would feature a two-week stay of four T-38s or F-5s and a 40-sortie training program, which would give up to 20 host unit aircrews a minimum of two DACT missions each. The host units themselves designed the training program to meet their individual needs.

Red Flag and Its Offshoots

A TAC study prompted by a specially convened fighter symposium held at Nellis in late 1972 firmly established the importance of more realistic aircrew training. As the symposium's keynote speaker admitted, "Things have changed a lot and we [in TAC] have not kept pace." An official TAC journal later noted the symposium's focus on the idea that "we [Tactical Air Command] may have concentrated too extensively on improving the machine and have not spent enough effort on the man who must fly it or on the training which he must have to make that machine an exploitable advantage."[7]

Three years later, prompted by the ferment created by that landmark symposium, the new TAC commander, General Robert J. Dixon, inaugurated a sweeping change in Air Force fighter training. In 1975, he approved a remarkable brainchild of the late Colonel Moody Suter called Red Flag, a recurring large-force training exercise aimed at providing maximum operational realism under peacetime conditions. Both the Vietnam war and earlier experiences showed that the first 10 combat sorties flown by a pilot are likely to be the main determinants of his subsequent wartime survival. The pilots who made it through the initial missions alive were those who were well prepared going in and who learned quickly. Those who did not have or soon develop such traits became statistics. The intent of Red Flag was to give aircrews the functional equivalent of their first 8 or 10 combat missions in a realistic, yet supervised and safe, peacetime environment.

What was at first called Operation Red Flag got started at Nellis in December 1975. It entailed a mock war engaging tactical air forces from throughout the country aimed at providing realistic training to participating units. A typical Blue Force consisted of Air Force F-4s, A-7s, and F-111s and Air National Guard F-100s launched in realistic force packages to attack tactical targets, electronically simulated SAM sites, and AAA emplacements. It also typically included OV-10 forward air controllers (FACs), RF-4C reconnaissance aircraft, and F-105 Wild Weasel support, with A-7s providing close air support (CAS) and HH-53 combat search-and-rescue forces involved, along with a four-man team of survival experts from the Air Force's survival school at Fairchild AFB in Washington. Pilots designated as "downed" by simulated enemy fire would be brought by helicopter into the desert and left alone there to conduct an individual escape-and-evasion exercise, using only the equipment provided in their survival kits. The opposing Red Force consisted of Aggressor T-38s and F-5Es with GCI support. An EC-121 provided communications jamming of attacking Blue Force aircraft. During its first years, a Red Flag exercise was conducted once a month. A typical operation conducted in May 1977 featured 141 aircraft of 19 different types, flying more than 2,000 training sorties altogether.

An inevitable problem was that the Red Flag training environment became familiar to aircrews over time because of geographic constants and range size and boundary limitations. Nevertheless, the Nellis range com-

---

[7] Quoted in Marshall Michel, *Clashes: Air Combat over North Vietnam, 1965–1972*, Annapolis, Md., Naval Institute Press, 1997, p. 289.

plex offered one of the few places where U.S. aircrews could integrate realistic communications jamming, high airspeeds, and novel tactics against diverse and unfamiliar targets. Its most distinctive feature was the opportunity for participating aircrews to be exposed to new and unforeseen situations in a highly fluid tactical environment.

To be sure, the clear-weather desert environment of Red Flag did not offer a replica of NATO's Central Region by any means. Apart from that, however, it was accurately described as "the heart-pumpinest, palm-sweatinest war we have," providing American and allied aircrews with an unparalleled opportunity to train to the limit of their ability.[8] That made for invaluable training, even if most aircrews throughout the tactical air forces (TAF) only got one two-week exposure to Red Flag a year.

Later, under the six-year tutelage of Dixon's successor at TAC, General W. L. Creech, a much-expanded training regime was implemented, led by Green Flag, a periodic mock-war exercise held at Nellis emphasizing electronic warfare and the suppression of enemy air defenses. A biennial Maple Flag program at Cold Lake, Canada, brought together selected Air Force, Navy, Marine, and Canadian fighter units for a week of intensive ground-attack and air-to-air training. Blue Flag, a nonflying activity conducted at Eglin AFB, Florida, concentrated on the myriad details of large-force mission employment planning. Checkered Flag became an exercise in which each fighter unit throughout the TAF planned and exercised for its real-world contingency tasking. Finally, starting in 1985, Copper Flag at Tyndall AFB, Florida, offered a thrice-yearly air defense exercise for aircrews and weapons controllers featuring realistic counterair scenarios not available at their home stations.[9]

In addition, Red Flag inspired increased efforts throughout the TAF to consolidate and disseminate tactics. Israeli pilots were prone to argue that tactics should never be written down because they then become doctrinaire and ossified. Yet there was much merit to building a manual for each aircraft that explained the full spectrum of its employment potential against all known varieties of targets and threats. That was done in Multi-Command Manual (MCM) 3-1, which was defined as "the most definitive source of tactics information" available to the TAF.[10] Two volumes described generic mission-planning considerations and threat capabilities and countertactics. Eleven more volumes provided operating specifics for each Air Force com-

---

[8] Major Gerald Volloy, "Red Flag in Perspective," *USAF Fighter Weapons Review*, Spring 1979, pp. 1–5.

[9] See Major Timothy J. Brennan, "TAC's New Flag," *USAF Fighter Weapons Review*, Summer 1985, pp. 21–24.

[10] Captain C. M. Westenhoff, "Tactics—The Key to Success: MCM 3-1," *USAF Fighter Weapons Review*, Fall 1985, pp. 2–4.

bat aircraft. These volumes were updated annually at a TAF-wide conference on MCM 3-1, with inputs from both Nellis and field operating units.

The cumulative experience gained throughout the TAF as a result of seven years of recurrent Red Flag seasoning led to a landmark large-force exercise in 1982 called Operation Bright Star, which was a Rapid Deployment Force (RDF) operation conducted from the United States to Egypt. In a representative deployment package, twelve A-10s flew nonstop from Myrtle Beach AFB, South Carolina, to the Cairo West air base, with multiple inflight refuelings along the way. Within 30 hours of their departure from the United States, four of the A-10s were flying tactical missions in the western desert of Egypt. The deployed aircraft and pilots operated for 17 days in bare-base conditions, working with Egyptian army and air force units against real Soviet SAMs and other equipment. Navy and Marine aircrews also participated in Bright Star and likewise benefited from the novel training opportunity it provided.

Concurrently, an RDF Red Flag exercise was conducted at Nellis. It was the most complex Red Flag exercise to have been held up to that time, with some 6,000 planned sorties aimed at rehearsing for a contingency in Southwest Asia. The overall intent was to determine combat capability requirements unique to that theater, in light of known adversary characteristics, operating distances, preconditions for ensuring force survival, the capabilities the designated rapid-deployment air forces actually had, and what more they might need to meet combat requirements for Southwest Asia. In consonance with such exercises, Air Force planners began to get serious about large-force employment tactics in the mid-1980s, with a view toward integrating maintenance and ground support, intelligence, communications, en route planning, and tactical application once a force was committed. The experience gained from these undertakings made it clear that the organization, execution, and control of such large-force packages entailed unprecedented complexities.

A final training improvement initiated in 1984 was the Weapon System Evaluation Program (WSEP) aimed at providing live missile-fire training for F-4, F-15, F-106, and CF-18 aircrews from the U.S. Air Force's fighter units and from the Canadian forces. Called Combat Archer, this activity at Tyndall AFB allowed participating aircrews to fire a total of more than 700 live radar and infrared air-to-air missiles a year against maneuvering target drones. The program gave aircrews a chance to experience a live missile firing under operationally realistic conditions and to observe at first hand the indispensability of proper radar technique, missile checks, and other procedures required to get off a valid shot. A typical WSEP intercept under GCI control began with a target at a known altitude 25 to 30 miles away. Failed intercepts brutally drove home lessons never to be forgotten about procedural errors, envelope limits, and the opportunity costs of poorly developed air-to-air skills. Soon afterward, a comparable air-to-ground WSEP was initiated on the Eglin AFB live tactical ranges. Called Combat Hammer, it allowed ground-attack aircrews realistic experience at destroying tanks with the AGM-65 Maverick missile and other precision weapons, along with the use of jammers, flares, and chaff against surface radar emissions.

Additional Training and Tactics Developments

Another important post-Vietnam innovation was a shift to specialized aircrew training in a new approach called the Designed Operational Capability (DOC) system. That change was likewise prompted by concern sparked by the Air Force's poor performance in air-to-air combat over North Vietnam. One of the many recommendations that emanated from TAC's fighter symposium held at Nellis in 1972 was that aircrew training should be optimized by reducing the number of roles required in multimission combat aircraft. That recommendation was based on the long-overlooked premise that there was no correlation between mere flying time logged and combat proficiency gained. In recognition of it, the symposium concluded that sorties and mission events rather than flying hours should henceforth constitute the main measures of merit of the Air Force's training program.

Under the new specialized system, each fighter squadron was assigned a primary and secondary DOC aimed at optimizing training for either the air-to-air or the surface-attack role. In this scheme of training, aircrews would concentrate on one or the other of these roles but not both, maintaining a less developed capability in the secondary role. In addition, the training program was built so as to differentiate among three levels of proficiency— basic proficiency, mission-capable proficiency, and mission-ready status.

In parallel with the new DOC approach, the Air Force further adopted new standards for determining each aircrew member's mission qualifications and training needs. These standards, developed systematically for each aircraft type, were formalized in a document called MCM 51–50, which became the guidebook for Air Force fighter training worldwide. Not only did MCM 51–50 specify in detail what events and with what frequency each aircrew needed to fly in order to satisfy each of the three DOC proficiency levels, but also it had the added advantage of giving squadron commanders an empirically based picture of each pilot's proficiency status at any moment, and thus a means for tailoring the squadron's training program to meet the identified needs of each aircrew.

Concurrently with the evolution of the DACT program, there was a related push, both at Nellis and elsewhere, to develop more effective air-to-air tactics than those used over North Vietnam. As early as 1971, Air Force innovators had begun to question the rigid welded-wing, or "shooter-cover," tactics of the Vietnam era and espouse what the Navy called "loose deuce" and the German Luftwaffe Fighter Weapons School at Luke AFB, using the F-104, called "double attack." As described in Chapter 2, this approach allowed for free and engaged roles for fighters in a two-ship element, along with tactical role reversals as necessary to provide mutual support while pursuing an enemy. The double-attack concept entailed a system of teamwork aimed at getting mutually supporting pilots to talk to each other freely and continually over the radio, to maximize the coordination of their positioning against an opponent. In earlier welded-wing tactics, as the common complaint jokingly went, the wingman was typically expected not to be heard from by his leader other than to call out, in the last resort, either "Mayday!" or "Lead, you're on fire!" In the new approach, all aircraft were freed to be shooters, with none wasted as mere lookouts for the leader. The new approach made a minimum of two aircraft self-sufficient in air combat.[11] The engaged pilot was now cleared to fight more than one target, not having to execute relative to his leader. This new concept was called "fluid two."[12]

The aerial attack flight of the USAF Fighter Weapons School at Nellis took an aggressive approach to refining and applying the sort of fluid-two tactics that had been validated earlier by the Navy over North Vietnam. The Aerospace Defense Command's Interceptor Weapons School at Tyndall AFB developed similar "Six Pack" tactics for the F-106, which had recently been reequipped with a new bubble canopy for better visibility out of the cockpit and an internal 20-mm cannon to increase its air-to-air effectiveness. These and other innovations were eventually written into the fighter pilot's bible, MCM 3-1, and promulgated to all fighter units worldwide.

Air combat maneuvering instrumentation (ACMI) went operational at Nellis in the summer of 1977, with a similar capability later introduced at Tyndall and Luke in the United States and also in Europe and the Pacific. The Navy had earlier pioneered this innovation in connection with Topgun at Miramar. The new system entailed a fully instrumented electronic range, with each participating aircraft carrying an AIM-9–sized pod affixed to a missile rail for transmitting instantaneous flight data to downlinks through-

---

[11] See Major Vincent P. Roy, "Double Attack Revisited," *USAF Fighter Weapons Review*, Spring 1971, pp. 27–32.

[12] The evolution of Air Force tactics from the classic shooter-cover approach through loose deuce to fluid two was treated in exquisite scholarly detail by then-Major Barry D. Watts, USAF, in "Fire, Movement and Tactics," *Topgun Journal*, Fall/Winter 1979, pp. 4–24, and in "A Comparison of 'Team' and 'Single-Ship' Approaches to Aerial Combat," *Bulletin of the ANG Fighter Weapons School*, Spring/Summer 1980, pp. 6–69. By far the most thorough unclassified treatment anywhere of post-Vietnam air combat tactics from basic fighter maneuvers to massed engagements between large numbers of opposed fighter aircraft of dissimilar type, written by a professional for professionals, is Robert L. Shaw, *Fighter Combat: Tactics and Maneuvering*, Annapolis, Md., Naval Institute Press, 1985.

out the range complex and back to the Range Control Center at Nellis via microwave relay, to feed a comprehensive, real-time, all-aspect picture of the ongoing training exercise. It opened up an entirely new medium for air-to-air combat and large-force employment training, permitting mass debriefings with total recall of all aircraft performance and weapons firing data. That, in turn, enabled aircrews to gain intimate and total familiarity with air-to-air missile envelopes.[13]

Among other things, this training innovation enforced more careful aircrew checks for proper switch settings, since it clearly indicated the cause for a missile's failure to fire if any switches were improperly positioned. Related developments that offered a disproportionately high payoff in reinforcing learning included the use of captive AIM-9 missiles with live seeker heads, cockpit tape recorders to preserve radio voice communications during engagements, and gun camera film and head-up display (HUD) videotape recorders to take most of the ego and guesswork out of postflight debriefings and allow substantiated lessons to be drawn and recorded after each mission. No one could argue with the hard facts that these training aids produced.

For its part, the Navy continued to pursue Topgun at Naval Air Station (NAS) Miramar, which had stabilized by the early 1970s into a 30-day course featuring 23 air-to-air training sorties. Students accepted into the program mastered the technique of systematic and thorough mission debriefing, including the use of cockpit videotapes and a methodical reconstruction of all engagements in pursuit of clear learning objectives. The approach to debriefing was coldly analytical, with no room allowed for emotion or boasting. In marked contrast to the movie characterization that made Topgun both a household word around the world and a synonym for macho airmanship, who won or lost in these engagements was not important. What mattered was understanding what had happened and duly learning from it.

With this newly heightened emphasis on realistic training in both the Navy and the Air Force, it was finally recognized by airmen for the first time in years, at least in American practice, that the pilot and his personal attributes and skills, rather than the aircraft or the weapon system, constituted the main ingredient in the formula for success in air combat. As retired Navy Captain Jerry O'Rourke put this point with uncompromising bluntness, "A fighter pilot must use his airplane right up to its limits in his routine flying, be it combat or training for combat. These fine edges between what the plane can do and what it cannot are his ballpark. The mark of the true professional is his ability to get into that ballpark and drive his enemy

---

[13] For more on this, see Major Chuck Turner, "ACMI Update," *USAF Fighter Weapons Review*, Summer 1977, pp. 17–22.

out. So he must *use* his airplane and his weaponry right up to these limits. If he doesn't—if he reserves a little cushion for safety, or for the wife and kids, or for any lack of personal confidence—he's not really a fighter pilot, and, when combat comes, he'll soon be beaten by one who is."[14]

Heightened emphasis was also placed on getting better at ground-attack tactics, with a shift away from relatively nondemanding medium-altitude training toward low-altitude scenarios in a simulated high-threat environment. The physical and mental stress such missions placed on aircrews often went well beyond that experienced in air combat training. As one weapons instructor described it, the challenge entailed "defending against and/or killing bandits during the execution of high speed terrain-following navigation and target acquisition and destruction, while maintaining mutual support to detect and outfly other bandits or SAMs and avoid areas of concentrated AAA—the whole thing being done comm-out, of course. It's a demanding mission and not for the faint of heart or those behind the power curve."[15] Threat avoidance techniques included low-level terrain masking to reduce the chance of being detected by enemy radar and random hard maneuvering (or "jinking") during departure from a defended target area to complicate any attempted enemy AAA or man-portable infrared missile shots.

Of course, the seminal adage that "you should train like you plan to fight" remained constrained to honor commonsense limitations imposed by peacetime safety considerations. Efforts to accommodate that need came in the form of rigorous rules of engagement, such as minimum separation distances between aircraft, avoidance of clouds, altitude restrictions for maneuvering, and prebriefed reactions to unplanned events, such as a stray aircraft entering a designated block of maneuvering airspace. There was a constant struggle during the early days of this training revolution to reconcile the demands of realism with such safety restrictions and rules of good

---

[14] Captain Jerry O'Rourke, USN (Ret.), "Fighters That Never Got to the Fight: Part II," *Proceedings*, U.S. Naval Institute, Annapolis, Md., April 1982, pp. 76–77. This view has long been axiomatic in the Israeli Air Force. As one of its manuals once noted, "Our strength is based mainly on the pilot and not on the weapon system. . . . Top-grade pilots will achieve magnificent results even with less superior aircraft, but the bad pilot in a good aircraft has no impact on the aircraft's performance. More so, there is a great probability that the pilot will kill himself." Quoted in Jeff Ethell, *F-15 Eagle*, Modern Combat Aircraft, No. 12, London, Ian Allen, 1981, p. 107. Recognition of the decisive role of the pilot in determining air combat outcomes, however, is probably as old as fighter aviation itself. It has best been summed up in the classic maxim of the Luftwaffe's fighter commander in World War II, General Adolf Galland, that "only the spirit of attack born in a brave heart will bring success to any fighter aircraft, no matter how highly developed it may be."

[15] Captain Clyde Phillips, "Air-to-Surface: Target Destruction with Force Survival," *USAF Fighter Weapons Review*, Spring 1977, p. 53.

judgment. Nevertheless, despite a notable rise in the accident rate for a time as a result of this more aggressive and demanding training, both General Dixon and General Creech in succession, bit the bullet and courageously accepted the cost, while working overtime to reduce the accident rate to the lowest level practicable.

Mastering the Low-Altitude Environment

In the wake of the 1973 Yom Kippur war, some individuals, both in Israel and in the West, argued that the high rate of Israeli aircraft losses to Arab SAMs and AAA had signalled the arrival of a new era in which fighters would no longer be able to operate effectively over the battlefield. That was plainly an overstatement, even at the time. All the same, there was much to be said for the observation of a U.S. Air Force F-4 Wild Weasel pilot that the Israeli experience "would seem to indicate that hostile air is no longer the primary barrier to the gaining of air superiority over the battlefield," and that the United States and its allies had entered an era in which ground-based air defenses had displaced enemy fighters as the main threat preventing control of the air over enemy terrain.[16]

Indeed, the increased density of the surface-to-air threat brought about by the proliferation of enemy SAM and AAA defenses, with lethal overlapping envelopes ranging from near-ground level to 70,000 ft or more, rendered it far more difficult than before for NATO air power to rove hostile airspace and deliver munitions at will. As a result, ground-attack aircrews were driven more and more to low-level penetration for survivability and to close-in standoff attack where SAM or AAA defenses made direct overflight of a target a virtual death act.[17]

The challenge presented by the need to penetrate enemy air defenses at low altitudes was not merely terrain avoidance, but complex mission management and execution in a completely merciless environment. It is difficult to exaggerate the manifold demands that such flying imposes on a pilot, particularly in the heat of combat. On any such highly task-saturated mission, a flight leader must think simultaneously about managing his formation, cross-checking his navigation system by means of visual pilotage,

---

[16] Major Donald J. Alberts, "A Call from the Wilderness," *Air University Review*, November–December 1976, p. 40.

[17] One tactic for avoiding direct overflight of a target in delivering free-fall bombs entailed the use of lateral delivery and escape maneuvers. Two such options explored for the F-16 included very-low-angle low-drag release and lateral toss bomb, both of which enabled an aircraft penetrating at low altitude to remain clear of weapons fragmentation, though with some degradation in delivery accuracy.

[69]

setting up armament control switches, clearing for enemy fighters, and remaining outside of overlapping enemy SAM and AAA envelopes—all *in addition* to maintaining terrain avoidance at altitudes as low as 100 ft and at speeds of 540 nautical miles per hour or more, while continually maneuvering for spacing or threat avoidance and striving to meet a preplanned time on target within seconds.

To cope with these mission demands, the Air Force developed a so-called step-down approach to low-level training based on the "comfort-level" theme, which aimed at gradually acclimating a pilot to the high-speed, low-altitude environment by ramping down his permitted low-level limit first to 500 ft, then to 300 ft, and finally to 100 ft, where most mission segments in the highest-threat areas near heavily defended targets would have to be flown. It further developed stringent currency rules regarding each pilot's low-level qualifications, which dictated how low the pilot was permitted to fly at any time.[18]

Finally, recognizing both the difficulty and the inherent danger of these multiple demands, Air Force leadership stepped out aggressively during the mid-1980s in seeking an appropriate blend of technology application and tactics development that might help pilots return to medium and higher altitudes where they could avoid the risks of the low-altitude environment, improve their prospects of successful target acquisition, and increase their overall mission effectiveness. Owing to the advent of precision standoff munitions and of more effective means of suppressing enemy SAMs, the Air Force, Navy, and Marine Corps eventually acquired the wherewithal to make good on that effort.

What It All Bought in Hindsight

These improvements in the operational prowess of American aircrews, particularly during the early years after Vietnam, were largely the doing of the veterans of air combat in Southeast Asia like Generals Momyer, Dixon, and Creech, among numerous others, who finally rose to positions of senior Air Force and Navy leadership armed with what Richard Hallion called a

[18] For a time, the Air National Guard's Fighter Weapons School at Tucson, Arizona, experimented with a novel approach to low-level training based on a philosophy different from that then endorsed by the Air Force. In contrast to the Air Force's "comfort-level" approach, the Guard took a different tack based on the proposition that most pilots who inadvertently fly into the ground do so both "comfortably" and completely unaware of impending catastrophe, usually while their attention is momentarily diverted from terrain avoidance to looking at a chart, resetting a switch in the cockpit, or perhaps most commonly, looking across the circle or over their shoulder during a hard turn at low altitude. This program focused instead on task-saturation management and stressed that when pilots were in the most critical portion of a low-level mission, they needed to concentrate on looking out the front of the aircraft where their attention properly belonged.

"never-again" mindset and determined to ensure that "the procedural, organizational, doctrinal, and equipment shortcomings of the Vietnam era were redressed."[19] By the mid-1980s, owing to the new stress on realistic training and the requisite funding provided by the administration of President Ronald Reagan, the average annual flying time allotted to Air Force fighter pilots was more than 230 hours, up from a yearly average of around 150 hours during the mid-1970s—and more than twice the prevailing average in the Soviet Air Force. That was important because of the intimate connection between the frequency of training sorties flown and a pilot's combat proficiency. All told, such initiatives as Red Flag, ACMI, and 10 years of intensive training by all the services worldwide had finally produced a new generation of American combat aircrews whose skills, in the words of a former Aggressor squadron commander, could be honestly described as "second to none."[20]

Relatedly, a sharp decline in the aircraft accident rate between 1975 and the early 1990s bore out a point long argued by airmen the world over—that training to the limits dictated by the needs of operational realism produces not only more combat-capable pilots but also safer pilots. From 1975 to 1995, the annual number of Class A mishaps (accidents involving a fatality, the loss of an aircraft, or equipment damage amounting to $1 million or more) for all services decreased from 309 to 76. For the Air Force, the number dropped from 99 to 32. The mishap rate per 100,000 flying hours between 1975 and 1995 fell from around 4.3 to 1.5 for all services, and from 2.8 to 1.4 for the Air Force. In the most critical category of fighter and attack aviation, the incidence of mishaps had fallen by 61.5 percent since 1975, with the curve flattening out, for the most part, by 1985 even as the number and intensity of sorties increased.[21] In contrast, in routine peacetime training during the 1950s and early 1960s, TAC routinely lost upward of 14.6 aircraft per 100,000 flying hours.[22] In addition to greatly enhanced combat readiness, the new training approach introduced after Vietnam also produced, along with more reliable aircraft and a heightened stress on safety in peacetime training, a windfall dividend in reduced aircraft losses that had not even been anticipated, let alone planned for.

[19] Richard P. Hallion, *Storm over Iraq: Air Power and the Gulf War*, Washington, D.C., Smithsonian Institution Press, 1992, p. 56.
[20] Lieutenant Colonel Mike Press, "Aggressor Reflections," *USAF Fighter Weapons Review*, Summer 1981, p. 4.
[21] See James Kitfield, "Flying Safety: The Real Story," *Air Force Magazine*, June 1996, p. 57.
[22] As now-retired Air Force General Charles Boyd recalled in 1991, during the days of the F-86, the Air Force lost one of those aircraft a day, on average, every day for three years. See his "United States Air Power Inbound to the 21st Century," in Alan Stephens, ed., *Smaller but Larger: Conventional Air Power into the 21st Century*, Canberra, Australia, RAAF Air Power Studies Center, 1991, p. 92.

MODERNIZING THE EQUIPMENT INVENTORY

The two decades that separated Vietnam and Desert Storm were also a time of unprecedented dynamism in the strengthening of the hardware ingredients of American air power. Leading the modernization of the fighter inventory was the introduction of the Navy's F-14 and F/A-18 and the Air Force's F-15 and F-16, each of which offered capabilities well beyond anything available in then-existing Soviet fighters. Among the unique performance attributes of these new fourth-generation aircraft were track-while-scan radars, thrust-to-weight ratios permitting both rapid acceleration and good vertical performance, and unmatched maneuverability for close-in air combat.[23]

Another novel feature of the new generation of American fighters was increased endurance per pound of fuel consumed, owing to improvements in both aerodynamic and engine efficiency. An approach pioneered in the F-16 entailed the use of relaxed stability margins and computerized flight controls, which permitted some control surfaces to be reduced in area and allowed the aircraft's center of gravity to be moved farther aft, with a consequent reduction in drag—particularly around Mach 1, where transonic rise in drag tends to impede acceleration severely.

Not only were the new fighters more capable, but also they were more user-friendly to their aircrews. The F-4 had been designed with notoriously poor cockpit "switchology," with weapons selection and arming switches scattered about with little coherence or ergonomic logic. This required the pilot's attention to be excessively focused inside the cockpit, wasting precious moments during the most critical stages of maneuvering engagements. Numerous opportunities to shoot down MiGs over North Vietnam were lost because of that. To remedy it, all the new U.S. fighters were configured with a "hands on throttle and stick" arrangement, which enabled the pilot to keep his eyes and attention focused outside the cockpit where they belonged during crucial moments of combat. Selectable information on the head-up display further helped to reduce needless distractions.

In the realm of ground attack, the A-10 was introduced into the Air Force inventory as a dedicated antiarmor platform to provide friendly ground forces with direct fire support by means of electro-optical and imaging in-

---

[23] The first generation of jet fighters was exemplified by the U.S. F-86 Sabre and the Soviet MiG-15. The second generation was led by the U.S. F-100 Super Sabre and the Soviet MiG-19. The third generation was characterized by the U.S. F-4 Phantom II, the Soviet MiG-21, and the French Mirage IIIC. The fourth generation, which equips most modern air forces today, is represented by the U.S. F-14/15/16/18 class of fighters and the Russian MiG-29 and Su-27. The U.S. Air Force's stealthy F-22 Raptor, now scheduled to enter service in 2005, is the first of the fifth generation of fighters.

frared Maverick air-to-surface missiles and a 30-mm cannon, the latter of which fired high-velocity rounds of depleted uranium capable of penetrating the aft portion of a tank turret. Although this aircraft was slow and ungainly compared to the more elegant and versatile fighters being deployed alongside it, it was optimized for the antiarmor mission and offered the beginnings of what was to become a major force multiplier against the Warsaw Pact's numerically superior legions of tanks. It was also to become the principal hardware item responsible for clinching what, for a time at least, amounted to a near-symbiotic relationship between the Air Force and the Army, as a later section of this chapter explores in more detail.

For defense suppression, the F-4G was introduced in 1978 as a replacement for the F-105G Wild Weasel. Equipped with rebuilt smokeless J-79 engines to reduce the aircraft's visual signature to ground gunners, it was designed to carry the new Standard ARM (antiradiation missile) and HARM (high-speed antiradiation missile). The heart of the F-4G's defense-suppression capability was the APR-38 (and later APR-47) threat sensor, which offered both azimuth and range information on the location of hostile radars.

For night and adverse-weather interdiction, a decision was announced in early 1984 that the F-15E would become the Air Force's new dual-role fighter, following a flight evaluation of F-15 and F-16 derivatives. Developed to supplement and ultimately supplant the F-111, the aircraft entered operational testing and evaluation in the summer of 1988 and attained initial operational capability at Seymour Johnson AFB, North Carolina, in the fall of 1989. Equipped with conformal fuel tanks that nearly doubled the aircraft's internal fuel-carrying capacity, the F-15E offered a greatly extended range and payload capability and the consequent ability to be deployed with reduced or no tanker support.

A final platform of truly revolutionary impact that made its debut during this two-decade period of air power enhancement was one that did not even figure in public discussion at the time, because of the extreme secrecy that shrouded its development from the very outset. That was the F-117 stealth attack aircraft designed and produced by Lockheed Corporation's renowned "Skunk Works," which earlier had developed the radically innovative U-2 and SR-71 high-flying reconnaissance jets. As applied to combat aircraft, stealth development was prompted by growing concern over the mounting difficulty of penetrating the increasingly formidable array of Soviet radar-guided SAMs that provided an overlapping threat envelope from near-ground level to as high as 125,000 ft in the case of the SA-5.[24] In light of

---

[24] The qualification "as applied to combat aircraft" is appropriate, because low observability has long been the stock in trade of America's nuclear attack submarines, which in a real sense can be considered the first "stealth fighters."

the export of many of these systems to various Soviet client states around the world, the concern involved not only penetrating Soviet airspace in case of nuclear war but also operating American combat aircraft comfortably in virtually any plausible high-intensity threat setting. As noted at the outset of this chapter, a preview of this emergent challenge was provided by the surprisingly effective performance of Soviet-supplied air defenses by Egypt and Syria against the Israeli Air Force (IAF) during the first half of the 1973 Yom Kippur war. Because of the IAF's loss of more than a third of its combat aircraft inventory to these defenses in 18 days, the fear was that an East-West conventional war involving comparable aircraft against similar ground defenses in Central Europe might reduce NATO's air forces to an intolerably low level over a similar period of time.

Lockheed earlier had pioneered low observability to radar through the shaping and skin treatments imparted to the Mach 3 SR-71, a remarkable aircraft roughly the size of a B-58 bomber yet with a radar cross section no larger than that of a Piper Cub. The stealth breakthrough that promised to give fighter-sized aircraft a radar cross section smaller than that of a hummingbird, however, sprung, ironically enough, from an inspiration a Lockheed mathematician gained from reading an obscure article written by one of the Soviet Union's leading radar experts. Eventually that inspiration led to what the acclaimed producer of the F-117, the late Ben Rich, unabashedly characterized as a "major technological breakthrough" that enabled the development of an aircraft with a radar cross section between 10 and 100 times lower than that of any existing American or Soviet fighter.

At first, the Air Force was reluctant to embrace the exotic idea of stealth, captivated as it was by the tactic of high-speed, low-level penetration of defended enemy airspace and committed as it was to the B-1 bomber, which relied on that penetration mode for survivability and was nearing a production decision. With modest funding, however, Lockheed successfully flew the first Have Blue technology demonstrator under tight security wraps on December 1, 1977, and quickly learned that it had indeed accomplished a fundamental breakthrough. The intent of the F-117's design was to minimize the aircraft's detectability by enemy radars and infrared sensors through a radical reduction of the aircraft's radar cross section and the use of baffles and tiles in the engine exhaust system to eliminate telltale heat signatures. The first effect was achieved through the use of special coatings and a flat-plate design that exacted a 20-percent penalty in aerodynamic performance and left the aircraft with an unrefueled radius of less than 600 miles, yet rendered the F-117 untouchable by any existing enemy radar-based defensive system.[25] The first production variant was delivered to the Air Force in 1982, and the F-117 went operational the following year at a secret air base

---

[25] Ben R. Rich and Leo Janos, *Skunk Works*, Boston, Little, Brown, 1994, p. 81.

near Tonopah, Nevada. Operated solely at night either in pairs or autonomously, the aircraft was built to carry two 2,000-lb laser-guided bombs (LBGS) internally and to provide its own laser target designation. In all, 59 were produced.

By 1988, the tightly closed F-117 community at Tonopah had developed a mature combat capability with its secret and mysterious aircraft. Accordingly, the Air Force determined that the time had come to expand its training activities to include other operating units and to start working the aircraft more routinely into existing force employment and contingency plans. Since that would necessitate at least a partial breach of the security wall that thus far had kept the program hermetically sealed from all but a few, the Defense Department reluctantly decided that it had little choice but to disclose the aircraft's existence so that such efforts could get under way. Until that time, although the F-117 had increasingly become the hidden trump card of American conventional air power, both its physical appearance and its numerical designator had remained tightly guarded secrets, with public discussion of "stealth" consigned almost exclusively to the realm of speculation among aviation buffs and fiction writers.

The first operational use of the F-117 took place on the night of December 20, 1989, when two such aircraft were employed in support of the hunt for the elusive Panamanian dictator, Manuel Noriega, on a mission to deliver ordnance close enough to two barracks to stun but not kill the Panamanian troops sleeping inside them. The aim points were in open fields roughly 150 ft from the barracks buildings. Because of adverse winds and weather in the target area as the scheduled time on target approached, the pilots swapped targets just before mission launch and dropped their precision weapons on aim points different from those originally planned. As a result, the bombs failed to achieve their desired effect, even though they went exactly where they had been aimed and even though the F-117s accomplished their attack undetected.[26] Nevertheless, press commentary afterward suggesting that the bombs had "missed their target" got stealth off to a bad footing in the public eye.

Even as the aircraft was publicly exposed in ever-more tantalizing detail beginning a year before the abortive Panamanian mission, it would not be until its bravura performance during the initial nights of Operation Desert Storm a year later that its unique capabilities would be fully appreciated even by air power professionals, let alone by the defense establishment as a whole. Nevertheless, viewed in hindsight, it was one of the most pivotal contributions of the 1980s to the revolution in the lethality and effectiveness of American air power. It both pioneered and validated a new technology

[26] General Merrill A. McPeak, USAF (Ret.), *Selected Works, 1990–1994*, Maxwell AFB, Ala., Air University Press, August 1995, pp. 2–3.

and concept of operations that, by the late 1990s, would come to find application not only in fighter aircraft, but also in bombers, cruise missiles, air-delivered munitions, and even surface naval vessels and attack helicopters.

Accompanying these trends in aircraft modernization was a parallel growth in the variety and quality of munitions for aerial combat and surface attack. For air-to-air combat, the principal improvement was the introduction of the AIM-7F and AIM-9L upgrades of the basic Sparrow and Sidewinder missiles used in Vietnam. The first of these was guided by a semi-active radar and offered beyond-visual-range capability. The latter was an infrared guided weapon for close-in combat. Both provided the capability of being fired at a target from any aspect within the missile's lethal parameters. They outperformed by a considerable margin any counterparts then available to Soviet and Warsaw Pact air forces. The AIM-9L, in particular, occasioned a quantum change in the lethality of infrared air-to-air missiles. Its all-aspect capability made it effectively a point-and-shoot weapon, capable of being fired head-on prior to the point at which converging friendly and enemy fighters closed to dogfight range. That meant that any U.S. or allied fighter armed with it no longer needed to maneuver into a firing position behind an enemy aircraft to be effective, which translated into a first-shot advantage and a heightened prospect of achieving a quick kill—both assets worth their weight in gold in close-in aerial combat.

Major advances also were made in the realm of air-to-surface weapons. For years, the Air Force had stood accused, not unfairly, of stressing platforms over munitions in its acquisition planning. As a result of that skewed emphasis, it had increasingly come to be dominated by latest-generation fighters and avionics, yet with few ordnance options other than general-purpose high-explosive bombs based on technology dating back to World War II. By the late 1970s, however, the pendulum had begun to swing the other way with the Air Force Systems Command's establishment of an Armament Division at Eglin AFB, Florida, expressly chartered to develop non-nuclear munitions to meet a wide spectrum of operational needs. In the mid-1980s, the Air Force introduced no fewer than 10 new ground-attack weapons, with plans in hand to field another 6 by 1990. It also increased its procurement of conventional munitions by a factor of four between 1981 and 1987. After years of neglect, the vector was finally pointed in the right direction.

In the surface-attack arena, the main outgrowth of Air Force and Navy initiatives first tested in Vietnam centered on continued improvements in weapons accuracy and lethality, both in powered and unpowered precision-guided munitions (PGMs) and in wide-area submunitions. The resultant reduction in the number of bombs needed to destroy a target largely did away with the need for ground-attack aircraft to be configured wall-to-wall with so-called Hollywood bomb loads. That, in turn, made possible increased range for a given mission profile, increased aircraft survivability owing to the prospects of destroying the target on the initial pass from standoff range, and increased sortie effectiveness as a result of enhanced munitions performance.

New ground-attack munitions entering the Air Force and Navy operational inventories included the GBU-15 precision-guided 2,000-lb bomb (along with the AGM-130, a rocket-powered version offering increased standoff range); the AGM-88 HARM for attacks against enemy SAM radars; the Durandal runway-attack munition procured from the French for disabling enemy runways; the imaging infrared AGM-65 Maverick missile for killing tanks and other vehicles; the CBU-87 combined-effects munition, a cluster bomb intended for use against enemy troop concentrations and other soft area targets; the Gator mine dispenser for impeding the mobility of second-echelon forces and other enemy rear-area assets; an improved variant of the Mk 84 2,000-lb general-purpose bomb; and the Harpoon missile for antiship attack. The mid-1980s also saw the development of the GBU-24 penetrator weapon, which consisted of a 2,000-lb BLU-109 bomb core with an attached laser seeker for attacking and destroying deeply buried enemy command posts and other hardened facilities.

Airfield attack, all but impossible during the 1970s owing to enemy hardening measures and the impracticality of disabling runways and aircraft shelters with conventional gravity bombs, returned to the fore as a serious deep-attack mission with the advent of the first-generation Durandal and, later, standoff LGBs. Until the advent of precision munitions that could be released from medium altitude, the ability of U.S. and allied air power to damage enemy airfields was limited. Conventional high-explosive bombs were never very effective for runway cratering, since they needed to be dropped at dive angles of up to 30 degrees to produce physical destruction. (At lower release angles, they would merely ricochet off the concrete.) That steep a dive required a fairly high-altitude roll-in, exposing the attacking aircraft to enemy ground fire for an uncomfortably long period. Depending on the weather, it could also place the attacking aircraft inside a cloud layer, preventing the pilot from seeing the target.

At least partly offsetting that lack of a standoff attack capability was a significant improvement in the ability of U.S. aircraft to carry out precision delivery of free-fall weapons. The head-up display in the F-16 and F/A-18 multirole fighters presented the pilot with a continuously computed impact point for free-fall bombs whenever that mode was selected, enabling almost any pilot with a steady hand to place bombs consistently on target. As an example of how dramatic the change was, according to the Air Force's director of operational requirements at the time, then-Major General John M. Loh, Air Force A-7 and F-16 pilots rated combat-ready attained an overall circular error average of 4 feet in all scored conventional bombing events, more than 10 times better than F-100 and F-4 pilots achieved on comparable missions involving low-altitude weapons release during the Vietnam era.[27] In contrast, during the earlier days of manual bombing in aircraft like the F-4, almost daily missions to the weapons range were required for pilots to maintain a qualifying level of proficiency. The operational effectiveness of this capability was pointedly demonstrated on June 7, 1981, when eight Israeli F-16s, each armed with two unguided Mk 84 2,000-lb bombs, attacked Iraq's Tuwaitha nuclear reactor on a carefully planned low-level strike mission, with all but one aircraft putting bombs on target and eliminating it as a threat.

Yet another advantage offered by precision weapons delivery avionics was that "multimission" finally became a realistic operational goal. In previous years, as reflected in the DOC training system described earlier, so-called swing fighters with both air-to-air and ground-attack tasking like the F-4 generally allowed pilots to develop well-honed skills in only one area or the other because of the complexity of the training demands associated with each. With the arrival of the F-16, air-to-ground proficiency became easier to acquire and maintain, meaning that multirole pilots could spend more time polishing their techniques for the more demanding air-to-air arena, with a consequent increase in their proficiency at both missions. Of course, merely once-a-month weapons range sorties to "keep the systems peaked" and to pay lip service to multimission capability were never credible options, for the continued demands of surface-attack mission planning, low-level navigation, and threat avoidance called for perhaps a third to a half of a typical unit's training sorties to be devoted to air-to-ground applications. Nevertheless, both the aircraft and the avionics introduced to operational status beginning in the mid-1970s increasingly rendered "multimission" not just a hollow slogan but a realistically attainable capability.

Other avionics improvements generally fell into three categories: (1) systems intended to enhance friendly situation awareness; (2) systems aimed at undermining or denying enemy situation awareness; and (3) systems designed to help task-manage an increasingly burdensome cockpit workload. Developments in the first category centered on better radars with greater range and jam resistance and more operating modes to deal with a growing variety of tactical situations. One such capability, first pioneered in the Navy's F-14 and later incorporated into advanced models of the F-15 and F-16 and in the F/A-18, was a multiple track-while-scan radar allowing the pilot to monitor an entire enemy formation and to sort and select targets for an initial attack from beyond visual range, while using track information to plan a favorable entry into a subsequent within-visual-range fight.

[27] Benjamin F. Schemmer, "Smarter Planes as Well as Smarter Bombs Boost USAF's Tac Air Arsenal," *Armed Forces Journal International*, June 1986, p. 69.

Relatedly, better offboard target information was provided by new information, surveillance, and reconnaissance (ISR) and battle management platforms in the form of the E-3 airborne warning and control system (AWACS) and the E-8 joint surveillance target attack radar system (JSTARS). After some initial growing pains with operational integration, AWACS eventually came to be considered a de facto "third wingman" for fighter pilots, and JSTARS promised to provide accurate real-time location and targeting information on moving enemy armor and vehicular traffic. An important related improvement was the deep battlefield surveillance and data-link capability offered by the TR-1 reconnaissance aircraft (an upgraded U-2).

Improved radar warning receivers provided information on types of radar posing a threat, their operating modes, and their range and bearing from the targeted aircraft. For aerial combat, the introduction of noncooperative target identification systems enabled accurate electronic assessment and sorting of multiple radar contacts and eased substantially the former requirement for offboard clearance to fire by allowing fighter pilots to designate their own targets. To further aid in the air control mission, the EC-130 Compass Call system was fielded to jam enemy GCI transmissions to airborne fighters, reflecting a belated recognition that a key Soviet vulnerability was the dependence of Soviet pilots on GCI directives to conduct their mission. To negate enemy efforts to return the favor in kind, the Have Quick and improved Have Quick II ultra-high-frequency (UHF) radio was installed on all combat aircraft to counter enemy attempts at jamming communications through the use of high-speed automatic random frequency hopping.

A major achievement ushered in during the 1980s to deny the Warsaw Pact a night sanctuary was the opportunity for effective night and under-the-weather attack against enemy armor and other time-urgent targets afforded by a novel system called LANTIRN, an acronym for "low-altitude navigation and targeting infrared for night." The initial TAC statement of need for this capability issued in 1979 called for a system that would provide the TAF with "an improved 24-hr capability to acquire, track, and destroy ground targets."[28] Initially intended for the single-seat F-16 and A-10 and ultimately mated with the Block 40 F-16C and F-15E, the system incorporated two externally mounted pods. The first, a navigation pod, contained a terrain-following radar and forward-looking infrared (FLIR) sensor capable of projecting a daylight-quality image of the world out in front on a wide field-of-view head-up display. The second, a targeting pod, contained a more narrowly focused FLIR for target identification, plus a self-contained laser designator for precision delivery of conventional guided munitions.

The introduction of the LANTIRN system allowed night and under-the-

[28] Acquisition Plan Number 80-1A-63249F, LANTIRN, USAF Aeronautical Systems Division, March 1980.

weather operations using manual and automatic terrain-following modes down to 200 ft and at speeds of 500 nautical miles per hour and above. With approximately 100 navigation pods and 32 targeting pods delivered by 1990, it promised to impart to the F-16C and F-15E the same night terrain-avoidance capability possessed at that time only by the Air Force F-111 and the Navy A-6. It further promised a capability for night bombing, at least against some target types, as good as that only available before for daytime missions.[29] The net effect of this capability was to open up a greatly expanded operating envelope for the combat air forces. By denying the enemy a night sanctuary, it portended an increase in sortie effectiveness, greater leverage from any given number of aircraft, and a reduced requirement for total numbers of aircraft in a theater of operations. Because of the system's complexity and cost (with some $3.8 billion spent on it as of 1991), however, the Air Force had to settle for a compromise in its capability, by ultimately abandoning the originally planned automatic target recognizer and accepting one target hit per pass in lieu of the initial requirement for six.[30]

Finally, the late 1970s and 1980s saw a surge of long-overdue attention in all services toward the unglamorous but essential needs of resource management and operational support. After all, satisfactory combat results required not just adequate weapons stocks and aircrew proficiency but also adequate sortie availability. It was a poorly appreciated fact that the mere doubling of a combat aircraft force's sortie rate could nearly double the overall productivity of the force, all other things being equal. More sorties per aircraft per day promised substantially increased leverage if those sorties were uniformly combat-effective.

Toward that end, determined efforts were made in the latest generation of fighters to make aircraft less dependent on an elaborate logistics infrastructure by reducing the number of parts, increasing the accessibility of critical components, using line-replaceable avionics modules, and providing onboard systems that reduced the need for ground servicing. As a result of such efforts, besides increased concentration of fire, the new platforms promised to offer more sustained force application through improved reliability and maintainability. The generation of fighters represented by the Air Force's F-15 and F-16 and by the Navy's and Marine Corps's F/A-18 offered far better in-commission rates than their predecessors because of the increased durability of their avionics and the greater ease of repair permitted by exchanging line-replaceable modular units. Much of that heightened reliability resulted from the accompanying shift from an electro-

---

[29] See Glenn W. Goodman, Jr., "LANTIRN Pod Approved for High-Rate Production," *Armed Forces Journal International*, January 1987, p. 20.
[30] Susan J. Bodilly, *Case Study of Risk Management in the USAF LANTIRN Program*, Santa Monica, Ca., RAND, N-3617-AF, 1993, pp. 3, 54–55.

mechanical era to a microelectronics era. Because it incorporated technology from the latter generation, the F-16, for example, was able to fly upward of 65 percent more sorties than the F-4 of the previous generation, and it required only some 20 maintenance man-hours per flying hour, compared to 41 for the F-4.[31]

This enhanced maintainability and reliability was only a recent design feature in modern combat aircraft development, and it contributed significantly to the confidence of commanders that their high-technology equipment would perform as expected when and as asked. Back in the "bad old days" of the F-4 and earlier-model F-111s, the reliability of the overall weapon system, defined as the mean time between failure of various essential onboard subsystems, was often shorter than the average duration of a combat sortie. That meant that a certain percentage of scheduled aircraft would never make it to the target area because something critical to the mission, such as the radar, would fail en route, forcing mission planners to build a margin of additional aircraft into a strike package simply to ensure that enough aircraft would make it to the target to get the job done. With the reliability and maintainability improvements designed into the new fourth-generation fighters, in contrast, combat aircraft were typically likely to land after a sortie in what is called Code One condition, namely, with all their systems in proper working order and the aircraft ready to launch again after being refueled and reloaded with weapons, with no repair required.

REFINING DOCTRINE AND CONCEPTS OF OPERATIONS

A third major area of improvement in the capability and versatility of American air power after Vietnam entailed a better matching of assets to tasks through more effective concepts of operations and force employment strategies at the theater level. At the start of the 1980s, Edward Luttwak complained about how "Anglo-Saxon military terminology . . . knows of *tactics* (unit, branch, and mixed) and of *theater strategy* as well as of *grand strategy*, but includes no adequate term for the *operational* level of warfare," even though issues relating to that level of warfare had long constituted the predominant focus of the military classics.[32] Luttwak saw it as an unfortunate eccentricity that U.S. defense leaders not only did not speak in these terms but also did not even *think* in them. In contrast, Soviet military doctrine—borrowing heavily from its Prussian forebears going as far back as Clause-

---

[31] See Mark K. Moore, "Reliable Electronics and Weapons Performance: Finally a Match?" *Armed Forces Journal International*, September 1986, pp. 88–90.

[32] Edward N. Luttwak, "The Operational Level of War," *International Security*, Winter 1980/81, p. 61.

witz—was heavily invested in what it called "operational art" as the key to victory in theater war.

Yet at the same time, this situation had begun to change substantially by the mid-1970s, with the emergence of new American initiatives, both intellectual and institutional, to deal with the gathering Soviet conventional threat to NATO. The initiatives were prompted by a growing recognition that the only chance NATO had of successfully defending against the Warsaw Pact's superior numbers and offensive doctrine lay in a synergistic marshalling of the alliance's air and ground assets against identifiable weak spots in the Pact's concept of operations.

In the aftermath of the Yom Kippur war in 1973, the U.S. Air Force began to get serious about gaining a better feel for the qualitative aspects of the Soviet threat. Inspired by the same sort of thinking that had occasioned the establishment of the Aggressor program, an Air Force pioneer in the field of enemy weapons and tactics wrote that in addition to knowing the details of Soviet equipment, "We must understand his logic techniques and the philosophy to which they are applied; his environment and the nature of his military and professional education; his military structure; his hardware and ordnance and the basics of how he plans to use the hardware."[33] Toward that end, the Air Staff in 1974 established a low-profile Net Assessment Task Force on Soviet Vulnerabilities and chartered it to look beyond the superficial order-of-battle numbers and tough-sounding rhetoric of Soviet offensive doctrine to the soft spots and vulnerabilities in Moscow's operational repertoire that could be exploited by properly focused NATO countermeasures. Its director, then–Brigadier General Jasper A. Welch, Jr., captured well what needed to be said on that score when he later noted, in his characteristic droll manner, that "there is a certain unbecoming fatalism about routinely allowing the Soviet military a free ride on their existing vulnerabilities just because we 'might' be wrong or they 'might' fix them."[34]

Despite the best of such efforts, the American habit of focusing on the easy quantifiables rather than on the more elusive but no less important intangibles of enemy capability occasioned a systemic tendency throughout the U.S. intelligence community to overestimate the operational prowess of Soviet forces deployed opposite NATO. All the same, a creative core of operators and operationally minded intelligence officers in the Air Force and, later, in the Navy offered a valuable antidote to the general instinct of the intelligence bureaucracy to place excess weight on the technical performance of enemy weapons at the expense of due attention to such factors as train-

[33] Major Gail Peck, "Enemy Weapons and Tactics: An Introduction," *USAF Fighter Weapons Review*, Fall 1973, p. 27.

[34] Major General Jasper A. Welch, Jr., USAF, "A Conceptual Approach to Countering Invasion Threats to NATO," unpublished manuscript, June 1976.

ing, doctrine, leadership quality, and proficiency, which were of no less interest to those operators concerned not just with sizing up enemy weapons but also with doing battle with them.

The Forging of Closer Air Force–Army Ties

Perhaps the key initial role in bringing the Army and Air Force to respond jointly to the Soviet military challenge opposite NATO was played by General Dixon, who tooked the lead upon assuming the reins of command at TAC in declaring that "the tactical air forces must be user-oriented"; that, as in any producer-consumer relationship, "this is a give-and-take business"; and that tactical air suppliers "have to know exactly what the Army wants, and the Army must know what can—and cannot—be done. Close coordination and cooperation must exist and be extended throughout the development, preparation and operations of air and ground components." Realizing this in practice, Dixon added, presented "a demand and an opportunity to evaluate the total Air Force/Army relationship to ensure that we have the right 'mix' for the future."[35]

Within two weeks of his arrival at Langley AFB in October 1973, General Dixon made good on these sentiments by opening a formal dialogue with his Army counterpart at nearby Fort Monroe, Virginia, General William Depuy, the commander of the Army's Training and Doctrine Command (TRADOC). Notably, this occurred two years *before* the beginning of Red Flag. The purpose of the dialogue, said Dixon, was to forge "an unprecedented cooperative effort to develop concepts, procedures and tactics in order to make the most efficient and effective use of existing forces."[36]

The groundwork for this initiative had been laid several weeks earlier by the respective Army and Air Force chiefs of staff at the time, Generals Creighton Abrams and George Brown. The two chiefs had fought together in Southeast Asia, and they understood the criticality of sustaining in peacetime the good working relationship the two services had developed during the Vietnam war. Each, respectively, urged Depuy and Dixon to seek a way to carry out "the commonality of purpose which existed so clearly in Vietnam . . . into the entire fabric of relations between the two services."[37] As General Dixon put it, both services had a commendable history of working in unison in past wars, during which "conflicting doctrines were put aside and workable ad hoc procedures were established to provide effective,

---

[35] General Robert J. Dixon, USAF, "The Range of Tactical Air Operations," *Strategic Review*, Spring 1974, p. 24.

[36] General Robert J. Dixon, USAF, "TAC-TRADOC Dialogue," *Strategic Review*, Winter 1978, p. 45.

[37] Letter of General Creighton W. Abrams, USA, to General William E. Depuy, USA, October 5, 1973, cited in ibid., p. 46.

efficient integrated joint firepower." Yet between wars, he pointed out, "the daily interaction lessened or vanished, the doctrinaires and budgeteers asserted themselves, [and] arguments over roles and missions emerged or were deliberately advanced by those seeking to divide the military services." In such a cutthroat bureaucratic environment, he added, "competing parochial interests often replaced logic as the common denominator in the force structure development and weapon acquisition process."[38]

Dixon grounded the TAC-TRADOC dialogue on the hard fact, as he put it, that "neither the Army nor the Air Force alone can win a significant conflict; they can only win as a team." He further stressed that the tempo and violence of a modern conventional war in Europe would not permit the development of the needed teamwork after the opening rounds were fired and that any such partnership had to be forged and nurtured in peacetime— and not, moreover, just between the respective service leaders, but at all levels in both services. Beyond pursuing an effective joint combat repertoire, he added, an important by-product of such a relationship would be that the two services could articulate force structure needs to the Defense Department and Congress "in unison and in a logical and plausible fashion."

To implement and institutionalize such a relationship, Dixon and Depuy established a joint entity called the Air-Land Forces Application (ALFA) directorate, which was tasked with working out joint procedures and operational concepts regarding the allocation of combat responsibilities, determining the essential elements of the air-land battle, and understanding what was required from all participants to win in joint conventional warfare. ALFA faced an early hurdle in that the Air Force was not harmonized with the Army's approach to concept development and validation. A solution was found by consolidating TAC's studies and wargaming activities at the Tactical Fighter Weapons Center at Nellis, which already had the responsibility for tactics development and, owing to the Nellis range complex, had the wherewithal immediately at hand for operationally testing joint concepts. Furthermore, the Nellis training facilities were complemented by the proximity of the Army's National Training Center at Fort Irwin, California, which offered a comparable venue for realistic land-warfare training. Using these collocated facilities, the Air Force and Army proceeded to conduct integrated, large-force training exercises against simulated enemy defenses in both Red Flag and Red Banner scenarios, to observe, evaluate, and quantify air-land battle operations. (Red Banner was the Army's counterpart to Red Flag.)

The introduction of the A-10 tank-killer into line service prompted further Air Force cooperation with the Army, reflected in an early example by the JAWS I (joint attack weapons systems) test at Fort Benning, Georgia, and

[38] Ibid., pp. 45–46.

the JAWS II test at Fort Hunter Liggett, California, in the fall of 1977. This joint-service experiment pitted the A-10 in numerous CAS scenarios with Army AH-1 Cobra and OH-58 Scout helicopters. The experience was said to have helped fighter pilots learn how to "talk Army" and Army people how to "talk fighter pilot" (which was not quite the same as "talk Air Force"). The combined kill ratios achieved by the A-10 and helicopters working together were four to five times greater than those achieved when these platforms were employed separately. The tests featured real-time scoring instrumentation and an illusion of live battle through the use of simulated smoke and dust. Sorties were launched in reaction to on-call CAS requests and were controlled by an Army battle captain and an Air Force FAC riding in the Army controller's helicopter. Both the A-10 and the Cobra made maximum use of terrain-masking tactics, with the Cobra firing TOW missiles (the acronym standing for "tube-launched, optically-tracked, wire-guided") and the A-10 firing Maverick missiles and the 30-mm GAU-8 cannon. Mutual support tactics were tested in the presence of both surface-to-air defenses and simulated enemy fighters, with a Cobra, in one instance, destroying a simulated SAM site that was tracking an A-10. As an Air Force participant in the exercise later commented, "Respect grew for both sides of the team, friendships were made, and a cooperative attitude appeared."[39]

AirLand Battle Doctrine and FOFA

In the event of an all-out surprise attack, the mounting Soviet conventional threat to NATO outlined at the beginning of this chapter portended a collapse of NATO's forward defenses even before the alliance could reach a decision to escalate to nuclear use. That spotlighted a number of concerns regarding the adequacy of the Army's existing "active defense" doctrine. One was that it was overly reactive, in effect ceding the operational initiative to Warsaw Pact forces. Another was that it focused excessively on concentrating allied firepower at the assumed point of anticipated Soviet breakthrough, rather than relying on maneuver to exploit Soviet weaknesses in lieu of frontally challenging Soviet strengths. A third concern was that this reliance on attrition warfare threatened to exhaust defending NATO forces before the attacking Soviet first echelon could be neutralized.

By the late 1970s, these concerns had begun to force new looks, both within the U.S. Army leadership and at Supreme Headquarters Allied Powers Europe (SHAPE), at new concepts that made the most of emerging deep-look and deep-attack technologies. As a result, Army thinking began evolving from its defensive, attrition-oriented mold struck in the 1976 version of

[39] Captain John Lieberherr, "A Little Warthog in All of Us," *USAF Fighter Weapons Review*, Fall 1978, p. 11.

Army Field Manual (FM) 100–5, *Operations*, to a more aggressively counteroffensive orientation envisioning an extended battlefield in which both
air and land units would fight the close battle and, using emerging surveillance and target acquisition systems, seek simultaneously to engage enemy
units not yet in contact with friendly forces. The intent of this new doctrinal
approach was to exploit the enemy's vulnerabilities, delay his advance, and
disrupt his timetable, ideally to the point of breakdown and total collapse.
As General Depuy's replacement as TRADOC commander, General Donn
Starry, stated the point in a landmark article, "Deep attack is not a luxury; it
is an absolute necessity for winning." [40]

Under General Starry's leadership, the Army in 1982 issued an updated
version of FM 100–5 that formally promulgated the new AirLand Battle
(ALB) doctrine, focusing on the counteroffensive and engaging second-echelon enemy forces. By one informed account at the time, the underlying idea
was that the second echelon would be broken up by a battle conducted deep
in the enemy's rear that would be fought simultaneously with the close-in
battle, employing a concept of operations "that required that planners not
only anticipate enemy vulnerabilities but view this two-part battle as one
engagement." [41]

In April the following year, the respective Army and Air Force chiefs of
staff, Generals Edward "Shy" Meyer and Charles Gabriel, endorsed a joint-
service memorandum of agreement spelling out in detail how each service
would work with the other in developing and applying the details of ALB.
After extensive discussion, the Joint Force Development Group commissioned by this memorandum issued a list of what later became known as the
"thirty-one initiatives," which spoke to a broad spectrum of issues such as
theater air defense, CAS, counter-helicopter tactics, electronic warfare, joint
munitions development, command and control, and interdiction that have
since defined the context of Air Force–Army planning for joint warfare. One
of those initiatives engaged Strategic Air Command (SAC) in a deep theater
conventional interdiction role for the first time since Vietnam, paving the
way for the involvement of the B-52 as a central player in preparing the
battlefield for future joint-force ground operations wherever they might occur worldwide. [42]

Concurrently, the new Supreme Allied Commander for Europe (SACEUR),
Army General Bernard Rogers, tasked the planning staff at SHAPE to develop a strategy for FOFA aimed at delaying, disrupting, and destroying

---

[40] General Donn A. Starry, USA, "Extending the Battlefield," *Military Review*, March 1981, p. 32.

[41] John L. Romjue, "The Evolution of the AirLand Battle Concept," *Air University Review*, May–
June 1984, p. 10.

[42] See General John T. Chain, Jr., USAF, "Strategic Bombers in Conventional War," *Strategic Review*,
Spring 1988, pp. 23–32.

Warsaw Pact forces from just beyond the so-called close battle to as far into the enemy's rear as existing target acquisition systems, delivery platforms, and conventional munitions would permit. In contrast to ALB, this strategy was optimized not for the corps level, with a view toward synchronizing deep-attack operations with the ground commander's scheme of maneuver, but rather for the higher-level theater commander's need for the centralized application of deep-strike capabilities to break up the momentum of an attack and ensure that second-echelon forces were kept separate from those in the initial echelons so that the latter could be kept at a level manageable by defending NATO forces.

This difference in focus made for an inner tension between the Army and Air Force that would later make its influence felt in a significant way during Operation Desert Storm. At its core lay the issue of where within the battle-space of a given theater of operations to dedicate the bulk of friendly deep-attack operations. Being an Army doctrine with a purely corps-level orientation, ALB was concerned only with the corps commander's domain of interest, namely, with enemy forces no more than 72 hours away. That meant a depth of operations of only 30 to 50 miles from the Forward Line of Troops (FLOT). In contrast, FOFA reflected more traditional air power thinking, which stressed the criticality of centralized air allocation on a theater-wide basis. Stated differently, air power in ALB was viewed as supplemental to the corps commander's organic means of attack, whereas in FOFA, it was treated as an independent *strategic* asset aimed not merely at fighting the forward ground battle, but at addressing the problem of engaging enemy echelons throughout an entire theater of operations.

These independently developed doctrines were not inherently in conflict with one another. However, absent a clear agreement on rules of allocation that reconciled the ingrained tension between the corps commander's local needs and the theater commander's imperative of maintaining centralized control of air power for theater-wide use, the doctrines reflected a disjuncture that, in the words of one well-informed treatment of the issue, bore "profound implications for how the ground war can be fought."[43] According to that analysis, the most pressing unsettled problem was that "the right balance must be struck between providing adequate air interdiction to support the ground commander's scheme of maneuver and assuring that air allocation achieves the most decisive effects theater-wide."[44] It was an issue that would persist all the way to Desert Storm and beyond.

[43] Boyd D. Sutton, John R. Landry, Malcolm B. Armstrong, Howell M. Estes III, and Wesley K. Clark, "Deep Attack Concepts and the Defense of Central Europe," *Survival*, March–April 1984, p. 60.
[44] Ibid., p. 62.

Revealed Problems

These two doctrines suffered three prominent shortcomings. First, both ALB and FOFA were ahead of their time, in that each depended on precision standoff weapons and new ISR systems that were still in their infancy and had not yet come on line. Second, both ALB and FOFA assumed a linear battlefield and that Soviet war plans depended on the use of second-echelon forces for battlefield success.[45] Third, ALB was not a joint-service doctrine. Although its name implied a compact between the Air Force and the Army, it was in fact a unilaterally developed Army doctrine that was configured toward land warfare. Its codification in the 1982 edition of FM 100–5 recognized that without the participation of air forces, "the Army cannot win against a large, modern, mechanized enemy force," and General Starry conceded that "many of the acquisition means and most of the attacking means will come from air forces."[46] At the same time, it expressly cast air power in a supporting role. In this outlook, moreover, the Army was backed by at least some in the most senior Air Force leadership. For example, as late as September 1990, as the buildup for the impending Gulf war was well under way, General Charles Donnelly, a former commander in chief of USAFE, wrote in the Army's monthly professional journal that the commander of allied air forces in Europe "must be ever mindful that air power is a support element."[47]

Nevertheless, it was in this third area where the seeds of greatest potential interservice trouble lay. To begin with, there was anything but a consensus between the Air Force and the Army on even the most basic principles of implementation. The memorandum of agreement signed by Generals Meyer and Gabriel only represented an understanding that the two services would cooperate in "joint tactical training and field exercises based on the AirLand Battle doctrine."[48] However, as an Air Force commentator observed at the time, it did "not acknowledge AirLand Battle as the sole governing principle for joint training and exercises." Nor did it "concede unequivocal primacy of AirLand Battle doctrine over established Air Force doctrine."[49]

[45] These weaknesses were recognized and spelled out in detail in Colonel William G. Hanne, "Doctrine, Not Dogma," *Military Review*, June 1983, pp. 11–25. For further elaboration, see also Major Jon S. Powell, "AirLand Battle: The Wrong Doctrine for the Wrong Reason," *Air University Review*, May–June 1985, pp. 15–22.

[46] Starry, "Extending the Battlefield," p. 47.

[47] General Charles L. Donnelly, USAF, (Ret.), "An Air Commander's View of Operational Art," *Military Review*, September 1990, p. 81.

[48] Department of the Army and Department of the Air Force, *Memorandum of Understanding on Joint USA-USAF Efforts for Enhancement of Joint Employment of the AirLand Battle Doctrine*, Washington, D.C., April 21, 1983.

[49] Major James A. Machos, "TacAir Support for AirLand Battle," *Air University Review*, May–June 1984, p. 16.

In effect, ALB not only represented a broadening of the ground commander's image of the battlefield, but also reflected an explicit effort by the
Army to gain greater control of the air assets to be used in the now-extended
battlespace within his purview. To be sure, it looked toward better planning
for and utilization of the slice of allied air assets allocated to the corps commander's area of responsibility. Nevertheless, it cut against the grain of Air
Force and NATO doctrine at the strategic level, which called for the centralized control of air assets above the corps level to ensure their most effective
use throughout the entire theater. Unlike ALB, the latter was concerned with
fighting a theater-wide war rather than discrete battles. The imbalance between these views was readily apparent in the disconnect between the corps
commander's concern with his own battle problem and the higher-echelon
air component commander's concern with operational needs across the entire theater. The dominance of ALB over more classic interdiction strategy in
air allocation decisions, by fragmenting the theater air campaign, would undermine the ability of the air component commander to mass resources to
engage and destroy enemy ground-force concentrations as needed throughout the theater.

A related problem posed by the Army's extended-battlefield concept was
its creation of ambiguities regarding the proper placement of the line separating traditional roles for acquiring and engaging targets. In pristine air
warfare doctrine, air operations in direct support of the ground battle were
to be controlled by and coordinated with the ground commander, whereas
control of air operations beyond the reach of the ground commander's organic strike assets was the exclusive prerogative of the theater air component commander, with no need to coordinate with engaged ground commanders as a rule. The Army's extended-battlefield concept, however, had
the effect of pushing the Fire Support Coordination Line (FSCL), that is, that
predetermined line on the battlefield ahead of friendly forces inside which
any friendly air-to-ground operations must be coordinated with the appropriate ground-force commander, out from some 8 to 10 miles to as far as
30 to 50 miles from the FLOT, encroaching directly into the deeper reaches of
the battlespace where air power was the more effective means of employing
force.

From the Air Force's perspective, the way out of this dilemma lay in the
so-called single-manager concept aimed at enabling the theater joint-force
commander to employ his air assets through a single designated air component commander. Its underlying intent was to prevent a recurrence of
the divided lines of authority that had contributed to other factors in undermining the effective application of air power in Vietnam. The initial
command-structure discussions of the Rapid Deployment Joint Task Force
in the early 1980s envisaged having *four* operational components—Army,
Air Force, Navy, and Marine Corps—with naval aviation remaining under
the Navy's control. Such retrograde thinking ran diametrically opposed to

the single-manager concept, which eventually emerged in time for Desert Storm.

Three years later, TRADOC's commander conceded that the 1982 edition of FM 100-5 did not reconcile the Air Force's theater-wide view of air support with the Army's corps-level conception of the air-land battle and further indicated that the new 1986 version had endeavored to recognize that future campaigns "will be joint undertakings with mutually supporting air and ground functions." He also admitted still-unresolved procedural issues between the two services and tacitly highlighted one such issue in declaring that while FOFA calls on little by way of ground forces, "AirLand Battle also employs available air and other assets but relies predominantly on ground forces to affect the close operation." [50] By leaving open what exactly constituted the "close operation" and where the line was to be drawn between it and deeper operations requiring less air-ground integration and coordination, the Army planted seeds for a problem that would later erupt heatedly in Desert Storm.

Commenting on this issue at the time, then–Air Force Lieutenant General Merrill McPeak observed that although the two services were indeed at the threshold of "a period of greatly increased joint effectiveness on the tactical battlefield," some friction points needed serious attention before that goal could be realized in practice. In particular, McPeak declared that the ambiguity associated with the placement of the FSCL meant that were the Air Force to insist on not doing interdiction inside it, "it would be possible to create a doctrinal 'no-mission zone.'" To avoid getting caught in such an untenable situation, he suggested drawing a sharp line between CAS, with its requirements for ground control, and battlefield interdiction, which should be treated as anything *but* "a kind of close support." McPeak agreed that there was "no reason not to fly properly coordinated interdiction missions inside the FSCL." He further granted that although the requirement for "detailed integration" in that instance decidedly weakened the flexibility of air power, it was "worthwhile to trade off flexibility when the safety of friendly troops is at stake." Yet he also warned that TAC and TRADOC had gone beyond mere "coordination" to a notion that, in effect, gave the ground commander "a leading role in selecting and prioritizing BAI [battlefield air interdiction] targets on both sides of the FSCL." [51]

Several years earlier, some Air Force airmen had already begun to recognize that U.S. air power was acquiring more than just the rudiments of an effective capability against deep strategic targets, such as massed second-

[50] General William R. Richardson, USA, "FM 100-5: The AirLand Battle in 1986," *Military Review*, March 1986, pp. 7–9.
[51] Lieutenant General Merrill A. McPeak, USAF, "TacAir Missions and the Fire Support Coordination Line," *Air University Review*, September–October 1985, pp. 65–72.

echelon forces, the prompt destruction of which could potentially "be a greater aid to our ground forces than the traditional close air support they expect."[52] Such early Air Force thinking entailed handwriting on the wall for what would eventually become a sharp divergence between Air Force and Army views on the most intelligent use of air power in conducting the deep battle, with the Army hewing to its classic image of air power as a supporting combat element and airmen increasingly coming to appreciate the emerging promise of new technologies to give air power an independent strategic role in achieving desired battlefield effects in support of theater operations.

By the mid-1980s, however, as Richard Hallion later noted, the United States and its NATO allies had finally acquired the beginnings of "a coherent body of thought on tactical air power that had been sorely missing a decade ago."[53] That development was helped greatly by Moscow's invasion of Afghanistan in 1979, which abruptly ended any remaining U.S. illusions regarding the underlying nature of Soviet motivations and which prompted a sharp shift in the Carter administration's attitude toward force structure and readiness needs. Within the services, as TRADOC's historian John Romjue pointed out, it reinforced an already well-advanced refocusing of attention toward the moral and human dimensions of battle, introducing into U.S. military doctrine "the clarifying notion of the operational level of war and . . . a return to the fundamental principles of attaining victory." That stood in sharp contrast to the now-discredited management conception of warfare, which had reached its pinnacle during the McNamara era by misguidedly seeking "measurable quantitative outcomes as the linchpin of military success," at the disregard of those "immeasurable but enduring principles constant in the experience of men in battle, such as leadership, initiative, and the commander's intuitive sense of time and maneuver."[54]

EARLY TESTS OF MATURING AIR POWER

The U.S. defense establishment had three opportunities during the 1980s to observe in application what many of the investments described earlier had to offer by way of a more capable air weapon. The first came vicariously when Israel's air force in 1982 employed the latest U.S.-produced equipment in a casebook SAM suppression operation and MiG sweep over Lebanon's Bekáa Valley against Syrian forces, in the process engaging a threat that all

[52] Lieutenant Colonel Hiram Hale Burr, Jr., "The Modernization of Soviet Frontal Aviation: What Does It Mean?" *Air University Review*, January–February 1981, p. 34.
[53] Hallion, *Storm Over Iraq*, p. 75.
[54] John L. Romjue, "AirLand Battle: The Historical Background," *Military Review*, March 1986, p. 55.

but mirrored in microcosm what the Soviets maintained opposite NATO in Central Europe. The second and third occasions involved situations in which U.S. air power itself was summoned to show its capabilities. One was an all-Navy day strike against Syrian proxy forces in Lebanon in 1983. The other was a joint Navy and Air Force night attack against far better defended Libyan targets around Tripoli and Benghazi in 1986, in response to a rash of Libyan terrorist provocations against American interests around the world.

Israel's use of the latest generation of American hardware to such telling effect against Syria's SAMs and fighters over the Bekáa soon became enshrined as the performance standard against which future U.S. air operations would be measured whenever the time came. In contrast, the first American test a year later ended up being a humiliating wake-up call which indicated both to the Navy and to everyone else that merely possessing capable weaponry meant nothing, in and of itself, about how effectively that weaponry might be employed in combat. Owing in part to the chastening effect of the Navy's less-than-satisfying performance over Lebanon in 1983, the joint Air Force–Navy raid against Libya three years later produced a more encouraging outcome. If the example set by Israel in 1982 offered convincing proof of what a first-rate air weapon, properly used, was capable of doing, the two subsequent U.S. air operations, each in its own way, contributed no less to the ultimate refinement of American air power that helped give the coalition's leadership the going-in confidence it needed when it came time to play for higher stakes in Desert Storm.

The Bekáa Valley Precedent

Dramatic proof of what the new technology could accomplish if skillfully wielded was offered by the crisply executed Israeli air operation against Syrian SA-6s and MiGs over the Bekáa Valley in June 1982. The spark that prompted it was an assassination attempt the month before against the Israeli ambassador in London, which left him gravely wounded and occasioned limited Israeli retaliatory strikes against Palestine Liberation Organization (PLO) positions in southern Lebanon. That action, in turn, triggered PLO artillery attacks against Israeli civilian settlements in Galilee and a substantial reinforcement of existing Syrian SA-6 missile emplacements in the Bekáa Valley, the first of which had been deployed in late April the year before.

Using these developments as a pretext, the Israeli Defense Forces (IDF) launched a massive combined-arms assault aimed at destroying the PLO as a military force and neutralizing any Syrian combat assets in Lebanon that might interfere with that effort. The air portion of the campaign began three days later with a coordinated surprise attack against the Syrian SA-6 net-

[92]

work in the Bekáa Valley. That, in turn, led to an extended showdown between Israeli and Syrian fighters in what later was widely acclaimed to have been the largest single air battle since World War II.

The target complex consisted of 19 SA-6 batteries deployed at several locations in the Bekáa Valley, an agricultural plain in central Lebanon some 10 miles wide by 25 miles long and flanked on both sides by ridgelines up to 6,500 ft high. Key mission-support elements included several E-2C surveillance aircraft orbiting off the coast of Lebanon, a Boeing 707 electronic intelligence (ELINT) platform, and numerous ground and airborne jammers (the latter aboard CH-53 helicopters).[55] The functions of the E-2C were to provide gap-filler support for Israeli ground radars, monitor the airspace over the target area and beyond into Syria, and provide vectoring and battle-management assistance to Israeli fighters in the event that Syrian MiGs rose to challenge the SAM suppression operation.[56] The 707, for its part, was poised to monitor Syrian SA-6 radar activity. Finally, Israeli jammers were to be employed against voice and data-link transmissions between Syrian fighters and GCI sites and perhaps also against other threat emitters, such as enemy aircraft and SAM radars.

According to Western press accounts at the time, the SAM attack operation was carried out by a combination of F-4s with Shrike and Standard ARM missiles, F-16s with standoff munitions and conventional bombs, and a variety of other systems, notably artillery and ground-launched surface-to-surface missiles.[57] The attack reportedly commenced with a wave of remotely piloted vehicles (RPVs) launched as decoys to trigger an activation of the SA-6 engagement radars. As expected, the Syrians rose to the bait, showed poor target discrimination and firing discipline, and initiated a massed launch of SAMs against the incoming drones. Once positive SAM activity was confirmed and target location was established by the 707, the SA-6 radars deployed in the southern part of Lebanon were attacked by artillery from Israeli ground units that had moved rapidly forward, as well as by Israeli ground-launched battlefield missiles. The SAM radars farther

---

[55] Drew Middleton, "Soviet Arms Come in Second in Lebanon," *New York Times*, September 19, 1982.

[56] "Washington Roundup: Mideast Air Battle," *Aviation Week and Space Technology*, June 28, 1982.

[57] Among the more suggestive press accounts of IAF tactics employed in the Bekáa Valley operation are Clarence A. Robinson, Jr., "Surveillance Integration Pivotal in Israeli Success," *Aviation Week and Space Technology*, July 5, 1982, pp. 16–17, and Russell Warren Howe, "DoD Opts for Untested U.S. Drone," *Washington Times*, September 28, 1982. See also Richard Homan, "Israel Inflicts Heavy Air, Missile Losses on Syria," *Washington Post*, June 10, 1982; Michael Getler, "Superior Weapons, Pilots, Tactics Seen as Key to Israeli Victories," *Washington Post*, June 11, 1982; David B. Ottaway, "Israel Said to Master New Technology to Trick and Destroy Soviet-Made Missiles," *Washington Post*, June 14, 1982; Charles Mohr, "New Wars Show the Powers of Military Basics," *New York Times*, June 18, 1982; and Craig Oliphant, "The Performance of Soviet Weapons in Lebanon," *Radio Liberty Research*, RL 68/83, February 7, 1983.

north, outside IDF artillery and missile range, were simultaneously attacked by F-4s using Shrike, Standard ARM, and Maverick missiles. Finally, once the Syrian SAM radars had been neutralized by a combination of electronic countermeasures (ECM) and physical destruction, F-4s and F-16s employing low-level penetration and terrain-masking tactics entered in simultaneous attacks from multiple directions, delivering standoff munitions, cluster bomb units (CBUs), and general-purpose bombs against surviving radar vans and SA-6 missile launchers.[58]

In the course of this highly orchestrated strike, which reportedly took only ten minutes, Israeli forces destroyed 17 of the 19 SA-6 sites in the Bekáa Valley, as well as several SA-2 and SA-3 sites. Throughout the operation, orbiting Scout and Mastiff RPVs provided continuous real-time video surveillance of ongoing events for the ground-based strike force commander. The Boeing 707 continued to monitor enemy radar emissions and transmitted threat data to attacking fighters. Chaff and flare countermeasures were used extensively by all Israeli aircraft operating within the Syrian air defense envelope. A total of 57 SA-6s were reportedly fired during this attack sequence, all to no effect. In the end, the IAF accomplished the mission without losing a single aircraft. The two surviving SA-6 sites, as well as some additional batteries that were replenished with new equipment overnight, were destroyed in a similar raid the following day.

Predictably, the Syrian Air Force scrambled a large number of MiGs to engage the attacking Israeli fighters. Anticipating this, the IAF had positioned several F-15 and F-16 combat air patrols (CAPs) west of the Bekáa Valley to intercept any Syrian fighters that might attempt to disrupt the SAM suppression raid. By one account, the Israeli Scout RPV used its electro-optical zoom lens and digital data link to provide real-time video imagery of Syrian fighters as they taxied into position for takeoff. The E-2C, with its 200-mile surveillance range, was able to pick up the MiGs on radar as soon as they lifted off the runway and relayed intercept vectors to the IAF fighter CAPs. Once the enemy fighter formations were airborne, their radio communications were massively jammed, depriving them of any contact with their GCI controllers. The Israelis also used some F-15s in a tactical airborne warning and control system (AWACS) mode to provide gap-filler support for the E-2C and to assist other fighters.

The resultant confrontation was by far the largest in the history of Middle East air warfare. At its height, some 60 Syrian and 90 Israeli fighters reportedly were airborne simultaneously in the combat arena. The IAF enjoyed the combined advantages of tactical initiative, numerical preponderance, superior aircraft and weapons, better aircrew proficiency, and confident

---

[58] Paul S. Cutter, "ELTA Plays a Decisive Role in the EOB Scenario," *Military Electronics/Countermeasures,* January 1983, pp. 135–137.

knowledge of where the Syrian threat would be concentrated. Using their look-down radars and all-aspect missiles (both of which the Syrians lacked), Israeli fighters simply picked off any MiGs that ventured past a pre-established line.[59] Although the IAF later maintained that it took no shots at Syrian fighters from beyond visual range, it evidently made extensive use of blind-side tactics by employing the E-2C to vector F-15s and F-16s into beam attacks against Syrian MiGs where their radar warning systems were reportedly least effective. Altogether, the IAF downed 23 Syrian fighters during this battle while sustaining no losses of its own. The following day, Israeli fighters shot down 15 more MiGs. By the end of July, the IAF had destroyed 85 Syrian aircraft (half MiG-21s and half MiG-23s) in a cumulative series of aerial engagements without losing a single aircraft to enemy fighter action. The result was a complete rout that established a new high for IAF kill ratios in air combat.

Understandably, that experience attracted keen interest on the part of the U.S. defense establishment, for it offered the first full-scale test of the latest generation of air weaponry that had been introduced into U.S. forces since the end of the Vietnam war. Its distinctive features included effective joint-force combat in a severe electronic warfare environment and a masterly blend of the same high-technology hardware with exceptional training and concepts of operations that American airmen had worked so hard to develop during the preceding decade.

The IDF was careful to caution against drawing overly sweeping "lessons" from its Bekáa achievement because of several factors that rendered the Lebanese air war unique.[60] For one thing, the operation was extremely limited in scope, intensity, objectives, and numbers of participants. Second, the Syrian SAM threat consisted largely of fixed SA-6s whose positions were well known by Israeli intelligence. That made for far less of a challenge than what NATO air forces would confront against integrated Warsaw Pact air defenses in Central Europe—or that the IAF itself would have had to face in any major air war over the Golan Heights. Finally, the IAF commanded numerical superiority and maintained the operational initiative at all times. Neither circumstance would have been likely to favor Israel so resoundingly in any full-scale war against an entire Arab coalition.

That said, the IAF performed well in the Bekáa Valley campaign by any measure—so well, in fact, that its leaders were reportedly surprised to have

---

[59] George C. Wilson, "Israel Proves U.S. Arms Effective, General Says," *Washington Post*, June 17, 1982.

[60] Indeed, the IAF commander at the time, Major General David Ivry, declined to participate in press interviews after the Bekáa Valley offensive because of his concern, as reported by a respected Israeli defense journalist, that his remarks might inadvertently be used to feed unwarranted Israeli "self-aggrandizement . . . spilling over into euphoria." Zeev Schiff, "The Danger of Mistaken Conclusions," *Ha'aretz* (Tel Aviv), August 27, 1983.

come through it virtually unscathed. By the end of September, it had amassed a total score of some 29 SAM sites destroyed in seven raids and 85 Syrian MiGs downed for only 2 Israeli aircraft losses to enemy ground fire. The impressiveness of that performance prompted a long-awaited U.S. Air Force fact-finding mission to Israel a year later, led by the deputy chief of staff for plans and operations at the time, Lieutenant General John Chain, to "go to school" on the Bekáa experience and ensure that the right lessons were incorporated into the now much-improved American air combat repertoire.[61]

It would be another nine years before American forces would encounter a test of comparable dimensions in the skies over Iraq. Yet the results of the Bekáa Valley shootout offered grounds for guarded Air Force and Navy assurance that their investments in training, technology, and tactics over the preceding decade had been vindicated by Israel's performance in what was, to all intents and purposes, a windfall preview of how the American air weapon might fare against the Soviet conventional threat. Viewed in hindsight, the real "lessons" of the Bekáa example did not concern weapons so much as concepts of force employment. Reduced to basics, it was the result of a confrontation between two radically divergent operational philosophies, in which the Syrians were simply outflown and outfought by vastly superior Israeli opponents. Without question, Israel's sophisticated American hardware figured prominently in helping the IAF emerge from the Bekáa Valley with a perfect air-to-air score. Nevertheless, the outcome would most likely have been heavily weighted in Israel's favor even had the equipment available to each side been reversed. At bottom, the Syrians were not done in by the AIM-9L's expanded launch envelope, the F-15's radar, or any combination of such Israeli technical assets in the first instance, but rather by the IDF's constant retention of the initiative and its clear advantages in leadership, organization, tactical adroitness, and adaptability.

A Rude Awakening over Lebanon

As much as Israel's success over the Bekáa was embraced by American airmen as a role model for the intelligent use of modern air power, the first opportunity the United States had to apply the air weapon in anger since Vietnam indicated that few lessons had been absorbed over the ensuing decade when it came to putting it all together. That ill-fated occasion grew out of the deepening American "presence" in Beirut that began shortly after the 1982 Lebanon war, with U.S. Marines deployed by the Reagan administration in a peacekeeping role to protect the threatened pro-American govern-

---

[61] After much Israeli resistance, this finally occurred in the spring of 1983. See Bernard Gwertzman, "Israelis to Share Lessons of War with Pentagon," *New York Times*, March 22, 1983.

ment of President Amin Gemayel. The lack of a clear and consistent rationale for that U.S. mission was brutally underscored on October 23, 1983,
when a terrorist bombing of the Marine barracks at the Beirut airport killed
241 Marines and wounded 100 more. That was but the latest in a long series
of escalating attacks on the multinational peacekeeping presence in Lebanon at the instigation of Syria.

Remarkably, that affront did not trigger an American reaction. What instead prompted a U.S. air reprisal in the end was the ineffectual firing of an
SA-7 missile by Lebanese terrorists against an F-14 reconnaissance mission
to monitor terrorist-training activities in the Shouf Mountains. Although
that, in and of itself, seemed anything but an appropriate pretext to warrant
such a reprisal, President Reagan nevertheless ordered a U.S. retaliatory
strike. To his credit, in contrast to Lyndon Johnson's proclivities during the
earlier years of the Vietnam war, he did not dictate either a time or any operational specifics, leaving all such details to the military.

For its part, surprisingly enough, the U.S. military repeated every conceptual and planning error of Vietnam by opting for a tit-for-tat response
that was guaranteed to have no coercive or military effect. Prompted by its
determination to apply timely punishment to avenge that perceived affront,
the Joint Staff moved briskly to lay on a retaliatory air attack at targets "associated with missile firings at U.S. aircraft on December 3." Alerted ahead
of time that a strike order might be coming down at any moment, the on-
scene naval air commander aboard the carrier USS *Independence*, Rear Admiral Jerry Tuttle, initiated planning for an attack by aircraft from both the
Independence and the USS *John F. Kennedy*, with a time-on-target of 1100 local time the following morning. As frantic efforts ensued to load aircraft
with munitions for the following morning's anticipated launch, a new set of
targets was issued by the U.S. European Command (EUCOM) in Stuttgart,
which required a downloading of high-explosive bombs and their replacement by CBUS. In the midst of this feverish activity, at 0530 the following
morning, EUCOM issued an order for a launch time of 0630. That meant that
the tasked air wing now had an insufficient number of aircraft properly
loaded and no aircrews even assigned, let alone briefed.

In the end, the air wing succeeded in launching 28 aircraft, a mix of A-6s
and A-7s, although none with the proper munitions load and with no aircrews properly briefed. In what Secretary of the Navy John Lehman later
described as a "classic twenty-year-old Vietnam 'aluminum cloud' alpha
strike," the mission was marked by no surprise, no deception, and no use of
countermeasures.[62] A Soviet ELINT trawler operating within easy view of
the *Independence* monitored the entire operation and undoubtedly commu-

---

[62] John F. Lehman, Jr., *Command of the Seas: Building the 600-Ship Navy*, New York, Charles Scribner's
Sons, 1988, p. 329.

nicated warning to the targeted Syrian terrorists. Upon arriving in the target area, the attacking aircrews found the sun directly in their faces and the targets themselves obscured by the shadows of the surrounding mountains. This necessitated a low weapons-release altitude in order for the attacking pilots to acquire and positively identify the targets visually.

From the moment the attacking aircraft crossed the Lebanese shoreline, they encountered nonstop AAA barrages and SA-7 and SA-9 missile launches. The inconsequential targets were effectively struck despite these attempted defensive countermeasures. However, during their departure from the target area, two of the A-7s from the *Independence* were hit by ground fire, with the pilot of one, the air group commander, being forced to eject. He was promptly rescued and returned to his ship, but the crew of a downed A-6 from the *Kennedy* was less fortunate. The pilot never separated from his ejection seat and died instantly on impact with the ground. The bombardier-navigator was captured and held prisoner, to great propaganda effect, by Syrian proxies in Lebanon until he was released (to Jesse Jackson) after a month in captivity.

The embarrassment caused for the United States by the poorly organized operation drove home unmercifully the fact that despite all the progress that had been made in rebuilding the U.S. air posture since 1973, some abiding lessons of Vietnam had not been learned and assimilated. Prominent among these had to do with the convoluted chain of command between Washington and the on-scene shooters, which proved itself incapable of planning and conducting an air strike effectively. Others entailed a lack of clarity of objectives, a failure to match means with ends, and virtually no progress by either Navy operators or EUCOM planners in growing out of their tit-for-tat Vietnam mindset. As Secretary Lehman harshly concluded, even had the air wing commanders been freed to do anything they wanted by way of retaliation, they would not have planned the sort of precision night attack that was employed far more successfully three years later against Libya. Instead, he said, "Left to their desires, the task force simply would have added more aircraft and loaded more bombs and gone later in the day, with possibly greater losses. To their credit, however, they undoubtedly would have picked better targets." [63]

The failed Lebanon raid, however, did have an upbeat ending in a sense two years later, when, at Lehman's instigation, the Navy finally established at NAS Fallon, Nevada, a training operation for fleet squadrons analogous to Red Flag, along with a Strike Leader's Attack Training Syllabus, or SLATS, at a new facility called the Strike Warfare Center, or "Strike U" for short. Prompted by the revelation that not just the civilian policy community but the uniformed military establishment was not yet ready for the prime time

[63] Ibid., p. 337.

of modern air employment, the aim of this program was to extirpate once and for all the obsolete massed daylight bombing tactics retained since Vietnam and to make the most of the all-weather precision attack capabilities that the Navy now had in the A-6E and F/A-18.

In this initiative, just as the Air Force lagged behind the Navy in improving its air-to-air repertoire a decade earlier, the Navy lagged behind its own Marine Corps, which several years earlier had developed a similar program of large-force, realistic air warfare training managed by Marine Aviation Weapons and Tactics Squadron One (MAWTS-1) at Marine Corps Air Station (MCAS) Yuma, Arizona. In addition to offering a twice-yearly Weapons and Tactics Instructor (WTI) course for Marine aviators much like the USAF Fighter Weapons School at Nellis, MAWTS-1 provided a superb venue for realistic intelligence assessment and threat integration, strike planning, and combined air and ground force training on an instrumented range, complete with ACMI and realistic surface-to-air threat simulators like those maintained throughout the Nellis range complex. Playing catch-up, the Navy finally moved to implement a new training regimen in which each air wing before deploying would spend three weeks at Fallon conducting day- and night-mission planning and weapons and tactics training on Fallon's instrumented range, in which weapons deliveries were scored and errors were exposed for all to see in mass debriefings.

No less important, the Navy also set up a new threat-assessment center in Suitland, Maryland, called SPEAR, for "Strike Projection Evaluation and Anti-Air Research." Heavily staffed by handpicked operators, including combat-experienced aircrews, this new enterprise was given the charter to improve the sophistication and quality of Navy tactical intelligence on Soviet and Third-World air and SAM threats. Much in the manner of several similar Air Force undertakings (notably an Air Staff activity called Project CHECKMATE) that had been initiated during the second half of the 1970s, this analysis cell was heavily focused on realistic assessment, with particular emphasis on exploitable enemy vulnerabilities. As the next chapter will show, its ultimate vindication was its correct appraisal of the capabilities and weaknesses of the Iraqi integrated air defense system (IADS) immediately prior to the start of Desert Storm.

With that, and the establishment of "Strike U" as the Navy's acknowledged center for advanced tactics development and validation, the combat air arms of the Air Force, Navy, and Marine Corps had finally converged on a postgraduate level of training and tactics that both fully exploited the current generation of conventional munitions and realistic training facilities and brought U.S. combat crews to an unprecedented level of proficiency and technical competence. With the added advantage that emanated from regular participation in each other's programs, the three services went a long way toward developing a common language in the realm of fighter operations, as well as a practiced ability to work together when necessary. Although the full payoff of this was not to be felt until the opening hours of Desert Storm, growing trouble with Libya's erratic ruler, Moammar Gaddhafi, was soon to give the Air Force and Navy an interim chance to show what they had gained from their efforts over the preceding decade at building a blend of training, technology, and tactics where the whole could fairly be said to be more than the sum of the parts.

El Dorado Canyon Sharpens the Edge

The first real opportunity for U.S. strike aviation to show its capabilities in combat was provided by a steadily mounting series of terrorist attacks and other provocations by Gaddhafi in the mid-1980s. Typical of such brazen acts was Libya's declaring a so-called "Line of Death" at the 32nd parallel across the Gulf of Sidra and its sending up of Su-22 fighters to fire on U.S. Navy F-14s that deigned to violate it. Seemingly undaunted when two of these Libyan fighters were dispatched by two F-14s, Gaddhafi continued his provocations at every opportunity, including attacks on an American military shopping mall in Frankfurt and later attacks on the Rome and Vienna airports.

The Reagan administration was finally goaded into action when a suspected Libyan terrorist squad bombed the La Belle discotheque in West Berlin, a known haunt of U.S. troops, killing 2 Americans and wounding more than 50. As a retaliatory measure, President Reagan directed the National Security Council (NSC) to select appropriate targets for a U.S. reprisal and authorized the Joint Staff to organize and plan the attack. The targets were selected this time not to "send a message" or otherwise deliver any tit-for-tat response, but to do visible and felt harm to the Gaddhafi regime. The five targets chosen by the NSC included the Azziziya barracks in Tripoli, which was known to contain both the command center of Libyan intelligence and a residence of Gaddhafi; a terrorist-training facility and the Uqba Bin Nafi air base (formerly the U.S. Air Force's Wheelus Air Base) near Tripoli; and a terrorist encampment and military airfield near Benghazi.

Almost before the mission planning had begun, leaks from Washington let it be known that the Reagan administration was up to something regarding Libya. These leaks naturally had the effect of generating Libya's Soviet-built air defense network to a state of high alert. By the time the mission was laid on, however, Libya had relaxed its guard. The city lights remained on and Libya's defenses were down when the attack hit in the early morning of April 15, 1986 at 0200 local time.

This time, in contrast to the ineffectual Navy attack against terrorist sites in Lebanon three years earlier, the operation was planned to be carried out at night and to call on both active defense suppression and the use of PGMs. The joint strike package was divided between the Tripoli target complex and the Benghazi complex, with 18 F-111Fs from the 48th Tactical Fighter Wing based at Lakenheath, England, and additional Navy suppression of enemy air defenses (SEAD) aircraft tasked against the former and a Navy-only package of A-6s, A-7s, and F/A-18s from the carriers USS *America* and USS *Coral Sea* taking the latter. Both packages were backed up by EA-6B jammers, EA-3 ELINT aircraft, E-2C surveillance aircraft, and F-14 and F/A-18 fighter cover in an operation reminiscent of what the Israelis had organized for the Bekáa Valley four years earlier. Whether or not those who planned and conducted the operation would have admitted it, clearly some useful lessons from the Bekáa had been quietly assimilated by both services along the way.

In a carefully planned communications-out operation, Navy A-7s suppressed Libyan SAM defenses with HARM attacks simultaneously in both target complexes, followed six minutes later by Air Force F-111s carrying Pave Tack target designator pods for delivering LGBs against the targets around Tripoli and by Navy A-6s and A-7s conducting nonprecision attacks against the Benghazi target complex. Although the defenses around the two complexes were as dense and overlaid as anything that Soviet forces maintained in Eastern Europe, only 1 U.S. aircraft (an F-111) was lost, perhaps as a result of having flown into the water during a high-speed exit from the target area at low altitude rather than as a consequence of having been hit by enemy fire. Because of exacting rules of engagement with respect to target identification to avoid collateral damage, 4 of the 18 F-111s did not release their weapons. All targets were hit effectively, however, with only one known instance of collateral damage—to the French embassy in downtown Tripoli, which was situated near a designated weapon impact point. Doubtless aware of what they would face in trying to mount a serious defense against this air armada, Libyan air force leaders did not launch a single fighter to try to oppose it.

One can only speculate about how much more successful this operation would have been had the stealthy F-117 been used instead of, or in addition to, the more conventional aircraft that were employed in the end. As reported several years later by the aircraft's producer, Ben Rich, the initial plan, in a top-secret order signed personally by Secretary of Defense Caspar Weinberger, was for 8 to 12 F-117s to fly from the east coast of the United States straight to Libya, using inflight refueling, and to attack the five target sets at 0300 on the assigned morning of the strike. Senior officers at TAC headquarters had advised the secretary that the aircraft was more than capable of performing the mission, with one four-star general adding, "This was why the system was built." As the final countdown began, however,

Weinberger abruptly changed his mind, on the reported premise that it was still too early to reveal the aircraft's revolutionary capability to the Soviet Union. Within an hour of the F-117 detachment's planned departure to the east coast, its inclusion in the mission plan was scrubbed.[64]

Even with the limited success of Operation El Dorado Canyon, as the raid against Libya was code-named, there remained uncertainties about how well the Air Force's and Navy's night operations, precision weapons delivery, and SAM-suppression capabilities would work on a larger scale against an adversary that was similarly equipped and better able to use such assets. Yet El Dorado Canyon earned a place for itself as a modest milestone in the transformation of American air power. Although some basic employment matters were reportedly botched despite months of detailed planning, it nevertheless represented a concerted marshalling of much of what the Air Force and Navy had done since the end of the Vietnam war to improve their strike capabilities.[65] The equipment wielded against Libya was the most advanced that the two services had used in combat up to that point, and it worked, despite some problems in execution, as it was designed and intended to work. For their part, both the Air Force and Navy aircrews who participated in the operation were as well primed for combat as any peacetime training regime could possibly permit. Apart from the deserved confidence the two services gained from the performance of their equipment, perhaps the greatest contribution of El Dorado Canyon was what it did to give Air Force and Navy leaders a better appreciation of the progress they had yet to make in order to organize and successfully execute a complex air operation under the most challenging threat circumstances.

[64] Rich and Janis, *Skunk Works*, p. 96.
[65] According to the deputy commander for operations of the F-111 wing that took part in El Dorado Canyon, these planning mistakes included allowing for only 30 seconds of spacing between attacking aircraft, even though it took a full minute or two for the debris of a 2,000-lb bomb to clear. They also included dropping LGBs on the closest aim point first, thus ensuring that the next aircraft in trail would have trouble seeing and identifying its target. By this account, only 4 of 18 LGBs dropped by the F-111s hit their targets. Colonel Robert E. Venkus, USAF (Ret.), *Raid on Qaddafi*, New York, St. Martin's Press, 1992, p. 146.

[4]

Desert Storm Revisited

Operation Desert Storm was a watershed event in modern American military history. From a political perspective, its outcome fell far short of being "the most decisive victory in the 20th century," as one pundit called it immediately after the cease-fire.[1] Yet the allied coalition's rout of the Iraqi army in just six weeks with so few friendly losses (only 148 American combat fatalities out of more than 500,000 military personnel deployed to the theater) represented something new in the application of force. Indeed, more Americans lost their lives to routine accidents during the five-month Desert Shield buildup than to hostile fire during the six weeks of actual fighting.[2]

By now, the essential facts of what happened in the 1991 Gulf war have been more than amply reported, owing to a multitude of efforts to assemble and assess the pertinent data on the war experience. In particular, the U.S. Air Force's Gulf War Air Power Survey (GWAPS), a five-volume undertaking modeled on the U.S. Strategic Bombing Survey conducted after World War II, was carried out, among other reasons, to provide "an analytical and evidentiary point of departure for future studies of the air campaign."[3] Granted, there are still-inaccessible Iraqi records that might yet shed new light on Saddam Hussein's motivations and what factors influenced them during the course of Desert Storm. Those aside, however, there is, in all likelihood, no remaining Rosetta stone waiting to be discovered that might fun-

---

[1] Patrick Buchanan, "Would Red Army Fold So Swiftly?" *Washington Times*, March 4, 1991.

[2] William Neikirk, "Accidents Killed Most GIs in Gulf," *Chicago Tribune*, March 24, 1991.

[3] Thomas A. Keaney and Eliot A. Cohen, *Revolution in Warfare? Air Power in the Persian Gulf*, Annapolis, Md., Naval Institute Press, 1995, p. xii. This is the commercially published version of the GWAPS summary report originally released in 1993.

damentally alter what we now *think* occurred of note in that war.[4] A year after the war ended, Anthony Cordesman noted how "many of the facts that seemed reliable right after the war," such as the effectiveness of U.S. Army Patriot surface-to-air missiles (SAMS) in intercepting incoming Iraqi Scud missiles and the number of Scuds destroyed on the ground by coalition air attacks, were being shown to be wrong—proof positive, in his view, that "instant history [was] invariably shallow history."[5] Today, however, the basic facts of Desert Storm are no longer in dispute. What remains in contention are their meaning and implications.

One problem with attempting to come to grips with such questions is their tendency to lead one to read too much into a single historical case. From that, it is but a short step to the complacent urge to think of discrete events like Desert Storm as literal scripts for *all* future contingencies. Yet another pitfall in seeking definitive answers from such unique occurrences concerns whether such answers are even there to be found, in and of themselves, in any recognizable form. In this regard, Sir Michael Howard cautioned that "history, whatever its value in educating the judgment, teaches no 'lessons,' and the professional historian will be as skeptical of those who claim that it does as professional doctors are of their colleagues who peddle patent medicines guaranteeing instant cures. . . . Historians may claim to teach lessons, and often they teach very wisely. But 'history' as such does not."[6] Those qualifications duly noted, however, there is a strong case to be made that the Gulf war attested to a notable increase in the ability of U.S. air power to swing combat outcomes in comparison to more traditional force elements. There is also a case to be made that the contribution of U.S. air power to the allied victory in Desert Storm constituted enough of a departure from past experience to suggest that a new relationship between air and surface forces in joint warfare may be in the offing.

How the Air Campaign Was Born

In response to Iraq's invasion of Kuwait on August 2, 1990, President Bush moved with dispatch to form an international coalition to counter that act of aggression, with the main goal of forcing a complete and unconditional

[4] The most detailed single-volume reconstruction of opening-night air operations, as well as of the pace, scale, and flow of the air war in general, may be found in Williamson Murray, *Air War in the Persian Gulf*, Baltimore, Md., The Nautical and Aviation Publishing Company of America, 1995. This study was written as a GWAPS supporting volume.

[5] Anthony H. Cordesman, "The Fog of War and the Fog of Politics," *New York Yimes Book Review*, April 5, 1992.

[6] Michael Howard, *The Lessons of History*, New Haven, Yale University Press, 1991, pp. 11–13.

withdrawal of Iraqi forces. Toward that end, Army General H. Norman Schwarzkopf, the commander in chief (CINC) of U.S. Central Command (CENTCOM) on whom operational responsibility for the situation fell, announced that should a showdown prove unavoidable, the coalition's objectives would be not only to liberate Kuwait but also to destroy Iraq's ability to wage war, including its ability to produce and employ weapons of mass destruction.[7]

An element of happenstance figured in the genesis of the air campaign plan that ultimately swung the war's military outcome. Indeed, the plan that evolved might not have germinated in the first place had Schwarzkopf not asked the Air Force vice chief of staff, General John M. Loh, for early Air Staff help in putting together an air option. Ordinarily, Loh would have turned to the Air Staff's deputy chief of staff for plans and operations, Lieutenant General Jimmie V. Adams, to organize a response to Schwarzkopf's request. Adams, a protégé of Tactical Air Command's (TAC's) commander at the time, General Robert D. Russ, shared TAC's view that the proper role of Air Force air power was to support U.S. land forces. In all likelihood, he would have enlisted a heavy TAC hand in shaping the Air Staff's reply.[8] However, since Adams was on leave at the time, Loh's request instead eventually worked its way down to Colonel John A. Warden III, the Air Staff's deputy director of plans for warfighting concepts.

Warden had long argued for an operational-level approach to air campaign planning. Rising to the challenge he had just been handed, he and his staff developed a draft plan in response to Loh's tasking that called for a six-day air campaign against 84 designated "strategic" targets to incapacitate Iraq's leadership and destroy key military capabilities. That draft plan, called Instant Thunder to distinguish it from the earlier failed Rolling Thunder campaign against North Vietnam, was organized around so-called centers of gravity, the simultaneous destruction of which would, or so it was believed, compel Iraq to comply with U.S. wishes. Later GWAPS reported that Warden's plan "stopped just short of declaring that Instant Thunder alone would force Iraq to withdraw from Kuwait."[9]

The plan was briefed first to Schwarzkopf and then to the chairman of the Joint Chiefs of Staff (JCS), General Colin Powell, both of whom reacted favorably to its seeming promise. Yet it was rejected summarily by the newly

---

[7] CINCCENT briefing, "Offensive Campaign: Desert Storm," August 24, 1990, cited in Keaney and Cohen, *Revolution*, p. 22.

[8] Michael R. Gordon and Bernard E. Trainor, *The Generals' War: The Inside Story of the Conflict in the Gulf*, Boston, Little, Brown, 1995, p. 79. See also Colonel Richard T. Reynolds, USAF, *Heart of the Storm: The Genesis of the Air Campaign against Iraq*, Maxwell AFB, Ala., Air University Press, 1995, pp. 30–31, 77–82.

[9] Keaney and Cohen, *Revolution*, pp. 29–30.

designated joint force air component commander (JF ACC), Lieutenant General Charles A. Horner, who thought Warden's approach was flawed in its failure to include Iraqi military forces. At the outset, Horner's own inclination, at Schwarzkopf's express direction, was to prepare an air plan more suited to CENTCOM's immediate mission of defending Saudi Arabia against a further Iraqi ground advance.[10] As allied air forces in the theater gradually gained the requisite offensive strength, however, he eventually embraced a conception of air strategy more focused on the operational level of war. He further selected Air Force Brigadier General Buster C. Glosson to refine and implement it.

One of the Air Staff planners who had assisted Warden in designing Instant Thunder, then–Lieutenant Colonel David A. Deptula, was retained in Saudi Arabia by Horner and became one of his key deputies. As a result, the core idea of Instant Thunder was quietly retained, although the name itself was never heard again. In the end, that core idea became the lead part of a far more inclusive air campaign plan aimed at achieving four operational-level goals that, for the sake of convenience, were described in terms of phases: a "strategic" component, the suppression of enemy air defenses (SEAD) in the Kuwaiti theater of operations (KTO), preparing the battlefield, and air support to the eventual ground campaign. In fact, as Horner recalled afterward, there was a certain artificiality about these four phases in that they were delineated mainly so that the campaign plan "could be briefed to and understood by generals . . . who did not have an air power background." Horner added, "In reality, there were no distinct phases, all operations were going simultaneously, [and] there was an emphasis in our tempo or level of effort of our air operations at different times to achieve different objectives."[11] Initially defensive in focus during the early stages of the Desert Shield buildup, the air campaign's concept of operations quickly became supremely offensive in character.

By mid-September, CENTCOM had both a workable plan and the required air elements in place to begin dislodging Iraq from Kuwait by targeting leadership and command and control; nuclear, biological, and chemical weapons facilities; electrical, military, and oil production facilities; lines of communication such as bridges and railroads; air defenses; and—of crucial importance—Horner's addition of Iraqi ground forces deployed in the KTO and southern Iraq. Although still far from ideal, it was all that CENTCOM would have for several months by way of a usable option in the event that Iraq were to make some unforeseen move. For its part, the land component of Desert Storm had only begun to take shape and would not be ready for at least another four months.

---

[10] Communication to the author from General Charles A. Horner, USAF (Ret.), May 15, 1997.
[11] Ibid.

Significantly, the air campaign plan ultimately arrived at had nothing in common with the contingency plans that CENTCOM had previously developed. The earlier plans envisaged air attacks against Iraqi leadership and command and control nodes in Baghdad as the *final* part of a campaign rather than as the opening gambit. Moreover, until late 1989, U.S. planning for a Southwest Asia contingency had focused almost exclusively on the Soviet threat. Only with the subsiding of the cold war did CENTCOM turn its attention to Iraq as a possible future aggressor against the Arabian peninsula. Even then, CENTCOM's contingency planning was focused primarily on halting an Iraqi ground advance. Little thought was given to the potential use of U.S. conventional air power as a strategic weapon. In no way did it reflect the scale, intensity, or planned duration of Operation Desert Storm.

Although the details remained to be filled in, the four-phase concept of operations developed at Horner's instigation was identical to the one that was ultimately implemented during the war itself. The first phase was essentially Instant Thunder, buttressed by additional sorties aimed at preventing the reinforcement of Iraqi forces already in Kuwait. It was far more extensive in its coverage of Iraqi targets, however, owing to the subsequent development of better target intelligence and the allocation of considerably more strike assets by the Bush administration. The Instant Thunder plan had only 150 attack aircraft at its disposal. In contrast, the opening phase of the air campaign proposal briefed to President Bush in October employed more than 400 combat aircraft. The plan's initial phase reflected decided elements of classic air power theory in its hope of using air strikes to increase the likelihood of a "loss of confidence in the government" by the Iraqi people.[12] However, because of the more-than-adequate number of combat aircraft that had been made available before the war commenced, the first three phases would be undertaken concurrently, with emphasis placed on neutralizing Iraq's air defenses as a precursor to other attacks. A central organizing goal of the plan was to create friction in the Iraqi system, not necessarily by taking out every target of interest in detail, but rather by searching for functional effects, creating disorientation and confusion, and destroying Iraq's capacity for collective action.

Both CENTCOM and the leadership in Washington were comfortable with the emerging air campaign plan almost from the start. The initial proposal for the ground offensive, however, envisaged an allied assault led by just a single U.S. Army corps, the only U.S. ground component that was available at the time, in a single, very shallow left hook into heavily fortified Iraqi positions. When Schwarzkopf later concluded that he could not divide his troops for a flanking attack unless he got substantial reinforcements, and told President Bush that if the single left hook failed, the coalition would be

---

[12] OPORD (Operations Order) 91-001, quoted in Keaney and Cohen, *Revolution*, p. 33.

left without a coherent armored striking force, he was given VII Corps in addition to the XVIII Airborne Corps. In granting CENTCOM that additional ground increment, Bush simultaneously doubled the U.S. air deployment, thus guaranteeing, for the first time, a clear surfeit of air power.

That said, things could have been considerably worse. For its part, TAC remained wedded to its near-symbiotic tie to the U.S. Army through its long involvement with AirLand Battle doctrine, even though TAC's leaders rarely lost an opportunity to point out that AirLand Battle was Army doctrine, not Air Force doctrine. Moreover, TAC's leadership was still heavily caught up in Vietnam-era thinking with respect to the role of air power in joint warfare. Had TAC had its way, the plan that went to CENTCOM for final approval might well have produced a needless replay of the failed Vietnam strategy. Early in August after Iraq's invasion of Kuwait, TAC had proposed a concept of operations that sought to start "with demonstrative attacks against high-value targets . . . [and then] escalate as required until all significant targets are destroyed." According to its authors, such a strategy would allow "time and opportunity for Hussein to reevaluate his situation and back out while there is still something to save."[13] Such a repetition of the attempted sending of "messages" that lay at the root of the failed U.S. application of air power in Rolling Thunder might well have produced a desert quagmire for the coalition. On top of that, some in the Navy sought, for a time at least, to push for a distribution of route packages between the Air Force and Navy along Vietnam lines, as well as a rollback campaign against Iraqi air defenses that would have worked agonizingly from the outside in rather than engaging it simultaneously. However, Horner rejected both TAC's and the Navy's proposals. As Williamson Murray later noted with respect to this whole process, much of the credit for the ultimate success of the air war rested on "idiosyncratic factors that placed individuals in control of CENTAF [Central Command Air Forces] and within its planning process who either intuitively understood or who were willing to be educated in the possibilities that an operational-level air campaign could offer."[14]

In a broader sense, much of the credit for the air war's success also rested on the reforms that had been instituted earlier by the Defense Reorganization Act of 1986, more commonly known as the Goldwater-Nichols Act after its two sponsors, Senator Barry Goldwater of Arizona and Representative Bill Nichols of Alabama. The main events that triggered that legislation were the failed Iranian hostage rescue mission of April 1980, the botched U.S. invasion of Grenada in 1983, and the terrorist bombing of the U.S. Ma-

[13] Fax message from TAC/XP (Director of Plans, Headquarters TAC) to AF/XOX (Director of Plans, Headquarters USAF), "CENTCOM Air Campaign Plan," August 11, 1990, quoted in Murray, *Air War in the Persian Gulf*, pp. 19–20.
[14] Ibid., p. 314. CENTAF was the Air Force component of CENTCOM.

rine barracks in Beirut later that same year. Each of these episodes, quite apart from the tragic loss of life they occasioned, caused considerable embarrassment to the United States as a direct consequence of problems widely attributed, at least in part, to the long-standing inability or unwillingness of the four U.S. services to work harmoniously either in the policy arena or at the operational level. As one of the first serious looks at the legislation later explained its intent, the Goldwater-Nichols Act sought to find a way to "improve and rationalize the efficiency of a Rube Goldberg contraption passing for a defense establishment" by formalizing new rules that might help the system function with less self-generated friction.[15]

The net effect of Goldwater-Nichols was to strengthen the authority of the JCS chairman, as well as that of the CINCs of the joint U.S. warfighting commands around the world, at the expense of the separate uniformed services, whose roles were reduced essentially to organizing, training, and equipping their respective forces rather than employing them in combat. In the case of Desert Storm, this shift in authority made for the first instance in which the long-espoused "single manager for air" concept could be applied and tested in actual practice. Although Horner, as Schwarzkopf's JFACC, did not technically exercise formal "command" over the air assets of the Army, Navy, or Marine Corps deployed to the Gulf, he did wield operational *control* over them to an extent that empowered him to task them as he deemed appropriate to support the CINC's air apportionment decisions. In that respect, as another assessment later concluded, the 1986 Goldwater-Nichols Act could be fairly described as "the godfather of the success of the Gulf war."[16]

Once it solidified, CENTCOM's air campaign plan was embodied in an Air Tasking Order (ATO) that brought together the assets of four U.S. services and five coalition partners into a single, carefully balanced, daily air employment schedule. As described by GWAPS, it "matched aircraft sorties with missions, targets, times, and all the coordinating instructions necessary for units to accomplish the specific tasks."[17] Army helicopters operating below 500 ft were exempted from JFACC jurisdiction, as were naval aircraft during overwater flight and Marine aircraft tasked with direct support of Marine ground operations. All other aircraft in all U.S. and allied services were directly subordinated to JFACC control.

Most of the involved players agreed that the ATO was overly cumbersome. Some complained that at 200 pages or more in standard message format, it was too long and too hard to digest. The Navy had a special problem in be-

---

[15] Vincent Davis, "Organization and Management," in Joseph Kruzel, ed., *American Defense Annual, 1987–1988*, Lexington, Mass., D. C. Heath, 1987, p. 197.

[16] James A. Winnefeld and Dana J. Johnson, *Joint Air Operations: Pursuit of Unity in Command and Control, 1942–1991*, Annapolis, Md., Naval Institute Press, 1993, p. 137.

[17] Keaney and Cohen, *Revolution*, pp. 28–29.

ing obliged to fly a computer disc bearing a file copy to each of its six carriers every day because its communications system could not receive the ATO electronically. Nevertheless, the ATO was indispensable for several important reasons, not least of which concerned the need to deconflict airspace over both enemy and friendly territory, considering that more than 2,000 combat and support sorties were being flown every day, with often as many tanker hook-ups to sustain them. Also, more than 900 discrete radio frequencies were assigned to specific aircraft groupings in the daily ATO so that aircrews might avoid inadvertently jamming one another through competing voice communications on the same channel. In the end, participating aircrews used different equipment, often different tactics, and sometimes widely differing operating styles. Yet all managed to work from a common playbook, often with such a density of operations that if a prebriefed time on target was missed by more than five minutes, the late-arriving formation would be forced to abort its mission en route so that the next attacking aircraft could get in unhindered by other friendly aircraft operating in the general vicinity of the target.

THE GAINING OF AIR CONTROL

On paper at least, Iraq's defenses appeared formidable. Its highly centralized integrated air defense system (IADS), code-named KARI (French for "Iraq," spelled backward), entailed four air defense sectors, each with a sector operations center connected to subordinate intercept operations centers and with acquisition and tracking radars at more than 100 sites. After Moscow, Baghdad was surrounded by the densest concentration of air defenses of any city in the world. The rest of Iraq was likewise replete with overlapping SAMs and antiaircraft artillery (AAA) threat envelopes. For its part, the Iraqi Air Force (IQAF), equipped with late-generation French and Soviet fighters, was among the world's largest. Leading its inventory were three squadrons of MiG-29s, the Soviet Union's premier close-in air combat fighter and one widely acknowledged to constitute an aerodynamic match for the F-15 and F-16.[18]

The Iraqi fighter pilot, however, was a different story. Although there was little hard evidence that might attest to his likely aggressiveness in a complex situation, IQAF aircrews had long been trained by the Soviet Union. Despite some French influence associated with the Mirage F1, they mainly operated in accordance with Soviet doctrine, with its stress on close control from the ground and its tendency not to emphasize hard maneuvering in aerial combat. In light of that, the IQAF was expected to perform more or less

[18] David A. Fulghum, "U.S. Mounts Swift Response to Iraq's Invasion of Kuwait," *Aviation Week and Space Technology*, August 13, 1990, pp. 18–21.

as the Syrian and Egyptian air forces had in previous Middle East wars against Israel.

During the final countdown, many allied aircraft slated to fly in the initial attack waves were placed on ground alert. The declared reason was to ensure against an Iraqi preemptive attack against Saudi Arabia before the United Nations (UN)-imposed January 15 deadline for Iraq to evacuate Kuwait. The actual reason was to allow adequate rest for the flight crews and reconfigurations of aircraft stores without telegraphing the coalition's operational intentions to Saddam Hussein. Earlier, coalition aircrews had conducted repeated large-force employment rehearsals beyond the view of Iraqi and Jordanian radar. Almost from the beginning of Desert Shield, the coalition had also flown daily deceptive sortie surges, complete with airborne tanker tracks, orbits of E-3 airborne warning and control systems (AWACS), and fighter combat air patrols (CAPs). Iraqi intelligence became habituated to this pattern, and that contributed to the allied achievement of tactical surprise. The coalition's chief air planner and fighter operations commander, General Glosson, later stated that the allies had maintained total tactical surprise until the first bombs landed on Baghdad.

Negating Iraq's Air Defenses

War began for Iraq at 0238 local time on January 17, only 19 hours after the UN deadline for Saddam Hussein's withdrawal from Kuwait had expired. In response to President Bush's directive to Schwarzkopf to pick a start date "as close to January 15 as possible," the duty captain in the CENTAF weather shop recommended an H-hour of 0300 over Baghdad because the illumination from the moon would be least at that time.[19] The opening shots, 22 minutes prior to H-hour, were Hellfire missiles fired from U.S. Army Apache helicopters against two Iraqi acquisition radar sites that provided early warning to Iraqi air and missile defenses. That opened a corridor enabling F-15Es to attack fixed Scud surface-to-surface missile sites at the same time the first allied bombs would be hitting Baghdad. Nine minutes prior to H-hour, with the first bombs dropped during the war, a pair of F-117s (2 of 10 in this initial attack) took out the interceptor operations center some 160 miles southwest of Baghdad to which the two early-warning posts reported. The F-117s proceeded thereafter to attack a second target, the Iraqi western-sector air operations center, 20 minutes later. These F-117 attacks blinded Iraq's air defenses and crippled key control nodes where such efforts mattered most for ensuring the success of follow-on attacks.

The most pressing challenge facing the allied attack force on opening night was to neutralize Iraq's extensive network of lethal SAMs. These SEAD

---

[19] Communication to the author from General Charles A. Horner, USAF (Ret.), May 15, 1997.

missions featured some of the most demanding air operations of the entire war. The F-4G with the AGM-88 high-speed antiradiation missile (HARM) did most of the actual shooting, with jamming support provided by EF-111s, EC-130s, and EA-6Bs. Marine F/A-18s also were utilized heavily on opening night in backing up the SEAD campaign with preemptive HARM attacks. These attacks were further supported by BQM-74 jet-powered drones and tactical air-launched decoys (TALDs) to stimulate and confuse Iraq's acquisition and tracking radars, much as the Israelis had done over the Bekáa Valley against Syria's SA-6s in 1982. The underlying concept of operations was to use a combination of tactical surprise and deception (by means of the decoys and drones) from the opening moments of the war to force the largest possible number of Iraqi SAM batteries to disclose their positions to coalition HARM shooters by activating their radars.

Initial efforts of the allied defense-suppression campaign focused on neutralizing Iraq's radar-directed medium- and high-altitude SAMS so as to open up a sanctuary for coalition aircraft above 10,000 ft.[20] At one point during these attacks, more than 200 HARMS were in flight simultaneously. During the first four hours of the war, nearly 100 Iraqi air defense radar emissions were logged by coalition sensors. That number later dropped to 15 and became only "sporadic" thereafter.[21] In all, more than 500 HARMS were fired during the first 24 hours of the war. Iraqi air defenders quickly learned that to activate their radars meant to invite a deadly attack.

Almost half of the nearly 2,000 HARMS fired over the course of the war were expended during the first week. After that, merely the threat of a HARM launch (often by nothing more than a well-timed bogus "Magnum" radio call by an allied aircrew to indicate a HARM in the air) sufficed to keep most enemy SAM radars either in standby mode or shut down entirely. By the sixth day of the war, Iraqi SAM, AAA, and early-warning radar emissions were down 95 percent. Later, once Iraq's early-warning radar and SAM crews had been intimidated into operating in less-than-optimal modes during those occasions when they did seek to employ radar-guided SAMs, coalition defense-suppression operations shifted from preemptive to reactive HARM launches to economize on HARM expenditure. With KARI's radar operators now fully intimidated against activating their radars by the initial attacks, SEAD operations moved from suppression to the physical destruction of enemy defenses, using general-purpose bombs, Maverick missiles, and CBU-87 cluster bombs.[22]

---

[20] John D. Morrocco, "Allies Attack Iraqi Targets; Scuds Strike Israeli Cities," *Aviation Week and Space Technology*, January 21, 1991, pp. 20–22.
[21] David M. North, "Carrier-Based U.S. Aircraft Flying Third of Desert Storm Strikes," *Aviation Week and Space Technology*, February 4, 1991, p. 27.
[22] Captain Dan Hampton, USAF, "Combat Defense Suppression: The F-4G/F-16C Wild Weasel at War," *USAF Fighter Weapons Review*, Summer 1991, pp. 4–6.

In all, more than 100 coalition fighters flew defense-suppression sorties the first night. By the U.S. government's estimate, the heart of the Iraqi IADS was taken out within the first hour. General Glosson's stated goal was the effective neutralization of Iraq's command and control within 24 hours of the start of combat operations. The coalition actually achieved that objective in the first eight hours.[23] After the first night, individual air defense sectors were forced into autonomous operations, and KARI no longer functioned as an integrated system. The entire system was rendered nonoperational in 36 hours. Hardened SAM and interceptor operations centers were negated within four days. Instead of rolling back enemy defenses, the latter were attacked simultaneously, and in a way from which Iraq never recovered.

After the war, General Horner was quick to emphasize that the SEAD campaign had been anything but a turkey shoot, since "the Iraqis had a sophisticated and very capable air defense system."[24] Nevertheless, owing to superior training, tactics, and equipment, the coalition's loss rate to Iraqi surface-to-air defenses in the end was only one aircraft per 1,800 combat sorties—14 times lower than the U.S. loss rate during Linebacker II. The Navy's Strike Projection Evaluation and Anti-Air Warfare Research (SPEAR) threat-assessment cell accomplished an outstanding analysis of the KARI system. On the eve of the war, SPEAR analysts identified critical nodes and vulnerabilities in what GWAPS called "perhaps the best assessment of the Iraqi air force and air defense system."[25] One vulnerability was the orientation of Iraqi AAA on preset azimuths for barrage firing. Another was the orientation of KARI radars and tactics toward the west (against Israel) and east (against Iran), rather than toward the south (Saudia Arabia) from which the allied attacks mainly came. For good reason, GWAPS later characterized the SEAD operation as "one of the clear success stories" of the Gulf war.[26]

Neutralizing Iraqi Air Power

The counterair portion of CENTCOM's air campaign plan entailed both clearing the skies of Iraqi fighters and attacking them on the ground to keep them from interfering with allied air operations and attacking the coalition's rear. As expected, CENTCOM established dominance over Iraq's fighters almost instantly in the initial air engagements. U.S. Air Force F-15Cs accounted for most of the air-to-air kills, with timely intelligence, threat warning, and airborne battle management provided by E-3 AWACS and RC-135 Rivet Joint aircraft orbiting to the south, out of harm's way. Deprived of

[23] Comments on an earlier draft by Lieutenant General Buster C. Glosson, USAF.
[24] Lieutenant General Charles A. Horner, "Desert Shield/Desert Storm: An Overview," *Air Power History*, Fall 1991, p. 7.
[25] Keaney and Cohen, *Revolution*, p. 109
[26] Ibid., p. 119.

any tactical coherence owing to widespread allied communications jamming and attacks against key command and control nodes, Iraq's fighters rose in disorganized formations on the first night, only to find themselves promptly dispatched by head-on missile shots. There was no reported Iraqi countermaneuvering in any of these engagements. In most cases, the downed Iraqi pilots never knew what hit them. It did not take Iraq's air commanders long to see the handwriting on the wall, indicating in no uncertain terms that to fly meant to die.

With few exceptions, this was the pattern of air combat for the first week, after which the IQAF ceased being an active player in the war. Most of the 33 allied air-to-air kills registered were accomplished by the AIM-7, with the AIM-9 playing a secondary role. More than 40 percent of those kills were the result of beyond-visual-range (BVR) missile shots. The E-3 AWACS and associated electronic identification techniques helped to underwrite BVR tactics with little risk of causing inadvertent fratricidal "blue-on-blue" engagements. All of these assets and tactics had been created and progressively refined over the two decades spanning Vietnam and Desert Storm. Although Iraq's pilots were trained according to the same operational doctrine that North Vietnam's had been a generation earlier, the contrast in outcomes could not have been more pronounced.

In a masterpiece of understatement, a Navy SPEAR assessment before the war similarly described IQAF tactics as "predominantly conservative, elementary, and generally not up to Western standards."[27] Indeed, Iraqi fighter employment was so hapless on most occasions that coalition aircrews began to joke before long that the IQAF had a departure control but no approach control and that the three most fearsome words to an Iraqi fighter pilot were, "Cleared for takeoff!" In seeming testimony to this, the IQAF in one instance had eight fighters holding short of the runway for takeoff. After the first two were downed by BVR missile shots in the face only seconds after becoming airborne, the other six promptly taxied back to their shelters and shut down.[28] The intimidation effect registered on the IQAF by CENTCOM's absolute command of the air was so pronounced that in contrast to the coalition's 69,000 "shooter" sorties throughout the war, the IQAF flew fewer than 500 altogether. There were only two known cases of Iraqi penetrations of coalition airspace, when two Mirage F1s attempted a low-level attack on January 24. Both were downed in prompt succession by a Saudi F-15.[29]

---

[27] Quoted in Murray, *Air War in the Persian Gulf,* p. 67.

[28] A GWAPS interview with Major General Buster Glosson, April 14, 1992, quoted in ibid., p. 130.

[29] The Royal Saudi Air Force later recovered the maps from the downed Mirages and informed Horner that the ordnance they carried was air-to-ground and that the target was a large oil refinery southwest of Dhahran. Communication to the author by General Charles A. Horner, USAF (Ret.), May 15, 1997.

In the end, the IQAF proved to be an inconsequential player in the war. Before the start of hostilities, it was averaging 55 shooter and 40 support sorties a day. After the war began, it launched 25 fighters the first night and 8 got shot down. It averaged 30 combat sorties a day during the first week, and 14 more got shot down. In contrast, no coalition air-to-air losses were confirmed, although there was one possible air-to-air loss (as noted earlier, a Navy F/A-18 to an unobserved MiG-25 infrared missile) the first night.[30] After the 25th day, the IQAF ceased flight operations entirely, aside from five aircraft that fled to Iran the day the ground war commenced.

Understandably, there was disappointment as the coalition's air-to-air pilots found themselves deprived, by the refusal of the IQAF to come up and fight, of an opportunity to validate in combat what they had learned during 15 years of Red Flag and similar realistic peacetime air combat training around the world. That said, it would be wrong to conclude that the quest for air supremacy did not play a vital role in shaping the outcome of Desert Storm. From the beginning, there had been a valid concern over the possibility of an Iraqi attempt to slip through allied air defenses and gain a politically significant achievement by downing a tanker or AWACS, even on a suicide mission by high-speed ramming if necessary.[31] Fortunately, the early achievement of allied air dominance prevented that. True enough, there may not have been an epic air-to-air contest between the coalition and Iraq on the grand scale of the swirling fighter engagements that dotted the skies of France and Germany during World War II. Nevertheless, the combination of the F-15C and AWACS left an important mark on the Gulf war's outcome by eliminating any IQAF involvement by default. Asked afterward why an all-out aerial showdown between the coalition and Iraq never came to pass, General Horner remarked that Saddam Hussein simply "had no idea what air power is. . . . Any of my captains could have run his air force and caused much more trouble than he did."[32]

Although it soon became clear that the IQAF had no intention of seriously contesting the coalition in air-to-air combat, it remained uncertain whether it was out of the picture entirely or whether Saddam Hussein was intentionally husbanding it, either for the impending ground war or perhaps for

---

[30] According to one credible account, the F/A-18 strike force leader had identified an Iraqi MiG-25 operating near his area, established a radar lock, and requested clearance from the AWACS to fire. Clearance was denied on the ground that the AWACS controller could not see the alleged target. Later, the F/A-18 mission commander said, "I can't change physics, nor can anybody else. If [the MiG] was in their Doppler notch, they couldn't see it. They had no evidence a plane was there." Mark Crispin Miller, "Death of a Fighter Pilot," *New York Times*, September 15, 1992.

[31] "Allies Shift Air Attacks to Break Ground Units," *Aviation Week and Space Technology*, January 28, 1991, pp. 20–21.

[32] Quoted in Richard Mackenzie, "A Conversation with Chuck Horner," *Air Force Magazine*, June 1991, p. 60.

a Tet-like suicide offensive against exposed allied rear-area facilities in Saudi Arabia. That uncertainty put a heightened premium on the need to keep pressing the offensive against Iraq's aircraft by pinning them down or destroying them in their shelters on the ground. Initially, allied attacks against Iraqi airfields had concentrated on suppressing the generation of fighter sorties so as to forestall any Iraqi air reaction to the opening strikes. In these operations, B-52s dropped area-denial weapons with time-delay fuses, and RAF Tornados used their JP233 runway-denial weapons to crater runways and taxiways. Although those attacks were effective as far as they went, Iraq's skillful use of decoys and rapid runway-repair capabilities offered a stern reminder that it is difficult to shut down an airfield completely. Moreover, the fact that the JP233 required direct overflight of the targeted runway at only 200 ft above ground level, plus the high combat loss rate of the Tornado (six in all), raised a valid question about the suitability of that munition and delivery mode in heavily defended enemy airspace.

Once it was evident that the IQAF would not come out and fight, allied airfield-attack operations shifted on January 23 from disabling runways to the systematic destruction of enemy aircraft in their shelters. In the new antishelter strategy, a typical airfield attack featured 20 F-111s, each carrying four 2,000-lb Mk 84 laser-guided bombs (LGBs), making two passes each in an operation spanning some seven minutes in the target area, with a weapon impact on the average of every five seconds. F-117s also were key players in the antishelter campaign because they were the only other aircraft in the U.S. inventory configured to carry precision weapons capable of penetrating hardened aircraft shelters. On Day Nine, the IQAF finally began its flight to Iran after F-117s destroyed 23 of Iraq's most durable shelters at an airfield northwest of Baghdad. Altogether, 80 Iraqi aircraft fled in three days. In the end, around 375 of 594 shelters (63 percent) were destroyed at 44 airfields altogether. By that time, the IQAF had been rendered totally ineffective.

To all intents and purposes, allied control of the air over Iraq was achieved during the opening moments of Desert Storm. In stark contrast to the tentative onset of Rolling Thunder (and to what TAC, in all likelihood, would have counseled for the Gulf had it been given free rein by Horner and Schwarzkopf), virtually every target category in the master attack plan was hit on the first night, with the stress on simultaneity in attacking key targets so as to maximize the shock effect. Altogether, 812 combat sorties were flown in the first 24 hours. That made the opening round of Desert Storm the largest single air offensive to have been conducted anywhere in the world since the end of World War II.

The effect of allied air control operations during the first few days of the Gulf war was quintessentially strategic, for they deprived Iraq of any defenses or situation awareness. They also meant that no ground campaign needed to be launched until coalition air attacks had beaten down enemy ground forces to the desired level at arm's length. Indeed, so confident was CENTCOM in its control of the air over Iraq that well before the planned date of the ground push, it moved some in-flight refueling missions northward into enemy airspace to support the heavy flow of ground-attack aircraft that were being employed to prepare the battlefield.

Perhaps the clearest indication of what the gaining of air dominance meant for the coalition lay in the relative rate of allied combat aircraft losses over the course of the war. Allied sortie rates remained roughly constant throughout the six weeks of fighting. Yet the coalition incurred nearly *half* its aircraft losses (17) during the first week of Desert Storm, before Iraq's defenses had been fully neutralized and when low-level operations were required in order for some coalition aircraft to penetrate them. Another eight aircraft were downed during the final week of the war, when coalition aircrews resumed low-altitude operations to support the ground campaign. These losses were due mainly to fire by optically tracked AAA and infrared SAMs, whose existence and locations could not be detected from the air.

In all, CENTCOM's air campaign plan in its final form, as Williamson Murray observed, "represented an intellectual triumph over much of the cultural baggage that had distorted the air war against North Vietnam."[33] However, CENTCOM's prompt and decisive attainment of unchallenged air control raised the more basic question of how allied air power would acquit itself in seeing to the endgame a war that ultimately would be decided on the ground. In that respect, what ensued over the next month by way of effective air power employment was unprecedented in the evolution of joint warfare.

AIR POWER FIGHTS A LAND WAR

The suppression of Iraqi air defenses and the early neutralization of the IQAF were the most acclaimed aspects of the coalition's air power performance in Desert Storm. Yet those achievements, impressive though they were in and of themselves, were not what accounted for the central role played by air power in determining the war's ultimate outcome. On the contrary, they only secured a necessary buy-in condition for enabling U.S. air power to demonstrate its *real* leverage of greatest note, namely, the ability to engage an enemy army wholesale, and with virtual impunity, by means of precision attacks. Appreciation of this point is crucial to a correct understanding of what air power showed itself, for the first time in Desert Storm, capable of doing if properly used.

[33] Murray, *Air War in the Persian Gulf*, p. 43.

The leaders at CENTCOM intended from the outset to destroy as much of Iraq's warfighting capacity as possible before any ground offensive took place. General Schwarzkopf's declared goal was to reduce the effective potential of Iraqi ground forces in the KTO by 50 percent before the start of the ground invasion. That goal was stipulated as early as August 14, when the CINC's analysis group pointed out that for a single-corps offensive to succeed, such a level of enemy attrition would be essential. Initial planning focused on enemy troops and major items of equipment, with the target set later narrowed to tanks, armored personnel carriers, and artillery. Ultimately, Schwarzkopf's declared goal became reducing the "effectiveness" of Iraqi troops by 50 percent.

It remained unclear, however, how effective allied air power would be in this new tasking until the air campaign plan was actually executed. As yet a further planning complication, moreover, it was never self-evident exactly how one might determine the attainment of that goal. In grappling with what Murray called the "most opaque and controversial portion of the air campaign," CENTCOM's planners engaged in often intense argument over measures of effectiveness.[34] In the end, that determination became a judgment call by the CINC, although the quantitative measure ultimately settled on was the destruction of armor and artillery throughout the theater. In all events, as GWAPS later noted, the strategy arrived at by CENTCOM "called on air power to destroy ground forces to a degree not heretofore planned for any air force."[35]

Three factors coalesced to enable allied air power to draw down Iraqi forces to a point where once the ground offensive began, it could advance in the certain knowledge that it would be engaging a badly degraded opponent. The first was the freedom made possible by the SEAD campaign for allied aircraft to operate more or less at will in the medium-altitude environment, unmolested by Iraqi radar-guided SAMs or fighters. The second was the ability made possible by the eleventh-hour introduction of the E-8 joint surveillance target attack radar system, or JSTARS, to permit the JFACC to see and identify fixed and moving objects on the battlefield clearly enough, and on a large-enough scale, to make informed force committal decisions and execute lethal attacks against ground force targets by day or night. The third was the discovery during the air campaign's battlefield-preparation phase of the ability of aircraft equipped with infrared sensors and an LGB delivery capability to find and destroy dug-in enemy tanks one by one in large numbers. These factors, in combination, gave U.S. air power an edge in joint warfare against enemy ground forces that it had never before possessed on such a pronounced scale.

[34] Ibid., p. 229.
[35] Keaney and Cohen, *Revolution*, p. 40.

The Move to Medium-Altitude Operations

During the first three days of the air campaign, some coalition aircrews elected to employ NATO-type low-level attack tactics because Iraq's dense and closely internetted air defenses had yet to be neutralized. The intensity and volume of Iraqi barrage AAA fire, however, soon showed those tactics to be fraught with danger. That conclusion was driven home with a vengeance on Day Three when CENTCOM sought to demonstrate the ability of a massed "gorilla" of F-16s to operate over the capital city in daylight with impunity. This largest air attack package of the entire war, called Package Q, consisted of 72 F-16s supported by eight F-15s, eight F-4G Wild Weasels, and two EF-111 jammers, along with an EC-130 to jam enemy communications and an RC-135 to monitor electronic signals. Because of last-minute changes in the attack plan and the large size of the attack package, the operation quickly devolved into chaos. In the process, two F-16s were downed by radar-guided SAMs and both pilots were captured. Significantly, they both went down only after the F-4G Wild Weasels radioed that they were departing the target area because of low fuel.[36]

The early rush to launch Package Q in broad daylight into the heart of downtown Baghdad suggested initial overconfidence not only in the JFACC planning cell in Riyadh but also at the unit level. Accordingly, in response to the loss of the two F-16s, a halt was called to operations over Baghdad by all aircraft other than F-117s and cruise missiles. In addition, medium-altitude floors were extended to areas other than Baghdad, depending on circumstances and mission needs. The latter move was based on a confident belief that Iraq's radar-guided SAMs had been neutralized to a point where allied aircraft could safely operate above 10,000 ft. Initially, a medium-altitude floor of 15,000 ft was established. Only the F-15E, the F-111F, the LANTIRN (low-altitude navigation and targeting infrared for night)–equipped F-16C, and the RAF Tornado GR1, all equipped with automatic terrain-following radar, were cleared to operate at lower altitudes as mission needs dictated. For their part, Tornado aircrews continued to operate at low level as a matter of course because, as noted earlier, their JP233 runway-denial weapon required a release altitude of 200 ft.[37] In addition, because the large size of Package Q had made it unwieldy to the point of being unmanageable, Horner decreed that no force packages tasked anywhere against Iraq would consist of more than 25 aircraft. Because of its stealthiness, the F-117 was the only aircraft cleared to operate inside the Baghdad threat envelope after the third day of the air campaign. It was backstopped during

[36] Price Bingham, "Joint Mobile Target Engagement," unpublished draft, January 28, 1997, p. 4.
[37] Later, the absolute minimum altitude (or "hard deck," in pilot parlance) was lowered to 8,000 ft and finally to as low as necessary for mission needs once the ground war commenced.

daylight hours by intermittent attacks by Navy Tomahawk land-attack missiles (TLAM) to keep nonstop pressure on Saddam Hussein.

The decision to shift to medium-altitude operations throughout the theater was not a forced move but rather an option of choice that had been planned from the outset and made possible by the successful SEAD campaign to neutralize Iraq's radar-guided SAMs. As explained in Chapter 3, low-level tactics have always been considered something of a necessary evil in response to unavoidable surface-to-air threats. Although often mandatory in the case of well-defended targets and low-hanging weather, they have been rightly regarded as undesirable because of the difficulties they create for navigation and target acquisition and the palpable risk of inadvertently flying into the ground during highly task-loaded mission segments. In the Gulf war, they were not required, since the prompt neutralization of Iraq's radar-directed SAMs by intimidation made medium-altitude fighter employment a safe practice in a way that it never was in the skies over North Vietnam until late in Operation Linebacker II. From a survivability standpoint, the tactic paid off handsomely. During the Vietnam war, approximately 85 percent of all U.S. aircraft lost were downed by AAA fire. In contrast, AAA was ineffective in Desert Storm as a result of the maturation of medium-altitude tactics. To be sure, 71 percent of all coalition fixed-wing aircraft lost or damaged in the Gulf war were hit by AAA or short-range infrared SAMs.[38] However, the total number lost in Vietnam was in the thousands because U.S. aircraft were forced by the SAM threat to operate in the heart of the AAA envelope, whereas in Desert Storm, the number did not exceed two dozen because they were able to remain safely above it until the ground campaign began.

The freedom to operate from a medium-altitude sanctuary offered the coalition's air planners numerous tactical advantages. In addition to keeping friendly aircraft above the lethal envelope of enemy infrared SAMs and optically tracked AAA, it eliminated the danger of pilots inadvertently flying into the ground and also provided them a more extended view of the battlefield, which made for easier target acquisition and allowed more time to execute an attack. Finally, because of the increased standoff range it allowed, it often enabled pilots to attack ground targets that remained oblivious of impending disaster until the actual moment of weapon impact.

One significant consequence, which is addressed later in this chapter, was the considerable penalty levied on the accuracy of unguided bomb delivery from medium altitudes by "smart" airplanes like the F-16, which was caused by the often quadrupled weapon-release distances from the target. This problem was noted and duly acted on after the war by substantially in-

[38] Keaney and Cohen, *Revolution*, p. 52.

creasing the number of Air Force and Navy fighters capable of delivering LGBs. The point that matters most here about the move to medium-altitude operations, however, is that it gave coalition aircrews a round-the-clock perch from which to conduct a deadly campaign with impunity against helpless enemy ground forces.

Precision Engagement and the Battle That Didn't Happen

Once it had become clear to the Iraqi leadership that the allied air campaign might be open-ended and that Iraq's Scud attacks against Israel were not having their intended effect, Saddam Hussein initiated a desperate attempt at an asymmetric response, apparently hoping to draw allied forces into a slugfest on the ground that would begin sending body bags home and turn American opinion against the war. On January 29, he launched a ground attack from southeastern Kuwait toward Saudi Arabia aimed at the abandoned and unprotected Saudi coastal town of Al Khafji. Iraqi troops occupied the town for a day, in the process unknowingly trapping two U.S. Marine reconnaissance teams, but coalition ground forces quickly evicted them.[39] Soon afterward, allied sensors detected a second wave of Iraqi columns forming up in Kuwait to reinforce those that had initially attacked Al Khafji. Apparently Iraq's intent was to engage that part of the Arab joint-force command that was deployed along the northern Saudi coast and force an American entry into a ground war, trying at a minimum for a Tet-like gambit that would sufficiently bloody the nose of the United States to have a disproportionate political effect on the American home front.

Initially, the Tactical Air Control Center (TACC) did not react to these indicators of Iraqi forces on the move because its airborne sensors had been focused on areas to the west in support of the counter-Scud operation and because CENTCOM's leaders, despite the initial foray into Al Khafji, were not expecting Iraqi forces in Kuwait to launch a major move against Saudi Arabia. Once it became clear, however, that a sizable Iraqi ground advance was forming on the night of January 30, the senior officer in the TACC, Major General John Corder, swung JSTARS to the east and began diverting coalition fighters to engage moving ground targets in Kuwait.[40] Upon being apprised of the Iraqi troop activity, Horner proceeded to the TACC and instantly saw an opportunity shaping up to engage the Iraqi column before it made contact with allied ground forces. Affirming the decision to divert coalition air

---

[39] This occasioned one of the early misfortunes of the war when 11 Marines were killed in two light-armored vehicles that were taken out by inadvertent friendly fire, one from a Maverick missile fired by an A-10 and the other to surface fire, after the Marines had called in air strikes on the Iraqi probes.

[40] Communication to the author by General Charles A. Horner, USAF (Ret.), May 15, 1997.

power from its original tasking, he committed more than 140 aircraft against the advancing column, which consisted of the Iraqi 3rd Armored and 5th Mechanized Divisions.[41]

The ensuing air attacks continued throughout the night and well into the following day before the battle was over. As a result of the timely diversion of coalition fighters, the Iraqi forces never had a chance to mass and attack. The lead tank was quickly disabled, and the rest were substantially drawn down in defilade. Once the dust settled, coalition air power had completely debilitated the advancing Iraqi column, forcing the survivors to beat a ragged retreat. In all, 357 tanks, 147 armored personnel carriers, and 89 mobile artillery pieces, not counting additional items of equipment in Republican Guard units farther north, were reportedly destroyed in the air attacks. A captured Iraqi officer who had fought in the Iran-Iraq war later volunteered that his brigade had endured more punishment from allied air power in 15 minutes at Al Khafji than it had experienced in eight years of fighting against Iran.

The real hero of this air power success story was the E-8 JSTARS, which was still in the early stages of development at the time the war began. Two of these aircraft, in effect AWACS analogs for ground surveillance, had been brought into the theater only days before the start of the air war, in part on a recommendation by the Army's VII Corps commander, Lieutenant General Fred Franks. The previous fall in Germany, Franks had witnessed a demonstration of the system in an exercise called Operation Deep Strike, which was intended to simulate a Soviet ground attack against NATO. During the exercise, Franks called on JSTARS to identify and target for counterattack a simulated Soviet armored column that was being acted out by a Canadian tank convoy. He was greatly impressed by its capabilities, achieving some 51 tank "kills" as a direct result, and he later raved about the capability to Schwarzkopf. Informed by that experience, Franks played an important role in getting JSTARS pressed into timely service in Desert Storm.[42]

As it turned out, JSTARS proved indispensable in providing the JFACC with real-time intelligence and targeting information on advancing and retreating Iraqi ground forces. Before the events at Al Khafji, CENTCOM's leaders had valued the E-8 more for its surveillance capabilities than as a potential platform for controlling precision air strikes, since it was not designed to provide command and control. Yet it performed well in that role, with one aircraft airborne and operating every night. The E-8 was capable of viewing

[41] Keaney and Cohen, *Revolution*, p. 95.
[42] Peter Grier, "Joint STARS Does Its Stuff," *Air Force Magazine*, June 1991, p. 40. An earlier request by CENTCOM in August 1990 that a JSTARS aircraft be sent to the theater was turned down by the Air Force because the aircraft was still in the developmental testing stage. See Grant M. Hales, "The Tactical Air Command and Operation Desert Storm: A Case Study of Tactical Aircraft Employment," *Air Power History*, Winter 1991, p. 46.

the entire KTO in a single orbit, and combat aircraft controlled by it typically experienced a 90-percent success rate in finding and engaging assigned targets on the first pass. The efficiency of operations it permitted was such that attacking aircraft consistently ran out of munitions before they ran out of fuel. In one instance, 80 percent of an advancing Iraqi unit was disabled before it could move into position to attack allied ground forces.[43]

One weakness of note was that the E-8 was unable to distinguish between tracked and wheeled vehicles, a shortcoming slated to be fixed once the aircraft attains full operational status. Also, in some cases the radar imagery appeared to defy any interpretation that made sense. One line of seeming "enemy activity" north of Al Khafji turned out, on further investigation, to have been simply concertina wire swaying in the wind.[44] Nevertheless, the ability of the aircraft to detect and fix vehicular traffic under way with its moving target indicator (MTI), while scanning larger areas with its synthetic aperture radar (SAR), produced a unique synergy. As one JSTARS crewmember graphically described the operational implications, "We would see very, very large numbers in convoys coming down a road [with MTI]. It was mind-boggling. In fact, sometimes there were so many you couldn't even count them all. . . . Then all of a sudden you don't see any more traffic on MTI. What does that tell you? It tells you they've left the road or stopped. Then you would use your SAR and shazam! All of a sudden, we've got the exact number of vehicles, where they would be parked and we would relay that information to fighters and the Army and they were able to address the situation quickly."[45] In this manner, JSTARS redefined the meaning of using real-time battlespace awareness to make the most of a casebook target-rich environment.

The effect of JSTARS in cueing F-15Es and other allied aircraft against enemy vehicles with such deadly accuracy must have been read by the Iraqi high command as a grim omen, since the abortive attack on Al Khafji represented its first and last attempt at offensive ground operations. Owing to JSTARS and effective attacks by coalition aircraft, Iraqi ground attrition increased fourfold between January 29 and February 3 over the previous drawdown rate, according to CENTCOM reporting.[46] From then on, Iraq's forces hunkered down to absorb the coalition's punishment "like a tethered goat," in General Horner's colorful phrase. For his part, General McPeak neatly encapsulated the overarching significance of the role played by JSTARS and precision air attacks in preventing a larger confrontation that

[43] David A. Fulghum, "Desert Storm Success Renews USAF Interest in Specialty Weapons," *Aviation Week and Space Technology*, May 13, 1991, p. 85.

[44] John Boatman and Barbara Starr, "Eyes of the Storm," *Jane's Defense Weekly*, May 4, 1991, p. 735.

[45] Tony Cappacio, "Air Force's Eyes in the Sky Alerted Marines at Khafji, Targeted Convoys," *Defense Week*, March 18, 1991, p. 7.

[46] Keaney and Cohen, *Revolution*, p. 95.

could have had serious consequences for coalition ground forces when he declared, in his report to the Commission on Roles and Missions in 1994, that "history may judge that the most significant battle of Desert Storm was, in fact, the one that did not happen at Al Khafji."[47]

"Tank Plinking" and Its Impact

Not long after the showdown at Al Khafji, Pave Tack–equipped F-111Fs were swung to attack enemy armor in the KTO, using 500-lb GBU-12 LGBS, starting on the night of February 5. This attack tactic was neither pre-planned nor even remotely a part of the F-111's original concept of operations. The idea for it first crystallized in December 1990, before the onset of Desert Storm, in an in-theater workup exercise called Operation Night Camel. Its training missions pitted U.S. Air Force fighters equipped with infrared navigation and targeting pods in simulated attacks against armored forces of the U.S. Army's VII Corps. Their goal was to determine whether infrared-equipped aircraft could conduct night interdiction against enemy supply lines and deliver cluster munitions against enemy armor concentrations. A by-product of these Night Camel missions was the discovery that armored vehicles stood out distinctly on infrared displays between sunset and midnight because their rate of heat dissipation was slower than that of the surrounding desert sand. It also was determined that such aircraft could conduct successful night attacks against point targets from a medium altitude.

Although further explored during Desert Shield, the tactic was never resorted to in combat until it became clear that because of problems of reliable battle-damage assessment (BDA), allied intelligence could not confirm the destruction of enemy ground forces at a fast-enough rate to meet General Schwarzkopf's timetable for launching the ground offensive. A wartime operational evaluation on the night of February 5 proved so successful that 44 more sorties were scheduled the following night. From that point onward, 73 percent of all assigned F-111F sorties in the ATO were devoted to enemy ground forces, with aircrews flying 664 sorties altogether against Iraqi tanks over a 23-day period. Because the tactic was so reminiscent of taking pot-shots at tin cans with air rifles, F-111 aircrews promptly dubbed it "tank plinking."[48]

This entailed a fundamentally new mission for F-111F and F-15E aircrews that had never before appeared in any ground-attack tactics manual. As the

---

[47] General Merrill A. McPeak, USAF, *Presentation to the Commission on Roles and Missions of the Armed Forces*, Washington, D.C., Headquarters United States Air Force, September 14, 1994, p. 101.

[48] Not surprisingly, this flip term discomfited some U.S. Army tankers, and General Schwarzkopf directed Horner to instruct his aircrews to use a less irreverent expression, such as "tank busting." That stricture guaranteed that the term "tank plinking" would stick forever.

pilot who flew the number-two F-111F during the initial test mission on the night of February 5 remarked afterward, "If I had stood up at Staff College a year ago and proposed using the F-111F for this type of attack, I would probably have been laughed out of the room."[49] As one of two snapshot indicators of its effectiveness, F-111Fs on the night of February 6–7 successfully dropped more than 140 LGBs on Republican Guard armor and artillery. The following week, on the night of February 13–14, 46 F-111Fs dropped 184 GBU-12 LGBs and destroyed 132 armored fighting vehicles, for an overall kill rate of 72 percent. Throughout the course of the war, F-111Fs destroyed some 920 Iraqi armored fighting vehicles, out of an estimated total of 6,100.[50] As a measure of the tactic's effectiveness, CENTCOM credited all coalition aircraft engaged in "tank plinking" with a combined total of 1,300 confirmed kills by February 14.[51]

The impact of this new attack tactic on classic survival assumptions for ground forces was profound. Hitherto, the Iraqis had thought they could endure the air campaign by digging in during the day and massing only at night. However, as two F-111 crewmembers summed it up in a nutshell, what the JSTARS–precision engagement tactic and "tank plinking" combination showed was that "if armies dig in, they die. If they come out of their holes, they die sooner."[52] The effect on enemy behavior was to heighten the individual soldier's sense of futility. Many vehicles were simply abandoned by their operators once it became apparent that they could turn into death traps at any moment without warning. Viewed at the individual shooter-to-target level, tank plinking may have seemed only "tactical" to the casual observer. Yet as a concept of operations for combating an enemy army, it was decidedly strategic in both character and consequence. The peak kill rate it enabled was well above 500 Iraqi armored fighting vehicles per day, and it remained above that rate for several days in a row. In previous wars, such targets would have been relatively unthreatened by air attack.[53] The novel effect on enemy ground forces that tank plinking produced was what Price Bingham aptly described as "paralysis through intimidation."[54]

[49] Alfred Price, "Deadly Darkness," *Flight International*, July 10–16, 1991, p. 35.
[50] Roy Braybrook, "On Target! A Review of Precision Air Attacks in the Gulf War," *Air International*, October 1991, p. 179.
[51] Tony Capaccio, "Air Force Used Vintage Aardvarks to 'Plink' Tanks," *Defense Week*, March 4, 1991, p. 1.
[52] Majors Michael J. Bodner and William W. Bruner III, "Tank Plinking," *Air Force Magazine*, October 1993, p. 31.
[53] Major General Jasper A. Welch, Jr., USAF (Ret.), "Technology and Military Strategy: Looking Forward to the Uncertainty of the 1990s," paper prepared for a discussion series on air power and the new security environment, Washington Strategy Seminar, RAND, Washington, D.C., November 14, 1991, p. 4.
[54] Price Bingham, *The Battle of Al Khafji andd the Future of Surveillance Precision Strike*, Arlington, Va., Aerospace Educational Foundation, 1997, p. 20.

Allied Air Power in the Endgame

By mid-February, the air campaign had shifted from what Horner called the "gee-whiz" phase to the "hard work" portion.[55] By that time, the coalition's air assets had begun to focus in earnest on battlefield preparation, taking down the Republican Guard and interdicting lines of communication to the KTO in addition to reattacking selected infrastructure targets and continuing to hunt down mobile Scuds. As what one reporter called Desert Storm's "grim symphony of destruction" advanced ever closer to crescendo level, the chairman of the JCS, General Powell, declared that "air power has been the decisive arm so far, and I expect it will be the decisive arm through the end of the campaign, even if ground forces and amphibious forces are added to the equation." Powell added, in testimony before the Senate Armed Services Committee, "If anything, I expect air power to be even more decisive in the days and weeks ahead."[56]

After more than a month of nonstop aerial preparation, the allied ground assault finally pushed off at 0400 on February 24. Immediately before the commencement of the ground push, Horner declared at his morning staff meeting: "There are people's lives depending on our ability to help them, if help is required. . . . The pressure today is for us to provide support for the maneuvering forces on the ground. So be alert and aggressive. . . . I think the ground forces will do just exactly what they want to do, and they'll execute superbly. So make sure that the air is there where they need it, when they need it—that's your job. No excuses."[57] More than 3,000 allied air support sorties flew that day, most of them directly over the battlefield.

As the ground offensive neared, Horner ordered the implementation of what he called a "push CAS [close air support]" arrangement, based on an idea that he had briefed to Schwarzkopf in April 1990 before the Gulf crisis had erupted. That idea involved maintaining an even flow of interdiction sorties into the KTO around the clock, with a proviso that any of those sorties could be diverted by the TACC as necessary to service CAS requests made by the corps commanders. The underlying logic of this approach was to assure the corps commanders that they had on-call CAS sorties should they ever be needed, yet in a way that did not tie up coalition aircraft in a wasteful commitment to dedicated CAS to the exclusion of anything else.[58] As it turned out, CAS was rarely required in Desert Storm because allied air

[55] David A. Fulghum, "Desert Storm Highlights Need for Rapid Tactical Intelligence," *Aviation Week and Space Technology*, February 11, 1991, p. 19.

[56] Guy Gugliotta, "Air Assault on Entrenched Iraqis Seen as Pivotal Phase of Gulf War," *Washington Post*, February 6, 1991.

[57] U.S. CENTAF Office of History, "Daily Comments of Lieutenant General Horner," February 24, 1991, quoted in Murray, *Air War in the Persian Gulf*, p. 276.

[58] Communication to the author by General Charles A. Horner, USAF (Ret.), May 15, 1997.

power had already significantly reduced the enemy's fighting strength and commitment to battle. Although some nominally designated "CAS" missions were flown by coalition aircraft, those were directed mostly against reserve divisions and retreating Iraqi columns.

Even Marine aviation, whose main combat function is to support embattled Marines on the ground, had little occasion or opportunity to fulfill that function. Although some 70 percent of all Marine combat sorties flown in Desert Storm were logged as CAS missions, subsequent analysis indicated that only 14 percent of those were flown inside the Fire Support Coordination Line (FSCL), and that an even smaller number were flown against targets in anything like close proximity to friendly forces.[59] As GWAPS later reported, "Few situations presented themselves of 'troops in contact' to test how well close air support by U.S. fixed-wing aircraft or attack helicopters could be synchronized with ground fire-support systems."[60] This low incidence of CAS tasking in Desert Storm was a natural result of light enemy resistance, due to the earlier drawdown attacks by allied air power well before allied ground forces had begun their offensive. Some Marine and Army ground units faced sporadic tough resistance. As a rule, however, Iraqi ground opposition was disorganized and weak enough that organic allied ground force weapons were sufficient to handle it.

In retrospect, allied air attacks against Iraqi ground forces did not produce any sudden change in Iraq's capabilities. Rather, they undermined its fighting capacity through a gradual process of degradation that finally reached a breaking point. On the eve of the ground push, CENTCOM estimated that 39 percent of Iraq's tanks, 32 percent of its armored personnel carriers, and 47 percent of its artillery (the Army's biggest concern) had been destroyed or neutralized by air attacks, although this attrition was not evenly distributed across the enemy's force and some enemy units remained combat-capable. By the war's end, the Iraqi army had sustained around 76 percent attrition in tanks, 55 percent in armored personnel carriers, and 90 percent in artillery.[61]

The main cause of the Iraqi army's breakdown, however, was not this attrition of equipment per se so much as the individual soldier's loss of will and resolve to fight. Enemy prisoner of war (EPW) interrogations conducted after the cease-fire indicated a widespread sense of futility throughout the

---

[59] Cited in McPeak, *Presentation to the Commission on Roles and Missions of the Armed Forces*, p. 117.

[60] Keaney and Cohen, *Revolution*, p. 96.

[61] CIA and the Defense Intelligence Agency held to much lower estimates, but Schwarzkopf in the end went with a more subjective assessment of unit capability, even refusing to allow briefings that stressed specific percentages of attrition. By that approach, on the eve of G-day (the starting day of the allied ground attack), CENTCOM assessed rear-area division effectiveness at 75 percent but that of front-line divisions at below 50 percent. Ibid., pp. 91–92. All numbers are from the GWAPS summary report unless otherwise indicated.

ranks after the many long weeks of nonstop bombing. The EPWs reported an initial belief that the air campaign would last only several days. Such an expectation was consistent with the classic Soviet combined-arms doctrine in which Iraqi officers had been schooled. Once it had become apparent, however, that the air war could go on indefinitely, they lost any remaining sense of hope.[62] The EPW interviews further suggested that coalition air attacks had destroyed more than half of the Iraqi trucks in the KTO. Other vehicles were put out of commission because of a lack of spare parts, since air attacks also completely severed the Iraqi resupply capability within the KTO. As a result, most units were low on food and water, with no relief in sight.

The rate of enemy troop desertion caused by allied air attacks was assessed after the war at 25 to 30 percent. That figure was remarkably high, considering that Iraqi ground commanders had been given express orders to execute any suspected deserters on the spot. It suggested that those who fled preferred to take their chances with that danger than to risk what they perceived to be the near certainty of eventual death from the skies. Early deserters, on initial interrogation, correctly predicted that most remaining units would surrender at the first opportunity. Sometimes the mere arrival of an allied combat aircraft overhead prompted Iraqi troops to wave the white flag. As GWAPS concluded after a careful investigation, "Air power essentially paralyzed or demoralized the Iraqi heavy divisions on which the Iraqi strategy depended. . . . Those left with a will to fight were able to do little more than face the attack and return fire, with no hope of maneuvering or being reinforced or even achieving tactical success."[63]

Saddam Hussein only began withdrawing his troops from Kuwait after the onset of the allied ground push punctuated his fear that he might lose his entire army. That fact will forever stand as reason enough why a coalition ground offensive was indicated, even if only as a hedge against uncertainty. That said, however, the Iraqi army had begun to cave in much earlier, once its leaders had seen that the air war would give them no respite.[64] Although it is only conjectural at this point, Air Vice Marshal Mason maintained that "there is sufficient circumstantial evidence to suggest that Iraqi ground forces were, in fact, preparing to withdraw from Kuwait before the coalition ground offensive began," as indicated, among other things, by their alleged destruction of the Kuwait City desalination plant on an order

---

[62] Strongly supportive documentation for this assertion may be found in the extensive EPW interview data presented in Stephen T. Hosmer, *Psychological Effects of U.S. Air Operations in Four Wars, 1941–1991: Lessons for U.S. Commanders*, Santa Monica, Cal., RAND, MR-578-AF, 1996.

[63] Keaney and Cohen, *Revolution*, pp. 101–102.

[64] Several captured Iraqi officers opined afterwards that the allied ground operation had been superfluous, because if the air attacks had continued for two to three weeks more, Iraqi troop units would have been forced to withdraw from Kuwait as a result of their supplies having been cut off. Murray, *Air War in the Persian Gulf*, p. 300.

that had to have been given at least a day before the allied ground invasion began. In light of that, Mason proposed, "The jury should remain out [on whether allied air power alone compelled the Iraqi decision to withdraw] until Iraqi evidence is comprehensively and unequivocally made available."[65]

In all events, once the allied rout of the Iraqi army was well under way, the JFACC placed emphasis on chasing down and destroying retreating enemy ground elements, with allied fixed-wing aircraft receiving targeting cues either from JSTARS or from U.S. Air Force F-16 or Marine F/A-18D fast forward air controllers (FACs). A 2-mile stretch of escaping vehicles was halted at the Mutla Ridge west of Kuwait City, resulting in the so-called Highway of Death. In fact, however, that infamous scene mainly entailed a traffic jam of abandoned and destroyed vehicles, considering that reporters afterward counted only 200 to 300 dead Iraqis among them. Nevertheless, the false image of indiscriminate carnage it produced had a decisive effect on the coalition's leadership in Washington, for President Bush declared a cease-fire after only 100 hours of ground operations.

Viewing the course and outcome of Operation Desert Storm in hindsight, the persistent argument over whether air or ground power deserves more credit for the allied win is a bit like arguing over which blade in a pair of scissors is more responsible for cutting the paper. Clearly it took both assets to produce the final victory. However, owing in considerable part to air power's preparation of the battlefield, only 148 U.S. military personnel were killed and 458 wounded during the actual course of fighting.[66] After the war was over, General McPeak touched the heart of what is new about American air power today relative to other force elements, as attested by that performance, when he suggested that its true value ultimately lay in its potential to determine the fate of armies. Few U.S. ground commanders in the heat and confusion of Desert Storm's endgame were able to appreciate the strategic importance of "tank plinking" because their conception of warfare led them to believe that enemy artillery posed a greater threat and that their own tanks could take care of enemy armor. Yet as a telling testament to what worked best, the United States shipped nearly 220,000 rounds of tank ammunition into the theater, of which less than 2 percent was actually fired.[67]

On that account, the suggestion by retired Army Lieutenant General William Odom that U.S. Army tanks and attack helicopters, rather than coalition fixed-wing aircraft, accounted for a full "70 to 80 percent" of Iraqi

[65] Air Vice Marshal Tony Mason, RAF (Ret.), *Air Power: A Centennial Appraisal*, London, Brassey's, 1994, pp. 139–140.
[66] Donald Kagan, "Colin Powell's War," *Commentary*, June 1995, p. 45.
[67] Rick Atkinson, *Crusade: The Untold Story of the Perian Gulf War*, Boston, Houghton Mifflin, 1993, p. 342.

tanks destroyed is simply unsupported by the most authoritative U.S. government BDA data.[68] Indeed, a careful review of the evidence marshalled by the U.S. Air Force's GWAPS and by CIA imagery analysts after the war indicates that Odom exaggerated U.S. Army performance in this respect by at least a factor of two. In an informed counter to Odom's claim by the leader of the GWAPS task force on operations and effects, allied fixed-wing aircraft accounted for at least 61 percent of all destroyed Iraqi tanks by the war's end, most of which had been taken out before the ground advance began.[69] That left allied ground forces with credit for a maximum of 38 percent of known Iraqi armored vehicles destroyed, and even those only after allied air power, to all intents and purposes, had eliminated the Iraqi army from the fight.

PROBLEMS IN AIR TASKING AND AIR-GROUND COORDINATION

As noted earlier, Desert Storm finally saw a vindication of the "single-manager" concept for the command and control of U.S. air power in joint warfare. The success of the JFACC approach came close to capturing the essence of General Billy Mitchell's long-unrequited argument that the important thing was not "strategic bombing," in David MacIsaac's words, "but rather the centralized coordination of all air assets under the control of an autonomous air force command, freed of its dependency on the army. If that goal could be achieved, he [Mitchell] felt, everything else would fall into its proper place."[70] Although the JFACC idea first entered the lexicon of joint planning and operations during the mid-1980s, it was not realized in practice until the onset of Desert Shield. By then, for the first time in U.S. experience, there was now one commander for air operations, in contrast to the kaleidoscopic arrangement that had hampered the most effective use of air power in Vietnam, where there were as many as six often-competing controlling authorities.

All of the U.S. services accepted, at least in principle, the need for a single jurisdiction over allied air power in Desert Storm. Yet three of them (the Army, Navy, and Marine Corps) frequently chafed at the extent of authority given to the JFACC to select targets and to determine the details of flight operations. In particular, the JFACC arrangement aggravated the suspicions

---

[68] William E. Odom, "Transforming the Military," *Foreign Affairs*, July/August 1997, p. 62.

[69] Barry D. Watts, letter to the editor, *Foreign Affairs*, November/December 1997, p. 180.

[70] David MacIsaac, "Voices from the Central Blue: The Air Power Theorists," in Peter Paret, ed., *Makers of Modern Strategy from Machiavelli to the Nuclear Age*, Princeton, Princeton University Press, 1986, p. 631.

of the Army's corps commanders, who feared that their interests would not get due attention from airmen assumed to be bent on fighting their own private war.

The Ownership and Control Issue

Indeed, of all the coalition land force principals in Desert Storm, the corps commanders were the most outspoken critics of the JFACC arrangement by far. Gordon and Trainor reported that as Desert Storm unfolded, "The confrontation between the Army field commanders and the Air Force was not so much about the performance of air power as the Army's inability to control it."[71] The corps commanders suspected from the start that the JFACC's air planners were conducting their own war out of a conviction that air power alone would produce a coalition victory.

At first glance, it is not hard to see why. After all, the JFACC gave corps commanders little direct accommodation during the first two weeks of the war because the CINC's primary concern at that stage was to neutralize Iraq's air defenses and establish uncontested control of the air. Of 1,185 targets nominated by the Army during that period, only 202 (17 percent) made it into the ATO and only 137 (12 percent) were actually hit.[72] Indeed, of 3,067 targets nominated by the Army for the ATO throughout the entire war, only a little more than a third were actually attacked by coalition aircraft.[73] Of course, many of the scheduled ATO sorties were working the Army's problem indirectly by drawing down enemy ground forces in accordance with General Schwarzkopf's predetermined drawdown schedule. Second-echelon Republican Guard forces got more priority from Washington and Schwarzkopf than from the corps commanders because the former had determined those forces to be "strategic" targets. Since they lay outside of the corps commanders' doctrinal area of responsibility, however, they were "out of sight, out of mind" as far as the latter were concerned. As Gordon and Trainor observed, the corps commander was not mindful of the entire theater. Instead, he looked at the battlefield like a "giant bowling alley," concerned only with those enemy forces directly in front of his deployed troops and, beyond that, with those that were a day or two away.[74]

Despite the Army's increasingly vocal complaining over this issue, however, Horner scarcely needed to be convinced to divert his efforts from so-called strategic targets to attacks on Iraq's ground forces. As early as Janu-

---

[71] Gordon and Trainor, *The Generals' War*, p. 331.
[72] Ibid., pp. 319–320.
[73] Atkinson, *Crusade*, pp. 222–223.
[74] Gordon and Trainor, *The Generals' War*, p. 311.

ary 18, he told his staff that he was ready to proceed with dealing with the Iraqi army: "I would suspect that in the next few days we will finish up valid targets in Iraq and begin to really shift our emphasis to the military forces in Kuwait."[75] By January 29, Horner was committed to ongoing operations against the Republican Guard, stating, "It is not going to be spectacular. It's going to be a lot of hard work. It should not be inordinately hazardous. We are not going to get a lot of feedback until suddenly they're defeated. . . . When we have the Republican Guard in the bag, then we'll turn our attention to the ground forces in Kuwait."[76]

Horner's later "push CAS" arrangement once the allied ground offensive was ready to start further demonstrated that U.S. air power did not let CENTCOM's ground commanders down. On the contrary, there was more air power on call and ready during the 100-hour land offensive than any allied ground commander could possibly have needed or used. Admittedly, as final preparations were being made for Schwarzkopf's left hook into the KTO, Colonel Warden back in the Pentagon reportedly sought to spark a rear-guard effort to get the strategic air campaign restarted, arguing that it should be intensified so as to preclude the need for a ground offensive altogether. However, Horner would not hear of it in his determination to abide nothing beyond the most minimal distraction from his support to the impending ground campaign. As Murray observed, "Any serious diversion of this tasking was unthinkable and would have intensified an already difficult situation between Horner and ARCENT's subordinate commanders."[77]

Less generally understood and appreciated in this sometimes unseemly interservice tug-of-war over the ownership and control of ATO sorties was the fact that Schwarzkopf had approved all of the JFACC's target choices beforehand. As General McPeak was quick to note after the shooting stopped, Schwarzkopf as the CINC set the cadence of coalition operations, and all pieces of the war plan "were his concept, including the air piece." Under the joint-force command arrangement by which Operation Desert Storm was conducted, the main responsibility of the JFACC was to ensure an integrated and harmonious employment of all fielded air assets and capabilities. As early as November, Schwarzkopf was clear about his blessing of the JFACC concept and who had final authority for making air tasking decisions. He instructed his division commanders, "There's only going to be one guy in charge of the air: Horner. If you want to fight the interservice battles, do it

---

[75] U.S. CENTAF Office of History, "Daily Comments of Lieutenant General Horner," January 18, 1991, quoted in Murray, *Air War in the Persian Gulf*, p. 184.

[76] U.S. CENTAF Office of History, "Daily Comments of Lieutenant General Horner," January 29, 1991, quoted in ibid., p. 188.

[77] Ibid., p. 270. ARCENT was the Army component of CENTCOM.

[78] Atkinson, *Crusade*, p. 217.

after the war."[78] Likewise in McPeak's portrayal, the coalition had "one concept of operations—General Schwarzkopf's concept," and all force components "marched to the same set of orders."[79]

For his part, the commander of British forces in the Gulf, RAF Air Chief Marshal Sir Patrick Hine, likewise observed that "it was more the case in this war than any previous war that the Marines put their aviation under the operational control of an overall air commander, who happened to be in light blue. It was something they were perhaps not comfortable with, but were quite clearly directed to do by Schwarzkopf."[80] To their credit, as Murray noted, "Even army generals like Schwarzkopf and Powell were looking for broader applications of air power than just supporting 'the ground commander's scheme of maneuver.'"[81] Powell indicated early on that even if an air campaign alone were to succeed in evicting Iraqi forces from Kuwait, he did not want Saddam Hussein to retain his large army. As he put it, "I won't be happy until I see those tanks destroyed. . . . I want to finish it; to destroy Iraq's army on the ground."[82]

Nevertheless, by the account of Gordon and Trainor, CENTCOM's strategy was "more joint in name than it was in fact" as the war's end approached.[83] As Rick Atkinson later commented, the battle for who would control allied air attacks against Iraqi forces in the KTO was being waged with "internecine fury."[84] In a controversial February 18 situation report that made its way from Riyadh all the way to U.S. European Command (EUCOM) and Washington, the Army complained that "air support–related issues continue to plague final preparations for offensive operations and raise doubts concerning our ability to effectively shape the battlefield prior to the initiation of the ground campaign. Too few sorties are made available to VII and XVIII Corps and, while air support [note, *support*] missions are being flown against first-echelon enemy divisions, Army-nominated targets are not being serviced."[85] Among other things, the corps commanders were complaining that it was Iraqi artillery, and not armor, that needed "servicing" by allied air power, since Iraqi artillery outranged their tanks.

This "teapot tempest," as Atkinson described it, reflected, at one level, "a

[79] General Merrill A. McPeak, USAF (ret.), *Selected Works 1990–1994*, Maxwell AFB, Ala., Air University Press, August, 1995, p. 40.
[80] Air Chief Marshal Sir Patrick Hine, RAF (ret.), "Air Operations in the Gulf War," in Alan Stephens, ed., *The War in the Air, 1914–1994*, Canberra, Australia, RAAF Air Power Studies Center, March 1994, p. 319.
[81] Murray, *Air War in the Persian Gulf*, p. 22.
[82] Memorandum by Lieutenant Colonel Ben Harvey, USAF, "'Instant Thunder' Briefing to CJCS," August 11, 1990, quoted in ibid., p. 26.
[83] Gordon and Trainor, *The Generals' War*, p. 310.
[84] Atkinson, *Crusade*, p. 338.
[85] Ibid., p. 339.

wrangle over battle doctrine and the eternal struggle between creatures aerial and terrestrial." More deeply, however, it attested to an understandable,
if groundless, torrent of Army fears about "sending forth soldiers to meet a
formidable foe."[86] All the same, Horner went ballistic, extracting an apol-
ogy from the Army drafter of the message and imploring the Army's corps
commanders to remain patient. Glosson later confirmed that many of the
Army's nominated targets had been taken out without the ground commanders' knowledge, since killer scout pilots had often destroyed targets of
opportunity in designated kill boxes within the KTO that had not been indicated on the formal ATO tasking.

At bottom, the interaction between U.S. air and ground elements was
needlessly complicated by Schwarzkopf's dual-hatted role as both CINC and
de facto ground component commander. Because he was, in effect, his own
ground forces boss, Schwarzkopf could live comfortably in a close working
relationship with Horner—which, by all indications, he did. For his part,
Horner unswervingly followed Schwarzkopf's bidding on air sortie apportionment. Even the unanticipated Scud hunt did not force Horner's eye off
the ball in that respect. As early as January 18, the day the Scud diversion
began, Horner declared that the coalition's air assets needed to handle it
with dispatch "so that we don't allow him [Saddam Hussein] to pull our
minds off our primary job; that's taking down his military machine and getting him out of Kuwait."[87]

Yet the corps commanders were frequently not happy with Schwarzkopf's decisions and often blamed them unfairly on Horner. They were only
concerned with the enemy ground forces that directly faced them. In contrast, Schwarzkopf was more concerned with the heavy armor divisions
of the Republican Guard in the second and third echelons. Based on extensive interviews with many of the involved principals afterward, GWAPS concluded that "not realizing it was Schwarzkopf's apportionment, some
ground commanders blamed Horner or Glosson. The upshot resulted in
tension between ground commanders, who felt their needs were not being
met, and the JFACC and his staff, who were responding to the theater commander's direction."[88]

Arm-Wrestling over the Proper Placement of the FSCL

The contretemps over air tasking control was most visibly pronounced in
the testy postwar finger-pointing between Army and Air Force principals
over where the blame properly lay for allowing sizable parts of the Repub-

[86] Ibid., p. 340.
[87] U.S. CENTAF Office of History, "Daily Comments of Lieutenant General Horner," March 20, 1991,
quoted in Murray, *Air War in the Persian Gulf*, p. 170.
[88] Keaney and Cohen, *Revolution*, p. 130.

lican Guard to escape the KTO to Basra. Even before the ground push began, the Army's corps commanders had voiced displeasure over Schwarzkopf's refusal to permit them to extend the FSCL even an inch into enemy territory until the ground offensive was actually under way. On this point, GWAPS noted that "since the JFACC had the principal responsibility for preparing the battlefield, the corps commanders were not given the air control they had come to expect during the years of preparing for a potential war in Europe with the Warsaw Pact. But visions of that war had never included an enemy army that would sit for weeks while bombing fatally weakened it."[89]

That notwithstanding, as GWAPS also reported, XVIII Airborne Corps advanced the FSCL well north of the Euphrates River on February 27 in an express effort to avoid JFACC control and thus reserved an area for attack helicopter operations unconstrained by any requirement to coordinate with the JFACC. "The effect of this use of the FSCL," concluded GWAPS, "was to hamper air power's ability to destroy escaping Iraqi ground forces until the FSCL was finally pulled back after several hours."[90]

Indeed, during the final 14 hours of the war, the FSCL was pushed back and forth repeatedly as the two services sought maximum flexibility for their own forces. In the U.S. Army's official account of the last four days of Desert Storm, then–Brigadier General Robert H. Scales later complained that the ATO's "72-hr cycle seemed unresponsive to battlefield commanders, particularly to corps commanders, in both the early operation and in the frustrating last-day effort to destroy the Republican Guard inside Kuwait."[91] More specifically, Scales suggested that the 20–grid-line restriction imposed by CENTCOM air planners kept the 11th Aviation Brigade's helicopters from preventing the escape of Iraqi armor. As a result, he charged, the coalition was unable to exploit the "synergy of deep attack with the unique capability of Apache helicopters to kill large numbers of moving targets at night in conjunction with integrated air power attacks."

There is another side to this story, however. In his presentation to the Commission on Roles and Missions in September 1994, General McPeak indicated that on the third day of the ground operation, Army commanders had fixed the FSCL well beyond their ability to affect the close battle with their own organic artillery and attack helicopters, and that for 17 hours as a result, the XVIII Airborne Corps commander prevented the JFACC from interdicting the main resupply line connecting Baghdad and Kuwait. McPeak also noted that a similar extension of the FSCL inside the KTO by the VII Corps commander had the effect of creating a sanctuary from air strikes on

[89] Ibid., p. 134.
[90] Ibid.
[91] Brigadier General Robert H. Scales, Jr., USA, *Certain Victory: The U.S. Army in the Gulf War*, Washington, D.C., Brassey's, 1994, p. 368.

Republican Guard units, whose commanders took advantage of this opportunity to mount an escape to Basra. Although Schwarzkopf had specifically directed Horner to engage and destroy those elite forces, his ground force commanders, according to McPeak, "acting in accordance with established joint doctrine, unilaterally placed boundaries which effectively contradicted the CINC's theater priorities." That, said McPeak, showed vividly "what can happen when boundaries are set by people who do not have full authority over military operations on both sides of the seam."[92] One U.S. Air Force pilot who had served as an Air Liaison Officer with the 101st Airborne Division during Desert Storm later noted that a big part of the problem was an outdated conception of "close air support." As he bluntly put it, "What we really have is either air power applied in close proximity to troops or air power applied not in close proximity to troops. Definitions and lines on maps that don't allow the flexibility required by nonlinear battle plans should be scrapped."[93]

After the war, Schwarzkopf admitted that he had known little of this debate. As Atkinson noted, that attested to "how joint warfare fell short and how the services' ability to work together suffered from Schwarzkopf's inattention."[94] Fortunately, such occurrences were infrequent, and the few opportunities lost for allied air power as a result were not crucial to the war's outcome. Nevertheless, they spotlighted a needless source of Army–Air Force friction when it came to the most efficient division of labor.

As for the Army's charge of ATO "rigidity," Horner indicated unambiguously after the war that he would not allow his targeteers to plan operations beyond the first two days. "The captains and majors who did the planning," he said, "wanted to take it through the first weeks. But the problem is that modern war is so uncertain and so fluid that you must develop the capability to react. If we had built that plan beyond the first two days, we would have become slaves to it. . . . So what happened was our efficiency in air operations was very high the first two days, dropped off drastically the third and fourth days, and then began to gradually go back up. We then achieved levels of efficiency which would not have been possible if we hadn't given people the chance to learn how to operate in this uncertainty called war."[95] Horner further noted that his "longest timeline . . . had to do with retargeting the B-52s. That was three minutes. Anything inside of that we would never hesitate to change the plan in order to get more efficiency or to take advantage of information if something became available."[96]

---

[92] McPeak, *Presentation to the Commission on Roles and Missions of the Armed Forces*, p. 35.

[93] Major John M. Fawcett, Jr., USAF, "Which Way to the FEBA (and FSCL, FLOT, Troops in Contact, Etc.)?" *USAF Weapons Review*, Fall 1992, p. 26.

[94] Atkinson, *Crusade*, p. 413.

[95] General Charles A. Horner, USAF, "New-Era Warfare," in Stephens, ed., *The War in the Air*, p. 326.

[96] Ibid., p. 322. As an example in point, Horner recounted before the Senate Armed Services Committee after the war that in one instance, "we had a force going out against one target, and as the

In all, then, the Army had little to complain about, other than not having been properly kept in the loop by Schwarzkopf. Of all the occasions throughout the war in which ordnance was released or fired against discrete aim points, 1,370 munitions went against SAMS, 1,460 against presumed Scuds, and 2,996 against airfields. Those were essential to gaining air control and keeping Israel out of the war. However, only 260 went after leadership; 280, after electrical power; 37, against naval targets; 540, against oil facilities; 580, against telecommunications and command and control; 630, against the Iraqi IADS; 970, against military industry; 990, against nuclear, chemical, and biological weapons targets; and 1,170, against bridges and other transportation targets. In contrast, a full 23,430 weapon releases— 67 percent of the overall effort—from the beginning to the end of the war were dedicated exclusively against fielded Iraqi ground forces.[97]

Granted, those sorties were all conducted under Horner's control, in response to his understanding of his tasking from Schwarzkopf. Without such a single air manager, CENTCOM would have suffered a far-greater chance of inadvertent blue-on-blue engagements, as well as a real danger of leaks in the air defense umbrella over Saudi Arabia and Bahrain that might have enabled Iraqi aircraft to penetrate allied airspace. In the end, however, Schwarzkopf remained true to his ground commanders, going so far as to declare in a directive to Horner on January 31 that "target development and nomination during the early phases of the campaign were clearly led by the . . . [JFACC]. As we move into the battlefield preparation, maneuver commander input into the target selection process becomes even more important. Therefore, the opportunity for corps and other subordinate commanders to plan for and receive air sorties to fly against targets of their choosing must increase."[98]

These facts by now have been cited so widely by so many observers with no axes to grind that it seems past time to move beyond the continued cavilling over this issue that has kept some Army and Air Force partisans at such pointless loggerheads.[99] The simple truth is that Schwarzkopf's deci-

---

pilot was taxiing, we had someone run out, stop the flight leader's airplane [and hand] him a picture of a new target, and [we] sent the entire force to the new target." "Technology Allowed Rapid Retargeting of Air Assets: Gen. Horner," *Aerospace Daily*, May 22, 1991, p. 307.

[97] Keaney and Cohen, *Revolution*, p. 56.

[98] Ibid., pp. 131–132.

[99] Three years after the Gulf war ended, one now-retired Air Force three-star general who had just returned from participating in two major joint field training exercises with the Army as the vice commander of Air Combat Command lamented in frustration how "these Army guys who were in the desert are not 'happy campers.' Mainly they believe we didn't use air to support *their* (not the CINC's, but *their*) objectives and service *their* targets, and they believe the air campaign was disconnected from the campaign's objectives *in toto*. It's almost like they resented not being able to strike sooner and harder. Further, there is enormous lack of trust at all levels, which compounds the problem of learning." Personal letter to the author from Lieutenant General Stephen B. Croker, USAF, May 12, 1994.

sion not to appoint a separate joint-force land component commander and his assignment of that function to himself led to inescapable friction between the two services. As Murray pointed out, it "had important consequences in the Army's attitude toward the conduct of the air campaign," as the corps commanders watched the JFACC planners seemingly ignore their target nominations for most of the duration of the war. The net effect of the CINC's dual-hatting was that "for most of the war, Schwarzkopf short-circuited his targeting board's recommendations, while telling Horner and Glosson directly what they should strike in the KTO. The result, unfortunately, was considerable, and needless, misunderstanding between Army and Air Force."[100]

CAVEATS AND QUALIFICATIONS

As effectively as allied air power performed from the first night onward in Desert Storm, it would be not just a reach but a grave error to conclude that such performance has become the norm to be expected of air power in all future situations. In the initial rush to extract enduring "lessons" from the Gulf experience, many forgot the numerous aspects of the war that were unique to that setting and that will not recur in future showdowns.

Beyond that, allied air power was not uniformly successful in Desert Storm. Although ultimately it beat down Iraqi forces to a point where the coalition's ground assault could sweep through the KTO and rout what was left of Hussein's army with virtual impunity, there were disappointments in air power's performance against so-called strategic targets associated with Iraq's leadership and infrastructure, as well as shortcomings in air power's ability to deliver owing to deficient intelligence, to note only two of the many sources of friction that air power encountered. These unique aspects of the Gulf scenario and associated shortfalls in air power's return on promise in CENTCOM's strategy must be owned up to squarely in any attempt to draw useful generalizations from the Gulf experience about air power and its proper place in American defense planning.

Distinctive Features of Desert Storm

To begin with, the coalition was exceptionally lucky with respect to the going-in conditions that helped make things turn out as well as they did. For example, it possessed a generally accurate picture of the threat, which was crucial for the effective suppression of enemy air defenses. Such a luxury may not be so readily available in future confrontations. No less important,

[100] Murray, *Air War in the Persian Gulf,* p. 238.

CENTCOM had five and a half months to plan, build up its forces, and train in the theater to make the defeat of Iraq's army such a textbook success story. Desert Storm was definitely *not* a "come as you are" war. The allied leadership used every minute of time it had available to good effect.

From an operational viewpoint, the open desert environment offered a near-ideal employment arena for allied air power, although the distances to targets and recurrent foul weather added offsetting complications. Taking note of that, some suggested in the aftermath of Desert Storm that the right bumper sticker for air power should read, "We do deserts. We don't do mountains or jungles." It will be important for future technology application to ensure that this assertion is proved wrong. Although tellingly effective when finally used properly and with determination, allied air power application in Bosnia in 1994 and 1995 and against Yugoslavia in the 1999 air campaign for Kosovo (see Chapters 5 and 6) proved to be a greater challenge than it was against Iraq. And there will be more, not fewer, cases like Bosnia and Kosovo in the future.

There was also the important fact that the Soviet Union did not resupply military hardware and other consumables to Iraq. The United States fought North Vietnam for 10 long years a generation earlier, in part because Hanoi enjoyed a nonstop source of arms replenishments from two communist sanctuaries to the north. In contrast, the winding down of the cold war and Soviet President Mikhail Gorbachev's desire for improved relations with Washington served to ensure that Moscow would not provide similar support to Iraq. Owing to the international trade embargo and Moscow's compliance in halting its arms transfers to Baghdad, it was only a matter of time before Iraq would run out of critical supplies and fighting strength. Had the Soviet Union chosen to back Iraq militarily, CENTCOM's strategy would not have worked as effectively and the Gulf crisis would likely have taken a different course.

Fortunately, as it turned out, the success of Desert Storm was facilitated by an almost unprecedentedly cooperative international political setting. A firm UN Security Council mandate in the form of Resolution 678 authorizing allied forces to use "all means necessary" to eject Iraq from Kuwait, the existence of a broad-based multinational coalition, and Soviet diplomatic support were all essential to the campaign's outcome. The United States and its principal allies cannot always count on such cooperation in future crises.

Relatedly, the Bush administration's handling of the Gulf crisis enjoyed strong domestic support, including the backing of an initially reluctant Congress. It is sometimes suggested that the United States won the war against North Vietnam militarily but lost it on the home front. Be that as it may, President Bush avoided such a debacle in Desert Storm through steady leadership and careful consensus building. It is at least arguable that the profusion of yellow ribbons across the country that symbolized that popular support was, in a sense, as important to ensuring a successful outcome to Desert Storm as were all the LGBs that were dropped by the F-117. Such support is fragile and perishable, and one can never take it for granted.

In addition, there was the unsurpassed advantage that comes from having a strategically and tactically inept opponent, as well as Saddam Hussein's failure to move against Saudi Arabia while the United States was just beginning its Desert Shield buildup. That was a time when Iraq had a force on the ground in Kuwait that could have registered real gains against Saudi territory. Whatever the Saudi reaction might have been, there is no way that a few squadrons of American F-15Cs and F-16s alone could have halted a determined Iraqi armored assault on the ground. Any significant Iraqi military foothold in Saudi Arabia would have made an effective coalition response far more problematic.

In clear testimony to this, a major concern when the initial U.S. aircraft arrived in Saudi Arabia was the vulnerability of the F-15C base at Dhahran. With nothing but flat terrain and hard-packed sand to the north, an Iraqi ground push would have advanced on it rapidly. As one Air Force pilot reported, "We were uncovered—and I mean really uncovered. I think we could have achieved and maintained air superiority after the third day we were here—at which point all our jets had arrived. But the tanks could have rolled down from the border almost completely unimpeded."[101]

On top of that, the coalition was lucky in that once Saddam Hussein invaded and occupied Kuwait, he completely misjudged everything that mattered thereafter: about whether the United States would respond beyond words, about American staying power and domestic support once committed, about the cohesion of the allied coalition, about the stance of his former Soviet benefactors, about the effects of modern air power, about his defensive fortifications in and around Kuwait, and about the "mother of all battles" and his prospect of drawing the United States into a war of attrition that would run up high American casualties before it ended. In benighted smugness, Hussein brushed off the American stealth threat before the war, proclaiming that the U.S. Air Force's F-117 "will be seen by a shepherd in the desert as well as by Iraqi technology, and they [the Americans] will see how their stealth falls just like . . . any [other] aggressor aircraft."[102]

Of particular importance, the coalition enjoyed a basing infrastructure in the Gulf region that left almost nothing to be desired, largely owing to the military assistance that the United States had provided Saudi Arabia over the preceding four decades. The U.S. Army Corps of Engineers had been building bases ever since the end of World War II to Saudi orders for what

[101] Jeffrey M. Lenorovitz, "U.S. F-15s Log High Flight Rates in Saudi Arabian Deployment," *Aviation Week and Space Technology*, September 10, 1990, p. 26.
[102] Quoted in Norman Cigar, "Iraq's Strategic Mindset and the Gulf War: Blueprint for Defeat," *Journal of Strategic Studies*, March 1992, p. 19.

was clearly more capacity than the Royal Saudi Air Force, by itself, could ever use. The quality of the bases varied from full facilities (as at Khamis Mushait, to the far southwest, where the F-117s were stationed) to bare-base facilities (as at Al Kharj) that offered little more than runways, taxiways, and ramp space. But at least they provided the needed springboard from which to conduct an air campaign that could hardly help but win. Had CENTCOM been unable to base its aircraft within a reasonable operating radius from Iraq, the air war would have looked quite different and would have had a less assured outcome.

Base vulnerability was generally not a problem. True, there was low-key concern for a time over the possibility of terrorist penetrations and the potential for a suicide attack by the IQAF. Many coalition bases enjoyed little by way of passive defenses, such as hardened aircraft shelters, hardened storage for fuel and munitions, hardened avionics shops, and perimeter guards. By and large, however, CENTCOM did not have to worry about the security of the rear where it had built up its forces and from which it planned to operate. Widely aired video clips of American F-15s and F-16s lined up wingtip to wingtip at Al Kharj and other airfields in Saudi Arabia offered a telling portrait of uncontested air control at work. The Egyptians and Syrians lost nearly their entire air forces to Israel's preemptive air attack at the outset of the Six-Day War in 1967 for having been similarly exposed. In contrast, the coalition did not have to worry because the air defense of its rear was ensured by AWACS and a capable alert posture of fighters.

As it turned out, the air defense of Saudi Arabia remained a serious concern only during the earliest days of Desert Shield, when the threat of an Iraqi invasion was both credible and real. Once the war was under way, repeated coalition attacks against Iraqi air bases and the prompt downing of any Iraqi fighters that got airborne ensured that the IQAF's ability to threaten coalition targets was neutralized almost from the outset. Freed of concern over any serious danger of enemy air attack, the coalition was able to determine at will the timing and tempo of subsequent air operations.[103]

In all, such generous good fortune enjoyed by the coalition in Desert Storm warrants a measure of humility among those who were responsible for winning the war, to say nothing of those who would draw overarching conclusions from the coalition's victory. As the under secretary of defense for tactical warfare programs at the time, Frank Kendall, rightly cautioned after the war ended, "What we did not learn was how to defeat a modern, well-trained, well-motivated, well-led force in a dynamic environment. We did not learn how to engage in a combat scenario without any significant preparation time or how to engage in an air operation where you did not have a large indigenous infrastructure to depend on for support." Because

---

[103] Nevertheless, defensive fighter patrols were flown around the clock along the Saudi border as insurance just in case.

Iraqi fighters never intruded into Saudi airspace, the coalition's early warning, reaction time, and interception capabilities were never truly put to the
test. Beyond that, an understandable concern voiced by many was that "we
showed our hand. We demonstrated to the world the effectiveness of taking
out an opponent's command and control—his eyeballs and ears."[104] Such
revelations were not ignored by important onlookers around the world who
might test the United States and its allies in future confrontations.

Where Air Power Encountered Friction

The popular image of the Desert Storm air war remains one in which the
effects of allied air power often seemed barely short of technological magic.
The fact is, however, that the coalition's air planners experienced compound
surprises over the course of the war and that the execution of allied air operations was frequently anything but flawless. Barry Watts itemized just
some of the problems that cropped up: "Aircrews had to cope with equipment malfunctions, inadequate mission planning materials, lapses in intelligence on both targets and enemy defenses, coordination problems between strike and support aircraft (including a number of F-111F sorties
aborted on the third day of the war due to being unable to find tankers for
prestrike refueling), target and time-on-target [TOT] changes after takeoff,
unanticipated changes in prewar tactics, adverse weather, the traditional
lack of timely bomb damage assessment [BDA], and, in many wings, minimal understanding of what higher headquarters was trying to accomplish
from one day to the next."[105] Such problems, Watts added, were not unique
to U.S. air power, but they definitely left their mark on the Gulf war by creating "operational and strategic consequences, not just tactical effects."[106]

To begin with, although it had no effect on allied combat operations in the
end, important parts of the U.S. air posture were stretched extremely thin by
the Desert Storm commitment. Even allowing for the five months that the
coalition enjoyed to build up its forces in the Gulf region, U.S. airlift capabilities were stressed to the limit by the support needs levied by CENTCOM.
The United States moved more materiel to the Gulf by air during the first
five weeks of Desert Shield than it accomplished in 56 weeks of the Berlin
airlift.[107] All told, U.S. airlift operations transported 99 percent of the personnel and virtually all supplies and equipment during the first month, until sealift operations could begin taking care of the rest. However, the U.S.

[104] John D. Morrocco, "War Will Reshape Doctrine, But Lessons Are Limited," *Aviation Week and Space Technology*, April 22, 1991, pp. 38–43.
[105] Barry D. Watts, *Clausewitzian Friction and the Future of War*, McNair Paper No. 52, Washington, D.C., Institute for National Strategic Studies, National Defense University, October 1996, p. 38.
[106] Ibid., p. 51.
[107] Roger Roy, "Air Force Chief Expects Land Fight to End It," *Orlando Sentinel*, February 1, 1991.

Air Force's Air Mobility Command had to call up the Civil Reserve Air Fleet, for the first time ever in a live contingency, by Day Ten of the Desert Shield buildup to help carry the load.

The sharp end of U.S. air power likewise was committed to an unprecedented extent by the requirements of Desert Storm. True enough, only 27 percent of the Air Force's total inventory of combat aircraft were deployed to the Gulf for the impending showdown. However, that deployment included two-thirds of the F-117s, virtually all nonstealthy LGB-capable aircraft, 75 percent of the F-4G Wild Weasels, most reconnaissance and electronic warfare aircraft, and nearly half of the Air Force's tankers and airborne command posts. It further included half of the Air Force's and Navy's combined HARM inventories, 63 percent of their LGB stocks, and 43 percent of their cluster bomb unit (CBU) stocks. Had a second contingency of like magnitude later developed elsewhere in the world, CENTCOM would not have had the luxury of commanding all of these resources for Desert Storm.

Second, as noted earlier, the smart airplane–dumb bomb combination did not work at medium altitudes. F-16s with unguided free-fall munitions were able to achieve lethal accuracies routinely in peacetime training, using NATO-type low-level attack profiles with a pop-up and roll-in to a dive attack with a weapons-release altitude of 4,000 ft or less. Yet at the higher release altitudes used in Desert Storm, the increased slant range between aircraft and target occasioned a pronounced degradation in bombing accuracy due to the natural amplification of aiming errors. On top of that, winds aloft were often 100 knots or more, making for additional aiming errors. In all, some 8,700 F-16 sorties dropped unguided bombs, mostly from medium altitudes, with many weapon releases having had no effect because of this substantially diminished accuracy. Navy and Marine F/A-18s were similarly affected, as were all other nonprecision bomb-droppers. This was not, of course, a problem for the B-52s, which dropped their bombs from high altitudes on area targets such as Iraqi troop concentrations. But for fighters against point targets, it often precluded a mission-effective sortie.

Third, the weather over Iraq during Desert Storm turned out to be the worst in 14 years. Persistent cloud cover forced a high mission abort rate because of target obscuration. On the second and third days of the war, more than half of the scheduled F-117 sorties aborted en route to target or were cancelled for that reason. The extension of medium-altitude floors throughout the theater after Day Three further compounded the effects of bad weather, since the number of targets obscured by clouds increased from 1 to 2 percent with low-level penetration to 33 percent at medium altitude.[108] By Day Ten, the coalition was still on only the fifth day of the air campaign's

---

[108] On the other hand, the loss in accuracy of dumb bombs was compensated by a reduced rate of downed allied aircraft.

planned tasks. Three weeks into the war, a full half of the planned attack sorties into Iraq had been either diverted to secondary targets or cancelled because of weather. Weather frequently hampered the delivery of laser-guided munitions as well. Indeed, it was so bad that Glosson noted by the end of January that it had the campaign "absolutely beat down," to a point where it saw the "whole pace of the campaign disastrously affected." [109]

Fourth, the confusion factor, or what Clausewitz referred to as the "fog of war," occasionally affected coalition air operations, most tragically in the case of the allied troop fatalities caused by inadvertent friendly fire from attacking aircraft whose pilots had either been misdirected or failed to identify the target properly. In the case of air-to-air operations, the E-3 AWACS, among other things, was expressly tasked with helping to prevent such inadvertent blue-on-blue engagements. In at least one instance, however, it erroneously committed an F-15 pilot against his own wingman, with the possibility of a fratricidal loss averted only because of the superior situation awareness of the F-15 flight leader.[110]

Other problems grew out of shortcomings in intelligence support at all levels. Most notably in this regard, the widely publicized LGB attack by an F-117 on the Al Firdos bunker in downtown Baghdad on February 13, in which more than a hundred innocent Iraqi women and children were killed, starkly dramatized what an intelligence failure can do to undermine the effectiveness of air power. No one either in Riyadh or in Washington had the slightest inkling that the targeted bunker, a known military command center, also harbored civilian families who were seeking shelter at night. Nevertheless, the negative publicity and propaganda value extracted by Iraq from the ill-fated attack prompted a decisive halt to allied air operations against Baghdad until the last few days of the war, with predictable consequences for the effectiveness of the so-called strategic air campaign.

A related problem emanated from the JFACC's often not knowing what to attack, particularly with respect to Iraqi nuclear, biological, and chemical (NBC) capabilities and Scud missiles. In the case of NBC targets, the problem was one of not knowing fully what the target set included. For example, on the first night of the air campaign, the attack plan included two nuclear-related targets. Yet after the war, UN inspectors uncovered more than 20 previously unidentified sites involved in nuclear weapons development.

---

[109] Notes from Glosson's diary, quoted in Murray, *Air War in the Persian Gulf*, p. 178.
[110] In fairness to what AWACS contributed to the campaign's success as a whole, however, it bears noting that not just AWACS but also such provisions as IFF, rules of engagement, special instructions, and noncooperative target-recognition systems, among other things, interact to prevent fratricide and that maintaining superior situation awareness is what air-to-air flight leaders are trained and expected to do. Notwithstanding this particular case, AWACS, by all accounts, did a superior job from opening night onward in controlling coalition fighters and keeping them out of more trouble than they got them into by a wide margin.

According to GWAPS, postwar inspection revealed that the Iraqi program to produce weapons-grade uranium, design and build implosion devices, and acquire nuclear weapons was "more extensive, more redundant, further along, and considerably less vulnerable to air attack than was realized at the outset of Desert Storm."[111] Similarly, despite determined attacks on suspected Iraqi chemical-weapons storage sites, inspectors after the war found some 150,000 untouched chemical munitions.

Much the same can be said for another surprise that stemmed from the unanticipated way in which Iraq employed its Scud surface-to-surface missiles, in a clever stratagem that exerted a major influence on CENTCOM's prosecution of the air war. Although the Scud's accuracy and lethality were low enough to make the weapon inconsequential militarily, it assumed strategic dimensions almost instantly once Saddam Hussein began firing it at Israel on the second night, in a ploy to goad Israel into entering the war, thus ending Arab participation in the coalition. Accordingly, on direction from Washington, it became a high-priority target and soon occasioned what came to be called "the great Scud hunt."

Once it was over, the Scud hunt was widely acknowledged to have been the most frustrating and least effective aspect of the air war. To begin with, in the absence of badly needed real-time intelligence inputs, CENTCOM's planners did not know the exact number or location of Scud launchers maintained by Iraq. Further complicating allied targeting, more than 80 percent of the Scud launches took place at night. After the Iraqis had fired the missiles, they moved the launchers back to their hiding positions, usually remaining exposed only for minutes. In addition, Iraqi deception efforts were excellent, featuring decoys with such fidelity that inspectors after the war could not distinguish the real thing from a dummy beyond 25 yards away.

Given the nature of the tactical problem, which involved attacking at night over great distances, the F-15E, with its LANTIRN system and range and payload advantage, was determined to be the best-suited platform for the mission. Yet despite more than 1,400 strikes committed against Scud-related targets by that versatile aircraft, no Scuds were proved to have been destroyed by coalition air power throughout the course of the operation, even though F-15E aircrews reported destroying some 80 launchers altogether. The best that can be said is that some Scuds *may* have been destroyed. That bore out the fact that all of the precision attack capability in the world is irrelevant against an enemy determined to bend every effort not to cooperate in its own destruction.

On the positive side, the operation had at least an indirect effect in reducing the launch rate of the Scuds once it became clear to the Iraqis that a

[111] Keaney and Cohen, *Revolution*, p. 72.

determined hunt for them was on. Of 88 Scud launches altogether through-out the war, 33 occurred during the first seven days. The remainder of the war saw a threefold diminution in the level of launch activity, almost certainly owing to the intimidation effect of the F-15E attacks. In the end, through diligent and sometimes maddening U.S. diplomatic effort, Israel was persuaded to sit the war out and the goal of Iraq's stratagem was not realized. Nevertheless, the unanticipated diversion prompted by the Scud hunt tied up 20 percent of all F-15E sorties flown during the war that might have been used to better military effect elsewhere.

Interestingly enough, the greatest effect achieved against Iraq's Scuds was registered by British Special Air Service (SAS) troops and U.S. Special Operations Forces (SOF), who waged what the U.S. SOF commander in Desert Storm years later characterized as "a fairly successful small campaign" in the western desert. By this account, U.S. and British SOF operators destroyed or damaged upward of 8 to 12 Scuds on their launchers, with SAS troops reportedly taking out one or two with hand-held antitank missiles and U.S. armed Blackhawk helicopters getting 3 or 4 more. In addition, a U.S. SOF patrol got to within 600 feet of a convoy of suspected Scuds and guided in an element of F-15Es from a vantage point close enough where its members felt the heat from the ensuing explosions and got dusted off with debris. According to the SOF commander, then–U.S. Army Major General Wayne Downing, the single greatest SOF contribution to the Scud hunt was determining how and where the Scuds were getting into their firing boxes and then persuading Schwarzkopf to authorize CBU-89 Gators to be dropped to interdict their movement. Although the number of actual hard kills, if any, achieved as a result of this tactic was never determined, there was fair reason to believe that the effort was the signal event that subsequently inhibited the Scuds from being fired into Israel.[112] The notable irony is that this indirect effect of U.S. air power was enabled by courageous operators on the ground rather than by the more high-technology air- and space-based information, surveillance, and reconnaissance (ISR) systems that were readily available but inadequate to the task.

Finally, there were disappointments with respect to the "strategic" employment of air power in Desert Storm. As for the early attacks against infrastructure targets in and around the so-called Baghdad center of gravity, there had been an underlying hope among CENTCOM's air planners that such attacks would weaken Saddam Hussein's control over his people. Such hope proved to be groundless, however, since popular attitudes mattered for naught given the depth and pervasiveness of Hussein's grip on the country. Related efforts to "inconvenience the Iraqi population" through selected air attacks on urban-industrial targets were likewise conducted in vain.

[112] Communication to the author from General Wayne A. Downing, USA (Ret.), December 15, 1999.

Similarly, allied air attacks against electrical power and petroleum targets inflicted little lasting harm to Iraq. To their credit, they also produced little unintended collateral damage. However, as GWAPS reported, "No evidence exists to substantiate that the air campaign inflicted lasting infrastructure damage to Iraq's oil industry."[113] By the same token, allied air attacks on Iraqi refineries and oil storage facilities had no significant military impact, since Iraq's army collapsed before their effects could be felt.

More influential were the JFACC's attempts to target military command centers to show Iraqi troops the helplessness of their leaders and to undermine ground force cohesion and morale. Such attacks almost certainly achieved these results, and on a wide scale. However, the initial goal involved a considerable overreach in its stipulation that "when taken in total, the result of Phase I will be the progressive and systematic collapse of Saddam Hussein's entire war machine and regime."[114] That clearly did not occur. Saddam Hussein and his regime not only survived but remained in sufficient control to command sporadic Scud launchings throughout the war.

In the end, the so-called strategic part of the air campaign, namely, those sorties not directly aimed at taking down Iraq's air defenses, command and control links, and fielded ground forces, did little to affect the immediate course and outcome of the war. To be sure, many such attacks were planned from the outset more with a view toward underwriting President Bush's declared goal of ensuring the security and stability of the Gulf region for the longer haul. Nevertheless, with few exceptions, these attacks did not live up to expectations. According to GWAPS, they "clearly fell short of fulfilling the ambitious hope, entertained by at least some airmen, that bombing the [leadership and command and control] target categories might put enough pressure on the regime to bring about its overthrow and completely sever communications between the leaders in Baghdad and their military forces."[115] In light of that disappointing performance, one might argue in hindsight that at least many of the allied attacks against Iraq's infrastructure drew off both sorties and precision weapons that could have been put to better use against targets of more direct relevance to Iraq's fighting capacity. They also may have been unnecessary in retrospect.[116]

---

[113] Keaney and Cohen, *Revolution*, p. 65.

[114] COMUSCENTAF (Commander, U.S. Central Command Air Forces) Operations Order, September 2, 1990, cited in ibid., p. 37.

[115] Ibid., p. 60.

[116] On the other hand, there is an argument to be made that these attacks remained warranted despite their limited success rate, considering that they involved fewer than 10 percent of the total "shooter" sorties flown throughout the war. An especially compelling reason for going after important infrastructure targets and suspected weapons of mass destruction from the war's outset was to work toward their elimination before Iraq contrived a ploy to end the war early and thus escape further destruction.

Such disappointment, however, was tempered by a keen awareness on the part of the JFACC planners that the rest of the air campaign was producing impressive strategic results of its own against the Iraqi army, even if an eventual coalition ground assault proved necessary, in the end, to secure the results achieved by allied air operations.[117] Asked afterward whether he had hoped that the Iraqis would cave in before a ground push had to be unleashed, Horner replied, "Of course. I'm an airman."[118] However, he placed little stock in any such outcome, and that showed in the way he conducted the so-called strategic portion of the air campaign. The peak levels of allied air attacks against leadership targets were achieved during the first two nights, with such attacks tapering off sharply thereafter.

DESERT STORM AND THE NEW FACE OF AIR POWER

Viewed with the broadened perspective that naturally comes with the passage of time, the Bush administration's conduct of the Gulf war has now come to be seen by most observers as having been considerably less than a towering strategy success. Many of the loftier goals articulated by its leaders before the war, from Colin Powell's bold assertion with respect to the Iraqi army that "first we're going to cut it off, and then we're going to kill it" to CENTCOM's declared objective of destroying Iraq's NBC weapons capability, did not come to pass. Beyond that, a legitimate and still-active debate has arisen over the perspicacity of the administration's decision to terminate the ground war so abruptly at the 100-hour mark, at just the moment when allied air and ground operations were beginning to make the most of what military professionals call the exploitation phase of war. As one foreign policy commentator put it in hindsight, Bush "was determined to expel Saddam from Kuwait and destroy the Iraqi military. . . . He succeeded in the first aim, and failed badly in the second."[119] Analysts will no doubt argue for years to come over what difference it might have made with respect to the longer-term outcome had the coalition kept pressing the combined air and ground offensive at the same level of effort for even another 24 to 48 hours. Most, however, would probably acknowledge what one critic characterized as "the yawning disparity between Desert Storm's unarguably impressive military accomplishments, especially at the operational and tac-

---

[117] Indeed, in one of the more memorable lines of the Gulf war, then–Lieutenant Colonel David Deptula, the senior Air Force target planner under Generals Horner and Glosson, remarked during the height of the coalition's air attacks against Iraqi ground forces, "We're not preparing the battlefield; we're *destroying* the battlefield."

[118] A GWAPS interview, March 10, 1992, quoted in Keaney and Cohen, *Revolution*, p. 79.

[119] James Chace, "New World Disorder," *New York Review of Books*, December 17, 1998, p. 61.

tical levels of combat, and its increasingly apparent failure to have engendered desirable political change in the Persian Gulf region."[120]

Yet as a more narrow exercise in the application of air power, Operation Desert Storm was anything but inconclusive. On the contrary, the ability of U.S. air assets to establish air dominance so quickly over a well-endowed opponent who knew a fight was coming and then to draw down his army to a point where coalition ground forces could consummate a virtually bloodless win in a mere 100-hour sweep through the KTO represented an achievement that is guaranteed to keep the Desert Storm air campaign prominently listed in the roster of air power success stories. Not only did it bear out all the efforts made since Vietnam to build a mature American air posture, its success in keeping allied ground force casualties so remarkably low suggests that the time may have come for considering a fundamentally new approach to the relationship between air- and surface-delivered fires in modern warfare.

To begin with, the success of the air campaign clearly attested to the wisdom of the sustained U.S. investment in realistic air combat training since Vietnam. Red Flag, Topgun, and similar exercises worldwide had taught a generation of American aircrews to conduct large-force operations in a high-threat environment as though it were second nature. The result was to make for a natural transition from the peacetime training environment to war.

The investment in low observability to enemy radar, or "stealth," was likewise vindicated under fire. After the war ended, General Horner frankly stated, "We had some initial uncertainties. We had a lot of technical data about stealth technology, but I had no way of knowing that we wouldn't lose the entire fleet on the first night. Those boys were going in there naked, all alone. We were betting everything on the data. As it turned out, they flew every night, and we did not suffer battle damage to any of the F-117 aircraft."[121] Without the tactical surprise made possible by the stealthy F-117, Iraq's air defenses would have been far more effective, and the cost in coalition aircraft lost would have been commensurately higher. Moreover, as GWAPS later observed, F-117 attacks on key nodes of KARI eventually provided "virtual stealth" to other attacking aircraft by disabling enemy air defenses, especially the early-warning and acquisition radars, and making the attackers more survivable as a result. Until then, because of their lack of low observability, other strike aircraft depended heavily on electronic counter-

---

[120] Jeffrey Record, *Hollow Victory: A Contrary View of the Gulf War*, Washington, D.C., Brassey's, 1993, p. 8.
[121] General Charles A. Horner, USAF (ret.), speech to business executives for the National Security Education Fund, Washington, D.C., May 8, 1991.

measures (ECM) support, to a point where the unavailability of escort jammers often meant a mandatory mission abort.

Some stealth detractors levied charges afterward that the F-117 had been forced to rely on support jamming from EF-111s to survive inside the Baghdad threat ring. Some EF-111s that were backstopping an attacking flight of F-15Es on opening night did move forward to jam Iraqi acquisition and tracking radars. But by the time they were instructed to turn their jammers on at 0258, the initial F-117s were already within Iraqi radar range, with the first F-117 bomb having landed seven minutes earlier. Some F-117 pilots noted afterward that any dedicated jamming support by EF-111s operating in close proximity would have been tactically unsound in any event, since it would have spotlighted the presence of the F-117s. Without question the F-117s received an intended windfall benefit from the jamming that was going on primarily to support nearby nonstealthy strike activity.[122] However, as much as they may have gained by way of enemy distraction and confusion as a result of their having been integrated into a larger strike package that included support jamming, the F-117s did not require such dedicated ECM support to survive and operate in defended enemy airspace.

In all, the combination of real-time surveillance and precision attack capability that was exercised to such telling effect by air power against Iraqi ground forces at Al Khafji and afterward heralded a new relationship between air- and surface-delivered firepower in joint warfare. One aspect of this transformation concerns what the resulting synergy does to enable the defeat of an enemy army through *functional* effects rather than through a more classic drawdown in detail by way of attrition. Just as the earlier SEAD campaign was able to neutralize Iraqi radar-guided SAMs not by physically destroying them but by intimidating their operators from turning on their radars, so the precision attacks made possible by JSTARS and other systems put potentially hostile armies on notice that they can no longer expect a night sanctuary or any place to hide. At the same time, they served notice that any attempt to move, day or night, will equally ensure a swift and lethal attack. In so doing, the events at Al Khafji presaged a new role for air power in saving friendly lives by substituting precision air attacks for ground forces within reach of enemy fire.

Needless to say, such characterizations are anything but reflective of mainstream thinking in the U.S. land warfare community. In the final chapter of his official account of the U.S. Army's contribution to Desert Storm, General Scales portrayed the four-day ground offensive as the "largest single land battle in American history won in the shortest time."[123] A skep-

[122] For further details, see Murray, *Air War in the Persian Gulf*, pp. 106–108. See also Tony Capaccio, "Air Force Strikes Back at F-117 Skeptics," *Defense Week*, November 18, 1991, p. 3.
[123] Scales, *Certain Victory*, p. 383.

tic might reply that this putative "largest single land battle in American history" was in fact little more, in the end, than a huge four-day mobility exercise with live-fire rules of engagement.[124] That would be grossly unfair to all those allied troops who actually participated in the 100-hour land advance through southern Iraq into Kuwait. It scarcely diminishes the superb performance of coalition air power in Desert Storm to acknowledge that allied ground units also excelled in completely sweeping a large and well-endowed opponent off the battlefield in a matter of hours. In the process, allied forces fought a number of high-intensity engagements in which they thoroughly shredded what were thought to be well-armed and well-trained Iraqi division-size formations. During these engagements, they destroyed hundreds of Iraqi tanks, armored personnel carriers, and artillery tubes for the loss of only a few armored vehicles and their crews.

At issue, however, is not how good the allied ground units and equipment were, which is uncontested, but rather what operational and strategic difference they made in determining the war's outcome. It is at least arguable that they cut so cleanly through Iraq's fielded forces in the KTO *not* principally because of their superior hardware and training, but rather because prior air preparation gave them a largely unopposed advance into Kuwait. There is no denying the unmatched combat capability and prowess of U.S. land forces. Yet the fact that matters most about its "100-hour victory" in Desert Storm is that the U.S. Army did not confront significant ground opposition.

There has been a continuing push from some quarters to make technology the hero of Desert Storm and to conclude that technological magic accounted for such a lopsided win by the coalition. That tendency reflects what Stanford historian Joseph Corn described as a pervasive strain of "technological utopianism" in American culture, dominated by an implicit belief that any problem can be solved if only the proper technology can be identified and applied.[125] Yet that almost surely is going to prove to be a hollow argument once the historians have the final word.

True enough, the coalition's pronounced technological edge over Iraq made an important difference in shaping the course and outcome of the war, and a few allied "silver bullets" had an impact far disproportionate to their numbers in ensuring the relative effortlessness of Desert Storm. These included the F-117, the HARM missile, the APR-47 threat sensor aboard the F-4G, LGBs, and JSTARS, among other platforms, munitions, and systems. Without them, the war would have proved far more costly for the allies.

---

[124] Indeed, the ground push was so unopposed that by one account, Army Apache helicopters came close to running out of fuel when the tanks they were supporting outraced their supply lines. See Andy Pasztor and James M. Perry, "As the Gulf War Begins Its March into History, Analysts Praise Success but Study the Failures," *Wall Street Journal*, March 6, 1991.

[125] See David Lauter, "High-Tech War Hopes Overdrawn," *Los Angeles Times*, February 5, 1991.

However, this observation requires an important qualification. Two points expressed by the late Secretary of Defense Les Aspin while he was still chairman of the House Armed Services Committee warrant special mention in this regard: "One, the equipment worked and was vindicated against its critics. Two, we know how to orchestrate its use in a way that makes the sum bigger than all the parts."[126] The second point in Aspin's statement is no less important than the first. Although by all accounts the F-117 was indispensable in achieving tactical surprise and minimizing the coalition's losses to enemy ground fire, to cite only one case in point, the real force-multiplication leverage that swung the final outcome in Desert Storm came from the way the coalition's diverse assets were brought together in synergistic combination by allied planners.

To sum up, high technology was a significant but not single-handedly determining factor in the coalition's success in Desert Storm. Superior training, motivation, proficiency, leadership, tactical cleverness, and boldness in execution were no less important in producing the final outcome. One need only consider the immensely difficult balancing act of getting 400 coalition fighters airborne and marshalled at night in radio silence, refueled (often several times), and working under tight time lines without a missed tanker connection, let alone a midair collision or other catastrophic accident, to appreciate how aircrew skill and the ability to adapt under stress were critically important to the air campaign's outcome. Without these and other intangibles, all the technology in the world would have been for naught.

The Desert Storm experience showed what high-technology weapons, coupled with good leadership and training, can do against less well-endowed forces. Yet ultimately the war was not about weapons systems or "technology," even though certain weapons and other combat-support systems were indeed star performers. It was more fundamentally about consensus building and the orderly formation of national goals; about diplomacy and leadership in the pursuit of those goals; and about astute planning and coordinated action by skilled professionals in the employment of military power, notably air power in this case, to achieve them once diplomacy and economic sanctions failed to carry the day. Insofar as the success of Desert Storm heralded a "revolution" in warfare, the revolution was in the fusion of *all* these ingredients into a winning combination.

---

[126] Representative Les Aspin, "Desert One to Desert Storm: Making Ready for Victory," address to the Center for Strategic and International Studies, Washington, D.C., June 20, 1991, p. 5.

The transformation begins. An F-4C Phantom mounting a Pave Knife laser designator pod on its left inboard wing station and a 2,000-lb laser-guided bomb on the left outboard station is readied by USAF ground crews for a weapons delivery test flight. (Photo courtesy U. S. Air Force)

Early effects of precision strike. Four USAF F-4Ds of the 8th Tactical Fighter Wing used 2,000-lb laser-guided bombs during a single mission in May 1972 to destroy three spans of the Paul Doumer rail and highway bridge over the Red River in Hanoi. (Photo courtesy U.S. Air Force)

Close air support. A 750-lb bomb is released from a 1950s-vintage USAF F-100D Super Sabre on a mission to provide emergency relief for an embattled U.S. Army unit pinned down by the Viet Cong in the Mekong Delta south of Saigon in August 1965. (Photo courtesy U.S. Air Force)

First of the fourth generation. The Navy's highly maneuverable F-14A Tomcat fleet air superiority fighter, which entered service shortly after the U.S. involvement in Vietnam ended, is shown here heading southwest over San Diego en route to an air-to-air training area off the coast of Baja California. (Photo courtesy U.S. Navy)

Inflight refueling. A USAF F-16A multirole fighter joins up underneath a KC-135 tanker to take on fuel during an early endurance flight over the United States aimed at simulating a deployment to a U.S. air base in West Germany. (Photo courtesy Lockheed Martin Corporation)

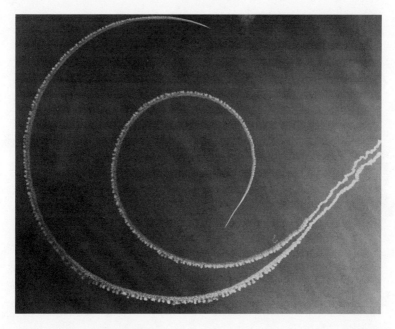

A new look in agility. The unprecedented maneuvering edge of the F-16 is graphically shown here in a turn performance comparison with an F-4E. The F-16, forming the inner contrail, completed a 360-degree turn in about half the radius and three-quarters the time required by the older F-4E. (Photo courtesy U. S. Air Force)

Aggressors at the ready. Four USAF F-5E fighters sit line-abreast on the flight line at Nellis AFB, Nevada, in preparation for a bimonthly Red Flag training exercise, in which they will simulate Soviet-flown MiG-21s as adversary threats against U.S. combat aircraft participating in the exercise. (Photo courtesy U.S. Air Force)

A Hornet with extra sting. The Navy's F/A-18 multirole fighter is shown here configured for aerial combat with a centerline fuel tank and a weapons load of 6 AIM-9L Sidewinder heat-seeking air-to-air missiles and 2 AIM-7F Sparrow semiactive radar homing missiles. (Photo courtesy U.S. Navy)

Lethal weapon. This swing-wing F-111F carries four AGM-130 powered variants of the GBU-15 electro-optically guided 2,000-lb bomb developed for precision attack against hardened enemy targets. The aircraft excelled in nightly attacks against Iraqi tanks and airfields during Operation Desert Storm. (Photo courtesy U. S. Air Force)

New eyes for the air war. The first E-3 AWACS fully equipped with production avionics takes off on its initial test flight. The aircraft carries a long-range surveillance radar and associated systems capable of providing a comprehensive real-time picture of air activity in a theater of operations. (Photo courtesy Boeing Company)

Strike Eagle. The two-seat F-15E, a variant of the USAF's F-15C air superiority fighter developed for the long-range night and adverse-weather interdiction missions, flew numerous nightly sorties against Iraqi armored units and other ground targets during the 1991 Persian Gulf war. (Photo courtesy U.S. Air Force)

Arming up to go tank trolling. The USAF's ungainly but effective A-10 tank killer was designed around its massive GAU-8 Gatling gun, which is capable of firing 30-mm armor-piercing shells made of depleted uranium at a rate of up to 6,000 rounds a minute. (Photo courtesy U.S. Air Force)

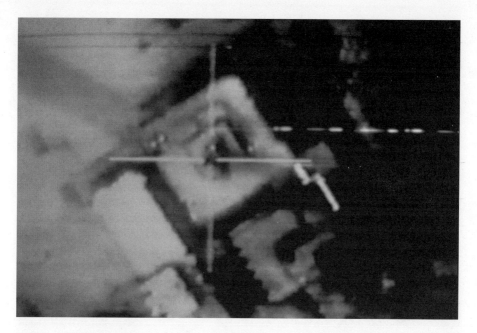

Mature air power shows its hand. This image taken from the infrared sensor of a USAF F-117 stealth fighter on a night mission early during Desert Storm shows the aircraft's laser designator locked onto the Iraqi air force headquarters building as a 2,000-lb laser-guided bomb guides toward its impact point. (Photo courtesy U.S. Air Force)

An untouchable returns home. A stealthy F-117 is towed back into its hardened shelter at Khamis Mushait air base in southern Saudi Arabia after recovering unscathed from a night deep-attack mission against key Iraqi military and infrastructure targets in heavily defended downtown Baghdad. (Photo courtesy U.S. Air Force)

"You should have seen the size of the fireball. . . ." A usaf F-16C pilot reconstructs a key ground-attack mission event shortly after landing in Saudi Arabia following the first night of coalition air attacks against Iraq in Operation Desert Storm. (Photo courtesy U. S. Air Force)

Making day out of night. This two-seat F-16B on a day test mission mounts imaging infrared AGM-65 Maverick missiles under each wing and navigation and targeting pods for its LANTIRN system under the air intake, giving the aircraft an effective night and under-the-weather attack capability. (Photo courtesy U.S. Air Force)

Dumb bomb, smart airplane. The two-seat F/A-18D, a variant of the basic Hornet produced solely for the Marine Corps, is shown here dropping a 2,000-lb free-fall bomb. The aircraft's avionics suite enables passable accuracy with so-called dumb munitions dropped at lower release altitudes. (Photo courtesy Boeing Company)

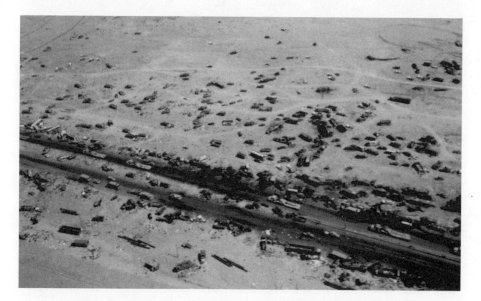

An enemy routed. Often called the "Highway of Death," this scene might be better labeled the "mother of all traffic jams." Hundreds of Iraqi vehicles attempting to flee Kuwait on the last day of the Gulf war were interdicted by allied air power, but most had already been abandoned before coming under attack. (Photo courtesy U.S. Air Force)

Global reach. A USAF C-17 Globemaster III designed for operating into austere forward locations nears touchdown on an aluminum-matted runway at an expeditionary airfield at the Marine Corps' Air Ground Combat Center at Twentynine Palms, California. (Photo courtesy Boeing Company)

All services are air power players. Initially fielded to help halt a Soviet armored assault against NATO, the Army's AH-64 Apache attack helicopter distinguished itself in Desert Storm by firing the first shot on opening night with a Hellfire missile against a forward-deployed Iraqi air defense radar. (Photo courtesy Hughes Helicopters)

No sanctuary for the enemy. In its combat debut, the USAF's stealthy B-2 bomber repeatedly delivered up to 16 satellite-guided 2,000-lb bombs against up to 16 dispersed targets during Operation Allied Force, including on nights when all other attacks had to be cancelled because of weather. (Photo courtesy U.S. Air Force)

To own the skies anew. This prototype of the USAF's stealthy F-22 Raptor fifth-generation air combat fighter slated to achieve initial operational capability beginning in 2005 shows off the distinctive fuselage shaping that helps contribute to its low radar signature. (Photo courtesy Lockheed Martin Corporation)

America's first-generation space warriors. Air Force Space Command officers conduct round-the-clock operation of U.S. communication satellites. The contribution of space systems to joint warfare has become so significant that a Space Division has been added to the USAF Weapons School. (Photo courtesy Lockheed Martin Corporation)

[5]

Into the Post–Cold War Era

As the relatively swift success of Operation Desert Storm well attested, the decade preceding it had seen a wide-ranging growth in the efficacy and lethality of the American air weapon. These improvements, mostly evolutionary but some entailing true breakthroughs in performance, accounted for much of the seeming ease of the allied joint-force victory against Iraq. Yet Desert Storm also marked a transition from the cold war, with its well-defined operational and force posture requirements, to a new era of diminished defense funds and uncertain challenges to international security.

Earlier in 1989, the fall of the Berlin Wall led to the collapse of the Warsaw Pact and the disintegration of the Soviet state, along with the military threat that Soviet communism had long presented to the Western allies. These developments, in turn, occasioned the disappearance, almost overnight, of a highly stable planning factor that had largely governed the character of American and NATO forces for more than three decades. Following the dissolution of the Soviet threat, the long American preoccupation with nuclear deterrence became displaced by a new need to prepare for a resurgence of regional conflict around the world. Rather than continue configuring U.S. forces for the possibility of a global strategic showdown, American defense planners now set as their goal the need to be prepared for two simultaneous "major regional contingencies," or MRCs as they came to be called. These equated, in effect, to another Desert Storm–level confrontation with Iraq and a full-scale conventional war on the Korean peninsula.

At the same time, the end of the cold war accelerated a gradual decline in American defense spending, initiated late in the Reagan administration and continued by the Bush administration, to a level lower in both constant dollars and percentage of gross domestic product than any experienced in the United States since before the outbreak of the Korean war. That, along with a diminished external threat, occasioned a force drawdown that reduced the Air Force fighter inventory from 39 to 20 wing equivalents (13 active and 7 in the Air National Guard and Air Force Reserve), the Navy from 15 to 11 carrier air wings (10 active and 1 reserve), and the Marine Corps to 4 air wings (3 active and 1 reserve). In terms of force size, the Air Force's fighter and attack aircraft inventory went from 4,200 aircraft in 1991 to almost half that number in 1996. Navy and Marine fighter and attack aircraft likewise declined in number from 2,200 to around 1,200.[1]

Part of this drawdown simply reflected the gathering obsolescence of certain older aircraft that had been in the inventory for more than two decades. For example, the last of the Navy's workhorse A-6 medium bombers, first flown during the early 1960s, were retired in 1997, as were most of the initial batch of F-16A/B fighters that entered Air Force service in the late 1970s. Also, both the F-111s and F-4Gs were finally put to pasture in 1996, in large part because of the high cost of maintaining those still capable but now tired and aging aircraft. The night and extended-range precision strike mission performed so well by the F-111F in Operation Desert Storm was picked up by the F-15E, which offered the added advantage of having an air-to-air capability on a par with that of the F-15C.

The end of the cold war further occasioned a decline, by nearly half, in the number of American overseas air bases. On top of that, the disappearance of the Soviet threat contributed to a reduced American willingness to make the needed investments to hedge against only dimly foreseeable challenges that might arise a decade or more hence. Yet despite this retrenchment, the onset of the post–cold war era saw a dramatic rise in the incidence of low-intensity conflicts worldwide, along with a growing American appetite for involvement in regional peacekeeping activities as the world's sole surviving superpower. From 1991 to 1994, the Air Force participated in 194 global military operations other than war, almost twice the number of such operations it was tasked to perform during the preceding five years that coincided with the end of the cold war.[2] The ensuing commitment of U.S. forces and personnel in concurrent deployments around the world inevitably forced a need to do more with less.[3]

On the plus side, the reduced size of the U.S air posture in the post–cold

---

[1] Secretary of Defense William J. Perry, *Annual Report to the President and the Congress*, Washington, D.C., Government Printing Office, March 1996, p. 179.

[2] Alan Vick, David Orletsky, Abram N. Shulsky, and John Stillion, *Preparing the U.S. Air Force for Military Operations Other Than War*, Santa Monica, Cal., RAND, MR-842-AF, 1997, p. 16.

[3] As one possible indicator of the poor training value imparted by the long hours of flying uneventful combat air patrols over Bosnia and Iraq in support of U.S. contingency operations, the failure rate for students flying basic fighter maneuvers syllabus sorties at the USAF Weapons School between 1995 and 1996 almost doubled from 21 to 37 percent. Peter Grier, "Readiness at the Edge," *Air Force Magazine*, June 1997, p. 58.

war era was offset in considerable part by qualitative improvements that made that force posture more capable than ever. For one thing, almost every U.S. combat aircraft was equipped with the wherewithal for dropping precision-guided weapons. For another, the advent of stealth, as first demonstrated on a meaningful scale by the F-117 during the Gulf war, was further entrenched by the subsequent deployment of the Air Force's second-generation B-2 stealth bomber, which entered line service in 1993. Beyond that, new munitions introduced into the forces since Desert Storm increased the lethality of U.S. air power in both ground-attack and air-to-air roles, and the Air Force's bomber component completed its transition from a predominantly nuclear to a predominantly conventional tool of war. Finally, the Air Force, Navy, and Marine Corps all instituted new concepts of operations after Desert Storm to help ensure the continued relevance of their air assets in the post–cold war era.

THE OPERATIONAL IMPACT OF STEALTH

The most significant advance in recent military aviation technology has been the introduction of low observability to enemy radar and infrared sensors, more commonly known as "stealth." In the crucial area of surface-attack operations, this design feature has greatly increased the likelihood of unobserved penetration to a target by an approaching aircraft.[4] Indeed, the much-reduced radar cross section of a stealthy air vehicle has increased the latter's survivability against enemy radar-directed surface-to-air missiles (SAMs) by shrinking the effective engagement envelopes of such SAMs by 95 percent or more. It permits an aircraft to fly at medium altitudes above the lethal envelopes of infrared SAMs and antiaircraft artillery (AAA) and, provided that some important operating limitations are respected, to perform combat missions in hostile airspace undetected.[5]

Equally important, stealth has obviated the need to amass large force

[4] This section draws on the informed early tutorial on low observability and its combat potential by Major General Jasper A. Welch, Jr., USAF (Ret.), "Assessing the Value of Stealthy Aircraft and Cruise Missiles," *International Security*, Fall 1989, pp. 47–62.

[5] As the principal designer of the B-2 has since written with regard to these limitations, stealth in actual practice is a combination of low observability and *tactics*, the latter of which entail close attention to mission doctrine, maneuver, sensor operation, and weapon application in addition to relying on the aircraft's inherent low-observability properties. "When appropriate tactics are employed," he added, "survivability will be assured with or without supporting ECM." By implication, when appropriate tactics are *not* employed, the survivability of a nominally stealthy aircraft is anything but assured. John Cashen, "Stealth (and Related Issues)," paper prepared for a conference titled "Control of the Air: The Future of Air Dominance and Offensive Strike," sponsored by the Australian Defense Studies Center, Canberra, Australia, November 15–16, 1999, p. 4.

packages for most applications of air power. A typical nonstealth attack package in Desert Storm required 38 Air Force, Navy, Marine, and Saudi aircraft to enable 8 of those aircraft to deliver bombs on three aim points. Yet at the same time, only 20 stealthy F-117s simultaneously attacked 37 aim points successfully in the face of a far more challenging Iraqi surface-to-air defensive threat. The difference was more than a 1,200-percent increase in target coverage with 47-percent fewer aircraft.[6] In operations against enemy air defenses and airfields during the critical opening hours of a high-intensity conflict, even modest numbers of stealthy aircraft can be disproportionately effective by allowing air control to be gained quickly, neutralizing SAM and fighter defenses, and paving the way for nonstealthy aircraft to continue most of the hard work against enemy ground targets by means of precision standoff attacks. Such aircraft further offer the ability to carry an air control campaign deep into enemy territory from the outset of combat, something that was generally not possible in high-intensity wars prior to Desert Storm.

Stealthy aircraft also reduce the need for defense suppression and fighter escort. In raids into the most heavily defended parts of the Hanoi-Haiphong complex during the last year of the Vietnam war, some 80 percent of the Air Force and Navy sorties flown were combat support sorties. Similar large-force packaging was required in early attacks into Iraq by nonstealthy aircraft before air dominance was achieved by the coalition. The nonstealthy F-15E required the help of precursor defense-suppression attacks, dedicated support jamming, fighter cover, and radar warning through the airborne warning and control system (AWACS), all of which substantially increased the cost per pound of ordnance delivered on critical targets. Yet apart from its dependence on tankers for inflight refueling, the F-117 operated virtually autonomously in Desert Storm, relying mainly on its low observability and on conservative tactics for survival.

The difference between these two examples is revealing for what stealth portends with respect to destroying critical targets with a minimum of cost and risk. By virtue of its ability to bring an aircraft to weapons-release parameters undetected so long as proper tactics are employed and the aircraft's vulnerabilities are kept in mind, stealth now enables both strategic and tactical surprise, at least in some scenarios, by allowing attacking aircraft to engage unalerted enemy forces. In contrast, nonstealthy platforms generally provide timely warning for the target under attack, increasing their own vulnerability while decreasing their likely effectiveness. All other things equal, low observability further ensures an increase in a stealthy aircraft's effective operating radius, owing to its capacity for enabling the air-

[6] Commission on Roles and Missions, *Future Bomber Force*, Arlington, Va., Aerospace Education Foundation, May 1995, p. 2.

craft to operate at fuel-efficient speeds and altitudes and for reducing the need for weight-adding and space-occupying electronic countermeasures (ECM) that otherwise would be required for self-protection against enemy defenses.

Granted, stealth does not render a combat aircraft fully invisible along the lines of the fanciful Romulan cloaking device of "Star Trek" fame. What it does do is reduce substantially the range at which an enemy's radar and infrared sensors can detect a platform from various look angles and to complicate the tracking of any stealthy vehicle that may be momentarily detected by enemy sensors. The net effect is to narrow significantly any defender's window of opportunity for successfully engaging and downing an attacking stealth platform. Low observability to radar means that stealth platforms can be operated in high-threat areas with less intense concern for surface-to-air defenses and can fly on headings and at altitudes aimed at maximizing opportunities for early target acquisition. One cannot, however, operate such platforms with *complete* abandon. Even the most advanced stealth aircraft must be flown in specific attitudes to radars to preclude their being detected in time to be put at risk, as the downing of an F-117 by a Serbian SA-3 missile on the fourth night of Operation Allied Force in 1999 (see Chapter 6) attested all too painfully. As a senior Air Force officer cautioned, stealthiness "significantly reduces your vulnerable area, but it does not give you the freedom to ignore the threats."[7] At some angles, even the most stealthy aircraft will be at least fleetingly detectable by airborne and surface radars, although the former will typically be at a disadvantage.

True enough, one can ask whether the outlook for stealth countermeasures may be promising enough over the longer haul to render the next generation of combat aircraft (the stealthy F-22 and Joint Strike Fighter now slated to enter service during the first decade of the 21st century) merely a passing advantage for the United States. Throughout the ages, it has been an iron law of weapons development for new concepts to be negated eventually by offsetting countermeasures. Naturally, in the case of low observability to radar, one can assume that adequately endowed adversaries will seek aggressively to unmask such aircraft either through more-capable radars or through sensors based on other physical principles, such as infrared, visible light, and acoustics.

Yet today's stealth technology, when coupled with astute tactics grounded in accurate and up-to-the-moment intelligence, has rendered existing early-warning and engagement radars, as well as the weapons that depend on them, all but useless. The resultant ability it has provided joint-

---

[7] David A. Fulghum, "Expanding Roles May Shield F-22," *Aviation Week and Space Technology*, January 6, 1997, p. 43.

force commanders to conduct precision attacks with near impunity against an opponent's core instruments of power, whether they be deployed forces or infrastructure targets, has imparted a new edge to U.S. air power. In the process, it has changed the face of joint warfare. Stealthy aircraft like the F-117 and B-2 allow joint-force commanders to conduct vital operations in the most heavily defended enemy airspace that *no* number of less capable aircraft can perform at an acceptable risk. Not only can smaller numbers of such aircraft produce strategic effects early in a war, but also they can increase the value of nonstealthy aircraft by providing the latter a safer envelope in which to operate over hostile terrain. Indeed, once air control is established and enemy radar-directed SAMs have been neutralized, even stealthy aircraft can operate in a nonstealthy manner, if need be in special circumstances, by carrying external bombs to join more traditional strikers in consummating the ground-attack portion of an air campaign.

THE ADVENT OF THE B-2

The low-observable technology pioneered in application by the F-117 in Desert Storm advanced significantly during the early 1990s with the successful flight testing and subsequent deployment of the long-range B-2 stealth bomber. That aircraft, essentially a high-technology flying wing, was first unveiled in 1988 after more than a decade of development in great secrecy. Its introduction into the bomber force gave the United States, for the first time, the ability to conduct precision attacks with surprise against the most heavily defended targets anywhere in the world.

Originally developed during the height of the cold war as a means of penetrating highly echeloned air defenses and attacking strategically relocatable targets such as mobile intercontinental ballistic missiles (ICBMs) in the Soviet Union, the B-2 was first planned for a production run of 132 aircraft. That number was later reduced to 75 in April 1990, less than six months after the fall of the Berlin Wall. Once the unraveling of the Soviet Union began in December 1991 following the failed coup attempt the previous August, the planned buy of B-2s was cut back again to merely 20 aircraft. Later, the Clinton administration allowed the initial B-2 flight test air vehicle to be upgraded into an operational bomber, increasing the planned total force to 21.

Despite this small force size, the aircraft brings a new capability to joint warfare. To begin with, the B-2 combines stealth for safe penetration of radar-directed defenses with intercontinental range, a large weapons payload, and the consequent ability to conduct precision attacks against critical targets anywhere in the world, as its almost nightly performance without a hitch during NATO's 78-day air campaign against Yugoslavia in 1999 (see Chapter 6) amply confirmed. The B-2's low observability offers leverage for opening up penetration corridors by taking out key air defense nodes with high confidence and little risk. Because it can strike with complete surprise, the B-2 can impose functional effects on an opponent by creating a situation in which he can never know for sure when he may find himself under attack. As for its destructive potential and operational reach, the B-2 can carry more than 10 times the payload of the F-117 to five times the latter's unrefueled range.[8] Its weapons bay can carry the full spectrum of current-generation conventional munitions for accurate attack against point targets. By the year 2000, all B-2s will have been converted to Block 30 standards, with enhanced stealth characteristics and the ability to drop precision munitions yet to be fielded.

The biggest problem to date with respect to availability for mission tasking has entailed maintaining the B-2's low-observable features in day-to-day operations, given the delicacy of its radar-absorptive skin treatment, which requires close and constant attention to ensure its ability to negate enemy radar emissions.[9] In particular, the aircraft's surface finish has shown itself to be susceptible enough to the deleterious effects of high-speed flight through rain as to require unusually labor-intensive work to maintain its stealth properties. Yet the initial bad press the aircraft received in 1997 and 1998 as a result of that problem, to a point where it had become an object of outright ridicule, was soon forgotten once the problem was duly addressed and the B-2 surpassed all expectations during its combat debut over Kosovo in 1999. It has recently shown a mission availability rate of 69 percent, with a mature rate of 80 percent now a reasonable prospect.[10]

Clearly, at $40 billion in sunk cost for a planned force of only 21 aircraft, the B-2 has proved itself expensive beyond precedent for a combat aircraft. However, as the former air commander for Desert Storm, General Charles Horner, testified to Congress not long afterward, "The bottom line is not dollars per aircraft but overall capability per dollar." A revealing preview of the increased combat leverage portended by the B-2's performance in Operation Allied Force was provided in a demonstration of the newly operational global positioning system (GPS)-aided targeting system (GATS) and GPS-aided munition (GAM) on the Nellis range complex in 1996 by three B-2s, in which the aircraft delivered 16 satellite-guided munitions altogether against 16 dispersed targets, destroying or disabling each. The weapons were released from above 42,000 ft at a standoff range of five to seven nau-

---

[8] Lieutenant General Charles A. Horner, USAF, testimony before the House Appropriations Committee, *Department of Defense Appropriations for 1992, Part 5*, 102nd Congress, 1st Session, Washington, D.C., Government Printing Office, 1991, p. 469.
[9] See William B. Scott, "Follow-On B-2 Flight Testing Planned," *Aviation Week and Space Technology*, June 30, 1997, p. 48.
[10] Cashen, "Stealth (and Related Issues)," p. 12.

tical miles.[11] That demonstration attested to the fact that American air power has now approached the point at which one can speak routinely of the number of aim points that can be engaged with a single sortie rather than, as was the case in past generations, how many sorties would be required to destroy one target with any confidence.[12]

A New Generation of Munitions

Low observability in fighters and bombers has proved to be an effective force multiplier through its ability to increase survivability and the element of surprise. It permits the holding of highly defended targets at risk, while sharply reducing the delivery vehicle's exposure to hostile fire. Yet in and of itself, stealth only gets the platform to within striking range of a target. The other half of precision engagement requires munitions capable of finishing the job.

Laser-guided bombs (LGBs) largely swung the outcome of the 1991 Gulf war by shutting down Iraq's integrated air defense system (IADS), keeping its air force out of the fray, and destroying its fielded armor. Of the 85,000 tons of bombs dropped by the coalition altogether, fewer than 10 percent (some 8,000 tons) were precision-guided munitions (PGMs). Yet that same small percentage of PGMs reportedly accounted for more than 75 percent of the significant damage achieved and was indispensable for ensuring the effectiveness of the earliest strikes carried out while Iraq's integrated air defenses remained intact.[13] Compared to unguided bombs such weapons offer an increase in their likelihood of hitting the intended aim point by as much as a factor of a thousand. Coupled with onboard or offboard laser target designators, they have rendered aircraft like the F-16 and F/A-18 effective against point targets from medium altitudes, correcting one of the most pronounced shortcomings of those two aircraft during Desert Storm. According to a 1993 Defense Science Board study, the Gulf war experience showed that "for many target types, a ton of PGMs typically replaced 12–20 tons of unguided munitions on a tonnage per target kill basis."[14]

[11] William B. Scott, "B-2 on Track to Achieve Initial Combat Status in 1997," *Aviation Week and Space Technology*, December 16, 1996, p. 74.

[12] In yet another preview of its operational application in Allied Force, the B-2 successfully drop-tested inert 4,700-lb GAM-113 earth-penetrating munitions using its GATS, which offered a launch-and-leave capability with an average miss distance of 20 ft. See William B. Scott, "B-2 Drops GPS-Guided 'Bunker-Buster,'" *Aviation Week and Space Technology*, April 21, 1997, p. 64.

[13] See "Precision Weapons Right for the Times," *Aviation Week and Space Technology*, July 29, 1996, p. 86.

[14] Office of the Under Secretary of Defense for Acquisition and Technology, *Report of the Defense Science Board on Tactical Air Warfare*, Washington, D.C., Department of Defense, November 1993, p. 17.

Developments for Precision Surface Attack

New precision munitions now available are headed by the GBU-31 joint direct attack munition (JDAM). Directed to target by means of the space-based GPS, this 2,000-lb weapon offers near-precision levels of accuracy against point targets, irrespective of weather or visibility, thereby circumventing the problems of weather and smoke and debris in the target area that often prevented the effective use of LGBs during Desert Storm. On more than one occasion, then–Brigadier General Buster Glosson, the chief air campaign planner in Desert Storm, complained that weather was a greater impediment to effective allied strike operations than the Iraqi Air Force. In finally transcending this problem, the introduction of a family of inertially guided, GPS-aided bomb kits that provide a consistently accurate attack capability against fixed targets regardless of weather has made for a major increase in the combat leverage of conventional air power.

In addition, the Air Force's first sensor-fused weapon, the CBU-97, entered full-rate production in July 1996. This munition contains 10 BLU-108 submunitions containing four Skeet antiarmor warheads, for a total of 40 submunitions, each of which can scan two-thirds of an acre for targets of opportunity. A full canister of such submunitions can engage vehicular targets within an area two football fields wide by four long. First qualified on the F-16, it has demonstrated consistent success at multiple armored vehicle kills per aircraft pass, both day and night and in adverse weather. It will enable joint-force commanders to attack enemy ground targets in ever larger numbers consistently and accurately from the relative safety of medium altitudes.[15]

Since Desert Storm the Navy has continued its acquisition of the standoff land attack missile (SLAM), a modified antiship Harpoon with an AGM-65 Maverick imaging infrared seeker and Walleye data link for man-in-the-loop control. This precision weapon, developed mainly for the F/A-18, is guided by real-time GPS updates and is steered to target during the final moments of flight through the missile's electro-optical sensor. Next in line for deployment in both Air Force and Navy squadrons is the joint standoff weapon (JSOW), a long-range, aerodynamically efficient glide munition with an autonomous navigation capability and all-weather target attack capability. An improved variant will carry sensor-fused submunitions for accurate standoff attack against enemy armor.

The GATS/GAM test conducted at Nellis AFB by Air Force B-2s in 1996 high-

---

[15] See Glenn W. Goodman, Jr., "Tenacious Tank Killers," *Armed Forces Journal International*, November 1996, pp. 20–24. See also William B. Scott, "U.S. on Track with Glide Bomb," *Aviation Week and Space Technology*, July 22, 1996, pp. 54–58.

lighted an increasingly important policy issue with respect to the relative merits of using cruise missiles versus guided air-delivered munitions for extended target coverage in future joint combat operations. As the former Air Force chief of staff, General Ronald Fogleman, observed in this regard, "The deficiency we have right now in the cruise missile system is the cost per shot. If you want to get somebody's attention at $1.5 million a pop, you can shoot those things and get their attention, but if you want to conduct an air campaign, you're going to bankrupt the country quickly by doing that."[16] Using air-delivered GPS-guided munitions like GATS/GAM and JDAM makes possible an even better effect for as little as $15,000 a shot. One of the main shortcomings of the Tomahawk land-attack missile (TLAM) from a tactical perspective is its relatively small punch compared to that provided by a 2,000-lb bomb, which offers twice the explosive power.

In addition to GPS-guided weapons offering an accurate through-the-weather ground-attack capability, the Air Force has begun to acquire the wind-corrected munition dispenser (WCMD), an accuracy-enhancing modification of the CBU-87 combined-effects munition, CBU-89 Gator, and CBU-97 sensor-fused weapon. This weapons module measures wind speed throughout the munition's time of flight and applies continuous guidance corrections to cluster bomb dispensers, improving their accuracy from higher release altitudes. Already, such infrared homing submunitions can be delivered from standoff ranges against such targets as tanks, hot artillery tubes, vehicles, and power generators for enemy radars and electrical equipment. Once acquired in enough numbers to support an extended air campaign, they will provide combat aircraft a considerable increase in leverage by permitting multiple target kills per pass. Taken together, this enhanced effectiveness adds up to a world qualitatively different from that which was shown on Cable News Network during Desert Storm a decade ago. In having moved U.S. forces a generation beyond the era of electro-optical and laser guidance while, at the same time, having essentially conquered weather as an operating limitation, it represents a new threshold crossed by American air power in its ability to achieve strategic effects in joint warfare.

An Advance in Air Combat Capability

The weapon development of greatest note for aerial combat since Desert Storm was the introduction of the AIM-120 advanced medium-range air-to-air missile (AMRAAM), the first true "launch and leave" missile with a fully

---

[16] General Ronald R. Fogleman, USAF, "The Contribution of Long-Range Bombers to America's Deep-Strike Capability," speech to the de Toqueville Group, Washington, D.C., September 13, 1996.

active homing radar.[17] The initial AMRAAM requirement was generated during the mid-1970s, when Air Force projections of the Soviet air-to-air threat dictated a beyond-visual-range (BVR) capability more effective than that offered by the AIM-7F Sparrow. The latter, with its semiactive radar homing seeker, required the pilot to keep the target illuminated by his air intercept radar throughout the missile's time of flight as the missile guided itself to target on the reflected radar waves. This constraint had the effect of making the pilot both predictable and vulnerable to attack by another fighter or SAM. It further worked to make medium-range air-to-air engagements, by one account, "little more than a function of which pilot fired first," all other things equal.[18] Only one AIM-7 could be fired by any aircraft per engagement, making for an unfavorable exchange ratio at best. In contrast, AMRAAM allows a fighter to engage multiple targets simultaneously. This so-called fire-and-forget capability has freed pilots from the discomfiting situation of having to fly a predictable flight path throughout the missile's time of flight. As a result, it permits multiple kills per engagement.

The development of AMRAAM was plagued for years by the tendency of its fins to fail on F-15 AIM-7 stations and by the need to pack a great deal of capability into a small volume, since the size and weight of the missile were constrained by plans to mount it on the F-16's wingtip missile rails, necessitating a weight limit of 350 lb. (The 500-lb AIM-7 was too heavy to be placed on that station.) The requirement included a launch-and-leave capability; a capability for multiple-target attack; a look-down, shoot-down capability against low-flying targets surrounded by ground clutter; an electronic counter-countermeasures capability; and the ability to be carried by the F-14, F-15, F-16, and F/A-18, as well as by the British Tornado F3 and Sea Harrier and the German F-4F. A full-scale development (FSD) contract was awarded to Hughes Aircraft Company in 1981, with FSD commencing in September 1982. The development schedule was heavily driven by the Air Force's desire to have the missile ready for use when the first F-16s were deployed to Europe in 1985. Because of repeated schedule slippages, however, the initial operational deployment of the missile only came six years after that original planned date.

The AMRAAM was first battle-tested over Iraq in December 1992 when an Air Force F-16 flying a combat air patrol (CAP) mission in Operation Southern Watch downed an Iraqi MiG with the AIM-120 at the missile's absolute

[17] Earlier, the Navy had developed and deployed the AIM-54 Phoenix long-range missile with such a capability, but it was very expensive, was designed solely to protect carrier battle groups against standoff Soviet bombers carrying cruise missiles, and could only be carried by the F-14.
[18] Kenneth R. Mayer, *The Development of the Advanced Medium-Range Air-to-Air Missile: A Case Study of Risk and Reward in Weapon System Acquisition*, Santa Monica, Cal., RAND, N-3620-AF, 1993, p. 14.

minimum range. Several weeks later, another F-16 scored a second AIM-120 kill over Iraq while flying on a similar mission in Operation Provide Comfort. Since then, the AMRAAM (now commonly referred to as the "slammer" in pilot parlance) has become standard in Air Force F-15 and F-16 squadrons and Navy and Marine F-14 and F/A-18 squadrons worldwide. It has radically altered the nature of air combat by making BVR engagements the rule rather than the exception and by substantially increasing the effectiveness of forward-aspect missile shots, especially against opposed aircraft not comparably armed.

COMPLETING THE SHIFT TO A CONVENTIONAL BOMBER FORCE

Well before the cold war ended, Strategic Air Command's (SAC's) leadership had come to recognize that the bomber force had more to offer than merely contributing to the nation's nuclear deterrent. Confirmation of this thinking was provided in 1988 by General John T. Chain, Jr., SAC's commander in chief (CINC), when he declared that SAC's bomber force "provided an existing asset which can significantly add to this nation's capability to conduct successful conventional operations."[19] Chain acknowledged that the main reason why SAC's bombers had not been thought of as conventional assets was because of their intimate and all-but-exclusive association with the nuclear mission. Yet in light of the Soviet conventional threat to NATO and such concepts as AirLand Battle and Follow-On Forces Attack (FOFA) described in Chapter 3, he saw a compelling rationale for employing bombers in theater war given the requirement for prompt power projection; the need for long-range, quick-reacting, and massed air-delivered firepower; and the ability of such firepower to narrow the numerical asymmetry between NATO and Warsaw Pact ground forces. He further cited the use of SAC's B-52s in a conventional role for eight years in Vietnam as a precedent for such an expanded mission set.

Three pillars of conventional wisdom, Chain wrote, would have to be knocked down before SAC's bombers could genuinely be said to have become a part of the nation's conventional force posture. The first was the deeply rooted notion that SAC's bombers had been built for nuclear use only. The second was that the term *strategic* meant "nuclear" and that SAC's bombers were exclusively tied to the nuclear mission. The third was that "theater" warfare was solely the domain of "tactical," or fighter, aircraft. In so characterizing the cold-war grip that had long hindered more creative thought about the conventional value of the bomber force, he spotlighted an

[19] General John T. Chain, Jr., USAF, "Strategic Bombers in Conventional Warfare," *Strategic Review*, Spring 1988, p. 23.

abiding deficiency in American thinking about air power more generally, namely, the tendency to use the term *strategic* to describe weapons and targets rather than actions and effects.

What finally prompted SAC's willingness to consider the idea of using bombers in a conventional role in high-intensity war was the growing concern over how best to halt echeloned waves of attacking Warsaw Pact armored forces across the North German Plain—or, in a different scenario, columns of Soviet tanks pouring down the mountain passes of northern Iran in a thrust to seize the oil fields of Southwest Asia. Because of their large weapons load, SAC's bombers were seen as offering considerable added value in such a disruption strategy. As early as 1988, the B-52G was configured to carry the tactical munitions dispenser, which allowed the aircraft to deliver a whole new family of submunitions. These included the combined-effects munition against soft area targets, air-delivered mines against surface lines of communication, the direct airfield-attack cluster munition (DAACM), and sensor-fused weapons like Skeet. Plans also were approved for the B-52G to carry the AGM-86 conventional air-launched cruise missile (CALCM) offering a precision attack capability analogous to that of the Navy's TLAM, only with considerably greater punch because of its larger warhead. The main problem with these employment options was that the aircraft lacked the needed survivability inside defended airspace to be operationally credible in that role.

It was only with the experience of Desert Storm that the potential of the bomber force for conventional operations became clearly evident. Once the coalition's repeated suppression of enemy air defenses (SEAD) had neutralized Iraq's radar-guided SAMs and opened up a medium-altitude sanctuary, B-52s were free to roam Iraqi skies more or less at will, dropping Mk 82 bombs by multiples of thousands on Iraqi troop positions. Within the first week of the war, SAC had committed 20 bombers to the joint-force air component commander (JFACC), with Schwarzkopf demanding still more. Yet still the bombers were wedded to a SAC mentality, and their crews were having difficulty getting bombs consistently on target. As the new CINCSAC, General George Lee Butler, later reflected, SAC's bombers by the end of Desert Storm "had achieved a proficiency level approaching that of the end of World War II."[20] He added, "At that point I understood something with absolute certainty. If we had to do the Persian Gulf six or seven years from now, and all SAC could do was come with B-52s and drop banded high-drags [i.e., bands placed around the retardation fins from World War II bombs to keep the fins from deploying] from 40,000 ft, then we would not be invited to participate."

---

[20] General George Lee Butler, USAF, "Disestablishing SAC," *Air Power History*, Fall 1993, p. 8.

Butler attributed this problem not only to the bomber's persistent connection to the nuclear mission but also to sac's continuing reluctance to consider anything else. Early during his tenure as c inc while the dust of Desert Storm was still settling, he concluded that "sac could never—in its current organization—be a fully competent conventional war-fighting organization." He further proposed to the Air Force chief of staff, General McPeak, that the time had come "to disestablish Strategic Air Command and meld its assets with tac [Tactical Air Command] to form a new Air Force warfighting organization." In light of sac's less-than-optimal integration with the rest of the Desert Storm air campaign, Butler said, "I finally came to the conclusion that at the core, Strategic Air Command was a nuclear outfit, had always been, was, and would always be. I knew that unless that perception changed, the air assets that traditionally had been assigned to sac would wither and be lost."[21] Butler affirmed that one of the opportunity costs of the cold war was that sac had been pigeonholed as a nuclear-delivery enterprise solely. He conceded that some B-52s had been released for conventional missions in Southeast Asia only after a "tremendously emotional" debate within sac. However, he added that once the Vietnam war was over, the bombers came home and went right back into the nuclear role, with the result that "virtually all that wartime experience was lost." Even his predecessor, General Chain, said Butler, had hit a brick wall in his effort to alter the complexion and orientation of the institution. Chain succeeded in getting 31 bombers committed to a conventional role and wanted to do more, but "the system wouldn't tolerate it."

Since the disestablishment of sac and tac in June 1992, major progress has been made in bringing Air Force bombers into the conventional role and making them a credible addition to the U.S. long-range strike capability. Whether this would have been possible had the Soviet-American nuclear competition persisted remains an open question. However, it also is a moot point. Under the new Air Combat Command, the time-honored usaf Fighter Weapons School has since been redesignated the usaf Weapons School, to include a B-52 and a B-1 division and regular participation of bombers in the school's biennial mission employment phase. The transition has not been entirely effortless, nor is it complete. Fighter and bomber aircrews still do not speak a common language or think in a common modality. Nevertheless, for the first time they are working together in mission planning and day-to-day operational training as respected and coequal partners in the air power equation.[22]

---

[21] Ibid., p. 4.

[22] For a detailed overview of the bomber force's potential contribution to a joint-force commander in future theater conflicts and the many trade-off issues involved in optimizing it for such application, see Glenn C. Buchan, "The Use of Long-Range Bombers in a Changing World: A Classical Ex-

As a result, the bomber force has brought significant growth to the nation's long-range strike capability. In late 1994, two B-1Bs and two B-52Hs conducted nonstop missions from their bases in North and South Dakota to Kuwait, where they dropped more than 50,000 lb of ordnance on derelict tanks and armored personnel carriers at a weapons range only 8 miles from the Iraqi border.[23] The B-1B is now assigned solely to conventional missions. After years of developmental trouble, it is now well down the road toward becoming the backbone of the future bomber force. Under the conventional munitions upgrade program, it has been configured to carry the entire family of cluster munitions, offering the aircraft great leverage against area targets and armored concentrations in permissive airspace. It also has been equipped with the ALE-50 towed ECM decoy to improve its survivability in low- to medium-threat SAM environments.[24] A single B-1B with a full load of 30 CBU-87s—more than five times the payload of an F-15E—offers an unrefueled combat radius of 1,500 to 1,700 nautical miles at fighter speeds for engaging soft targets, troop concentrations, tanks, and armored personnel carriers.[25]

OPERATIONAL CONCEPTS FOR THE POST–COLD WAR ERA

In parallel with the force drawdown that has so heavily affected U.S. air power since the end of the cold war, the services have implemented some important changes aimed at gaining greater leverage from their declining hardware assets. Not long after the Gulf war ended, the Air Force, in particular, eliminated many subordinate commands and reduced its number of major commands. Motivated by the success of the ad hoc "provisional" wings that had been cobbled together for specific combat needs in Desert Storm, it also moved to establish three so-called composite wings after the war at the instigation of its chief of staff at the time, General McPeak. The showcase example of that concept was the 366th Wing at Mountain Home AFB, Idaho, a unique organization with a mixed inventory of 36 "shooter" aircraft made up of B-1 bombers, F-15C air superiority fighters, and F-15E and F-16 ground-attack aircraft, along with an E-3 AWACS and

---

ercise in Systems Analysis," in Paul K. Davis, ed., *New Challenges for Defense Planning: Rethinking How Much Is Enough*, Santa Monica, Cal., RAND, MR-400-RC, 1994, pp. 393–450.

[23] See "B-1s, B-52s Conduct Kuwaiti Bombing Exercise, *Aviation Week and Space Technology*, November 7, 1994, p. 29, and William B. Scott, "B-1B Demonstrates Global Reach," *Aviation Week and Space Technology*, November 14, 1994, pp. 21–22.

[24] "Decoy Tested for B-1B," *Aviation Week and Space Technology*, June 30, 1997, p. 52.

[25] Captain Ronald P. Morrell, "Employing CBU-87s in the B-1," *USAF Weapons Review*, Winter 1996, p. 12.

several KC-135 tankers to provide combat support. The wing's assigned mission was to provide an air intervention capability, using solely its organic assets, for rapid response anywhere an American presence might be deemed important.[26]

McPeak's successor, General Fogleman, decided not to pursue the composite wing idea further because of its high cost and the added maintenance burden it imposed by having so many different types of aircraft assigned to a single unit. He disestablished two of the three composite wings initially set up by McPeak, namely, those that had been formed to provide dedicated air support to Army rapid deployment units. Fogleman deemed them unnecessary on the reasonable grounds that direct air support to allied ground operations had not been a significant requirement in Desert Storm and did not represent the likely face of future war. Because of its orientation toward force projection and indirect fire against fielded enemy ground forces, Fogleman saw the 366th as the only peacetime composite wing that made sense. More to the point, he used it as a conceptual baseline for a new and more flexible "air expeditionary force" (AEF) that could be built out of pieces from various different units for deployment on short notice as required.

Toward an Expeditionary Air Force

One of the more arresting lessons driven home by the Desert Shield deployment of forces that preceded the 1991 Gulf war was that the United States lacked a sufficiently agile capability for dealing with fast-breaking overseas challenges to U.S. security. Over time, recognition of that deficiency led to a perceived need for a more responsive mobility posture, eventually spawning an Air Force determination to think increasingly in expeditionary terms, or as some generals put it, in terms of "going rather than staying." The intent of the resulting AEF concept, largely a brainchild of then–Lieutenant General John Jumper while on assignment as the air commander for U.S. Central Command (CENTCOM), was to provide a force projection tool aimed at deterring and, if need be, halting aggression by blunting an enemy ground offensive that could be a prelude to an MRC.[27]

The AEF idea is, in a sense, a revival of the now all-but-forgotten Composite Air Strike Force, an almost identical concept developed and institutionalized in TAC's 19th Air Force for a time during the mid-1950s to deal with so-called brushfire wars before the nuclear commitment of TAC's fighters had become fully entrenched. In essence, the AEF seeks to provide

---

[26] General Merrill A. McPeak, USAF (ret.), *Selected Works 1990–1994*, Maxwell AFB, Ala., Air University Press, August 1995, p. 132.

[27] Much of the information presented in this section derives from Paul Killingsworth, "Enhancing the Effectiveness of Air Expeditionary Forces," briefing at RAND, Santa Monica, Cal., August 18, 1997.

the Air Force with a midway solution between fighting from permanent overseas bases, which are growing in increasingly short supply, and reliance on operating from the continental United States.[28] As envisaged in one of its earlier variants, a typical AEF might be composed of 35 to 40 aircraft drawn from three or four wings worldwide, including 6 bombers (B-52s, B-1Bs, or B-2s), 12 air-to-air fighters (F-15Cs or F-16Cs), 12 air-to-ground aircraft (F-15Es or Block 40 F-16CGs), and 6 SEAD fighters (Block 50 F-16CJs equipped with high-speed antiradiation missiles [HARMs]). Airlifters, consisting of up to 14 C-141s or C-17s, also would constitute an important part of the deployment package. The overall strike capability offered by such an entity would be somewhat greater than that provided by a single U.S. Navy carrier battle group. More important, it could establish a fighting presence in a threatened area far more quickly than a carrier could. (It goes without saying that at least minimal access to serviceable airfields in a prospective theater will be essential for the concept to work.) The envisaged goal is for an AEF to be ready to engage in combat within 24 to 48 hours of receiving an execute order and to continue surge operations for at least seven days, followed by withdrawal or augmentation thereafter.

The AEF concept remains in a developmental stage and has yet to be proved in combat. The cost-effectiveness of the concept also has yet to be assessed, and numerous questions bearing on its practicality remain to be answered satisfactorily. The latter concern the prerequisites for getting aircrews ready to deploy on short notice, securing overflight clearances, and putting bombs on target within a mere 24 hours of a deployment decision. Air base access presents yet another unsettled issue, as do the requirements for base preparation, unit reconstitution, logistics coordination, force protection upon arrival, and insurance of adequate command and control and information, surveillance, and reconnaissance (ISR) support. Even a 48-hour timeline, along with assembling a unit's personnel and equipment promptly upon arrival in the theater and configuring and generating aircraft for immediate combat employment, will be demanding in the face of such challenges.

That said, the Air Force took the major step in 1998 of reorganizing itself into 20 expeditionary wings spread over 10 corresponding air bases, with a view toward providing both greater deployment predictability and a more equitable spread of deployment burdens among its overstressed units and personnel than was ever achievable under the preexisting system of ad hoc reaction to shifting worldwide demands. Under the new arrangement, each AEF will be made up of some 250 aircraft, with around 75 of those deployed

---

[28] For an overview of the origins and early evolution of this thinking, see Colonel Brian E. Wages, USAF (Ret.), "The First with the Most: USAF's Air Expeditionary Force Takes the Offensive on Power Projection," *Armed Forces Journal International*, September 1996, pp. 66–71.

abroad as necessary to maintain an air presence and with such low-density/ high-demand aircraft as the B-2, F-117, and various surveillance and command and control assets like the U-2, AWACS, and joint surveillance target attack radar system (JSTARS) being kept at their bases in the United States for immediate on-call deployment as operational needs may demand. One account characterized this arrangement as "the biggest shift any branch of the armed services has made in an effort to adjust to the post–cold war world."[29]

If the now-maturing AEF concept is to be of use to a joint-force commander, it will have to demonstrate its ability to blunt an enemy ground push short of the enemy's objectives and hold the line during the ensuing buildup for more sustained combat operations. This, in turn, will require exploiting to the fullest the most recent advances in information availability and air-delivered firepower. It will further require acceptance by theater CINCs of an approach to joint warfare in which early "close" battle between opposed ground forces is supplanted by the use of friendly ground forces *not* to engage their enemy counterparts directly, but rather to cause a "heavying up" and consequent slowing down of enemy troops so they can be engaged in detail by air power, as was done during and after the battle of Al Khafji in Desert Storm.

With the right weapons load, Air Force bombers may be able to contribute materially to the halt phase directly from the continental United States while an AEF is being established in the theater. The latter will require prior achievement of local air control, as well as a negation of any nuclear or chemical weapons threats to rear-area air bases and air and naval ports of debarkation. It also will require adequate information availability and cueing through such assets as JSTARS, along with lethal firepower in enough numbers to make a difference. Ultimately, AEF exercises will need to be conducted routinely in peacetime to institutionalize the requisite support, build confidence among the theater CINCs in their potential, and demonstrate their deterrent and combat potential. Over the longer haul, with smaller and smarter munitions entering the Air Force's weapons inventory, desired effects may be achieved with fewer sorties, thus reducing both combat aircraft and lift requirements.

Navy and Marine Developments

Naval aviation likewise has undergone major organizational and doctrinal changes since Desert Storm. The end of the cold war clearly foreshad-

---

[29] Thomas E. Ricks, "Air Force to Reorganize into 10 Units, Marking Post–Cold War Strategy Shift," *Wall Street Journal*, August 3, 1999. See also Adam Hebert, "Air Force Set to Name 10 Air Wings as Lead Expeditionary Force Units," *Inside the Air Force*, February 12, 1999, p. 1.

owed an end to the Navy's long-standing focus on sea control. Virtually none of Desert Storm's combat characteristics bore even a remote relationship to the Navy's assumptions as reflected in its Maritime Strategy throughout the 1980s. There were no opposed surface naval forces or air threat to challenge the Navy's carriers, and naval air capabilities that had been developed for open-ocean engagements, such as the long-range AIM-54C Phoenix missile carried by the F-14 fleet defense interceptor, were of little relevance to the coalition's air-to-air needs—although admittedly the F-14s were not assigned to the choicest CAP stations because, having been equipped for the less crowded outer air battle in defense of the carrier battle group, they lacked the onboard target recognition systems that CENTCOM's rules of engagement required for the denser air traffic environment of Iraq.[30] As the former vice chairman of the Joint Chiefs of Staff (JCS), Admiral William Owens, put it bluntly, "For the Navy, more than any other service, Desert Storm was the midwife of change."[31]

Since there is no longer a credible open-ocean challenger to U.S. naval preeminence, the Navy leadership has adopted a new outlook in which planning for open-ocean engagements has been supplanted by a new focus on littoral operations. The amended doctrine that emerged from this ferment was codified in a Navy white paper promulgated in September 1992 called *"Forward . . . from the Sea."* That document placed major emphasis on power projection and explicitly envisioned U.S. naval forces as working jointly with Air Force and Army elements to control events ashore.[32] In this new approach, which reflects a fundamental shift from sea to land control, the underlying premise is that naval forces will concentrate primarily on influencing events on a joint battlefield. Part and parcel of it has been a shift in focus toward interoperability with other services, with the possibility of Army helicopters operating from Navy carriers being but one example. The prevalent view today, as the 1992 white paper's title suggested, is that naval forces will maneuver *from* the sea rather than *on* it. Importantly in this respect, Admiral Owens stressed that "naval aviation must see itself as a component part of the full air power the nation can bring to bear on military problems, especially in support of land and air campaigns."[33]

Partly in keeping with this new outlook and partly in response to short-comings identified during the 1991 Gulf war, the Navy has upgraded its

---

[30] James A. Winnefeld and Dana J. Johnson, *Joint Air Operations: Pursuit of Unity in Command and Control, 1942–1991*, Annapolis, Md., Naval Institute Press, 1993, p. 115.

[31] Admiral William A. Owens, USN (Ret.), *High Seas: The Naval Passage to an Uncharted World*, Annapolis, Md., Naval Institute Press, 1995, p. 4.

[32] On the origins and intent of that initiative, see the richly informed treatment by Captain Edward A. Smith, Jr., USN, "What ' . . . from the Sea' Didn't Say," *Naval War College Review*, Winter 1995, pp. 9–33.

[33] Owens, *High Seas*, p. 49.

precision strike capability by fielding new systems and improvements to existing platforms that have given it a degree of flexibility it lacked throughout Desert Storm. First among these has been the conversion of the venerable F-14 fleet defense interceptor into a true multimission combat aircraft through the incorporation of a LANTIRN (low-altitude navigation and targeting infrared for night) targeting pod, which now allows the aircraft to deliver LGBs both day and night. The Navy has modified 200 F-14s to carry the LANTIRN system, giving the aircraft a precision deep-attack capability and putting it in roughly the same league as that of the F-15E.

As for yet another deficiency highlighted in Desert Storm, naval aviation has since improved its command, control, and communications process so it can operate more freely with other joint air assets under the aegis of a single theater-wide Air Tasking Order (ATO). Notably, this includes having gained a long-needed ability to receive the ATO aboard ship electronically. In addition, the Navy has arranged for a more flexible mix of aircraft in a carrier air wing, which can now be tailored to a particular operational need, much like the Air Force's AEF concept. Under the new arrangement, carrier decks can be filled with aircraft flown in for contingency support within 24 hours, relying as needed on Air Force tankers en route. The Navy also learned from the less-than-optimal effectiveness of its attack assets in Desert Storm that being prepared to operate out of expeditionary airfields ashore whenever feasible can result in higher sortie rates and a higher ratio of combat-effective sorties than can be generated by operating off the ship.

The Navy's new look has also occasioned a closer integration of naval and Marine air assets that goes beyond the mere "coordination" that was the rule until recently. Marine air will henceforth be tied to a common operational game plan and tasked with working the same theater-level needs as the other services. This has demanded, in turn, a synergy of assets that can only be provided through physically blending naval and Marine air capabilities by putting Marine F/A-18s aboard carriers routinely. In what the Defense Department's 1996 annual report called "a new approach," F/A-18s, F-14s, AV-8s, and EA-6Bs of the Navy and Marine Corps have been placed into a common pool for satisfying the needs of specific deployments. Such integration has increased the flexibility of a JFACC to assign Navy or Marine combat squadrons to any suitable mission as needed and to spread the operations tempo burden more equitably between the two services.[34]

There also has been a growing Navy acceptance of the value of strategic air campaigns and the idea that naval air forces must be more influential players in them. As Admiral Owens stated, "The issue facing the nation's

---

[34] Perry, *Annual Report to the President and the Congress*, p. 172.

naval forces is not whether strategic bombardment theory is absolutely correct; it is how best to contribute to successful strategic bombardment campaigns."[35] The Navy well appreciates that its shortfall in available PGMs limited its effectiveness in Desert Storm. That gap has since narrowed considerably with the improvements to the F-14 noted earlier and by the equipping of more Navy and Marine F/A-18s with the ability to fire SLAMS. The Navy is slated to get JSOW in addition to SLAM for midrange precision strike, since SLAM is not effective against armor. Finally, the integration of Marine F/A-18 squadrons into carrier air wings not only has worked to improve the Navy's land-attack capability, but also has brought aboard ship a unique perspective on the uses of air power in land warfare, owing to Marine aviation's intimate connection to Marine infantry forces through its primary role as a supporting combat element in the Marine Air-Ground Task Force.

A New Rite of Passage over Bosnia

The first serious test of American air power in the post–cold war era was the successful conduct of U.S.-led NATO air strikes against Bosnian Serb forces in 1995 in support of UN peacemaking efforts in the Yugoslav civil war. The action that ultimately triggered NATO's response was a shelling attack against Sarajevo on August 28, 1995, which resulted in 38 civilians being killed. Confirmation of Bosnian Serb complicity in that attack led two days later to the unleashing of Operation Deliberate Force, an 11-day campaign of coordinated NATO air strikes against preapproved Serbian targets in Bosnia-Herzegovina. The purpose of the operation was to deter further Serbian attacks against declared UN safe areas and to respond as necessary to any such attacks until they ceased.[36]

The operation's essential elements had been preplanned over the preceding two months and fully coordinated among all scheduled participants. It took the shelling of Sarajevo, however, to give UN authorities the final impetus to action. The UN peacekeeping forces were moved out of threatened areas to give NATO air power the latitude it needed to engage the targets selected by NATO strategists. The main premise underlying and informing the air campaign was that fear of domination was the core vulnerability of the Bosnian Serbs. That, in turn, dictated an attack against their advantages,

---

[35] Owens, *High Seas*, p. 96.

[36] The most thorough available treatment of that operation is the final report of Air University's Balkans Air Campaign Study edited by Colonel Robert C. Owen, USAF, *Deliberate Force: A Case Study in Effective Air Campaigning*, Maxwell AFB, Ala., Air University Press, 1999.

notably their freedom to maneuver and their ability to supply their combatants, with the goal of transforming these into disadvantages.[37]

Operation Deliberate Force Scores a Win

The air campaign commenced at 0200 local time on August 30, with 43 allied strike aircraft attacking command and control sites, SAM and AAA sites, and supporting radar and communications facilities. The strike force was made up mostly of Air Force aircraft operating out of Aviano Air Base, Italy, with additional Navy and Marine aircraft from the USS *Theodore Roosevelt* on station in the Adriatic Sea. The declared intent of these initial attacks was to destroy all fixed and truck-mounted air defense positions in eastern Bosnia and to take down the Bosnian Serb IADS completely.[38] The target array was not, as the popular image of the fighting in Bosnia might have suggested, a rag-tag threat wielded by untutored rebels in a nasty civil war. It was a sophisticated Soviet-style IADS consisting of SA-2 and SA-6 radar-guided SAMs and AAA. It was operated, moreover, by former Yugoslav air defense professionals who had been trained to engage massed air attacks in the context of a major Warsaw Pact offensive and who knew from both radar and other sources where NATO's aircraft were at all times.

More than 300 strike and support sorties were flown during the first 24 hours, with attacks against 23 targets resulting in 90 weapon impacts. Among the most important early targets engaged were hardened Serbian underground command bunkers that had been designed for use during the cold war. These were taken out by F-15Es using GBU-10 2,000-lb LGBs. Later targets consisted of ammunition dumps, artillery positions, communications links, and supply storage areas, with a view toward reducing the Bosnian Serb army's ability to conduct further offensive operations. Additional targets included a number of key bridges used to support Bosnian Serb military activity, although without any underlying goal of destroying the entire Serbian infrastructure. AC-130 gunships and A-10s, along with the faster-moving fighters, worked selected aim points, with the AC-130 operating mainly at night against IADS and command and control targets. Serbian troop concentrations were kept strictly off limits, and there were highly restrictive rules of engagement beyond that.

For two days starting on September 2, NATO suspended the bombing in an attempt to test Serbian compliance with the alliance's demands. When none

---

[37] Lieutenant General Michael E. Ryan, USAF, "Deliberate Force: The Bosnian Air Campaign—Lessons for the Future," briefing at a conference titled "Canada's Air Power in the New Millennium" sponsored by the Canadian Forces Air Command, Winnipeg, Manitoba, Canada, July 30, 1997.
[38] Craig Covault, "Air Power Alters Bosnia Equation," *Aviation Week and Space Technology*, September 4, 1995, pp. 22–24.

was forthcoming, the attacks resumed on September 5. In a tactic highly reminiscent of what Israeli combined-arms forces did during the opening moments of the 1982 Bekáa Valley operation, air strikes against selected SAM and AAA emplacements were coordinated with artillery attacks by the UN Rapid Reaction Force, with NATO ground-based tactical air control parties providing that force with precise targeting data. As in Desert Storm, weather was a complicating factor in the air delivery of precision weapons, with thunderstorms topping out as high as 38,000 ft forcing an overall abort rate of 25 to 30 percent of all scheduled U.S. ground-attack sorties and 30 to 35 percent of those by other NATO participants. Nevertheless, the overall assessed average success rate of allied precision weapon attacks was around 60 percent, with the GBU-12 yielding the highest, at 76 percent.[39]

Portions of the Bosnian Serb IADS were sufficiently capable that NATO's air commanders and planners initially wanted to use the F-117 against the most demanding targets. Indeed, planning for the use of F-117s had progressed to the point where a detachment of the aircraft had begun taxiing to the runway at their home base at Holloman AFB, New Mexico, for deployment to the theater when the Italian government, at the last minute and highest level, denied permission for that high-profile U.S. asset to operate out of Aviano, in an understandable expression of pique over having been excluded from the so-called Contact Group despite all Italy had done to make its facilities available to UN and NATO forces.[40] NATO planners elected instead to use Tomahawk land-attack missiles against the most heavily defended IADS targets and standoff GBU-15 PGMs against the rest.

In all, roughly 70 percent of the weapons employed in Deliberate Force were LGBs and electro-optical guided bombs. Unguided munitions as well as Maverick and HARM missiles were also used, along with 13 Tomahawks that were targeted against several particularly well-protected Serbian IADS sites. The latter weapons were fitted with GPS receivers and other upgrades that rendered them more accurate than those employed during the Gulf war. In addition, Navy F/A-18s employed SLAMs to good effect.[41] After the campaign was terminated, 338 Serbian aim points spread over 56 discrete targets had been attacked by more than 600 precision weapons.[42] As in Desert Storm, the SEAD portion of the operation succeeded by intimidation in shutting down the Serbian IADS around Sarajevo and in much of the remainder of Bosnia. No radar-guided SAMs were fired after the operation be-

---

[39] "NATO Air Operations over the Balkans," SHAPE briefing charts, no date given.

[40] See Celestine Bohlen, "Italy Demands a Little Respect," *New York Times*, September 17, 1995, and Arturo Zampaglione, "Italy Blocks Stealth Fighters," *La Reppublica*, September 12, 1995.

[41] Craig Covault, "Precision Missiles Bolster NATO Strikes," *Aviation Week and Space Technology*, September 18, 1995, pp. 22–23.

[42] Rick Atkinson, "Deliberate Force," *Washington Post*, November 15, 1999.

gan, although NATO aircraft continued to draw fire from AAA and shoulder-fired infrared SAMS. [43]

Concern over collateral damage was extremely high, since even a single stray bomb resulting in a catastrophe on the ground would end instantly any UN confidence in NATO's ability to be precise. Accordingly, each weapon's desired mean point of impact (DMPI) was centrally controlled by the JFACC at Vicenza, Italy, with special attention given to such considerations as attack axis, time of day or night, aircraft system limitations, munitions capabilities, and possible secondary effects. Efforts were made as well to use the smallest weapon possible, such as a 500-lb rather than a 2,000-lb bomb, to minimize the undesired side effects of shrapnel and blast. Careful battle damage assessment (BDA) was conducted after each strike using a combination of mission reports, ground reports, cockpit video, postattack reconnaissance by U-2s and other air vehicles, and national imagery and signals intelligence (SIGINT). A senior U.S. intelligence officer later admitted that he had never seen better BDA results.

In the end, NATO's efforts to minimize unintended destruction paid off well. There were no Serbian complaints about noncombatant fatalities or other harm to innocents, since there was no collateral damage to speak of.[44] No civilians were reported to have died from the allied air attacks, and only a small number of Bosnian Serb military personnel were killed. In some cases, accuracy criteria were exacting enough that if a weapon did not hit within 7 ft of its target, it was not counted as mission-effective. The overall reported force effectiveness rate was 1.5 attack sorties flown and 2.8 PGMS expended per DMPI engaged, with 6.6 general-purpose bombs released per DMPI in the case of nonprecision attacks.[45]

In all, Operation Deliberate Force featured 3,515 sorties flown by 293 aircraft of eight NATO countries operating from 18 locations across Europe, along with the USS *Theodore Roosevelt* and, later, the USS *America*. Of that total, 750 were strike sorties. The majority of sorties flown (65 percent) were American. The remainder were flown mainly by the United Kingdom and France, with token participation by the Netherlands, Spain, Germany, Turkey, and Italy. Air tasking was conducted out of the NATO Combined Air Operations Center (CAOC) at Vicenza, with orchestration of the attacks from NATO AWACS aircraft and an EC-130 airborne command and control center.[46] Target detection, acquisition, and destruction proved to be more challeng-

---

[43] Barbara Starr, "NATO Strikes Strive to Stop Serb Shelling," *Jane's Defense Weekly*, September 9, 1995, p. 3.

[44] "NATO Air Forces Inflicted No Collateral Damage in Bosnian Air Campaign," *Inside the Air Force*, July 19, 1996, pp. 1–2.

[45] Ryan, "Deliberate Force: The Bosnian Air Campaign—Lessons for the Future."

[46] Craig Covault, "NATO Air Strikes Target Serbian Infrastructure," *Aviation Week and Space Technology*, September 11, 1995, p. 28.

ing than they had been in the Persian Gulf war. Nevertheless, the sensor and information systems that had worked so well in Desert Storm were more than adequate for enabling NATO air power to produce the results it did. The only aircraft lost during the 11-day operation was a French Mirage 2000D, which was downed by a shoulder-fired SA-7 infrared SAM while the fighter was operating at low altitude on the first day.[47]

This was NATO's first sustained air operation, as well as the largest military action to have taken place in Europe since World War II. Although limited in scope, it finally produced, after four years of unspeakable killing, a shaky truce in Bosnia that has persisted to this day. Operation Deliberate Force successfully achieved its designed objectives, including the restoration of safe areas from any threat of attack, the removal of offending heavy weapons, and the reopening of the Sarajevo airport and road access to Sarajevo for relief supplies. In so doing, it demonstrated that U.S. and allied air power possessed credible leverage for show-of-force roles short of war.

Measured against some of the earlier cases of air employment addressed in this study, Operation Deliberate Force did not constitute an especially historic event in the evolution of air power, even though it was no less effective than Desert Storm in helping to enable a strategic outcome on the ground. There were no surprises in its performance, and it did what it was expected to do once approved by the UN authorities. That said, as in the case of Israel's surprise attack on Iraq's nuclear reactor in 1981, it provided a textbook illustration of air power in action not to "win a war," but rather to achieve a discrete and important national goal. The result was a successful exercise in coercion. In underscoring the limited intent of the operation, General Fogleman stressed afterward that the aim of the NATO bombing was "not to defeat the Serbs, but simply to relieve the siege of UN safe areas and gain compliance with UN mandates and thus facilitate ongoing negotiations to end the fighting."[48]

In the end, the Bosnian Serb leaders acceded to NATO's demands by withdrawing specified heavy weapons from the Sarajevo exclusion zone. More important, the air attacks paved the way for the Dayton peace accords, which were initialled not long afterward on November 21 and signed in Paris on December 14. To be sure, it was not only allied air power but a confluence of other factors as well that ultimately drove the Bosnian Serb leadership to the negotiating table. The latter included increased allied artillery fire, the credible threat of a Croatian ground attack, and mounting diplomatic pressure and other sanctions. Nevertheless, Assistant Secretary of

---

[47] See "French Mirage Loss Highlights Threat," *Aviation Week and Space Technology*, September 4, 1995, pp. 22–23.

[48] General Ronald R. Fogleman, USAF, "What Air Power Can Do in Bosnia," letter to the editor, *Wall Street Journal*, October 11, 1995.

State Richard Holbrooke, who successfully negotiated the Dayton accords, later observed that although it had taken a Bosnian Serb outrage to trigger the launching of Deliberate Force in the first place, the air campaign had made a "huge difference" in helping to bring about an acceptable outcome.[49]

How the Bosnia Mission Almost Failed

However effective Deliberate Force may have been as an example of co-ercive diplomacy through air power, the main lesson to be recorded from it ought not be that achievement itself so much as the near-disastrous flirta-tion with failure that preceded it for more than two frustrating years of UN ineffectuality. That flirtation, reminiscent of every bad strategy choice the U.S. government made in Vietnam, should stand as a powerful reminder that however capable a tool modern air power may be, there is nothing pre-ordained about its ability to produce winning results.

Indeed, NATO air operations over Bosnia were only vindicated at the 11th hour by Deliberate Force. They began more than two years earlier with a hapless enterprise called Operation Deny Flight. That earlier operation, which commenced on April 12, 1993, entailed round-the-clock fighter pa-trols to enforce a declared no-fly zone, maintain a NATO air "presence," and provide on-call air support as needed in response to the unconscionable killing of innocents that the Yugoslav civil war had come to represent since it resumed, after more than three generations of quiescence under com-munism, in 1991.[50] Quite apart from the degradation in aircrew mission readiness they occasioned, owing to the many long hours spent merely bor-ing holes in the sky, those diffident and half-hearted sorties were, to all in-tents and purposes, pointless with respect to any tangible gain produced on the ground. Over the two years during which they occurred, they saw only limited contact with Bosnian Serb forces. For example, out of over 100 close air support (CAS) "presence" requests, only four authorized CAS attacks were conducted. There was a grand total of only five precision air strikes, one of which resulted in a temporary shutdown of a runway at Udbina by

---

[49] Richard Holbrooke, *To End a War*, New York, Random House, 1998, p. 104. The overarching ques-tion, however, remains whether that immediate outcome will translate into a long-term political settlement that vindicates the underlying policy motivation behind the air campaign. As in the case of Operation Linebacker II a generation ago, Operation Deliberate Force clearly coerced the oppo-nent to stop fighting and to agree to negotiate. As such, it offered resounding proof of air power's effectiveness when used with skill and determination. However, as a *Wall Street Journal* editorial noted two years later, whether the ensuing Dayton peace conference "was the result of statecraft or simply of shooting fatigue is open to interpretation. Whether Bosnia will see a lasting peace is an open question." "Korea's Hour," *Wall Street Journal*, August 5, 1997.

[50] Operation Deny Flight was preceded by Operation Sky Monitor, which, as its code name im-plied, was a passive NATO effort to follow the escalating Yugoslav civil war starting on October 16, 1992.

an attacking force of 30 NATO aircraft on November 21, 1994, in response to a launching of Serbian fighters from that airfield against Croatian targets inside a designated UN safe area.

Apart from that, as far as any practical effect it may have had on Serbian conduct, Operation Deny Flight was little more than a costly exercise in converting jet fuel into noise. As the commander of Allied Air Forces, NATO Southern Command, General Michael Ryan, later put it with studied tact, it entailed "a use of air power in a way we don't normally use air power," namely, under UN-imposed restrictions that were "very frustrating for us."[51] Among the many UN constraints that hampered the effective use of allied air power were a ban against attacking Serbian aircraft or air defenses at Udbina and UN authorization for NATO to engage only the Bosnian Serb air defense positions that had actually fired on NATO aircraft. In all, said General Ryan, the limitation of NATO air power to little more than "making noise" quickly inured Bosnian Serb leaders to the fact that NATO would not follow through on its repeated threats to unleash air strikes.

As a testament to the strategic amnesia that the UN's initial rules of engagement seemed to indicate, a British Sea Harrier was shot down near Gorazde within the first week of Deny Flight on April 16 by a handheld infrared SA-7 missile during the aircraft's third pass in a vain attempt to identify and destroy the single offending Serb tank that UN authorities had approved for attack. Because of a fatally flawed concept of employment, the aircraft's mission was ineffectual, its tactics were predictable, and its mode of use was in violation of every rule of rational force commitment that was consistently honored in Desert Storm.

The following year, in roughly similar circumstances, an Air Force F-16 was shot down by a radar-guided Serbian SA-6 on June 2 while orbiting in a by-then totally predictable high racetrack pattern southwest of Banja Luka. Subsequent indications suggested that the aircraft may have been lured into a trap. Bad enough, it was said not to have been equipped with the latest radar warning equipment. Worse yet, there were conflicting reports from the U.S. military about the extent of prior awareness of a SAM threat in the area, with the chairman of the JCS, General John Shalikashvili, stating that "we had absolutely no intelligence [of an active SAM threat]" and the Supreme Allied Commander in Europe, General George Joulwan, countering that the area had been a known "high threat environment" with an IADS.[52] Whatever the case, airborne U.S. electronic surveillance assets operating in the area reportedly acquired real-time indications of an active SA-6 tracking radar within range of the targeted aircraft but were unable to

[51] Ryan, "Deliberate Force: The Bosnian Air Campaign—Lessons for the Future."
[52] See "Washington Outlook," *Aviation Week and Space Technology,* June 12, 1995, p. 37. The F-16 pilot, Captain Scott O'Grady, was rescued a week later by a team of 40 Marines and a force of 40 mission and support aircraft.

communicate that awareness in sufficient time to prevent the shootdown. Secretary of Defense William Perry later conceded that he was "not satisfied . . . that we did the best job in transmitting and relaying the information to the person who most needed the information."[53] Immediately after the shootdown, NATO planners moved with alacrity to develop a credible counter-IADS attack option, and all subsequent Deny Flight missions were accompanied by SEAD assets. That scarcely lessened the fact, however, that the downing of the F-16 was an embarrassment to the United States and a setback for air power's hard-earned reputation for effectiveness.

During the weeks that ensued, recurrent allied threats to carry out air strikes in response to Serbian acts of aggression, followed by increasingly predictable backpedalling and inaction by the principal UN authorities, suggested that all involved at the highest levels had forgotten not only the United States's cardinal mistakes in Vietnam, but also the teachings of its remarkably successful use of air power in Desert Storm. In a reflection of the frustration felt by most American air commanders both on-scene and elsewhere, NATO's AWACS wing commander observed that during the more than two years of Operation Deny Flight, there had been no fewer than 5,300 recorded violations of the no-fly zone (albeit by helicopters), of which Air Force F-16s had downed only four Galeb light attack jets, one with an AIM-120 AMRAAM, in a single episode on February 28, 1994.[54] Even after Operation Deliberate Force was under way, signs of Vietnam-think continued to raise their head on occasion. For example, NATO aircrews were cleared to go after the runways and taxiways at the Udbina airfield, which they took out with pinpoint accuracy. Yet in a restriction highly evocative of the ban against attacking exposed SA-2 sites and MiGs in the Hanoi-Haiphong complex, they were directed to avoid the two dozen Serbian Galebs parked on the ramp.[55] When Deny Flight was finally concluded on December 20, after more than two years of UN effort to maintain an air "presence" over Bosnia, allied aircraft had flown 100,400 sorties, rivaling Desert Storm in total number.[56] Of these, however, a full third were passive CAP missions, with reconnaissance, in-flight refueling, command and control, and other support sorties accounting for another 30 percent.[57] Viewed in hindsight, only the 3515 sorties of Operation Deliberate Force, of which fully 70 percent were penetrating and directly combat-related, were counters as far as any practical payoff was concerned.

[53] Barbara Starr, "Deny Flight Shootdown May Put USAF on the Offensive," *Jane's Defense Weekly*, June 24, 1995, p. 24.
[54] Brigadier General R. T. Newell III, USAF, letter to the author, September 2, 1995.
[55] Ibid.
[56] A third of these were CAP missions and another 31 percent were designated as CAS. The remainder were mainly reconnaissance, airborne early warning, inflight refueling, and SEAD missions.
[57] Ryan, "Deliberate Force: The Bosnian Air Campaign—Lessons for the Future."

[6]

NATO's Air War for Kosovo

Between March 24 and June 7, 1999, the near debacle of Operation Deny Flight came close, at least for a time, to replaying itself out on a much grander scale. During that period, NATO, led by the United States, conducted an air campaign against Yugoslavia in an effort to halt the continuing human-rights abuses that were being committed against the citizens of its Kosovo province by Serbian strongman Slobodan Milosevic. As it turned out, that 78-day campaign, called Operation Allied Force, represented the third time in a row after Operations Desert Storm and Deliberate Force in which air power proved pivotal in determining a regional combat outcome during the 1990s. Yet notwithstanding its ultimate success, what began as a hopeful gambit for producing quick compliance on Milosevic's part soon devolved into a situation suggesting to many that those most responsible for the campaign had forgotten all they had learned—or should have learned—not only from Desert Storm and Deliberate Force but also from Vietnam. Among other things, Operation Allied Force was marred by repeated hesitancy on the part of both U.S. and NATO decisionmakers, some pronounced problems of mistrust between the United States and its NATO allies, a surprising incidence of interoperability problems between U.S. and other NATO air forces, and a potentially debilitating interservice conflict within the most senior command echelon of the U.S. contingent. All of that and more made NATO's air war for Kosovo a step backward in terms of efficiency when compared to Desert Storm.

The air campaign, essentially prompted by humanitarian concerns, had its origins in the steadily mounting Serbian atrocities against ethnic Albanians who made up the majority of Kosovo's population. The previous October, the Clinton administration had dispatched U.S. special envoy Richard

Holbrooke to Belgrade in a bid to persuade Milosevic to agree to negotiations on Kosovar autonomy and to accept a presence of international monitors on Kosovo soil. Milosevic assented to the negotiations and the monitors. Before long, however, the latter found themselves watching helplessly as the Serbian killing of Kosovar Albanians continued. In response, NATO declared this time that it would take all steps, including air strikes if necessary, to compel Serbian compliance in bringing about a settlement in Kosovo.

After two unsuccessful diplomatic attempts by the United States and NATO in February 1999 to induce Milosevic to desist, U.S. officials presented NATO's ambassadors in mid-March with a bombing plan that entailed a three-phase air campaign, yet expressly ruled out any backstopping by NATO ground forces. The first phase, intended to soften up Yugoslavia's integrated air defense system (IADS), would begin with suppression of enemy air defense (SEAD) missions and attacks on enemy command bunkers in Kosovo. The second phase envisaged attacks against military targets below the 44th parallel, which bisected Yugoslavia well south of Belgrade. Only in the third phase would the bombing, if need be, go after military facilities north of the 44th parallel and against targets in Belgrade itself. The plan's stated aim was to "reduce" Serbia's ability to continue abusing the Kosovars, with the declared goals of achieving a halt to Serbian ethnic cleansing in Kosovo; a withdrawal of all Serbian military, police, and paramilitary forces; the deployment of a NATO-led international peacekeeping presence; the return of all ethnic Albanian refugees and unhindered access by them to aid; and the laying of groundwork for a future settlement that would allow for Kosovar autonomy under continued Yugoslav sovereignty.

THE AIR CAMPAIGN

The operational setting of Yugoslavia contrasted sharply with that presented to coalition planners by Iraq in 1991. Defined by a series of interwoven valleys partly surrounded by mountains and protected by low cloud cover and fog, Serbia and Kosovo made for an arena smaller than the state of Kentucky (39,000 square miles), with Kosovo itself no larger than the Los Angeles metropolitan area. Its topography and weather promised to make for a unique challenge for NATO air power, compounded further by an enemy IADS that was guaranteed to make offensive operations both difficult and dangerous.

Yugoslavia's air defenses were dominated by an estimated 60 surface-to-air missile (SAM) batteries equipped with around 1,000 Soviet-made radar-guided SAMs, including the SA-2, SA-3, and SA-6, along with a profusion of man-portable infrared SAMs and some 1,850 antiaircraft artillery (AAA) pieces. Backing up these defenses, the Yugoslav air force consisted of 240 combat aircraft, including 15 MiG-29 and 60 MiG-21 fighter-interceptors. Although the Yugoslav air defense network fielded equipment that was at least 15 years old, its operators knew U.S. tactics well and had honed their techniques for more than four decades. They also had the benefit of more equipment and better training than the Bosnian Serbs had in 1995, and they maintained more-concentrated defenses than those wielded by Iraq in 1991. Before opening night, Pentagon planners were said to have estimated that NATO could lose as many as 10 aircraft in the initial wave of strikes.[1]

The campaign plan was conceived from the outset as a coercive operation only, with the implied goal of merely inflicting enough pain to persuade Milosevic to capitulate. It was expected by U.S. and NATO leaders that he would settle very quickly.[2] Indeed, so confident were those leaders that merely a symbolic bombing effort would suffice to persuade Milosevic to yield to NATO's demands that the initial attack was openly announced in advance, with U.S. officials conceding up front that it would take a day or more to program all of the Tomahawk land-attack missiles (TLAMs) to hit 60 planned aim points.[3]

Initial Attacks and Their Effects

Operation Allied Force commenced on the night of March 24. The first attacks were carried out solely by TLAMs launched by four U.S. ships, two U.S. submarines, and a British submarine in the Adriatic Sea and by AGM-86C conventional air-launched cruise missiles (CALCMs) launched by six Air Force B-52s flying outside of Yugoslav airspace. These cruise-missile attacks were followed by air strikes throughout the night against enemy air defenses. Targets included SAM batteries and radar and military communications sites in Kosovo and southern Serbia, plus a radar site at Podgorica, the capital city of Montenegro. Allied pilots were instructed to remain above an altitude floor of 15,000 ft at all times so as to take no chances with enemy infrared SAMs and AAA.

No SAMs were fired in self-defense the first night. However, numerous enemy fighters, including at least a dozen MiG-29s, were launched to intercept the attacking NATO aircraft. Two MiG-29s were downed by U.S. Air Force F-15Cs and one by a Royal Netherlands Air Force F-16. Only rarely did Serbian fighters rise to challenge NATO aircraft after that. In all, some 400 sor-

[1] Bruce W. Nelan, "Into the Fire," *Time*, April 5, 1999, p. 31.

[2] As Secretary of State Madeleine Albright declared in a television interview on the evening of March 24, "I don't see this as a long-term operation." Quoted in John T. Correll, "Assumptions Fall in Kosovo," *Air Force Magazine*, June 1999, p. 4.

[3] Jane Perlez, "U.S. Option: Air Attacks May Prove Unpalatable," *New York Times*, March 23, 1999.

ties were flown by NATO the first night. Of these, however, only 120 were actual strike sorties, which attacked a mere 40 Serbian targets all told.

Once it became clear that the air offensive was not having its hoped-for effect on Milosevic, NATO's military commander in chief, U.S. Army General Wesley Clark, received authorization from the North Atlantic Council, the political arm of NATO, to proceed to Phase II of the campaign, which entailed ramped-up attacks against a broader spectrum of fixed targets in Serbia and against fielded Serbian forces in Kosovo. Because of escalating Serbian atrocities on the ground, NATO went into this second phase of the campaign earlier than anticipated. Up to that point, the attacks had had no intended effect on Serbian behavior whatsoever. On the contrary, Serbia's offensive against the Kosovar Albanians intensified, with Serbian troops burning villages, arresting dissidents, and executing suspected Kosovo Liberation Army (KLA) supporters. It became increasingly clear that Milosevic's strategy was one of playing for time. The bombing campaign became a race between Serbian forces trying to drive the ethnic Albanians out of Kosovo and NATO forces trying to hinder that effort—or, failing that, to punish Milosevic badly enough to make him quit.

Despite the seeming escalation suggested by the campaign's shift to Phase II, the intensity of effort continued to average no more than around 50 strike sorties a night throughout the first week, in sharp contrast to the first week of Operation Desert Storm, in which the allied combat sortie rate had been as high as 1,000 a day. On top of that, more than half of the NATO aircraft launched against the few approved targets returned without any ordnance expended because of adverse weather in the target area.

After the second week, the focus of the campaign shifted from SEAD to interdiction, with predominant emphasis on Serbian lines of communication, choke points, storage and marshalling areas, and any tank concentrations that could be found. The attacks continued to be hampered by bad weather, Serbian dispersal tactics, and air defenses that were proving to be considerably more resilient than anticipated. In the absence of a credible NATO ground threat, which the United States and its NATO allies had ruled out from the start because of an assumed lack of popular willingness to accept casualties, Serbia's ground forces were able to survive the air attacks simply by dispersing and concealing their tanks and other vehicles.

By the end of the third week, out of unrelieved frustration over the campaign's inability to get at the dug-in and elusive Serbian troop positions, Clark requested that 300 more aircraft be committed to Operation Allied Force. That request, which would increase the total number of U.S. and allied aircraft assigned to the campaign to nearly 1,000, entailed more than twice the number of aircraft (430) that had been on hand when the campaign started on March 24—and almost half of what the allied coalition had had available to conduct the far more ambitious Operation Desert Storm eight years earlier. For the United States, it represented a 60-percent increase over the 500 U.S. aircraft already committed to the campaign.[4]

Earlier, Clark had asked for a more modest increment of 82 aircraft, which administration leaders granted without hesitation. This time, U.S. officials expressed surprise at the size of Clark's request and openly questioned whether it would be approved in its entirety.[5] The chief concern was that any increase of that magnitude would inevitably draw crucial assets, notably such low-density/high-demand aircraft as the E-3 airborne warning and control system (AWACS) and EA-6B Prowler, away from competing needs in the Persian Gulf and Korea. The service chiefs were said to have complained that Clark's requested buildup represented a clear case of overkill and that the U.S. European Command (EUCOM), which was conducting the U.S. portion of Operation Allied Force, was not making the most of the considerable assets already at its disposal.

As a part of his requested force increment, Clark also asked for a deployment of Army AH-64 Apache attack helicopters. Although Secretary of Defense William Cohen and the Joint Chiefs of Staff (JCS) eventually approved deployment of the other aircraft, they initially turned down the request for the Apache helicopters, on the avowed premise that since attack helicopters are typically associated with land combat, the introduction of any Apaches might be misperceived by the shakier allies as a precursor to a ground operation. A more serious, if unstated, concern was the survivability of the Apaches were they to be committed to combat in the still-lethal Serbian SAM and AAA environment. In the end, despite Army and JCS reluctance, Clark prevailed in his request for the Apaches and announced that 24 of them would be deployed to Albania. Pentagon spokesmen went out of their way, however, to stress that the Apaches were intended solely as an extension of the air campaign and not as any implied prelude to future ground operations.[6]

Meantime, in one of the first tentative strikes against enemy infrastructure, the main telecommunications building in Pristina, the capital city of Kosovo, was taken out by a cruise missile on April 8. Yet the campaign as a whole remained but a faint shadow of Operation Desert Storm, with only 28 targets throughout all of Yugoslavia attacked out of 439 sorties in one 24-hour period during the campaign's third week. As for the hoped-for "strategic" portion of the campaign against the Serbian heartland, NATO's

---

[4] Steven Lee Meyers, "Pentagon Said to Be Adding 300 Planes to Fight Serbs," *New York Times*, April 13, 1999.

[5] Elaine M. Grossman, "Clark's Firepower Request for Kosovo Prompts Anxiety among Chiefs," *Inside the Pentagon*, April 15, 1999, p. 1.

[6] Bradley Graham and Dana Priest, "Allies to Begin Flying Refugees Abroad," *Washington Post*, April 5, 1999.

political leaders still refused permission to attack the state-controlled television network throughout Yugoslavia.

Facing the Need for a Ground Option

Before the campaign was even a week old, indications began to mount that U.S. officials were starting to have second thoughts about the advisability of having peremptorily ruled out a ground option before launching into Allied Force. For example, the chairman of the JCS, Army General Hugh Shelton, remarked that there were no NATO plans "right now" to introduce ground troops short of a peace settlement in Kosovo.[7] In a similar hedged remark, Secretary Cohen pointed out that the Clinton administration and NATO had no plans to introduce any ground troops "into a hostile environment," leaving open the possibility that they might contemplate putting a ground presence into a Kosovo deemed "nonhostile" before the achievement of a settlement.[8] By the end of the second week, Secretary of State Madeleine Albright went further toward acknowledging Washington's growing appreciation of the attractiveness of a credible ground threat when she allowed that NATO might change its position and put in ground troops should the bombing succeed in creating a "permissive environment."[9]

Before long, however, a pronounced rift began to emerge between Clark and senior Pentagon authorities over Clark's insistence on stepping out aggressively toward undertaking concrete preparations for a NATO ground invasion. Despite their hedged comments, top Clinton administration decisionmakers continued to nurture hopes that the air campaign would eventually produce the desired response on Milosevic's part. Deep doubts that it would do so, however, prompted a steady rise in military support for developing at least a ground option, notably including support from many U.S. Air Force leaders involved in the campaign. By the start of the third week, a consensus had begun to form in Washington that ground forces might be needed, if only to salvage the increasingly shaky credibility of NATO.[10]

In advancing his case for a ground option, Clark acknowledged that his air commanders were no happier than he was with the absence of a NATO ground threat, noting how it was "sort of an unnatural act for airmen to fight a ground war without a ground component."[11] As the end of the campaign's

[7] Paul Richter, "Use of Ground Troops Not Fully Ruled Out," *Los Angeles Times*, March 29, 1999.

[8] Rowan Scarborough, "Military Experts See a Need for Ground Troops," *Washington Times*, March 30, 1999.

[9] Rowan Scarborough, "Momentum for Troops Growing," *Washington Times*, April 5, 1999.

[10] Dan Balz, "U.S. Consensus Grows to Send in Ground Troops," *Washington Post*, April 6, 1999.

[11] Michael Ignatieff, "The Virtual Commander: How NATO Invented a New Kind of War," *New Yorker*, August 2, 1999, p. 33.

second month approached, NATO finally appeared headed toward conceding at least the possibility of a land invasion, even though the Clinton administration would still not countenance even a hint of encouraging any public debate over the subject. In the end, the campaign's continued indecisiveness led Clinton, following the energetic lead of Britain's Prime Minister Tony Blair, to acknowledge for the first time that he would consider introducing ground troops if he became persuaded that the bombing would not produce the desired outcome. In clear contradiction to his earlier position on the issue, he asserted that he had "always said that . . . we have not and will not take any option off the table." That statement was later described by a U.S. official as testimony to an ongoing administration effort "to break out of a rhetorical box that we should never have gotten into."[12]

NATO *Finally Escalates*

As the campaign entered its fourth week, NATO's targeting efforts began to focus not just on fielded forces in Kosovo but also on what NATO officials had come to characterize as the four pillars of Milosevic's power—the political machine, the media, the security forces, and the economic system. New targets added to the approved list included national oil refineries, petroleum depots, road and rail bridges over the Danube, railway lines, military communications sites, and factories capable of producing weapons and spare parts.[13]

The first attacks against enemy radio and television stations in Belgrade took place on April 21, with three cruise missiles temporarily shutting down three channels after NATO had issued a warning to employees to vacate the buildings. With that escalation, NATO finally brought the campaign to Yugoslavia's political and media elite after weeks of hesitation, indicating that it was now emboldened enough to go directly after the business interests of Milosevic's family and friends. In the same attack, U.S. cruise missiles took out the offices of the political parties of Milosevic and his wife. Not long afterward, within two weeks of having attacked one of Milosevic's residences in Belgrade, NATO employed a 4,700-lb GBU-37 bunker-busting munition to attack another of his periodic retreats, this time the national command center, a multistory facility buried more than 100 ft underground.[14] Equipped with communications, medical facilities, living spaces, and enough food to last more than a month, it was designed to accommodate the entire Yugoslav general staff, top defense officials, and other civilian authorities.

---

[12] John F. Harris, "Clinton Says He Might Send Ground Troops," *Washington Post*, May 19, 1999.
[13] Eric Schmitt and Steven Lee Meyers, "NATO Said to Focus Raids on Serb Elite's Property," *New York Times*, April 19, 1999.
[14] Paul Richter, "Bunker-Busters Aim at Heart of Leadership," *Los Angeles Times*, May 5, 1999.

During the early morning hours of May 3, in possibly the most consequential attack of the campaign up to that point, Air Force F-117s dropped CBU-94 munitions on five transformer yards of Belgrade's electrical power grid, temporarily cutting off electricity to 70 percent of Yugoslavia. These munitions were similar to weapons delivered by TLAMs against the Baghdad electrical power network during the opening hours of Operation Desert Storm. The effects were achieved by means of scattered reels of treated wire that unwound in the air after being released as BLU-114/B submunitions, draping enemy high-voltage power lines like tinsel and causing them to short out. The declared intent of the attack was to shut down the installations that provided electrical power to the Yugoslav 3rd Army so as to disrupt military communications and confuse Serbian air defenses.[15] Very likely an unspoken intent was also to tighten the air campaign's squeeze on the Serbian political leadership and rank and file.

By the end of the seventh week, there began to be reports of Yugoslav officials openly admitting that the country was on the verge of widespread hardship due to the mounting damage that the campaign was doing to the nation's economy, which had already been weakened by almost four years of international sanctions imposed for Serbia's earlier role in the war in Bosnia.[16] The destruction of one factory in Krujevac that produced automobiles, trucks, and munitions resulted in 15,000 people being put out of work, plus 40,000 more who were employed by the factory's various subcontractors. Attacks against other factories generated similar effects on the Yugoslav economy. By the time the campaign had reached its halfway point, the bombing of infrastructure targets had halved Yugoslavia's economic output and deprived more than 100,000 civilians of jobs. Local economists reported that the effect was more damaging than that of the successive Nazi and allied bombing of Yugoslavia during World War II, when the country was far more rural in its economic makeup.[17]

Only during the final two weeks of the campaign did NATO finally strike with real determination against Serbia's electrical power–generating capability, a target set that had been attacked in Baghdad from the very first days of Desert Storm. The earlier "soft" attacks at the beginning of May with graphite filament bombs against the transformer yards of the Serbian power grid had caused a temporary disruption of the power supply by shorting out generators and disabling them rather than destroying them. This time,

[15] David A. Fulghum, "Electronic Bombs Darken Belgrade," *Aviation Week and Space Technology*, May 10, 1999, p. 34.
[16] Robert Block, "In Belgrade, Hardship Grows under Sustained Air Assault," *Wall Street Journal*, May 12, 1999.
[17] Steven Erlanger, "Economists Find Bombing Cuts Yugoslavia's Production in Half," *New York Times*, April 30, 1999.

on May 24, Belgrade's electrical power grid was severely damaged by high-explosive precision-guided munitions (PGMs). That attack affected the heart of the Yugoslav air defense network, as well as the computers that ran Yugoslavia's banking system. Until that peak in NATO's determination to bring the war home to the Serbian population, Clark later remarked, "This was the only air campaign in history in which lovers strolled down riverbanks in the gathering twilight and ate at outdoor cafes and watched the fireworks."[18]

Countdown to Capitulation

In what was initially thought to have been a pivotal turn of events in the campaign's effort against enemy ground forces, the KLA launched a counteroffensive on May 26 against Serbian troops in Kosovo. That thrust, called Operation Arrow, involved upward of 4,000 guerrillas, with the aim of driving into Kosovo from two points along the province's southwestern border and securing a safe route so that the KLA could resupply its beleaguered fighters. The attack was thwarted at first by Serbian artillery and infantry counterattacks, indicating that the Serbian army still had plenty of fight in it after 70 days of intermittent bombing by NATO. Three days after launching their assault, the rebels found themselves on the defensive, with some 250 KLA fighters pinned down by 700 Serbian troops near Mount Pastrik, a 6,523-ft peak just inside the Kosovo-Albanian border.

However, as the KLA's counteroffensive forced Serbian ground units to come out of hiding and marshal their forces to defend themselves, their movements were occasionally detected by allied sensors, even though enemy troops sought to maneuver in small enough numbers to avoid such detection. Allied sensor operators then transmitted the coordinates of suspected enemy troop concentrations to airborne forward air controllers (FACS) who, in turn, directed both unmanned aerial vehicles (UAVs) and fighters in for closer looks and ultimately for attacks on the Serbian units whenever possible.[19]

As the endgame neared, Russia's envoy to the Balkans, former Prime Minister Viktor Chernomyrdin, and Finnish President Martti Ahtisaari, representing the European Union, flew to Belgrade on June 2 and offered Milosevic a plan to bring the conflict to a close. Ahtisaari was brought into the process because allied leaders had been concerned that Chernomyrdin, operating alone, had not faithfully conveyed NATO's demands to Milosevic during his four previous visits to the Yugoslav capital. Two days later, the Yugoslav leadership accepted an international peace plan by

[18] Ignatieff, "The Virtual Commander," p. 35.
[19] Tony Capaccio, "JSTARS Led Most Lethal Attacks on Serbs," *Defense Week*, July 6, 1999, p. 13.

which it would accede to NATO's demands for a withdrawal of all Serbian forces from Kosovo, an unmolested return of the refugees to their homes, and the creation of self-rule for the ethnic Albanian majority that acknowledged Yugoslavia's continued sovereignty over Kosovo. The draft plan stipulated that once all occupying Serbian personnel had departed Kosovo, an agreed contingent of Serbs, numbering in the hundreds only, could return to provide liaison to the various peacekeeping entities, help clear the minefields that they had laid earlier, and protect Serb interests at religious sites and border crossings.

No sooner had this accord been reached in principle when NATO and Yugoslav representatives failed to agree on the terms for Serbian withdrawal. The talks degenerated into haggling over when NATO would terminate its air attacks and whether Belgrade would have more than a week to get its troops out of Kosovo. That breakdown suggested that the Serbs were looking for more time to continue their battle against the KLA. In response to this willful foot-dragging, NATO's attacks, which had been scaled back after Milosevic initially accepted the proposed plan, resumed their previous level of intensity.

At the same time, on June 7, Serbian forces launched a redoubled attack against the KLA in an area south of Mount Pastrik where they had been locked in an artillery duel since May 26. This time, owing to improved weather, a noticeable degradation of Serbian air defenses, and the effective role that the KLA had apparently played in forcing Serbian forces to come out of hiding, two B-52s and two B-1Bs dropped a total of 86 Mk 82s and cluster bombs on an open field in a daytime raid near the Kosovo-Albanian border where the enemy troops were thought to have been massed. The estimated number of Serbian troops was 800 to 1,200, with initial assessments suggesting that fewer than half of those had survived the attack.[20] Although that assessment was not immediately confirmed, the Serbian counteroffensive against the KLA came to a halt after that raid, which the Pentagon later called the single heaviest air attack against fielded enemy forces in the entire campaign.[21]

In the end, Yugoslavia acceded to an agreement authorizing a presence of 50,000 international peacekeepers commanded by a NATO general and with sweeping occupation powers over Kosovo. After 78 days of bombing, the agreement was signed on June 9, after which NATO ceased its attacks upon confirming that the Serbian withdrawal had begun. The UN Security Council then approved, by a 14 to 0 vote with China abstaining, a resolution putting Kosovo under international civilian control and the peacekeeping

---

[20] William Drozdiak, "Yugoslav Troops Devastated by Attack," *Washington Post*, June 9, 1999.
[21] R. Jeffrey Smith and Molly Moore, "Plan for Kosovo Pullout Signed," *Washington Post*, June 10, 1999.

force under UN authority. With that, President Clinton declared that NATO had "achieved a victory."[22]

WHY MILOSEVIC GAVE UP

As one might have predicted, disagreements arose after the cease-fire went into effect over which of the campaign's target priorities (fielded forces or infrastructure assets) was more crucial to producing the outcome. Contention also arose over the more basic question of the extent to which the air campaign as a whole had been the causal factor behind Milosevic's capitulation. On the one hand, there were those air power proponents of known views who were wont to conclude up front that "for the first time in history, the application of air power alone forced the wholesale withdrawal of a military force from a disputed piece of real estate."[23] On the other hand, there was the more skeptical view offered by the commander of the international peacekeeping forces in Kosovo, British Army Lieutenant General Sir Michael Jackson, who suggested that "the event of June 3 [when the Russians backed the West's position and urged President Milosevic to surrender] was the single event that appeared to me to have the greatest significance in ending the war." Asked about the effects of the air campaign, Jackson, an avowed critic of air power, replied tartly, "I wasn't responsible for the air campaign; you're asking the wrong person."[24]

Whatever the answer to the more narrow question about target priorities may turn out to be once the detailed force effectiveness assessments are completed, there is good reason to be wary of the broader intimation that air power all by itself swung the outcome in Belgrade. True enough, one can insist that air power "made it work" in the tautological sense that the campaign was an air-only operation and that in its absence, Milosevic's ethnic cleansing of Kosovo would undoubtedly have continued unimpeded.[25] Yet in all likelihood, numerous factors besides the direct effects of the air campaign interacted to produce the Serbian dictator's eventual decision to yield to NATO's demands.

For one thing, beyond the obvious damage that the air attacks had caused and the equally obvious fact that NATO could have continued bombing indefinitely and with virtual impunity, another possible element was the fact that the sheer depravity of Serbia's conduct in Kosovo had stripped it of

---

[22] Tim Weiner, "From President, Victory Speech and a Warning," *New York Times*, June 11, 1999.

[23] John A. Tirpak, "Lessons Learned and Re-Learned," *Air Force Magazine*, August 1999, p. 23.

[24] Andrew Gilligan, "Russia, Not Bombs, Brought End to War in Kosovo, Says Jackson," *London Sunday Telgraph*, August 1, 1999.

[25] Rebecca Grant, "Air Power Made It Work," *Air Force Magazine*, November 1999, pp. 30–37.

[191]

any remaining vestige of international support, including from its principal backers in Moscow in the end. On top of that was the added sense of walls closing in that must have been prompted by Milosevic's indictment as a war criminal by a UN tribunal only a week before his loss of Moscow's political support. Yet a third factor may have been mounting elite pressure behind the scenes. As the campaign began encroaching ever closer on Belgrade proper, Secretary Cohen reported that Serbian military leaders had begun sending their families out of Yugoslavia, following a similar action earlier by members of Yugoslavia's political elite and reflecting possible concerns among senior commanders that Milosevic had led them down a blind alley.[26] A related factor may have been mounting heat from Milosevic's cronies among the Yugoslav civilian oligarchy, prompted by the continued bombing of utilities and other infrastructure targets in and around Belgrade in which they had an economic stake and whose destruction increasingly threatened to bankrupt them.[27]

After all is said and done, we may *never* know for sure what dynamic ultimately caused Milosevic to admit defeat. Yet of all the considerations that ultimately converged to produce Milosevic's capitulation, the most discomfiting over the long haul may well have been what he perceived, rightly or wrongly, to have been the prospect of an eventual NATO ground intervention of some sort. Whatever NATO's declaratory stance on the ground-war issue may have been, its actions as the campaign progressed spoke louder than its words. A 32,000-strong NATO Stabilization Force, soon to number 50,000, patrolling Bosnia-Herzegovina and 7,500 additional NATO troops in Albania deployed to perform humanitarian work there made for an undeniable signal that a NATO ground presence of more than token size was forming in the theater. That presence included 2,200 combat-ready U.S. Marines aboard warships in the Adriatic and 800 more headed to Hungary to provide force protection for the Marine F/A-18s and Air Force A-10s that were operating out of the former Warsaw Pact air base at Taszar. There is every reason to believe that NATO's decision to enlarge the Kosovo peacekeeping force (KFOR) to as many as 50,000 troops was assessed by Milosevic as an indication that all options were being kept open. Such concern could only have been heightened by the unexpected role played by the KLA during the last two weeks of the campaign in driving Serbian troops out of hiding and making them more lucrative targets for NATO aircraft.

Taking advantage of a covert relationship between the Central Intelligence Agency (CIA) and the KLA, NATO had begun probing the capability

[26] Daniel Williams and Bradley Graham, "Milosevic Admits to Losses of Personnel," *Washington Post*, May 13, 1999.
[27] Paul Richter, "Officials Say NATO Pounded Milosevic into Submission," *Los Angeles Times*, June 5, 1999.

and extent of Serbia's ground defenses, an inquiry that very likely did not escape Milosevic's attention. In a related development, NATO engineers on May 31 began widening and reinforcing a key access road from Durres to Kukes on the Kosovo-Albanian border so that it could support the weight of a main battle tank. Earlier, Clark had authorized the engineers to strengthen the road to handle refugee traffic only, but they made it strong enough to support the Bradley armored fighting vehicle (AFV). This time, only three days before Milosevic finally called it quits, Washington gave Clark approval to send in another engineering battalion to make the road capable of supporting M1A2 Abrams tanks and artillery.[28]

Beyond that, Milosevic may have gotten wind of a secret NATO plan for a massive ground invasion code-named Plan B-minus, which was slated to be launched the first week of September if NATO's political leaders approved. In support of this plan, Britain had agreed to contribute the largest single national component (50,000 troops) to the envisaged 170,000-strong personnel contingent. Developed by a secret planning team at NATO's military headquarters in Mons, Belgium, Plan B-minus relied heavily on previous plans going back to June 12, 1998, which featured six land-attack options, including a full invasion of Serbia itself (Plan Bravo, with 300,000 NATO troops). The chief of Britain's defense staff, General Sir Charles Guthrie, later confirmed the outlines of this plan.[29]

Moreover, earlier on the same day that Milosevic eventually capitulated, President Clinton held a widely publicized meeting with his service chiefs for the express purpose of airing options for land force employment in case NATO decided it had no choice but to approve a ground invasion.[30] Immediately after that meeting, which left the issue unresolved, Clinton was said to have been planning to inform the chiefs that he was now ready to agree to a ground invasion should developments leave no alternative.[31] Clark later disclosed that Milosevic had ample intelligence to that effect, as well as "all the indicators that would have made him conclude that we were going in on the ground."[32]

In the end, Milosevic probably opted to accept NATO's demands simply out of a rational calculation that he had nothing to gain by holding out any longer. A ground invasion, whether or not it was immediately in the cards, could have meant Serbia's loss of Kosovo for good, posing the direst threat

---

[28] Dana Priest, "A Decisive Battle That Never Was," *Washington Post*, September 19, 1999.

[29] Patrick Wintour and Peter Beaumont, "Revealed: The Secret Plan to Invade Kosovo," *London Sunday Observer*, July 18, 1999.

[30] Jane Perlez, "Clinton and the Joint Chiefs to Discuss Ground Invasion," *New York Times*, June 2, 1999.

[31] For details, see Steven Erlanger, "NATO Was Closer to Ground War in Kosovo Than Is Widely Realized," *New York Times*, November 7, 1999.

[32] Priest, "A Decisive Battle That Never Was."

to Milosevic's political, and possibly even personal, survival. Even in the continued absence of a NATO ground assault, he knew that the air campaign could have continued for many more weeks, and even indefinitely if need be. In contrast, acceding to NATO's demands while there was still time allowed Milosevic to exploit the face-saving opportunity of claiming that the Yugoslav government would retain sovereignty over Kosovo, whatever autonomy might be granted to its ethnic Albanian majority.

AIR POWER'S ACCOMPLISHMENTS

Operation Allied Force was the first air campaign in which all three types of currently deployed U.S. heavy bombers saw combat use. Of some 700 combat aircraft committed to the campaign altogether, a mere 21 Air Force heavy bombers (10 B-52s, 5 B-1s, and 6 B-2s) dropped 11,000 out of the 23,000 bombs and missiles that were expended during the campaign's 78-day course.[33] Also of major note, the first night saw the long-awaited combat debut of the Air Force's B-2 stealth bomber, which flew nonstop to its targets directly from Whiteman AFB, Missouri, on 30-hour round-trip missions in its final Block 30 configuration. Each B-2 delivered up to 16 global positioning system (GPS)–guided GBU-31 joint direct-attack munitions (JDAMS) from 40,000 ft, usually through cloud cover, against hardened enemy targets, including command bunkers and air defense facilities.

To the surprise of many, the B-2 turned out to be the most consistently effective performer of the entire air campaign. Supported by EA-6B jamming, as were all other NATO combat aircraft that flew into hostile airspace, it was the first manned platform to penetrate Serbian air defenses the first night.[34] In addition to its normal load of JDAMS, the B-2 also carried the GPS-guided GBU-37 for special missions against deeply buried or superhardened targets.[35] In only 45 missions all told, the B-2 flew fewer than 1 percent of the total number of combat sorties in Allied Force, yet it dropped a full third of all the precision munitions expended during the campaign. It also proved

---

[33] David Atkinson, "B-2s Demonstrated Combat Efficiency over Kosovo," *Defense Daily*, July 1, 1999, p. 1. The parent 509th Bomb Wing based at Whiteman AFB, Missouri, had only six B-2s available for Kosovo, a number deemed sufficient to meet EUCOM's mission tasking. Nine of the total number of 21 B-2s were at Whiteman, but one was kept aside for training, one was undergoing upgrades, and one was in extensive maintenance, with the remainder completing their upgrades to the aircraft's definitive Block 30 status. Two flew on 15 nights and a single aircraft flew on 19 nights. "Missouri-to-Kosovo Flights for B-2 Not a Concern to Wing Commander," *Inside the Air Force*, July 2, 1999, p. 12.

[34] Dale Eisman, "Over Balkans, It's Beauty vs. the Beast," *Norfolk Virginian-Pilot*, April 26, 1999.

[35] Adam Hebert, "Air Force Follows Roadmap in Employment of Bombers against Serbia," *Inside the Air Force*, April 2, 1999, p. 2.

itself capable of operating effectively above weather that grounded all other allied combat aircraft.[36]

Once Serbia's air defenses became less of an ever-present threat, the campaign saw a heightened use of B-52s, B-1s, and other aircraft carrying unguided bombs. By the end of May, some 4,000 free-fall bombs, around 30 percent of the total number of munitions expended by heavy bombers altogether, had been dropped. They included the Mk 82 500-lb general-purpose bomb and the CBU-87 cluster bomb. In contrast to the indiscriminate carpet bombing that was all the B-52 could accomplish from high altitudes with free-fall bombs both over Vietnam and during Operation Desert Storm, the B-1 repeatedly demonstrated a capability to drop cluster munitions within a footprint only 1,000 ft long against enemy barracks and other military area targets.

More than in any previous air operation, UAVs were used in Allied Force for combat support, most notably for locating mobile SAMs, Serbian troop concentrations, and enemy aircraft parked in the open. Some were flown as low as 1,000 ft above Serbian troop positions to gather real-time imagery, which periodically enabled prompt attacks by Air Force A-10s and F-16s against often fleeting targets. Several were lost when commanders requested closer looks at such positions, forcing the drones to descend into the lethal envelopes of Serbian AAA and man-portable air defense systems (MANPADS). These losses did not evoke much concern, however, since the UAVs had been intentionally sent out on missions known beforehand to be especially dangerous. Despite the losses, UAVs offered EUCOM air commanders and planners the advantage of close battlespace awareness without any accompanying danger of incurring aircrew casualties.[37]

In the final tally, allied aircrews flew 37,465 sorties, of which 14,006 were said to have been strike sorties.[38] One-third of the 23,000 munitions expended were general-purpose Mk 82 unguided bombs dropped by B-52s and B-1s during the campaign's last two weeks. Between 3,000 and 5,000 of these munitions were delivered against some 500 fixed targets in Serbia and Montenegro. The remainder were dropped on what were thought to be fielded enemy forces in Kosovo. In a telling reflection of the extent of allied determination not to lose a single aircrew member, some 35 percent of the overall air effort was directed against enemy air defenses. Owing largely to that, only two allied aircraft were downed and not a single friendly fatality was incurred.

---

[36] Paul Richter, "B-2 Drops Its Bad PR in Air War," *Los Angeles Times,* July 8, 1999.

[37] "Despite Losses, Backers Say Unmanned Systems Excelling Over Kosovo," *Inside the Pentagon,* June 10, 1999, p. 1.

[38] General Wesley K. Clark, USA, "When Force Is Necessary: NATO's Military Response to the Kosovo Crisis," *NATO Review,* Summer 1999, pp. 16, 18.

FRICTION AND PROBLEMS ENCOUNTERED

Although air power prevailed in the end, some troubling questions arose well before the campaign's favorable outcome about the way in which it was conducted and about some operational problems that were encountered along the way. In one of the first disappointments, NATO analysts were unable at the end of the third week to confirm the destruction of a single tank or military vehicle, owing to the success of Serbian forces in dispersing and concealing their armor. That disappointment underscored the limits of conducting an air campaign against fielded enemy forces in wooded and mountainous terrain and in poor weather from above 15,000 ft and in the absence of any supporting allied ground threat. Had Serbian commanders any reason to fear a NATO ground invasion, they would have had little alternative but to position their tanks to cut off roads and other avenues of attack, thus making their forces predictable and targetable by NATO air power. Instead, having dispersed and hidden their tanks and armored personnel carriers (APCs), Serbian army and paramilitary units, with just 20 or more troops in a single truck, were free to go in to terrorize a village in connection with their ethnic cleansing campaign.

After the dust settled in early June, a preliminary NATO postmortem concluded that the air campaign had had almost no effect on Serbian military operations in Kosovo. The initial conclusion of NATO bomb-damage experts who went into Kosovo after the arrival of the KFOR peacekeeping force was that "only a handful" of enemy tanks, APCs, and artillery pieces had been damaged.[39] Moreover, the use of joint surveillance target attack radar system (JSTARS) and airborne infrared sensors to locate enemy tanks and other military vehicles that had worked so well in Desert Storm turned out to have been largely inapplicable in the very different setting of Kosovo. Once safely dispersed, Serbian army units turned off the engines of their tanks and other vehicles to save fuel; hid their vehicles in barns, churches, forests, and populated areas; hunkered down; and hoped to wait the air campaign out.

In the later aftermath of Allied Force, on-site surveys of bomb-damage effects by KFOR observers and other inspectors seemed to confirm that NATO's attacks against enemy ground forces accomplished considerably less than what had initially been thought, including at Mount Pastrik.[40] In its final tally as Operation Allied Force ended, the U.S. Defense Department settled on the number of destroyed tanks, APCs, and artillery pieces in Kosovo as

[39] Tim Butcher and Patrick Bishop, "NATO Admits Air Campaign Failed," *London Daily Telegraph*, July 22, 1999.
[40] Richard J. Newman, "The Bombs That Failed in Kosovo," *U.S. News and World Report*, September 20, 1999.

being 700 out of a total of 1,500.[41] However, nothing like a matching number of hulks was found by allied inspectors after the campaign ended. During their withdrawal, the Serbs took hundreds of tanks, artillery pieces, and APCs out of Kosovo. They also seemed spirited and defiant rather than beaten.

Although NATO initially claimed after the campaign was over that it had disabled 150 of the estimated 400 Serbian tanks in Kosovo, Clark later scaled that claim back to 110 disabled tanks after having determined that many tanks assumed to have been destroyed were, in fact, decoys that the Serbs had skillfully employed in large numbers. Another source spoke of aircraft head-up display videotapes showing targets with every appearance of being tanks and SAM sites collapsing instantly upon being hit.[42] The Serbs fielded numerous tank decoys made of milk-carton material. They also used wood-burning stoves with their chimneys angled to mimic artillery pieces. In some cases, water receptacles were found in the decoys, cleverly placed there to heat up under the sun to help replicate the infrared signature of a vehicle or hot artillery tube.[43]

These problems in what allied air planners called "flex targeting" of enemy ground forces, however, were more a predictable result of prior strategy choices than a reflection of any inherent deficiencies in the air weapon itself. Of more serious concern were other identified problems that indicated needed fixes in the realm of equipment, tactics, and operating practices. Those that aroused the greatest consternation were assessed deficiencies in the SEAD campaign, excessively lengthy information and intelligence cycle time, the unacceptably high incidence of inadvertent civilian casualties, and some serious revealed shortcomings in alliance interoperability. Also of special concern were the many problems spotlighted by the Army's plagued deployment of its Apaches to Albania and the full extent of U.S. overcommitment that the air campaign experience brought to light.

Frustrations of the SEAD Campaign

In contrast to the far more effective SEAD experience in Desert Storm, the initial effort to suppress Yugoslav air defenses in Allied Force did not go nearly as well as expected. The Serbs kept most of their SAMs hidden with

[41] Rowan Scarborough, "Pentagon Intends to Issue Final Count of Serbian Losses," *Washington Times*, July 9, 1999.

[42] Joseph Fitchett, "NATO Misjudged Bombing Damage," *International Herald Tribune*, June 23, 1999.

[43] Paul Richter, "U.S. Study of War on Yugoslavia Aimed at Boosting Performance," *Los Angeles Times*, July 10, 1999.

their radars not emitting, prompting concern that they were attempting to draw NATO aircraft down to lower altitudes where they could be more easily engaged. Because of that inactivity, it was not clear at the outset whether the communications links of the Serbian air defense net had been destroyed or whether Serbian SAM operators were intentionally husbanding their assets.[44] Either way, the enemy's refusal to make its SAMs cooperative targets forced allied aircrews to remain constantly alert to the radar-guided SAM threat throughout most of the air campaign, even as that altitude gave them a comfortable sanctuary against AAA and MANPADS threats.

As noted earlier, no SAMs were launched against attacking NATO aircraft the first night. The second night, a single SA-6 was fired but failed to score a hit. Later during the campaign, enemy SAMs were frequently fired in large numbers, with dozens hosed off in salvo fashion on some nights followed by only a few SAM launches on others. Although these unguided launches constituted more a harassment factor than any serious challenge to NATO operations, numerous times allied pilots were forced to jettison their fuel tanks to evade enemy SAMs in circumstances in which chaff employment had failed to negate the attack.[45] A common Serb tactic was to fire on the last aircraft in a departing strike formation, perhaps on a presumption that those aircraft would be unprotected by other fighters, flown by less-experienced pilots, and low on fuel with a limited ability to counter-maneuver.

The persistence of a credible SAM threat throughout the air campaign meant that NATO had to dedicate a larger-than-usual number of strike sorties to the SEAD mission to ensure reasonable freedom to operate in enemy airspace. That, in turn, meant fewer sorties for NATO mission planners to allocate against Yugoslav military and infrastructure targets. From the very start of the campaign, Serbian air defenders sought to sucker NATO aircrews down to lower altitudes to address mission objectives on the ground so that they could be brought within the lethal envelopes of widely proliferated MANPADS and AAA systems.

One of the biggest problems to confront attacking NATO aircrews on defense-suppression missions was target location. Because of the mountainous terrain, the moving target indicator and synthetic aperture radar aboard the E-8 JSTARS did not work well at oblique angles, nor did the sensors carried by the U-2 and RC-135 Rivet Joint electronic intelligence aircraft. The cover provided to enemy air defense assets by the interspersed mountains and valleys made for a severe complicating factor in that it allowed defending SAM and AAA units to lay low, set up a trap for unsuspecting NATO aircraft, and then shoot and quickly duck behind a ridgeline and disappear.

---

[44] Dana Priest, "NATO Unlikely to Alter Strategy," *Washington Post*, March 26, 1999.
[45] Richard J. Newman, "In the Skies over Serbia," *U.S. News and World Report*, May 24, 1999, p. 24.

Efforts to attack the internetted communications links of the Yugoslav IADS were hampered by the latter's extensive network of underground command sites, buried land lines, and mobile communications centers. Using what was called fused radar input, which allowed the acquisition and tracking of NATO aircraft from the north and the subsequent feeding of the resulting surveillance data to air defense radars in the south, the internetting enabled the southern Sector Operations Center to cue defensive weapons without having an active radar anywhere nearby. That may have accounted, at least in part, for why the F-16CJ and EA-6B were often less than ideally effective as SAM killers, since both employed the high-speed antiradiation missile (HARM) to home in on enemy radars that normally operated in close proximity to SAM batteries.[46] Whenever Serbian SAM operators activated their fire-control radars, they made themselves susceptible to being attacked by a HARM. For that reason, the use of fire-control radars by the Serbian air defense net was only sporadic at best, with the result that most HARM shots were reactive rather than preplanned.[47]

Whenever available intelligence permitted, the preferred offensive tactic entailed going for hard kills against enemy SAM sites using the Block 40 F-16CG and F-15E carrying laser-guided bombs (LGBs) and cluster bomb units (CBUs) rather than merely suppressing SAM activity with the F-16CJ and HARM. The problem with these so-called DEAD (destruction of enemy air defense) attacks was that the data cycle time had to be short enough so that the attackers could catch the emitting radars before they moved on to new locations. One report observed that Air Force F-16CJs were relatively ineffective in the reactive SEAD mode, since they orbited so far away from known SAM sites that the time required for them to detect an impending launch and get a timely HARM shot off exceeded the flyout time of the SAM aimed at the targeted aircraft.[48] As a result, whenever attacking fighters found themselves engaged by a SAM, they were pretty much on their own in defeating it.

In all, some 700 SA-3 and SA-6 SAMs were estimated to have been fired at NATO aircraft over the course of the campaign, many of those ballistically without any radar guidance. The dearth of enemy radar-guided SAM activity may have been explainable, at least in part, by reports that the Air Force's Air Combat Command had been conducting information operations by inserting viruses and deceptive communications into the enemy's computer system and microwave net. The commander of U.S. Air Forces in Europe

---

[46] Bill Gertz, "Remote Radar Allows Serbs to Keep Firing at NATO Jets," *Washington Times*, April 13, 1999.

[47] Robert Wall, "Airspace Control Challenges Allies," *Aviation Week and Space Technology*, April 26, 1999, p. 30.

[48] Lieutenant Colonel Philip Tissue, USMC, "21 Minutes to Belgrade," *Proceedings*, U.S. Naval Institute, Annapolis, Md., September 1999, p. 40.

(USAFE), General John Jumper, later confirmed that Operation Allied Force had seen the first use of offensive computer warfare as a precision weapon in connection with broader U.S. information operations. During Desert Storm, through taps of land lines passing through friendly countries, computer penetration, and high-speed decrypting algorithms, the United States was reportedly able to intercept and monitor Iraqi e-mail and digitized messages but engaged in no manipulation of enemy computers. During Allied Force, however, information operators were said to have succeeded in putting false targets into the enemy's air defense computers to match what enemy controllers were predisposed to believe. Such activities also reportedly occasioned the classic operator-versus-intelligence conundrum from time to time, in which intelligence collectors sought to preserve enemy threat systems that were providing them with a stream of information, while operators sought to attack them and render them useless to protect allied aircrews.[49]

The F-117 Downing

These challenges to the campaign's defense-suppression effort did not take long to register their first toll. On the fourth night of air operations, in the first combat loss ever of a stealth aircraft, an F-117 was downed at approximately 8:45 P.M. over hilly terrain near Budanovici, about 28 miles northwest of Belgrade, by an apparent barrage of SA-3s. Fortunately, the pilot ejected safely and was recovered within hours by a combat search-and-rescue team. A flurry of speculation afterward sought to explain how such an unexpected event might have taken place. Experts at Lockheed Martin Corporation, the aircraft's manufacturer, reported that unlike earlier instances of F-117 combat operations, the missions flown over Yugoslavia had required the aircraft to operate in ways that may have compromised its stealth characteristics. By way of example, they noted that even a standard banking maneuver can increase the aircraft's radar cross section by a factor of 100 or more, which may have been a factor considering that such turns were unavoidable in the constricted airspace within which the F-117s were forced to fly.[50] Another report suggested that the RC-135 Rivet Joint aircraft that was monitoring enemy SAM activity had been unable to locate the SA-3 battery that was thought to have downed the F-117 and may additionally have failed to relay to the appropriate command and control authorities timely indications of enemy SAM activity, much as occurred earlier in con-

[49] David A. Fulghum, "Yugoslavia Successfully Attacked by Computers," *Aviation Week and Space Technology*, August 23, 1999, pp. 31–34.
[50] James Peltz and Jeff Leeds, "Stealth Fighter's Crash Reveals a Design's Limits," *Los Angeles Times*, March 30, 1999.

nection with the F-16 shootdown over Bosnia in June 1995. Lending credence to that interpretation, the commander of Air Combat Command, General Richard Hawley, commented that "when you have a lot of unlocated threats, you are at risk even in a stealth airplane."[51]

Alternatively, the F-117 could have been illuminated by enemy acquisition radars while its weapons bay doors were momentarily open. During normal operation, the doors remain open only for a few seconds, not enough time to allow enemy radars to detect, lock onto, and track the aircraft. Should a door remain stuck in the open position or should a segment of radar-absorptive material that coats the aircraft be stripped away, however, that could increase the aircraft's radar cross section sufficiently to enable a successful missile intercept. Other speculation suggested that the aircraft may have dropped below a cloud deck and been silhouetted against it, rendering it possible for Serbian air defenders to track and engage the F-117 visually. Beyond that, it was hypothesized that Serbian acquisition radars may have been operating in a bistatic mode, with their transmitters located at one site and their receivers at another. That, at least in theory, could just remotely have enabled their operators to determine the aircraft's position.[52]

Although the Air Force has remained silent as to what confluence of events it believes occasioned the F-117's downing, press reports claimed that Air Force assessors had concluded, after conducting a formal postmortem, that a lucky combination of low-technology tactics, rapid learning, and astute improvisation had converged in one fleeting instant to enable an SA-3 not operating in its normal, radar-guided mode to down the aircraft. Enemy spotters in Italy doubtless reported the aircraft's takeoff from Aviano, and IADS operators in Serbia, as well as perhaps in Bosnia and along the Montenegran coast, could have assembled enough glimpses of its position en route to its target from scattered radars to cue a SAM battery near Belgrade to fire at the appropriate moment. The aircraft had already dropped one LGB near Belgrade, offering the now-alerted air defenders yet another clue. (The Air Force is said to have ruled out theories hinging on a stuck weapons bay door, the aircraft's having descended to below 15,000 ft, and its having been hit by AAA.)[53]

At least three procedural errors were alleged to have contributed to the

---

[51] "Washington Outlook," *Aviation Week and Space Technology*, May 3, 1999, p. 21. Asked whether the aircraft's loss was caused by a failure to observe proper lessons from earlier experience, Hawley added, "That's an operational issue that is very warm."

[52] William B. Scott and David A. Fulghum, "Pentagon Mum about F-117 Loss," *Aviation Week and Space Technology*, April 5, 1999, p. 32.

[53] Eric Schmitt, "Shrewd Serb Tactics Downed Stealth Jet, U.S. Inquiry Shows," *New York Times*, April 11, 1999. In subsequent testimony before the Senate Armed Services Committee, Secretary of the Air Force F. Whitten Peters did confirm that the aircraft had been downed by enemy SAMs. See Vince Crawley, "Air Force Secretary Advocates C-130, Predators," *Defense Week*, July 26, 1999, p. 2.

downing.[54] The first was the reported inability of the RC-135 Rivet Joint aircraft to track the changing location of the three or four offending SAM batteries. Three low-frequency Serbian radars that at least theoretically could have detected the F-117's presence were reportedly not neutralized because U.S. strike aircraft had earlier bombed the wrong aim points within the radar complexes. Also, F-16CJs carrying HARMs and operating in adjacent airspace could have deterred the SA-3 battery from emitting, but those aircraft had been recalled prior to the F-117's shootdown.

The second alleged procedural error entailed an EA-6B support jammer that was said to have been operating not only too far away from the F-117 (80 to 100 miles) to have been of much protective value, but also out of proper alignment with the offending threat radars, resulting in inefficient jamming. The options available were to jam over a large spectrum with little power output or to jam a more narrow frequency band with a lot of power. By this account, the EA-6B mission planners made the wrong tactical choice.

Last was the reported fact that F-117s operating out of Aviano had previously flown along more or less the same transit routes for four nights in a row because of a SACEUR ban on any overflight of Bosnia to avoid jeopardizing the durability of the Dayton accords. That would have made their approach pattern into Yugoslav airspace predictable. Knowing from which direction the F-117s would be coming, Serbian air defenders could have employed low-frequency radars for the best chance of getting a snap look at the aircraft. Former F-117 pilots and several industry experts acknowledged that the aircraft is detectable by such radars when viewed from the side or from directly below. U.S. officials also suggested that the Serbs may have been able to get brief nightly radar hits while the aircraft's weapons bay doors were fleetingly open. Whatever the explanation, the cost exacted by the downing was not merely the loss of a key U.S. combat aircraft, but its effect in dimming the F-117's former aura of invincibility, which for years had made for a U.S. asset of incalculable psychological value.

Shortcomings in Intelligence Cycle Time

Commanders and other campaign operators found themselves repeatedly frustrated by the amount of time it often took to cycle critical information about enemy air defense threats and other targets of opportunity from sensors to shooters that were positioned to engage them effectively. Although the requisite architecture was in place throughout most of the campaign once a flexible targeting cell was established by the end of the first

---

[54] See David A. Fulghum and William B. Scott, "Pentagon Gets Lock on F-117 Shootdown," *Aviation Week and Space Technology*, April 19, 1999, pp. 28–30, and Paul Beaver, "Mystery Still Shrouds Downing of F-117A Fighter," *Jane's Defense Weekly*, September 1, 1999, p. 4.

month, it lacked a sufficiently high-volume data link with enough channels to get the information where it needed to go quickly. Sometimes it took days to locate Serbian air defense emitters and to disseminate the resulting intelligence to NATO aircrews. That shortfall stood in sharp contrast to the Desert Storm experience, during which virtually any time an Iraqi threat emission was detected, a bomb or HARM would typically end up heading toward the offending source within minutes.

U.S. aircraft equipped with the joint tactical information distribution system (JTIDS) frequently were not allowed to rely on that asset but were obliged instead to use voice communications to ensure adequate situation awareness for all players, notably allied participants not equipped to receive JTIDS signals.[55] There were occasional instances of major success stories, such as the demonstration of the U-2's ability to be retasked in real time to image a reported SA-6 site; data-link the resulting imagery via satellite back to its home base at Beale AFB, California, within minutes for an assessment of the target's coordinates; and have the results transmitted back to the cockpit of an F-15E just as its pilot was turning inbound toward the target to fire an AGM-130. Although that example was not representative, it previewed the sort of fusion toward which the U.S. intelligence, surveillance, and reconnaissance (ISR) system is heading.

More typically, target images from Predator UAVs flying over Kosovo would be transmitted to the Combined Air Operations Center (CAOC) in real time, only to encounter difficulty being forwarded from there to operating units in time for them to be tactically useful. In addition, the JSTARS crew complement was found to be too small to accommodate many of the data-processing and reporting demands it was asked to handle. The aircraft was said to require either more battle managers integrated closely enough into the commander's loop so that targets could be identified and attacked in near-real time, or else wider-band data links to ground stations, where a larger number of mission specialists could do the analysis and handling.[56]

Another identified bottleneck was the classified internet link called SIPRNET (short for secret internet protocol routed network), operated by EUCOM's Joint Analysis Center at RAF Molesworth, England. Frequently

---

[55] David A. Fulghum and Robert Wall, "Data Link, EW Problems Pinpointed by Pentagon," *Aviation Week and Space Technology*, September 6, 1999, pp. 87–88. The JTIDS offers aircrews a planform view of their tactical situation, as well as a capability for the real-time exchange of digital information between aircraft on relative positions, weapons availability, and fuel states, among other things. It further shows the position of all aircraft in a formation, as well as the location of enemy aircraft and ground threats. Fighters can receive this information passively, without highlighting themselves through radio voice communications. See William B. Scott, "JTIDS Provides F-15Cs 'God's Eye View,'" *Aviation Week and Space Technology*, April 29, 1996, p. 63.

[56] David A. Fulghum, "Lessons Learned May Be Flawed," *Aviation Week and Space Technology*, June 14, 1999, p. 205.

real-time target information would be withheld from U.S. allies as U.S. of-ficials argued over who should be allowed to see what. There also was a problem with the unsatisfactorily slow operating speed of SIPRNET. Finally, the National Imagery and Mapping Agency (NIMA) was frequently slow to deliver overhead photography of proposed targets and of targets already at-tacked, slowing the battle-damage assessment process and decisions as to whether to retarget a previously attacked site. One informed source com-mented that ISR fusion worked better in Allied Force than it did during Desert Storm, but that it still rated, at best, only a grade of C-plus in light of what remained needed. In contrast, what generally worked well was the Air Force's "reach-back" procedure of using secure communication lines in the forward theater to tap into information sources in the intelligence commu-nity in Washington and elsewhere.[57]

Stray Weapons and the Loss of Innocents

Pressures to avoid civilian casualties and unintended collateral damage to nonmilitary structures were greater in Allied Force than in any previous campaign involving U.S. forces. Any targets even remotely considered to be politically sensitive were reviewed personally at the White House by President Clinton, Secretary of Defense Cohen, and General Shelton. Some proposed targets, irrespective of their perceived importance to campaign planners, were removed from the list because of their excessively close prox-imity to civilian buildings. Also in many cases, the recommended bomb size was reduced to minimize or preclude any chance of causing unintended damage. For example, of every five LGBs dropped by an F-117 during the campaign's opening night, one was a 500-lb GBU-12 instead of a 2,000-lb GBU-24, offering a lower likelihood of destroying the intended target but also less chance of causing collateral damage. Measures imposed to avoid causing noncombatant casualties were uncompromisingly exacting, and NATO pilots were instructed to return home with their weapons unless their target could be positively identified.[58]

Nevertheless, despite rules of engagement characterized by Air Force Major General Charles Wald as being "as strict as I've seen in my 27 years in the military," there were 30 reported instances throughout the campaign of unintended damage caused by errant NATO munitions, including a dozen highly publicized incidents in which civilians were accidentally killed.[59]

---

[57] Rowan Scarborough, "Kosovo Target Data Stalled in Transit," *Washington Times*, July 28, 1999.

[58] Nelan, "Into the Fire," p. 32.

[59] Joel Havemann, "Convoy Deaths May Undermine Moral Authority," *Los Angeles Times*, April 15, 1999.

The first significant loss of civilian lives occurred on April 12 when an elec-tro-optically guided AGM-130 released by an F-15E struck a rail bridge in Kosovo just as a passenger train full of noncombatants happened to be crossing it. Belgrade later reported that more than 55 civilians were killed in that incident. Later that week, attacks against presumed Serbian military ve-hicles at two sites in southwestern Kosovo near the town of Djakovica in-advertently killed as many as 64 ethnic Albanian refugees when Air Force F-16 pilots mistook civilian vehicles for a convoy.[60]

These and similar errors resulted in part from constraints imposed by the requirement that NATO aircrews remain at medium altitudes to avoid the most lethal enemy threat envelopes, which made visual discrimination be-tween military and civilian traffic all but impossible. Another contribut-ing factor was the recurrent presence of clouds and smoke over many areas of Serbia and Kosovo, which would sometimes drift in after an LGB was re-leased and block the laser beam that was illuminating a target, causing the weapon guiding on it to go ballistic. The extraordinary media attention given to these events attested to what can happen when zero noncombatant casualties becomes not only the goal of strategy but also the expectation. Owing to unrealistic efforts to treat the normal friction of war as avoidable human error, every occurrence of unintended collateral damage became overinflated as front-page news and treated as a blemish on air power's pre-sumed ability to be consistently precise.

Indeed, the added constraints imposed on NATO aircrews as a result of these occasional tragic occurrences indicated the degree to which modern air power has become a victim of its own success. During the Gulf war, cock-pit video images of LGBs homing with seemingly unerring accuracy down the air shafts of enemy bunkers were spellbinding to most observers. Yet thanks to that same seemingly unerring accuracy, such performance has since come to be expected by both political leaders and the public alike. Once zero collateral damage becomes accepted as a goal of strategy, air power gets set up to be judged by almost unreachably high standards. In-evitably, any collateral damage then caused during the course of a campaign becomes grist for domestic critics and the enemy's propaganda mill. An-thony Cordesman rightly noted how characterizations of modern precision bombing as "surgical" overlook the fact that patients still die on the operat-ing table from time to time.[61] Nevertheless, many proposed sorties in Oper-ation Allied Force were either cancelled outright or aborted at the last minute before any weapons were released because targets could not be pos-

[60] Rowan Scarborough, "As Strikes Mount, So Do Errors," *Washington Times*, May 11, 1999.
[61] Anthony H. Cordesman, "The Lessons and Non-Lessons of the Air and Missile War in Kosovo," unpublished draft, Center for Strategic and International Studies, Washington, D.C., July 20, 1999.

itively identified or because of the perceived risk of causing collateral damage. At best, that made for an inefficient air campaign compared to the standard set earlier in Desert Storm.

The Chinese Embassy Bombing

A particularly egregious case of unintended damage occurred when three JDAMS intended for the headquarters of a Yugoslav arms agency were dropped with flawless accuracy by a B-2 on the Chinese embassy in Belgrade. That colossal intelligence blunder was reminiscent of the ill-fated bombing of the Al Firdos bunker by an F-117 during Desert Storm, which accidentally killed more than a hundred Iraqi women and children who, unbeknown to U.S. intelligence, had been sleeping inside in the belief that it offered them shelter. The inadvertent bombing of the Chinese embassy caused a huge international uproar and dramatized yet again how seemingly tactical errors can have disproportionately strategic consequences. Among other things, the event triggered a diplomatic crisis of the first order between Washington and Beijing, disrupted moves to negotiate an end to the Kosovo conflict, and prompted a halt to any further bombing of targets in Belgrade for two weeks thereafter.

At least two failures accounted for the inadvertent bombing. First, CIA officials who nominated the intended target wrongly deduced where it was located in Belgrade. Second, those same officials were unaware that the actual targeted building was the Chinese embassy, which had been moved there from another site four years before. During Desert Storm, target planners almost always had knowledge of all off-limits buildings in and around Baghdad, including foreign embassies, and they put red circles around those buildings on planning maps to ensure that they would not be struck inadvertently. Gulf war planners were also more proactive in updating the no-strike list, to include having U.S. officials contact foreign governments directly whenever there was any doubt about the location of their embassies.[62] In this case, U.S. intelligence officials admitted afterward that they had relied on an outdated map of Belgrade. Some laid the blame on a budget-cutting decision by the Clinton administration in 1996 to fold the CIA's National Photographic Interpretation Center (NPIC) into the Defense Department's NIMA, which had prompted many of NPIC's most experienced analysts to resign in protest.

As it turned out, U.S. intelligence officers had the correct street address for the intended target, which was a Yugoslav weapons-producing agency

---

[62] David A. Fulghum and Robert Wall, "Intel Mistakes Trigger Chinese Embassy Bombing," *Aviation Week and Space Technology*, May 17, 1999, p. 55.

called the Federal Directorate of Supply and Procurement. Yet when over-head imagery was examined to match up the address with the intended tar-get, responsible individuals at CIA selected the wrong building. The actual target turned out to have been on the same street, only a block away to the south. The map used had been created in 1992 and updated in 1997. It did not, however, show the Chinese embassy at its current location, to which it had moved in 1996. No one in the planning loop thought to check the matchup of the target address with its presumed location because no one had any reason to believe that there was a problem. Afterward, Secretary Cohen said that the bombing had resulted not from a mechanical or human mistake but from "an institutional error."[63] Whatever the explanation, of all of NATO's incidents of collateral damage in Allied Force, the mistaken bomb-ing of the Chinese embassy was the most politically damaging by far.

The Apache Fiasco

As noted earlier, within days after Operation Allied Force commenced, General Clark had asked the Army to deploy a contingent of its AH-64 Apache attack helicopters to the combat zone to provide a better close-in ca-pability against enemy tanks and APCs than that offered by fixed-wing fighters, which remained restricted to operating at medium altitudes as a general rule. Clark initially had hoped to deploy this force to Macedonia, where the roads and airfields were better and the terrain was less challeng-ing. The Macedonian government, however, declined to grant permission because it was already swamped by the flood of Kosovar refugees, so Alba-nia was sought instead as the best available alternative. Within four hours, NATO approved Clark's request. It took more than a week, however, for the U.S. and Albanian governments to endorse the deployment.

At first glance, the idea of using Apaches to reinforce NATO's fixed-wing aircraft seemed entirely appropriate, considering that the AH-64 had been acquired by the Army expressly to kill enemy armor. In a normal weapons load, it mounts up to 16 Hellfire antitank missiles, 76 folding-fin antiper-sonnel rockets, and 1,200 rounds of 30-mm armor-piercing ammunition. With that armament, it gained deserved distinction by destroying more than 500 Iraqi armored vehicles during Operation Desert Storm. Yet in Desert Storm, the Apaches had deployed as an organic component of two fully fielded U.S. Army corps. In this case, the Army was being asked to cobble together an ad hoc task force more analogous to an Air Force air ex-peditionary force (AEF). The Army is not configured to undertake such ad

[63] Paul Richter and Doyle McManus, "Pentagon to Tighten Targeting Procedures," *Los Angeles Times*, May 11, 1999.

hoc deployments, and its units do not train for them. Instead, an Apache battalion normally deploys only as a part of a larger Army division or corps, with all of the latter's organically attached elements.

Accordingly, the Army was obliged by its own standard operating procedures to encumber the two Apache battalions with a decidedly top-heavy complement of ground forces, air defenses, military engineers, and headquarters overhead. As the core of this larger force complement, now designated Task Force (TF) Hawk, the Apaches were drawn from the Army's 11th Aviation Brigade stationed at Illesheim, Germany. The deployment package included, however, not only the two battalions of AH-64s, but also a number of UH-60 Blackhawk and CH-47D Chinook helicopters. Additional assets whose deployment was deemed essential to support the Apaches included a light infantry company; a multiple-launch rocket system (MLRS) platoon with three MLRS vehicles; a high-mobility multipurpose wheeled vehicle (HMMWV, or "humvee") antitank company equipped with 38 armed utility vehicles; a military intelligence platoon; a military police platoon; and a combat service support team. The Army further deemed it necessary to have its Apaches accompanied by a mechanized infantry company sporting 14 Bradley AFVs; an armor company with 15 M1A2 Abrams tanks; a howitzer battery with eight 155-mm artillery pieces; a construction engineer company; a short-range air defense battery with eight more Bradley AFVs armed with Stinger infrared SAMs; a smoke generator platoon; a brigade headquarters complement; and diverse other elements. In all, to support the deployment of a mere 24 attack helicopters to Albania, TF Hawk ended up being saddled with a support train of no fewer than 5,350 Army personnel.

To be sure, there was a legitimate force-protection rationale behind this accompanying train of equipment and personnel. Unlike the Marines, who deployed 24 F/A-18 fighters to Hungary only a few weeks thereafter and had them flying combat missions within days with nothing even approaching TF Hawk's overhead and support baggage, Army planners had to be concerned about the inherent risks of deploying a comparable number of Apaches on terrain that was not that of a NATO ally, that lacked any semblance of a friendly ground force presence, and that could easily have invited a Serbian cross-border attack in the absence of a U.S. ground force sufficient to render that an unacceptable gamble for Serbian commanders. As one might have expected with that much extra freight, however, the Apache deployment soon encountered multiple problems in execution. It was at first estimated that 200 Air Force C-17 transport sorties would be needed to airlift the assorted support elements with which the Apaches had been burdened. (The Tirana airport lacked the required taxiway and ramp specifications to accommodate the more capacious C-5.) In the end, it took more than 500 C-17 sorties, moving some 22,000 short tons in all, to transfer

TF Hawk in its entirety to Albania. Commenting later on the deployment, one Army officer complained that the Army is "still organized to fight in the Fulda Gap." Even the outgoing Army chief of staff, General Dennis Reimer, admitted in an internal memo to senior Army staff officers once the deployment package had finally been assembled in-theater that the manifold problems encountered by TF Hawk had underscored a "need for more adaptive force packaging methodology."[64]

In all events, the Apaches with their attached equipment and personnel finally arrived in Albania in late April. No sooner had the Army declared all but one of the aircraft ready for combat on April 26 when, only hours later, one crashed at the Tirana airfield in full view of reporters who had been authorized to televise the flight. (The 24th Apache had developed hydraulic trouble en route and remained on the ground in Italy.) Neither crewmember was injured, but the accident made for an inauspicious start for the widely touted deployment. Less than two weeks later, on May 5, a second accident occurred, this time killing both crewmembers during a night training mission some 46 miles north of Tirana. The aircraft was carrying a full load of weapons and extra fuel. A subsequent investigation concluded that the first accident had been caused by the pilot's having mistakenly landed short of his intended touchdown point.[65] The second was attributed to an apparent failure of the tail rotor, considering that the aircraft had been observed to enter a rapid uncontrolled spiral during the last moments before its impact with the ground.

As of May 31, the cost of the TF Hawk deployment had reached $254 million, much of that constituting the expense for the hundreds of C-17 sorties that had been needed to haul all the equipment from Germany to Albania, plus the additional costs of building base camps and port services and conducting mission rehearsals.[66] Yet despite Clark's intentions to the contrary, the Apaches flew not a single combat mission during the entire remainder of Operation Allied Force. The reason given afterward by the JCS chairman, General Shelton, was that Serbian air defenses in Kosovo, although noticeably degraded by early May, remained effective enough to warrant keeping the Apaches out of action until the SEAD campaign had "reduced the risk to the very minimum."[67] President Clinton himself later reinforced those reservations when he commented in mid-May that the risk to the Apache pi-

[64] Elaine M. Grossman, "Army's Cold War Orientation Slowed Apache Deployment to Balkans," *Inside the Pentagon*, May 6, 1999, p. 6.
[65] Paul Richter and Lisa Getter, "Mechanical Error, Pilot Error Led to Apache Crashes," *Los Angeles Times*, May 13, 1999.
[66] Ron Lorenzo, "Apache Deployment Has Cost Quarter Billion So Far," *Defense Week*, June 7, 1999, p. 6.
[67] Molly Moore and Bradley Graham, "NATO Plans for Peace, Not Ground Invasion," *Washington Post*, May 17, 1999.

lots remained too great and that because of recent weather improvements, "most of what the Apaches could do [could now] be done by the A-10s at less risk."[68]

In a final coda to the plagued TF Hawk experience, Shelton conceded in later testimony to the Senate Armed Services Committee that "the anticipated benefit of employing the Apaches against dispersed forces in a high-threat environment did not outweigh the risk to our pilots."[69] Shelton added that by the time the Apache deployment had reached the point where it was ready to engage in combat, Serbian ground formations were no longer massed but had become dispersed and well hidden. Moreover, he went on to note, the weather had improved, enabling Air Force A-10s and other fixed-wing aircraft to hunt down fielded enemy forces while incurring less risk from enemy infrared SAMS, AAA, and small-arms fire than the Apaches would have faced.

Beyond these problems associated with the deployment itself, there was a breakdown in joint doctrine for the combat use of the helicopters that was disturbingly evocative of the earlier competition for ownership and control of coalition air assets that had continually poisoned the relationship between the joint-force air component commander (JFACC) and the Army's corps commanders during Desert Storm.[70] The issue stemmed in this case from the fact that the Army has traditionally regarded its attack helicopters not as part of a larger air power equation with a theater-wide focus, but rather as an organic maneuver element fielded to help support the ground maneuver needs of a division or corps. Apache crews typically rely on their own gaining ground units to select and designate their targets. Yet in the case of Allied Force, with no Army ground combat presence in the theater to speak of, they would either have had to self-designate their targets or else rely on Air Force FACs flying at higher altitudes to designate the targets for them. The idea of using Apaches as a strike asset in this manner independently of U.S. ground forces was simply not recognized by prevailing Army doctrine. On the contrary, as prescribed in Army Field Manual FM 1-112, *Attack Helicopter Operations*, an AH-64 battalion "never fights alone. . . . Attacks may be conducted out of physical contact with other friendly forces," but they must be "synchronized with their scheme of maneuver." Manual FM 1-112 expressly characterizes deep-attack missions of the sort envisaged by Clark as "high-risk, high-payoff operations that must be exercised with the utmost care."[71]

[68] Robert Burns, "Use of Apache Copters Is Not Expected Soon," *Philadelphia Inquirer*, May 19, 1999.
[69] Sheila Foote, "Shelton: Risk Was the Key in Decision Not to Use Apaches," *Defense Daily*, September 10, 1999, p. 2.
[70] See David Atkinson and Hunter Keeter, "Apache Role in Kosovo Illustrates Cracks in Joint Doctrine," *Defense Daily*, May 26, 1999, p. 6.
[71] Elaine M. Grossman, "As Apaches near Combat, White House Seeks Diplomatic Solution," *Inside the Pentagon*, May 6, 1999, p. 7.

As a result of this mindset, the Army's V Corps commander, Lieutenant General John Hendrix, initially refused to cede tactical control over TF Hawk's Apaches to the CAOC in Vicenza, which, by standard joint operations practice, was overseeing all other air missions being flown by U.S and allied forces. More to the point, Hendrix, who as V Corps commander was also the ultimate commander of TF Hawk, would not allow any preplanned Apache sorties to appear on the EUCOM Air Tasking Order (ATO). The rift between Hendrix and Air Force Lieutenant General Michael Short, the JFACC, over operational control of the Apaches became so pronounced that it eventually had to go all the way to the JCS for resolution.

The agreement that was finally reached nominally included the Apaches with all other ATO missions, yet left to Hendrix's discretion much essential detail on mission timing and tactics. A window was provided in the ATO such that the Apaches would be time-deconflicted from friendly bombs falling from above and also assured of some fixed-wing air support. However, the agreement reached in the end was so vague that it allowed each service to claim that it maintained tactical control over the Apaches in the event they were ever committed to combat. For their part, Army officers insisted that fire support for the AH-64s would come *only* from MLRS and Army tactical missile systems (ATACMS) positioned on the Albanian side of the border. In contrast, Air Force planners maintained that excluding the Apaches from CAOC control would increase their level of risk by depriving them of support from such key battlespace awareness assets as JSTARS, Rivet Joint, Compass Call, and the EA-6B.[72]

In yet further testimony to the snake-bitten character of the TF Hawk deployment, it was acknowledged in an internal Army memorandum after the campaign ended that the aircrews that had been sent with the Apaches had been both undertrained and underequipped for their intended mission. In a report to the newly incoming chief of staff, General Eric Shinseki, Brigadier General Richard Cody, the Army's director of operations, resources, and mobilization, warned that because of those shortcomings, "we are placing them and their unit at risk when we have to ramp up for a real world crisis." Cody, who earlier had planned and executed the Army's highly successful Apache operations during the 1991 Gulf war, noted that more than 65 of the assigned aviators in TF Hawk had less than 500 hours of flight experience in the Apache and that none were qualified to fly missions requiring night-vision goggles. He further noted that the radios in the deployed Apaches had insufficient range for conducting deep operations and that the crews were, in the absence of night-vision goggles, dependent solely on their forward-looking infrared (FLIR) sensors. Given the rugged terrain, unpredictable weather, and poorly marked power lines that criss-crossed

[72] Elaine M. Grossman, "Army Commander in Albania Resists Joint Control over Apache Missions," *Inside the Pentagon*, May 20, 1999, pp. 7–9.

Kosovo, relying on FLIR alone, he suggested, "was not a good option." Moreover, he added, in order for the Apaches to fly the required distances and cross the high mountains of Kosovo, Hellfire missiles would have to be removed from one of their two wing mounts to free up a station for auxiliary fuel tanks. As for the MANPADS threat, Cody remarked that "the current suite of ASE [aircraft survivability equipment] was not reliable enough and sometimes ineffective."[73]

On his second day in office as the Army's new chief, General Shinseki acknowledged that the Army had been poorly prepared to move its Apaches and support overhead to Albania. Part of the problem, he noted fairly, was that the only available deployment site that made any operational sense had poor rail connections, a shallow port, and a limited airfield capacity that could not accommodate the Air Force's C-5 heavy airlifter. However, he admitted that the Army all the same was overdue to develop and act on a plan to make its heavy forces more mobile and its lighter forces more lethal.[74] In what may have presaged a major shift in Army force-development policy for the years ahead, he declared, "Our heavy forces are too heavy and our light forces lack staying power. Heavy forces must be more strategically deployable and more agile with a smaller logistical footprint, and light forces must be more lethal, survivable, and tactically mobile. Achieving this paradigm will require innovative thinking about structure, modernization efforts, and spending."[75]

One positive role played by TF Hawk once the KLA's counteroffensive began registering effects in late May was the service provided by the former's counterbattery radars in helping NATO fixed-wing pilots pinpoint and deliver munitions against enemy artillery positions. Its TPQ-36 and TPQ-37 fire-finder radars were positioned atop the hills adjacent to Tirana to spot Serb artillery fire and backtrack the airborne shells to their point of origin. Army EH-60 helicopters and RC-12 Guardrail electronic intelligence aircraft were further able to establish the location of Serb command posts whenever the latter transmitted. Although TF Hawk's Apaches and other combat assets never saw action, its ISR assets exerted a significant influence on the air campaign at one of its most crucial moments. The KLA's counteroffensive had forced the Serbs to mass their forces and maneuver, to communicate by radio, and to fire artillery and mortars to protect themselves. In response, the sensors of TF Hawk, operating in conjunction with the Army's Hunter UAVS, spotted Serbian targets and passed that information on to those in the command loop who could bring air-delivered ordnance to bear in a timely

---

[73] George C. Wilson, "Memo Says Apaches, Pilots Were Not Ready," *European Stars and Stripes*, June 20, 1999.

[74] Eric Schmitt, "New Army Chief Seeks More Agility and Power," *New York Times*, June 24, 1999.

[75] "Shinseki Hints at Restructuring, Aggressive Changes for the Army," *Inside the Army*, June 28, 1999, p. 1.

manner. "The result," said a retired Army three-star general, "was that NATO air power was finally able to target precisely and hit the Serb army in the field. The Kosovars acted as the anvil and TF Hawk as the eyes and ears of the blacksmith so that the hammer of air power could be effective."[76] Echoing this conclusion, USAFE's commander, General Jumper, confirmed that the counterbattery radars of TF Hawk had played "a very big part" in allied targeting during the final stages of the campaign.[77]

Interoperability Shortcomings

One of the most disturbing aspects of the air campaign experience was what it revealed about the extent of disconnect that had been allowed to develop between U.S air power and that of most other NATO allies who participated. One concern had to do with inadequacies in the equipment operated by the allies. To begin with, there was a pronounced dearth of interoperability with respect to rapid and secure communications. Only at Aviano were there some old STU-2 secure telephones that allowed the U.S. participants to transfer classified information quickly to allied units. (The STU-3 secure phone system used by U.S. forces was not available to the allies.) Other classified communications required passing a hard copy of the information by hand, repeating one of the worst command and control deficiencies that had been exposed earlier in Desert Storm, when the ATO had to be flown every day to each of the Navy's six participating aircraft carriers because the latter were not equipped to receive it electronically. In addition, many European NATO fighters lacked Have Quick–type frequency-hopping UHF radios and KY-58–like radios allowing encrypted communications. As a result, U.S. command and control aircraft were often forced to make transmissions to those fighters in the clear with respect to targets and aircraft positions, enabling the enemy to listen in and gain valuable tactical intelligence.

Second, among all participating allied air forces, only U.S., British, Canadian, and French combat aircraft had the ability to deliver LGBs. General Short frankly admitted that he could not risk sending the aircraft of many allied countries into harm's way because of concern for the safety of their pilots and for the civilian casualties that might be caused by inaccurately aimed weapons. Largely for that reason, around 80 percent of all strike sorties flown in Allied Force were carried out by U.S. aircraft.

Apart from the problem of incompatible radio links, the absence of a ro

---

[76] Lieutenant General Theodore G. Stroup, Jr., USA (Ret.), "Task Force Hawk: Beyond Expectations," *Army Magazine*, August 1999, p. 10.
[77] General John Jumper, USAF, response to a question at an Air Force Association Eaker Institute colloquy, "Operation Allied Force: Strategy, Execution, Implications," held at the Ronald Reagan International Trade Center, Washington D.C., August 16, 1999.

bust alliance-wide IFF (identification friend or foe) system made life doubly difficult for AWACS operators, as did the lack of a capability to detect which SAM systems were targeting allied aircraft. In addition, the small number of non-U.S. aircraft able to laser-designate targets inhibited the usefulness of many allied assets. Much of this discrepancy between U.S. and allied capability was a result of the fact that the European nations typically spend only half the annual U.S. rate on military procurement and a third of the annual U.S. rate on research and development.[78] Largely because of that asymmetry, the United States selected virtually every target attacked in Operation Allied Force and provided more than 80 percent of the 1,100 aircraft and almost all of the aerial intelligence employed in the campaign.[79]

The Wages of U.S. Overcommitment

Finally, the demands placed by Allied Force on U.S. equipment and personnel underscored the extent to which the U.S. defense posture had been stretched thin by the post–cold war force drawdown and concurrent quadrupling of deployment commitments worldwide. The first indicator was the unexpectedly high rate at which scarce and expensive consumables were being expended. After only the first week, the Air Force found itself running low on CALCMs, with the initial stock of 150 down to less than 100. The Air Force had had preexisting plans in hand to convert 92 additional nuclear-configured air-launched cruise missiles (ALCMs) to CALCMs, but that process was expected to take more than a year. For its part, JDAM was still in testing at the time it was committed to combat. As of April 20, less than a month into the campaign, there were only 609 remaining in stock.[80] The burdens placed by the campaign's demands on materiel of all kinds prompted a rising groundswell of military complaints that the consequences of seven years of underfunding were finally making their impact fully felt.[81]

A second indication of the extent to which the U.S. military had come to find itself strapped as a result of the force drawdown was the sharply increased personnel tempo that was set in motion by the campaign. In all, some 40 percent of the active-duty Air Force found itself committed to Operation Allied Force and to the concurrent Operations Northern and Southern Watch over Iraq. That was roughly the same percentage of Air Force per-

[78] John D. Morrocco, "Kosovo Reveals NATO Interoperability Woes," *Aviation Week and Space Technology,* August 9, 1999, p. 32.

[79] Barton Gellman and William Drozdiak, "Conflict Halts Momentum for Broader Agenda," *Washington Post,* June 6, 1999.

[80] David A. Fulghum, "Bomb Shortage Was No Mistake," *Aviation Week and Space Technology,* May 17, 1999, p. 55.

[81] See Rowan Scarborough, "Smaller U.S. Military Is Spread Thin," *Washington Times,* March 31, 1999.

sonnel that had been committed during Operation Desert Storm, when the total force was much larger. Among other things, the heightened person-nel tempo obliged President Clinton to approve a Presidential Selected Re-serve Call-up authorizing a summons of up to 33,102 selected reservists to active duty.[82]

Third, the demands of Allied Force placed a severe strain on such low-density/high-demand U.S. aircraft as JSTARS, AWACS, the U-2, the B-2, the F-16CJ, and the EA-6B. So many of these scarce assets were committed to the campaign that day-to-day training in home units suffered major shortfalls as a result. The most acute strains were felt in the areas of surveillance, SEAD, and combat search and rescue. Almost every Block 50 F-16CJ in line service was committed to support the SEAD campaign, necessitating a virtual halt to mission employment training in the United States. Similarly, Vice Admiral Daniel Murphy, the commander of the 6th Fleet, which provided the U.S. naval forces that were operating in the Adriatic, reported that there was an insufficiency of EA-6B jammers and that they, along with their aircrews, were being worn out by the campaign's demands.[83] Almost half of the ini-tial batch of 11 EA-6Bs used to spearhead the air campaign had been drawn from assets previously committed to Operation Northern Watch at Incirlik, Turkey. Navy and Marine spokesmen declined to admit that their EA-6Bs were being stressed to the danger point, but they did concede that they were being run ragged trying to marshal enough aircraft out of the total inven-tory of 124 to support the launching of Allied Force.[84]

An even greater demand was imposed on the Air Force's various ISR plat-forms, which left none unencumbered for day-to-day continuation training once the needs of Allied Force were superimposed on preexisting commit-ments. During the time in question, the Air Force had only four operational E-8 JSTARS aircraft, two of which were committed to Allied Force (it has since acquired a fifth). As a result, the JSTARS community found itself so stripped of its most skilled personnel that there was no instructor cadre left to work with new crewmembers who were undergoing conversion training. Some JSTARS aircraft were flown at more than three times their normal use rates, creating a major maintenance and depot backlog that would take months to clear up.

Finally, the Kosovo campaign exposed the extent to which U.S. forces were being stretched to the limit to support real-world commitments while also meeting the requirement to deter conflict in two potential major theater

[82] "U.S. Mobilizes Guard, Reserve for Balkan Duty," *Air Force Magazine*, June 1999, p. 16.

[83] Dale Eisman, "Kosovo Lesson: Navy Says It Needs More High-Tech Tools," *Norfolk Virginian-Pilot*, June 10, 1999.

[84] Greg Seigle, "Prowler Jammers Used to Aid NATO Air Assault," *Jane's Defense Weekly*, March 31, 1999, p. 4.

wars. In the prevailing defense lexicon, Kosovo was supposed to be only a "smaller-scale contingency." Yet the number of U.S. aircraft committed to the campaign quickly approached the level of a major theater war and exposed shortcomings in the availability of needed assets in all services. For example, the diversion of the USS *Theodore Roosevelt* from the Mediterranean to the Adriatic to support the air campaign deprived U.S. Central Command of a vital operational asset. Likewise, the later redeployment of the USS *Kitty Hawk* from the Pacific to the Persian Gulf deprived U.S. Pacific Command of a carrier in the western Pacific for the first time since World War II.

The Air Force was similarly forced to juggle scarce assets to handle the overlapping demands imposed by Kosovo, Iraq, and Korea. It positively scrambled to find enough tankers to support NATO mission needs in Allied Force. Ironically, both Kosovo and Iraq, in and of themselves, represented lesser contingencies whose accommodation was not supposed to impede the U.S. military's ability to handle two major theater wars. Yet the burdens of both began to raise serious doubts as to whether the two-major-theater-war construct, at least at its current funding level, was realistic for U.S. needs. For example, when EUCOM redeployed 10 F-15s and 3 EA-6Bs from Incirlik to support Clark's requirements for Allied Force, it was forced to suspend its air patrols over northern Iraq immediately. Air patrols to enforce the no-fly zone over southern Iraq were continued, but at slower operational tempo.[85]

LAPSES IN STRATEGY AND PLANNING

The desultory onset of Allied Force and its later slowness to register effects arguably reflected not, in the first instance, any inadequacies in the equipment used by NATO but rather some basic shortcomings in strategy. Indeed, during the six years that preceded the air campaign, there was a regression in the U.S. use of air power after the latter's casebook performance in Desert Storm. With the singular exception of the determined performance by allied air power in Operation Deliberate Force in 1995, a trend toward what came to be called "cruise-missile diplomacy" had instead become the prevailing U.S. pattern, owing to the ability of cruise missiles to deliver a punitive message without risking the lives of any U.S. aircrews.

The origins of this pattern went back to June 1993, when President Clinton first ordered the firing of several TLAMs in the dead of night against an empty governmental building in Baghdad in symbolic reprisal for confirmed evidence that Saddam Hussein had underwritten an assassination

---

[85] Elizabeth Becker, "Needed on Several Fronts, U.S. Jet Force Is Strained," *New York Times*, April 6, 1999.

attempt against former President George Bush. The trend was next reflected in the administration's unwillingness or inability to use air power decisively in dealing with Bosnian Serb atrocities throughout the two years antecedent to Operation Deliberate Force. It was subsequently attested to by the costly, yet apparently ineffectual, TLAM strikes launched by the administration against presumed assets of the terrorist Osama bin Laden in Sudan and Afghanistan. It culminated, finally, in the three-day Operation Desert Fox, a mini–air campaign that was finally executed against Iraq at the height of President Clinton's impeachment proceeding in December 1998. Less than a year earlier, a more serious campaign plan called Operation Desert Thunder, set in motion shortly after Iraq had expelled the UN's arms inspectors in January 1998, was aborted by Clinton literally at the last minute, as allied strike aircraft were taxiing for takeoff, in response to the extraction by UN Secretary General Kofi Annan of an 11th-hour, later unfulfilled, promise from Saddam Hussein to relent in permitting UN inspections.[86] In all cases, the declared emphasis was merely on "degrading" or "damaging," rather than destroying, enemy assets, seemingly such that the operation could be terminated at any moment in a manner allowing success to be declared.

That may have been the administration's going-in hope for Operation Allied Force as well. Not long after the effort began, however, Milosevic's defiance of NATO and his acceleration of the ethnic cleansing campaign in Kosovo denied NATO the quick settlement it had counted on and left it and the Clinton administration with no choice but to keep pressing with the air attacks until NATO unambiguously prevailed over the Yugoslav dictator. General Klaus Naumann, the chairman of NATO's Military Committee, admitted a month into the campaign that the allied leaders had initially assumed that it would be over "very quickly" and that no one at any level had prepared for Milosevic's ethnic cleansing push.[87] Because NATO's leaders on both sides of the Atlantic had banked on a quick win, no preparations were made whatever to anticipate what the consequences might be should Milosevic raise the stakes by accelerating his ethnic cleansing plans.

As one might have expected, senior U.S. military leaders soon began voicing off-the-record misgivings over the desultory pace of the campaign, its restricted target base, and its rules of engagement that all but proscribed any serious application of air power. One Air Force general spoke of officers in Europe who had characterized the air war to date as "a disgrace," adding that "senior military officers think that the tempo is so disgustingly slow it

[86] For an informed, if also sharply judgmental, account of this history, see Joshua Muravchik, "The Road to Kosovo," *Commentary*, June 1999, pp. 17–23. See also Lieutenant Colonel Paul K. White, USAF, *Crises after the Storm: An Appraisal of U.S. Air Operations in Iraq since the Persian Gulf War*, Military Research Papers No. 2, Washington, D.C., Washington Institute for Near East Policy, 1999.
[87] Carla Anne Robbins, Thomas E. Ricks, and Neil King, Jr., "Milosevic's Resolve Spawned Unity, Wider Bombing List in NATO Alliance," *Wall Street Journal*, April 27, 1999.

makes us look inept."[88] Another, harking back to the initial concept of operations developed for Desert Storm, complained, "This is not Instant Thunder, it's more like Constant Drizzle."[89] Yet a third Air Force general, reflecting the consensus of most airmen, commented that "the hammer is working just fine. But when the blueprints have to undergo revision each day by nineteen separate architects before it is determined where to drive the nail, one has to wonder what the final product is going to look like."[90]

To be sure, it was not as though NATO's uniformed professionals had been railroaded into an operation against Milosevic without having given it prior consideration. On the contrary, planning for an air campaign of some sort against Yugoslavia had begun as far back as June 1998. The commander of USAFE, General Jumper, reported that by the start of Operation Allied Force, no fewer than 40 alternative campaign options had been generated, including some that were highly critical of using air power without a supporting ground element to flush out enemy troops. Nevertheless, shortly after the campaign began, it became clear that the relatively seamless performance by the coalition in Desert Storm was not to be replicated in Allied Force. Instead, what unfolded was a highly dissatisfying application of air power that showed not only the predictable fits and starts of trying to prosecute an air campaign through an alliance of 19 members bound by a unanimity rule, but also some failures even within the campaign's U.S. component to operate by textbook norms and make the most of what air power had to offer.

Problems at the Coalition Level

In their joint statement to the Senate Armed Services Committee after the campaign successfully ended, Secretary Cohen and General Shelton insisted that Operation Allied Force "could not have been conducted without the NATO alliance and without the infrastructure, transit and basing access, host-nation force contributions, and most importantly, political and diplomatic support provided by the allies and other members of the coalition."[91] Be that as it may, the conduct of the campaign as a coalition effort came at the cost of a flawed strategy that was further hobbled by the manifold

[88] Rowan Scarborough, "U.S. Pilots Call NATO Targeting a 'Disgrace,'" *Washington Times*, April 1, 1999.
[89] John D. Morrocco, David Fulghum, and Robert Wall, "Weather, Weapons Dearth Slow NATO Strikes," *Aviation Week and Space Technology*, April 5, 1999, p. 26.
[90] William M. Arkin, "Inside the Air Force, Officers Are Frustrated about the Air War," *Washington Post*, April 25, 1999.
[91] Secretary of Defense William S. Cohen and General Henry H. Shelton, "Joint Statement on the Kosovo After Action Review," testimony before the Senate Armed Services Committee, Washington, D.C., October 14, 1999.

inefficiencies that were part and parcel of conducting combat operations by committee.

Those inefficiencies did not take long to manifest themselves. During the campaign's first week, NATO officials reported that up to half of the proposed strike missions had been aborted due to weather and "other considerations," the latter, in most cases, being the refusal of some allies to approve certain target requests.[92] Indeed, the unanimity principle made for a rules-of-engagement regime that often precluded the efficient use of air power. The standing list of rules of engagement from NATO was compounded by some 70 reported additions for Kosovo before the bombing even began. Beyond that, there was an understandable lack of U.S. trust in many allies where the most important sensitivities were concerned. The Pentagon withheld from the allies mission specifics for literally hundreds of sorties that entailed the use of F-117s, B-2s, and cruise missiles to ensure strict U.S. control over those U.S.-only assets and to maintain a firewall against leaks from any allies who might compromise those operations.[93]

Beyond the natural friction created by NATO's committee approach to target approval, the initial unwillingness of its leaders to endorse a more aggressive air campaign failed completely to capitalize on air power's potential for taking down entire systems of enemy capability simultaneously. In his first interview since the campaign began six weeks earlier, the JFACC, General Short, was frank in airing his sense of being constrained by the political limits imposed by NATO, pointing out that the graduated campaign was counter to all of his professional instincts.[94] Short further admitted that he was less an architect of the campaign than its implementor. He was particularly critical of NATO's unwillingness to threaten a ground invasion from the start, noting that that failure was making it doubly difficult for NATO pilots to identify their targets because of the freedom it had given Serbian forces to disperse and hide their tanks and other vehicles.

To be sure, there were occasions when allied military planners sought to do the right thing despite the inclinations of their political masters. For example, until the campaign's very last week, France's President Jacques Chirac personally opposed attacking Belgrade's electrical power grid with high-explosive munitions. In an effort to work around his early opposition, U.S. and French military officers searched for more palatable alternatives and finally came up with the idea of using the still-secret CBU-94 cluster munition, which could shut down Belgrade's power source for at least a few

---

[92] Thomas W. Lippman and Bradley Graham, "Yugoslavs Fire on U.S. Troops; 3 Missing," *Washington Post*, April 1, 1999.

[93] Bob Deans, "Pentagon Mum about Air Mission," *European Stars and Stripes*, April 27, 1999.

[94] Michael R. Gordon, "Allied Air Chief Stresses Hitting Belgrade Sites," *New York Times*, May 13, 1999.

hours by depositing carbon-graphite threads on the grid to short it out. Chirac agreed to that proposed alternative, and 70 percent of Yugoslavia's power was shut down for nearly a day on May 3. Although it was only the first step toward what was later to become a more resolute effort against enemy infrastructure targets, that attack moved NATO past an important threshold and brought the war more directly home to the Serbian people.[95]

Finally, Operation Allied Force was hampered by an inefficient target-planning process. Because NATO had initially expected that the campaign would last only a few days, it failed to get a smoothly running mechanism for target development and review established and in place until late April. The process involved numerous planners at the Pentagon and elsewhere in the United States, at NATO headquarters in Belgium, at EUCOM headquarters in Stuttgart, Germany, and at the CAOC in Vicenza, Italy, with each U.S. participant logging on every morning to the earlier-noted secure computer network called SIPRNET.

Daily target production began at the U.S. Joint Analysis Center at RAF Molesworth, England, where analysts collated and transmitted the latest all-source intelligence, including overhead imagery from satellites and from Predator and Hunter UAVs. With that information in hand, target planners at Supreme Headquarters Allied Powers Europe (SHAPE) and EUCOM would then begin assembling target folders, conducting assessments of a proposed target's military worth, and taking careful looks at the likelihood of causing collateral damage. In addition, lawyers would vet each proposed target for military significance and for conformity to the law of armed conflict as reflected in the Geneva Conventions. Finally, the most appropriate weapon types would be picked at the CAOC, and planners at NATO and EUCOM headquarters would then assign rules of engagement, recommended attack headings, and desired mean points of impact for selected munitions.[96]

Further compounding the inefficiency of this multistage and circuitous process, two parallel but separate mechanisms for target selection and planning were used. Any U.S.-specific systems involving special sensitivities, such as the B-2, F-117, and cruise missiles, were allocated by EUCOM rather than by NATO, and the CAOC maintained separate targeting teams for EUCOM and NATO strike planning. Commenting on the friction that was inevitably occasioned by this cumbersome system, General Short recalled in hindsight that he was constantly having to tell allied leaders to "trust me" regarding what U.S. assets would be doing and that he would have preferred to find a way of ensuring that the daily NATO air operations schedule reflected those U.S.-only systems in some usable way. As it was, their absence led on occasion to some significant force deconfliction problems, such as U.S. aircraft

[95] Dana Priest, "France Acted as Group Skeptic," *Washington Post*, September 20, 1999.
[96] Dana Priest, "Target Selection Was Long Process," *Washington Post*, September 20, 1999.

suddenly showing up on NATO AWACS displays when and where they were not expected.[97]

Problems at the U.S. Level

It was not only the alliance-induced friction that helped make for an inefficient air campaign. As Allied Force unfolded, it became increasingly evident that even the U.S. military was divided over the most appropriate targeting strategy. There was visible tension in this regard between General Clark and his air commander, General Short. Clark was said to have believed at the outset that there was a 40 percent chance that Milosevic would cave in within three days after the bombing started. Once that hope proved evanescent, NATO began scrambling for an alternate strategy, which quickly pitted Clark in an internecine battle with his Air Force subordinate over where the focus of the air attacks should be directed. Short had chafed from the very beginning at the slowness of the campaign to gather momentum, considering that three nights were required to get through the 52 targets that had been approved up to that point, all of which were air defense related and none of which were located anywhere near Belgrade. Short insisted that the most effective use of allied air power would be to ignore Serbia's fielded forces in Kosovo and to concentrate instead on "strategic" targets in downtown Belgrade, including key electrical power plants and government ministries.

As the commander of U.S. naval forces participating in Allied Force, Vice Admiral Murphy, recalled after the campaign ended, "There was a fundamental difference of opinion at the outset between General Clark, who was applying a ground commander's perspective . . . and General Short as to the value of going after fielded forces."[98] For his part, Short believed that it was a waste of valuable munitions, sorties, and time going after the Yugoslav 3rd Army in Kosovo because the latter was not an important vulnerability for Milosevic. However, Clark's view as to where the target priorities properly lay prevailed throughout most of the campaign.[99] His approach ended up producing what some Air Force critics later criticized as "ad hoc targeting," in which air strikes were demanded on the same day that they had

---

[97] John A. Tirpak, "Short's View of the Air Campaign," *Air Force Magazine*, September 1999, p. 45.

[98] Dana Priest, "Tension Grew with Divide over Strategy," *Washington Post*, September 21, 1999.

[99] In one reported exchange during a daily video teleconference, Clark insisted that NATO air power remain committed against enemy fielded forces in Kosovo, with Short countering that such missions were a waste of assets and should be supplanted by missions against downtown Belgrade. Noting that U.S. aircraft were about to attack the Serbian special police headquarters in Belgrade, Short said, "This is the jewel in the crown." To which Clark replied, "To me, the jewel in the crown is when those B-52s rumble across Kosovo." Short replied, "You and I have known for weeks that we have different jewelers." To which Clark responded, "My jeweler outranks yours." Ibid.

been approved, missions that had not yet been approved were assigned to the JFACC, and those same missions were later removed from the list at the last minute if they had not been approved by NATO's civilian authorities. The resulting confusion led the commander of allied forces in southern Europe, Admiral James Ellis, to complain, "We don't like this kind of process where something could be left on [the ATO] by omission."[100]

Although the methodology of effects-based targeting was well in hand among U.S. air power professionals, most of the attack planning that took place against approved targets was not driven by desired effects, but rather seemed to entail simply parcelling out sortie and munitions allocations by target category, without much consideration for how a target's neutralization might contribute toward advancing the campaign's objectives. A typical example was going after refineries, factories, and bridges unsystematically and in piecemeal fashion over time rather than as interconnected components of a larger entity whose simultaneous destruction might instantly undermine Yugoslavia's capacity to function effectively. Because of the apparent paucity of effects-based target analysis, NATO's military chiefs often encountered needless difficulty convincing their civilian superiors of the importance of many targets. The commander of USAFE, General Jumper, scored this problem when he later stressed the importance of effects-based targeting and faulted what typically happened instead, namely, what he called "campaign-by-target-list management," whereby planners simply took a list of approved targets and managed them on a day-to-day basis.[101]

On the plus side, the methodology used in *individual* target planning, now a bona fide science in its own right, had evolved to a point where target analysts could predict, for any given weapon type and impact angle, how far the blast effects would extend, how far shards of glass could be expected to fly, and even at what distance they would retain enough force to penetrate skin. The use of this methodology in arriving at a precisely determined weapon yield, aim-point placement, and weapon heading and impact angle to minimize unwanted collateral damage often proved decisive in persuading NATO's civilian leaders to approve attacks on many of the most politically sensitive targets.

Also on the plus side, the B-2's successful use of accurate JDAMs in Allied Force may have heralded a long-overdue end to the costly six-year U.S. habit of relying solely on cruise missiles as a seemingly risk-free way of delivering precision ordnance. Before the start of Allied Force, the Clinton administration had expended nearly 800 cruise missiles, all told, in various sig-

---

[100] Ibid.
[101] General John Jumper, USAF, comments at an Air Force Association Eaker Institute colloquy, "Operation Allied Force: Strategy, Execution, Implications," held at the Ronald Reagan International Trade Center, Washington, D.C., August 16, 1999.

nalling and punitive attacks against presumed terrorist targets and against Iraq. At a cost of approximately $1.5 million a shot, that added up to enough to pay for the purchase of more than 50,000 JDAMS.[102]

A First Cut at Kosovo "Lessons"

Because of the campaign's ultimate success in forcing Milosevic to yield to NATO's demands, many hastened to characterize it afterward as a watershed achievement for air power. One account called Operation Allied Force "one of history's most impressive air campaigns."[103] Another suggested that if the cease-fire holds, the United States and its allies would have accomplished "what some military experts had predicted was impossible: a victory achieved with air power alone."[104] These and similar views were aired by many of the same American newspapers that, for the preceding 11 weeks, had doubted whether NATO's strategy would *ever* succeed without an accompanying ground invasion.

It was not just outside observers, moreover, who gave such ready voice to that assessment. Shortly after the cease-fire, President Clinton himself declared that the outcome of Allied Force "proved that a sustained air campaign, under the right conditions, can stop an army on the ground."[105] Other administration leaders were equally quick to congratulate air power for what it had done to salvage a situation that looked, almost until the last moment, as though it was headed nowhere but to a NATO ground involvement of some sort. In their joint statement to the Senate Armed Services Committee after the campaign ended, Secretary of Defense Cohen and General Shelton, the chairman of the JCS, described it as "an overwhelming success."[106]

With all due respect for the unmatched competence of the aircrews in all services who actually carried out the campaign, it is hard to accept such characterizations as the right conclusions to be drawn from Allied Force. To begin with, they are at marked odds with the consensus views of the senior military professionals who, one would think, would be most familiar with air power and its limitations. Shortly before the campaign began, the four

---

[102] William M. Arkin, "In Praise of Heavy Bombers," *Bulletin of the Atomic Scientists*, July–August 1999, p. 80.
[103] William Drozdiak and Anne Swardson, "Military, Diplomatic Offensives Bring about Accord," *Washington Post*, June 4, 1999.
[104] Paul Richter, "Air-Only Campaign Offers a False Sense of Security, Some Say," *Los Angeles Times*, June 4, 1999.
[105] Pat Towell, "Lawmakers Urge Armed Forces to Focus on High-Tech Future," *Congressional Quarterly Weekly*, June 26, 1999, p. 1564.
[106] Cohen and Shelton, "Joint Statement."

U.S. service chiefs uniformly doubted in testimony before the Senate Armed Services Committee whether air strikes by themselves would succeed in compelling Milosevic to yield to NATO's demands.[107] Indeed, the Air Force chief of staff, General Ryan, admitted less than a week later, "I don't know if we can do it without ground troops."[108] After the campaign was over, the former commander of NATO forces during Operation Deliberate Force, Admiral Leighton Smith, remarked that the Kosovo experience should go down as "possibly the worst way we employed our military forces in history."[109] A former Air Force chief of staff, General Ronald Fogleman, likewise observed that "just because it comes out reasonably well, at least in the eyes of the administration, doesn't mean it was conducted properly. The application of air power was flawed." Finally, the JFACC, General Short, declared that "as an airman, I'd have done this a whole lot differently than I was allowed to do. We could have done this differently. We should have done this differently."[110]

Indeed, few campaign participants were more surprised by the sudden capitulation of Milosevic than the alliance's most senior airmen. By the end of May, most Air Force generals had come to conclude that NATO would be unable to find and destroy any more dispersed Serbian troops and equipment without incurring more unintended civilian casualties.[111] Moreover, General Short had reluctantly concluded that NATO's strategy was unlikely to break Milosevic's will and that there was a mounting need either to intensify the war or to accept Belgrade's terms for peace.[112] True enough, on the eve of the cease-fire, General Ryan predicted that once the campaign began seeking strategic rather than merely battlefield effects, Milosevic would wake up to the realization that NATO was destroying his country on the installment plan and that his ultimate defeat was "inevitable." The Air Force chief hastened to add, however, that the campaign had not begun in "the way that America normally would apply air power," implying his belief that there was a more efficient and effective way of going about it.[113] As a testament to widespread doubts that the campaign was anywhere close to achieving its objectives, planning was under way for a continuation of offensive air operations against Yugoslavia through December or longer if necessary—although it remains an open question whether NATO cohesion

---

[107] Bradley Graham, "Joint Chiefs Doubted Air Strategy," *Washington Post*, April 5, 1999.

[108] Quoted in "Verbatim Special: The Balkan War," *Air Force Magazine*, June 1999, p. 47.

[109] "Reporters' Notebook," *Defense Week*, July 19, 1999, p. 4.

[110] William Drozdiak, "Allies Need Upgrade, General Says," *Washington Post*, June 20, 1999.

[111] John F. Harris and Bradley Graham, "Clinton Is Reassessing Sufficiency of Air War," *Washington Post*, June 3, 1999.

[112] William M. Arkin, "Limited Warfare in Kosovo Not Working," *Seattle Times*, May 22, 1999.

[113] General Michael E. Ryan, "Air Power Is Working in Kosovo," *Washington Post*, June 4, 1999.

or popular support on either side of the Atlantic would have sustained such operations for that long.

To be sure, there is much to say about Operation Allied Force that is positive. To begin with, it did represent the first instance in which the application of air power coerced an enemy leader to yield with no friendly land combat action whatsoever. In that respect, its conduct and results well bore out a subsequent observation by Alan Stephens that "modern war is concerned more with acceptable political outcomes than with seizing and holding ground." [114] Moreover, although there were some unfortunate and highly publicized cases in which innocent civilians were killed by stray weapons, Secretary of Defense Cohen was on point when he characterized the campaign after the cease-fire went into effect as "the most precise application of air power in history." [115] At the end of May, General Clark reported that of all the precision munitions that had been expended throughout the campaign, 79 percent had hit their target, a higher percentage than had been expected.[116] In all, probably no more than 600 civilians, including noncombatants in Kosovo, died as a direct result of errant NATO air attacks.[117]

In contrast to Desert Storm, the campaign's attempts at denial did not bear much fruit. Allied efforts to attack fielded enemy forces were largely ineffective, in considerable part because of the decision made by NATO's leaders at the outset to forgo even the threat of a ground invasion. Hence, Serbian atrocities against the Kosovar Albanians increased even as the air campaign intensified. Yet ironically, also in contrast to the coalition's ultimately unrequited efforts to coerce Saddam Hussein into submission, punishment *did* seem to work against Milosevic in this case, disconfirming the common adage that air power can beat up on an adversary indefinitely but rarely can induce him to change his mind. Yet it does not follow that the targeting choices ultimately agreed to by NATO's political leaders represented the most astute application of air power, let alone a prescription for the future pursuit of coercion through punishment. As one critic later observed, "Bureaucratic, political, and diplomatic concerns were elevated above military

[114] Alan Stephens, *Kosovo, or the Future of War*, Paper No. 77, Fairbairn, Australia, RAAF Air Power Studies Center, August 1999, p. 21.
[115] Bradley Graham, "Air Power 'Effective, Successful,' Cohen Says," *Washington Post*, June 11, 1999.
[116] Neil King, Jr., "General Warns NATO to Expect More Bombing, Civilian Casualties," *Wall Street Journal*, May 27, 1999.
[117] That was the final assessment of an unofficial post campaign bomb-damage survey conducted in Serbia, Kosovo, and Montenegro by a team of inspectors representing Human Rights Watch. An Air Force analyst who was later briefed on the study commented that Human Rights Watch had "the best on-the-ground data of anyone in the West." "A New Bomb Damage Report," *Newsweek*, December 20, 1999, p. 4.

efficacy. The fact that foolish gambles sometimes pay off does not make them any less foolish."[118]

In sum, despite the campaign's successful outcome and through no fault of allied airmen, Operation Allied Force was a suboptimal use of air power by those responsible for the strategy that governed its application. The incremental campaign plan chosen by NATO's leaders risked squandering much of the capital that had been built up in air power's account since its success in Desert Storm nearly a decade before. Clark's early comment that NATO would "grind away" at Milosevic rather than hammer him hard and with determination attested powerfully to the watered-down nature of the strikes.[119] By metering those strikes with such hesitancy, NATO's leaders remained blind to the fact that air power's very strengths can become weaknesses if the air weapon is used in a way that undermines its credibility.[120] The opportunity costs incurred by NATO's anemic start of the campaign without any accompanying ground threat included, most notably, a failure to exploit air power's inherent shock potential and the encouragement it gave Serbian ground forces to disperse and hide while they had time. Almost without question, the first month of underachievement in the air campaign due to the misapplication of air power convinced Milosevic that he could ride out the NATO assault and encouraged him to expand his human-rights abuses against the Kosovar Albanians.[121]

Indeed, the way Operation Allied Force commenced violated two of the most enduring axioms of military practice: the importance of achieving surprise and the criticality of keeping the enemy unclear as to one's intentions. True enough, there was virtually no chance that either the U.S. Congress or public opinion on either side of the Atlantic would have permitted a more aggressive NATO strategy than the one ultimately adopted. This is especially true in the absence of more top-level leadership preparation and consensus-building than was provided by the Clinton administration in this case. Nevertheless, the acceptance by U.S. military planners and their civilian superiors of a strategy that ruled out a ground threat preemptively and that envisaged only gradually escalating air strikes to inflict pain was no less a recipe for downstream trouble just because it was the only strategy that NATO would collectively endorse. For U.S. defense leaders to have suggested afterward that NATO's attacks against fielded Serbian ground troops "forced [those troops] to remain largely hidden from view . . . and made them ineffective as a tactical maneuver force" and that the SEAD campaign

---

[118] "Pax Clintonia," *National Review*, June 28, 1999, p. 10.
[119] Eric Schmitt, "Weak Serb Defense Puzzles NATO," *New York Times*, March 26, 1999.
[120] For a fuller development of this point, see Daniel L. Byman, Matthew C. Waxman, and Eric Larson, *Air Power as a Coercive Instrument*, Santa Monica, Cal., RAND, MR-1061-AF, 1999.
[121] Jim Hoagland, "Stopping a Mass Murderer," *Washington Post*, June 6, 1999.

forced Milosevic to "husband his antiaircraft missile defenses to sustain his challenge" to NATO air operations was to make a virtue of necessity on two counts.[122] In fact, it was the absence of a credible NATO ground threat that *enabled* Milosevic's troops to disperse and hide, making it that much more difficult for NATO's aircrews to find and attack them. Their asserted ineffectiveness as a tactical maneuver force was quite beside the point, considering that tactical maneuver was not required for the ethnic cleansing of Kosovar Albanians, which those troops managed to sustain quite handily throughout most of the campaign's duration. And it would have been more honest to say that the Serbian tactic of carefully husbanding antiaircraft missile defenses throughout the campaign made those defenses a continuing threat to NATO's freedom to operate in Yugoslav airspace, undermining the effectiveness of many sorties as a result.

Accordingly, perhaps the most pressing question for the various "lessons-learned" enterprises that are now striving to make detailed sense of the air campaign has less to do with anything connected with platform or weapons performance than with the more basic strategy choices made by NATO's leaders and what those choices may suggest about earlier lessons forgotten, not only from Desert Storm and Deliberate Force but also from Vietnam. Had Milosevic been content to hunker down and wait out the bombing campaign, he could easily have challenged the long-term cohesion and staying power of the alliance. Fortunately for the success of the campaign, by opting instead to accelerate his ethnic cleansing of Kosovo, he left NATO with no alternative but to dig in for the long haul simply to ensure its own credibility.

As for what airmen and other observers should take away from Allied Force by way of lessons indicated and points worth pondering, the commander of the U.S. military contribution, Admiral Ellis, offered a good start when he declared in an after-action briefing to Pentagon and NATO officials that luck played the chief role in ensuring the campaign's success. Ellis charged that NATO's leaders "called this one absolutely wrong" and that their failure to anticipate what might occur, once their initial strategy of hope failed, occasioned most of the untoward consequences that ensued thereafter. These included the hasty activation of a joint task force, a race to find suitable targets, an absence of coherent campaign planning, and lost opportunities caused by the failure to think through unpleasant excursions from what had been expected. Ellis concluded that the imperatives of consensus politics within NATO made for an "incremental war" rather than for "decisive operations," that excessive concern over collateral damage created "sanctuaries and opportunities for the adversary—which were successfully

---

[122] Cohen and Shelton, "Joint Statement."

exploited," and that the lack of a credible NATO ground threat "probably prolonged the air campaign."[123]

One reason for NATO's overconfident belief that merely a few days of modest air strikes would be enough to compel Milosevic to desist in Kosovo may have been a questionable reading of the earlier Bosnian war and the role of Operation Deliberate Force in producing the Dayton accords in 1995. A false belief that air power alone had produced Milosevic's concession with respect to Bosnia may have helped inform NATO's miscalculation that he could be induced to knuckle under yet again in Kosovo after merely a few days of token bombing. As Adam Roberts noted with respect to the 1995 operation over Bosnia, "The mythologizing of that campaign ignored one inconvenient fact: that it followed a period of sharp Serb military reverses on the ground, including the mass expulsion of the Serbs from the Croatian Krajina. Also, the 1995 bombing was not against Serbia proper, and thus did not arouse the same nationalist response as would the bombing in 1999. The real lesson of those 1995 events might be a very different one: that if NATO wants to have some effect, including through air power, it needs to have allies among the local belligerents and a credible land-force component to its strategy."[124]

Indeed, that NATO prevailed in the end with only two aircraft lost and no combat fatalities surely reflected good fortune at least as much as the professionalism of its aircrews and their commanders. General Jumper explained afterward that "we set the bar fairly high when we fly more than 30,000 combat sorties and we don't lose one pilot. It makes it look as if air power is indeed risk free and too easy a choice to make." Amplifying on the same point, retired RAF Air Vice Marshal Tony Mason observed that seeking to minimize one's losses is both admirable and proper up to a point, yet it can lead to self-deterrence when efforts to escape the costs of war are pursued to a moral fault. Although force protection "must be a major concern for any force commander," Mason added, "my own view is that if Saint George's first priority with tackling dragons had been force protection, I don't think he would now be the patron saint of England."[125]

It is not too early to begin asking what the Allied Force experience implies for the future application of U.S. air power. Although the manner in which the campaign was conducted did not represent the ideal use of air power by any means, it nevertheless suggested that gradualism may be here to stay if

---

[123] Elaine M. Grossman, "For U.S. Commander in Kosovo, Luck Played Role in Wartime Success," *Inside the Pentagon*, September 9, 1999, p. 1.

[124] Adam Roberts, "NATO's 'Humanitarian War' over Kosovo," *Survival*, Autumn 1999, pp. 110–111.

[125] General John Jumper, USAF, and Air Vice Marshal Tony Mason, RAF (ret.), comments at an Air Force Association Eaker Institute colloquy, "Operation Allied Force: Strategy, Execution, Implications," held at the Ronald Reagan International Trade Center, Washington, D.C., August 16, 1999.

U.S. leaders ever intend again to fight within a coalition like NATO. As the vice chairman of the JCS, Air Force General Joseph Ralston, noted in a retrospective look at the experience, airmen will continue to insist, and rightly so, that a massive application of air power will be more effective than gradualism. Yet, Ralston added, "When the political and tactical constraints imposed on air use are extensive and pervasive—and that trend seems more rather than less likely—then gradualism may be perceived as the only option." [126] General Jumper likewise intimated that the United States may have little alternative but to accept the burdens of an incremental approach as an unavoidable cost of working with shaky allies in the future: "It is the politics of the moment that will dictate what we can do. . . . If the limits of that consensus mean gradualism, then we're going to have to find a way to deal with a phased air campaign. Efficiency may be second." [127] Insofar as gradualism may be the wave of the future, it means that airmen will have to discipline their natural inclination to bridle when politicians hamper the application of a doctrinally pure strategy, and to recognize and accept instead that it is, after all, political considerations that determine—or should determine—the way in which campaigns and wars are fought. [128]

On the plus side, the campaign's successful outcome despite its many frustrations suggested that U.S. air power may now have become capable enough to underwrite a strategy of incremental escalation irrespective of the latter's inherent inefficiencies. What made the gradualism of Allied Force more bearable than that of the earlier war in Vietnam is that in the more recent case, the allied advantages in stealth, precision standoff attack, and electronic warfare meant that NATO could fight a one-sided war against Milosevic with near impunity and achieve the desired result even if not in the most ideal way. [129] That was not an option when U.S. air power was a less developed tool than it is today.

The Kosovo experience further suggested some needed changes in both investment strategy and campaign planning. On the first count, the combination of marginal weather and the unprecedented stress placed on avoid-

---

[126] "Ralston Sees Potential for More Wars of Gradual Escalation," *Inside the Pentagon*, September 16, 1999, p. 1.

[127] "Washington Outlook," *Aviation Week and Space Technology*, August 23, 1999, p. 27.

[128] On this point, Air Vice Marshal Mason remarked that he had not "spent the past 25 years trying to persuade unbelievers of the efficacy of air power only to finish up whining because political circumstances made operations difficult." Personal communication to the author, October 22, 1999. In a similar spirit, the leader of USAFE's postcampaign munitions effectiveness investigation in Kosovo later suggested that airmen should "consider a politically restricted target list like the weather: complain about it, but deal with it." Colonel Brian McDonald, USAF, briefing at RAND, Santa Monica, Cal., December 14, 1999.

[129] See Colonel Phillip S. Meilinger, USAF, "Gradual Escalation: NATO's Kosovo Air Campaign, Though Decried as a Strategy, May Be the Future of War," *Armed Forces Journal International*, October 1999, p. 18.

ing collateral damage made for numerous days between March 24 and mid-May when entire ATOs had to be cancelled and when only the B-2, with its through-the-weather JDAM capability, could be used. That spoke for broadening the ability of other aircraft in all services to deliver accurate munitions irrespective of weather, as well as for ensuring that adequate stocks of such munitions are on hand to see the next campaign to completion. On the second count, the probability that coalition operations will be the rule rather than the exception in future years suggests a need to work out basic ground rules to the fullest extent possible *before* a campaign begins, so that once operators are unleashed, they can implement the plan with a minimum of political friction. As it was, Allied Force attested not only to the strategy legitimation that comes from the safety of numbers provided by working through a coalition, but also to the limitations of committee planning and least-common-denominator targeting. General Short commented that the need for 19 approvals of target nominations was "counterproductive" in many cases and that an appropriate conclusion was that "before you drop the first bomb or fire the first shot, we need to lock the political leaders up in a room and have them decide what the rules of engagement will be so they can provide the military with the proper guidance and latitude needed to prosecute the war."[130]

Finally, the United States displayed an ability in this case to apply coercion successfully through air power from a poorly prepared battlefield at a remarkably low cost in terms of noncombatant fatalities due to direct collateral damage.[131] Yet there is a danger that making a habit of such displays by accepting Allied Force as a model for future interventions could easily lead to an erosion of the United States' claim to global leadership. As Elliott Abrams cautioned in this respect, the picture "of a superpower willing to bomb but not to fight, willing to inflict a tremendous amount of pain on others to avoid the slightest risk to itself, under a leadership more sensitive to polls than to the moral considerations involved in deciding what is just—that is a picture that should repel us."[132] On the contrary, Allied Force should have underscored the fact that one of the most acute challenges facing U.S. policymakers in the age of a single superpower entails deciding when, and in what manner, to intervene in humanitarian crises that do not yet impinge directly on U.S. security interests.

---

[130] William Drozdiak, "Allies Need to Upgrade, General Says," *Washington Post*, June 20, 1999.
[131] A heated argument is now under way between defenders and critics of the Clinton administration's strategy for Kosovo over whether the approach taken, despite its low cost in terms of noncombatant lives lost to *direct* collateral damage, nonetheless produced an unconscionably high loss of civilian innocents to the Serbian ethnic cleansing campaign that it allegedly accelerated. For a snapshot summary of the positions on both sides, see Christopher Layne and Benjamin Schwarz, "For the Record," *National Interest*, Fall 1999, pp. 9–15, and Ivo Daalder, "NATO and Kosovo," *National Interest*, Winter 1999/2000, pp. 113–117.
[132] Elliott Abrams, "Just War. Just Means?" *National Review*, June 28, 1999, p. 18.

As for the oft-noted concern over the prospect of sustaining an unbearable level of friendly casualties had NATO opted to back up the air campaign with a ground element, there most likely would have been no need actually to *commit* NATO troops to battle in the end. By its implications alone, a serious Desert Shield–like deployment of NATO ground troops along the Albanian and Macedonian borders would have made their Serbian counterparts more easily targetable by allied air power. Had such a deployment commenced in earnest, it also may have helped to deter, or at least lessen, the ethnic cleansing of Kosovo by giving Serbian ground forces a more serious concern to worry about. In both cases, it could have enabled a quicker end to the campaign.

This suggests an important corrective to the seemingly unending argument between airmen and land combatants over the relative merits of air power versus "boots on the ground." Although Operation Allied Force reconfirmed that friendly ground forces no longer need inexorably to be committed to combat early, it also reconfirmed that air power in many cases cannot perform to its fullest potential without the presence of a credible ground component to the campaign strategy. As former Air Force Chief of Staff General Merrill McPeak instructively elaborated on this point, "In a major blunder, the use of ground troops was ruled out from the beginning. I know of no airman—not a single one—who welcomed this development. Nobody said, 'Hey, finally, our own private war. Just what we've always wanted!' It certainly would have been smarter to retain all the options. . . . Signaling to Belgrade our extreme reluctance to fight on the ground made it much less likely that the bombing would succeed, exploring the limits of air power as a military and diplomatic instrument."[133]

ON THE USES AND ABUSES OF AIR POWER

Viewed in hindsight, perhaps the most remarkable thing about Operation Allied Force is not that it defeated Milosevic hands down, but rather that air power prevailed *despite* a NATO leadership that was unwilling to take risks and an alliance that held together only with often paralyzing drag. Lesson one from both Vietnam and Desert Storm, which NATO's leaders failed to honor in Allied Force, should have been that one must not commit air power in "penny packets," as the British say, to play less-than-determined games with the risk calculus of the other side. Although it can be surgically precise when precision is called for, air power is, at bottom, a blunt instrument designed to break things and kill people in pursuit of clear and militarily achievable objectives on the ground. Not without reason have airmen re-

---

[133] General Merrill A. McPeak, USAF (Ret.), "The Kosovo Result: The Facts Speak for Themselves," *Armed Forces Journal International*, September 1999, p. 64.

peatedly insisted since Vietnam that if all one wishes to do is to "send a message," call Western Union. On this point, Eliot Cohen hit the nail on the head squarely when he compared air power's lately acquired seductiveness to modern teenage romance in its seeming propensity to offer political leaders a sense of "gratification without commitment."[134]

The Persian Gulf war of 1991 conclusively demonstrated that air power can be decisive when its limitations are understood and it is used without compromise toward the fulfillment of a clear and realizable plan. The goal of American involvement in Desert Storm, after all, was neither to punish Saddam Hussein nor to transform Iraq as a political entity, but to force a withdrawal of Iraqi troops from Kuwait and, to the extent possible, break the back of Iraqi military power once diplomacy and economic sanctions proved unavailing. That goal was unambiguous from the outset and remained so to the very end. Yet in Allied Force, as in the earlier case of Bosnia before the United States and NATO finally mustered the resolve to carry out Operation Deliberate Force, many allied leaders could be said to have forgotten that basic rule.

To admit that gradualism of the sort applied in Allied Force may be the wave of the future for any U.S. involvement in coalition warfare is hardly to accept that it is any more justifiable from a military viewpoint for that reason alone. Quite to the contrary, the incrementalism of NATO's air war for Kosovo, right up to its very end, involved a potential price that went far beyond the loss of valuable aircraft, munitions, and other expendables. It risked frittering away the near-mystical reputation for effectiveness that U.S. air power had finally earned for itself in Desert Storm after more than three years of unqualified misuse during the Rolling Thunder campaign over North Vietnam a generation earlier. As the Gulf war experience showed and as both Deliberate Force and Allied Force ultimately reaffirmed, U.S. air power as it has evolved since the mid-1980s can do remarkable things when employed with determination in support of a campaign whose intent is not in doubt. Yet to conjure up the specter of "air strikes," NATO or otherwise, in an effort to project an appearance of "doing something" without a prior weighing of intended targets or likely consequences is to misemploy the air weapon inexcusably. After years of false promises by its most outspoken prophets, U.S. air power has become a more capable instrument of force employment than ever. Even in the best of circumstances, however, it can never be more effective than the strategy it is intended to support.

[134] Eliot A. Cohen, "The Mystique of U.S. Air Power," *Foreign Affairs*, January/February 1994, p. 109.

[7]

The Synergy of Air and Space

Until the 1991 Gulf war, Air Force aviators and space officers lived and worked almost literally in separate worlds. That condition was a natural consequence of the almost completely dissimilar origins and personnel makeup of the two communities. Rated airmen, for their part, were quintessential "operators," associated as they were with combat flying and its concerns. In contrast, the Air Force's space professionals evolved not out of the flying community, but rather from the secret worlds of overhead reconnaissance and advanced-systems acquisition. Their early interests were devoted exclusively to supporting the nation's strategic leadership, with a predominant focus on the mission of nuclear deterrence. Naturally for that reason, their training and career development steeped them not in the warrior arts, but rather, for the most part, in applied science, engineering, and systems management. As a result, they brought a pronounced technical approach to their work, which made for an almost preordained divide between the air and space components of the Air Force. That divide became ever more apparent as military space systems increasingly emerged from their formerly compartmented netherworld into the light of day.

To be sure, the term *aerospace* was coined as early as 1958 by the Air Force's then–chief of staff, General Thomas D. White, as if to suggest an embryonic vision of air power eventually extending its reach into space. Appreciation of space as a medium from which combat operations might someday be mounted was further acknowledged by the Air Force a year later when the Air Staff's director of advanced technology, Brigadier General Homer Boushey, foresaw orbiting satellites as instruments not only of peaceful space patrol, mutual inspection, and attack warning, but also of bombardment.[1] For the most part, however, air and space remained separate domains of activity within the Air Force, each populated by individuals with widely dissimilar vocabularies and mindsets.

There even developed what must be acknowledged as something of a mutual disdain between the two communities as distinctions began to form between the "real men" who wore wings and flew jets and those in the emerging missile and space world, who all too often were shrugged off by their aviator brethren as "techies," "pocket rockets" (a pejorative reference to the missileer's badge), and "space cadets," or—worse yet—"space geeks." For their part, the proud but beset-upon professionals in the fledgling space community took due note of their rejection by the operators and, in natural fashion, circled the wagons and forged a self-protective sense of separate identity.

That, in turn, led many in the space community to press for apartness rather than closer integration with the flying Air Force, and indeed for the development of a separate organizational base and doctrine. The more assertive among them went so far as to fashion themselves as the new pioneers of the dawning space age, looking to the day when they might become the vanguard of an independent U.S. space force. The latter sentiment was reflected in a 1985 essay in the Air Force's professional journal by a midcareer space officer, who wrote that the very term "aerospace doctrine . . . inappropriately links our air and space doctrines." On the contrary, he insisted, space systems have characteristics fundamentally different from those of air-breathing systems, "which cause differences in the principles of war as they apply to possible conflict in space. Thus space is unique."[2] This officer suggested that "the environmental principles of aerospace war do not uniformly apply to space because the air and space environments are different." Given the distinctive characteristics of orbital operations, he declared, there is no doctrinal foundation for the term *aerospace*. He further asserted that existing space doctrine was "highly constrained by . . . the misapplication of air principles to space."[3]

It was only in the crucible of the 1991 Persian Gulf war, however, that the synergistic potential of air and space assets first began to be fully recognized and appreciated by airmen and space professionals alike. In manifold unexpected ways, space demonstrated what it could bring to the new face of air warfare as first displayed in Operation Desert Storm. In the end, the effective exploitation of space by U.S. Central Command (CENTCOM) and

---

[1] Brigadier General Homer A. Boushey, USAF, "Blueprints for Space," *Air University Quarterly Review*, Spring 1959, p. 18.
[2] Lieutenant Colonel Charles D. Friedenstein, USAF, "The Uniqueness of Space Doctrine," *Air University Review*, November–December 1985, p. 13.
[3] Ibid., p. 21.

other U.S. agencies occasioned a post–Gulf war blossoming of space aware-ness at all levels, which offered unprecedented promise, albeit in a way and along a route perhaps least expected by either space professionals or rated combat pilots.[4]

SPACE SUPPORT TO DESERT STORM

When Iraq invaded Kuwait on August 2, 1990, the first coalition assets to make their presence felt on scene were neither air, naval, nor land forces, but rather the U.S. space systems already on orbit high above the gathering storm. Although these assets played only a supporting role for coalition forces in the allied buildup and combat operations that followed, they were indispensable in determining the course and outcome of the war. Allied force enhancement through the medium of space came in the form of navi-gation and positioning support, communications, the provision of terrain and environmental information, weather reporting, indications and warn-ing, attack warning, and surveillance and reconnaissance. Each contribution by U.S. space systems was pivotal in ensuring the coalition's information dominance throughout the war.

On the first count, the Navstar global positioning system (GPS) came of age in Desert Storm by providing real-time navigation and targeting up-dates to numerous weapon types employed by coalition forces.[5] It proved particularly useful because of the undifferentiated terrain of the Iraqi desert, which presented unusually severe challenges to navigation.[6] Aircrews in combat aircraft equipped only with inertial navigation systems used hand-held GPS terminals to augment their less accurate analog navigational aids. Such GPS cues were especially useful to U.S. special operations forces, whose helicopter crews relied on them entirely for both day and night nap-of-the-earth penetrations into Iraq and Kuwait.

---

[4] For a thorough treatment of the antecedents to this development going back to the earliest days after World War II, see the Air Force Space Command's officially commissioned history by David N. Spires, *Beyond Horizons: A Half-Century of Air Force Space Leadership*, Washington, D.C., U.S. Government Printing Office, 1997.

[5] See Sir Peter Anson and Group Captain Dennis Cummings, RAF (Ret.), "The First Space War: The Contributions of Satellites to the Gulf War," *RUSI Journal*, Winter 1991, pp. 45–53.

[6] At the time, the GPS constellation had only 16 satellites in orbit, 5 short of the number required for full global coverage and 8 shy of the complete network, including 3 planned spares. One of the 16 satellites experienced a failure that threatened to degrade severely the war-support capability of the overall system. It remained off-line only until operators at Air Force Space Command's Falcon AFB developed the needed software to put it back in service. Walter Boyne, "A Great Tradition in the Making: The United States Air Force," *Aviation Week and Space Technology*, April 16, 1997, p. 134. For a snapshot overview of the GPS system and how it works, see also Peter Grier, "GPS in Peace and War," *Air Force Magazine*, April 1996, pp. 76–79.

A limited number of handheld GPS receivers were available for use by allied ground personnel as well. At first, only a few hundred of these, popularly known as "pluggers" (from PLGR, the acronym for "portable lightweight GPS receiver"), were on hand for coalition forces. By the war's end, there were thousands. As the value of these devices became clear and the demand for them peaked, the GPS program office made an emergency buy of 13,000 PLGRs for use on military vehicles, of which some 4,500 ultimately made their way to the theater.[7]

Because the GPS satellite constellation had not been fully completed at the time the Gulf war commenced in January 1991, there were seven time windows of up to 40 minutes each day during which fewer than the required minimum of four satellites were simultaneously in view of a receiver. These GPS "sad times," as they came to be called, obliged allied combatants to fall back on less capable systems and techniques or rely on less accurate GPS data. Nevertheless, GPS had a revolutionary impact on coalition operations throughout the Gulf war, perhaps most notably in facilitating the unerring 100-hour ground sweep across the flat and featureless Iraqi desert into the blind side of Iraqi troops hunkered down in the Kuwaiti theater of operations (KTO). All of this pointed toward a future in which such equipment would be standard for both air and surface operations.

As for allied communications, three satellites of the Defense Satellite Communications System (DSCS) constellation on high orbit enabled continuous high-capacity, high-data-rate, worldwide secure voice communications. These DSCS satellites supported 128 tactical terminals throughout the war. One of these satellites was moved from its orbit over the Pacific Ocean to the Indian Ocean to augment coalition communications, in the first instance of a Defense Department satellite having been repositioned to support combat operations. The data load was so heavy that commercial space systems capabilities were purchased to augment the dedicated military space capabilities. Ultimately, both these and the military's satellites provided the main conduit for 85 percent of all intratheater and intertheater communications. After the war ended, the chairman of the Joint Chiefs of Staff (JCS), General Colin Powell, declared that "satellites were the single most important factor that enabled us to build the command, control, and communications network for Desert Shield."[8]

With respect to overhead surveillance and monitoring, satellites of the Defense Meteorological Support Program (DMSP) provided commanders

---

[7] Curtis Peebles, *High Frontier: The United States Air Force and the Military Space Program*, Washington, D.C., Air Force History and Museum Program, 1997, p. 74.

[8] General Colin Powell, speech to the Armed Forces Communications Electronics Association, Washington, D.C., December 1990, cited in Lieutenant General Thomas S. Moorman, Jr., USAF, "Space: A New Strategic Frontier," *Airpower Journal*, Spring 1992, p. 19.

and planners with near-real-time weather information. Among other things, they enabled the remote analysis of desert soil moisture to help determine the best routes for CENTCOM's left hook into Iraq and Kuwait. As for combat intelligence and battle-damage assessment (BDA), classified national space reconnaissance platforms, along with other allied capabilities, were key contributors toward obtaining multispectral images of the theater and electronic intelligence. The last of these collection means focused on electronic intelligence turned out to be the least significant in the end, since the Iraqi command and control system and radar emissions from Iraq's integrated air defense system (IADS) went into a sharply reduced transmission mode within days of the war's commencement, in self-protective reaction to the incessant allied air attacks. Much of the difficulty that attended adequate BDA throughout the air campaign reflected procedural problems in the intelligence processing system and the enemy's concerted efforts to deny the coalition information rather than any inherent capacity limitations.[9] The American Landsat and French SPOT (for *satellite probatoire d'observation de la terre*) commercial remote sensing satellites were enlisted to provide additional imagery support for terrestrial observation, notably via broad-area views of sufficient resolution to enable the creation of tailor-made, yet unclassified, products for combat mission planning.[10]

A space surveillance system that proved to be crucial in dealing with the Iraqi Scud threat was the Defense Support Program (DSP) constellation of infrared-sensing satellites, which were able to detect the heat of the Scud's rocket exhaust plume within 30 seconds of launch. Although not originally designed to detect the launch of short-range ballistic missiles, DSP nonetheless helped greatly in alerting Patriot missile defense crews to an incoming attack. Owing to the fortuitous conduct by the Iraqis of three practice Scud launches during the course of the Desert Shield buildup, DSP operators were able to exploit those windfall events to tweak the system for better operations in a quick-response mode. As a result, Air Force Space Command (AFSPC) was ready when the first Iraqi combat use of Scuds occurred on the second night of Desert Storm.[11] The Scud's short time of flight from launch to impact (only seven minutes), however, limited the practical usefulness of such information, aside from its alerting value.

After the dust settled, the Air Force's chief of staff, General Merrill McPeak, described Operation Desert Storm as "the first space war," a characterization that was warmly embraced by many in the military space com-

[9] To be sure, another big part of the BDA problem was the limited observable damage caused by highly precise weapons.
[10] Dana J. Johnson, Scott Pace, and C. Bryan Gabbard, *Space: Emerging Options for National Power,* Santa Monica, Cal., RAND, MR-517-JS, 1998, p. 25.
[11] Peebles, *High Frontier,* p. 74.

munity.[12] Purists might demur on whether the strictly support functions performed by U.S. space assets in that war were sufficient to warrant such a categorical description. There is no denying, however, that the Gulf war represented the first instance in which the entire panoply of U.S. space assets was employed in direct, if considerably less-than-fully-integrated, support of combat operations at all levels. That amply bore out the more incontestable point by a British defense leader that Desert Storm "taught us that space has changed the whole nature of warfare."[13]

THE CREATION OF AN OPERATIONAL SPACE CULTURE

The unprecedented use of space systems for combat support in the allied campaign against Iraq and the surprising revelation of how crucial they were in shaping the course and outcome of almost all joint-force operations led to a dramatic change in the complexion and character of the military space community. At the outset of Desert Storm, commanders and planners had only limited insights into what space could do for them. For their part, space professionals had little insight into the kinds of support that terrestrially focused air, naval, and land warfighters needed. This mutual disconnect suggested a core problem with relationships and understanding between the two communities that sorely needed fixing. At bottom, the problem entailed harnessing U.S. space assets more closely in support of the needs of the warfighter—a challenge that had never been systematically embraced by *either* side. Fortunately, both airmen and joint-force leaders in general saw the outlines of a synergistic relationship between space and terrestrial operations that was ripe for further development and exploitation.

Although not prompted by any calculated master plan aimed at empowering Air Force operators, in effect, to shanghai the space establishment and recast it more in their own image, the appointment of General Charles A. Horner after Desert Storm to be commander in chief of the unified U.S. Space Command (CINCSPACE) proved to be a seminal event with respect to bringing the space and flying communities closer together. This was not, by any means, the first time that a fighter pilot had served as CINCSPACE. However, Horner's recent experience in the Gulf made for a unique difference. As the joint-force air component commander (JFACC) in Desert Storm, he had presided over air power's greatest combat accomplishment since World War II, made possible by the indispensable contributions of America's space

---

[12] General Merrill A. McPeak, USAF, briefing on Desert Shield and Desert Storm to the National War College, Fort Leslie J. McNair, Washington, D.C., March 6, 1991.
[13] Anson and Cummings, "The First Space War," p. 53.

assets. As a grateful beneficiary of those contributions, he well knew what potential he was inheriting in his new assignment.

One of the first milestones in the move to merge space with the warfighting community was a windfall inheritance by AFSPC of the Air Force's Minuteman and Peacekeeper intercontinental ballistic missiles (ICBMs) as a byproduct of the dissolution of Tactical Air Command (TAC) and Strategic Air Command (SAC). In the new organizational arrangement, Air Combat Command (ACC) brought together the Air Force's fighters and bombers and also found itself the new repositor of the Air Force's ICBM inventory. With the missiles making, at best, for an uncomfortable fit with ACC's primary air employment focus, however, they were soon transferred to AFSPC.

In hindsight, that move proved to have been inspired from the vantage point of both communities. The missileers found themselves, at long last, finally out from under the thumb of "airplane people" and embraced by a more sheltering community of like-minded professionals who spoke the language of space systems fluently. In turn, AFSPC found itself the sudden beneficiary of a surprise adoption of fellow nonrated airmen who also operated in the medium of space, yet supremely as warfighters with a combat mission as deadly serious as it was unlikely ever to be executed. The missileers brought to AFSPC not only a warfighting function but also the operational expertise that went with it, including combatant-oriented habits ingrained by the observance of such rituals as being part of a concrete war plan and generally thinking like professionals with a "shooter" role and not just a spectrum of support missions to carry out. The effect was to give the missileers a sense of identity with the space mission and the space technicians, for their part, a credible claim to warfighter credentials.

Growing awareness among Air Force leaders of the promise offered by such developments led, among other things, to the creation in 1992 of a Blue Ribbon Panel on Space as a part of the Air Force's initial analysis of Gulf operations. Chaired by then–Lieutenant General Thomas Moorman, at the time vice commander of AFSPC, the panel ratified what was already becoming more and more widely understood throughout the operational community, namely, that the Air Force's past emphasis in space development had been directed almost solely toward acquiring and operating satellite systems, with little attention given to exploiting those systems in the service of the terrestrial warfighter. One initiative prompted by this finding was the recommendation for creating an Air Force space applications and warfare center to develop new concepts and procedures for extracting greater value from existing space assets in support of air and joint-force operations.

Hard evidence of the operator hand at work in imparting a new vector to military space development was first provided by the establishment of the USAF Space Warfare Center (SWC) at Falcon AFB, Colorado, on November 1, 1993, during Horner's tenure as CINCSPACE. Modeled after the USAF

Weapons Center at Nellis AFB, Nevada, and Air Warfare Center at Eglin AFB, Florida, SWC promptly became the cutting edge of a determined effort to integrate space more fully into the daily operating routines of all the U.S. combat forces. Its avowed goal was not only to make space more relevant to the warfighter, but also to breed warfighters out of space professionals along the way. One of its principal functions is to develop new concepts for better applying U.S. military space equities in support of joint-force planning, operations, and training.

The Air Force's SWC was born out of a recognition that although space had been exploited more effectively than ever before in support of military operations in Desert Storm, there remained serious deficiencies, including an unacceptably slow cycle time for getting space-derived information from sensors into the hands of planners and warfighters. Another problem lay in the excessive compartmentation of highly classified information pertaining to U.S. space systems and their operational contribution, often producing such gridlock that the needed material frequently never made its way to those who needed it most.

The activities of SWC to date have included the development of tools to exploit the accuracy of GPS information for target location and accurate weapons delivery; the prompt transmittal of space-derived intelligence and weather products to operators; and the use of existing communications systems to deliver imagery, manifests, and mission taskings directly into the cockpits of airborne aircraft on combat missions. A particularly impressive demonstration of the potential offered by GPS for real-time strike mission targeting was provided in a test conducted out of Nellis AFB in 1994 called Strike II, in which an airborne F-15E was successfully vectored to attack a simulated mobile Scud missile launcher at night using satellite-derived target location coordinates.[14]

A related SWC activity involves cultivating a broadened base of knowledge and expertise in response to the 1992 Blue Ribbon Panel finding that then-extant resources were inadequate to support fully integrated air and space mission planning and execution. Innovations in this respect have included bringing space to Blue Flag campaign planning exercises at Eglin AFB, the establishment of a space training facility at Red Flag at Nellis AFB, and the addition of a Space Division (an evolution of the former USAF Space Tactics School) at the USAF Weapons School, also at Nellis. The latter activity now offers a space weapons instructor course, as well as hands-on training for aircrews in what space has to offer those at the sharp end of the lance, in particular how the bit streams from the wide variety of military and commercial space systems can be exploited by mission planners to help improve

---

[14] Briefing to the author by Brigadier General Glen W. Moorhead, USAF, "The Space Warfare Center," Falcon AFB, Col., April 4, 1997.

the effectiveness of air combat operations. The intent of these and related efforts is to build a cadre of "space-smart" operators, both rated and nonrated, and to seed them throughout the combat air forces at all levels, with the ultimate goal of generating an expanded base of space literacy among those with their fingers on the trigger.

Much of the ongoing integration of space with the military operational community can be chalked up to the fact that U.S. Space Command has now had five CINCs in a row whose career maturation occurred primarily in the world of combat flying. Horner was followed by General Joseph W. Ashy, likewise a fighter pilot with comparable background, having commanded NATO air operations over Bosnia before taking over the helm as CINCSPACE. Ashy, in turn, was replaced by General Howell M. Estes III, who once served as commander of the Air Force's F-117 wing and later was director of operations on the Joint Staff. Upon Estes' retirement in 1998, U.S. Space Command was taken over by General Richard B. Myers, who previously was the commander of Pacific Air Forces and also once headed the USAF Weapons School. Two years later, Myers was replaced by General Ralph E. Eberhart, yet another career fighter pilot who previously had commanded ACC.

One can imagine impassioned debate among airmen at all levels who have made the career transition to space whether it may yet take a succession of several more CINCs of similar background at U.S. Space Command to ensure that enough of a generational shift has occurred to render the continuing integration of space with joint-force operators irreversible. There is little question, however, that owing to the cumulative influence of Generals Horner, Ashy, Estes, Myers, and Eberhart in uninterrupted succession, a change of major note has been registered in both the orientation and the outlook of the military space community. For years, space people all but begged for attention and acceptance by the operational Air Force, and "space push" — often to little or no avail — was typically the rule. Since Desert Storm, this rule has changed unmistakably to "operator pull," with former fighter pilots in senior leadership positions setting both the tone and the example, no doubt to a mixed and still-uncertain reaction from some of the more tenured individuals in the space career field, who may privately wonder whether the apparent seizure of military space by these interlopers wearing wings has altogether been a welcome development.

Much road remains to be travelled before the rated and nonrated officers who have found themselves thrust together in the space community can be said to have learned to speak a common language. The relationship between the two groups is still uneasy in many respects, as old habits and thought patterns on both sides remain slow to evolve and as mutual suspicions linger. That said, the bringing of space to the service of the warfighter is no longer something to which the Air Force leadership merely pays lip service. Indeed, *all* of the uniformed services now depend heavily on the many and varied space support functions provided by the Air Force for their own mission performance. The commander of Army Space Command stated in 1997 that the success of the roadmap outlined in *Army Vision 2010* depends on it and that the Army After Next concept (see Chapter 8) will be gravely constrained without it.[15] With 50 percent of the surface naval fleet deployed at any time, the commander of Navy Space Command likewise acknowledged that the Navy is "functionally dead in the water without space."[16]

SPACE AS A NEW MEDIUM OF OPERATIONS

Throughout most of the cold war, military space systems were devoted almost exclusively to supporting the nation's nuclear readiness posture and intelligence collection requirements. Today, they have become indispensable in providing added leverage to U.S. and allied military forces across the board. As the Defense Department's annual report for fiscal year 1996 acknowledged, space assets have become a "major element of U.S. military power," and their use has evolved "from an initial focus on providing peacetime support for national decisionmakers and strategic nuclear operations to more extensive integration into overall force structure and broader application in support of the warfighter."[17]

The spectrum of military space missions starts with space support and progresses through force enhancement to space control and finally to force application. Because of equipment and treaty limitations, only the first two of these are currently being performed to any significant degree. The first, space support, essentially involves the launching and operating of spacecraft. To date, the high cost of access to orbit has been the single greatest limitation on the further military exploitation of space. In time, however, successor-generation launch alternatives should feature new means of lift at substantially reduced cost, which will enable access to space on an increasingly routine basis.

The second military space mission, that of force enhancement, embraces the spectrum of services that American space assets provided joint-force commanders in Desert Storm. Activities in this area include navigation, weather, communication, Earth resources monitoring, reconnaissance and surveillance, round-the-clock GPS operations, and missile attack warning

---

[15] Comments by Lieutenant General Edward Anderson, USA, to the 13th annual symposium of the U.S. Space Foundation, Colorado Springs, Col., April 3, 1997.

[16] Comments by Rear Admiral Patrick Moneymaker, USN, to the 13th annual symposium of the U.S. Space Foundation, Colorado Springs, Col., April 3, 1997.

[17] Secretary of Defense William J. Perry, *Annual Report to the President and the Congress*, Washington, D.C., Government Printing Office, March 1996, p. 205.

and characterization. Specific enhancement functions might include monitoring sea states and enemy naval movements, locating in real time enemy artillery and armor on the move, identifying and determining preferred routes of ground advance and attack, and providing real-time situation awareness to friendly ground forces to keep them from inadvertent encounters with enemy fire.

The third mission area, space control, is conceptually comparable to the notions of air and sea control. It entails ensuring the freedom to operate unmolested in space and denying an enemy the use of space. At present, the space control mission is almost completely undeveloped. About all the United States can do today to deny an enemy access to the data stream from space is to jam or physically destroy ground satellite stations. If and when space becomes a medium of hostile action, however, ensuring friendly access and denying enemy access will become more and more a security imperative, necessitating both defending against attack and negating enemy systems, whether on orbit or on the ground. Passive hardening of satellites offers an interim solution, but it is costly and can easily be countermeasured.

Once developed, the space control mission area will be dominated by passive missile detection and both passive and active space defense. Such capabilities will be natural extensions of today's multisensory tracking systems, antisatellite weapons, and embryonic decoy and deception technologies and concepts. As the wherewithal to provide it becomes increasingly available, space control will involve protecting U.S. and allied satellites as a first order of business. It will also involve operations to disable systems on orbit or transiting space, as well as disabling or destroying ground communications and control facilities for spacecraft.

Development of the force application mission will complete the Air Force's transition from an air instrument to a true air and space power. At present, any such effort would violate the threshold of political acceptability because of treaty limitations. However, it could ultimately lead to the deployment and use of such exotic weapons as space-based lasers to intercept ballistic missiles and destroy or neutralize other satellites. In the more distant future, force application may also involve the use of space-based nonnuclear, hyperkinetic weapons against terrestrial aim points, ranging from fixed high-value targets such as hardened bunkers, munitions storage depots, underground command posts, and other heavily defended objectives to surface naval vessels and possibly even armored vehicles and other ground force targets of interest.

Unimpeded access to space will become increasingly important as friendly economies come to depend on it. This implies a bright future for the space control mission. Already, the American defense establishment has well over $100 billion worth of satellites on orbit. In addition, there is a

$7 billion-a-year commercial industry in telecommunications and remote sensing, with other civil applications yet to be discerned likely to follow.[18] As ever more billions of dollars get invested in space-based platforms and systems, these assets will become economic centers of gravity that will pose attractive targets to potential troublemakers. Such equities will have to be protected.

To note the most telling example, GPS has become critical to the United States in multiple ways. As a case in point, the civilian air traffic control system is slated to become wholly dependent on it by the year 2012. Moreover, Congress has mandated that GPS receivers be incorporated into every major U.S. weapons platform by the year 2000 as a precondition of that platform's receiving funding authorization. Of particular importance, the joint direct-attack munition (JDAM) and follow-on systems that will constitute the core of America's all-weather precision engagement capability during the next decade and beyond will depend wholly on real-time GPS cueing for terminal guidance. For these reasons and more, there is every ground for legitimate concern that GPS will be both challenged and subverted toward hostile ends. This means that the United States will need the wherewithal beforehand to deny GPS signals to an opponent while, at the same time, applying timely antijamming and antispoofing measures to prevent itself from being denied access to GPS.

As launch costs become ever cheaper and access to space becomes ever easier for those with the requisite money and willingness to spend it, the possibility that rogue powers and would-be regional peer competitors will seek to exploit space will naturally grow. Once launch costs are reduced to only a fraction of what they are today, a sea change will occur in the spectrum of threats both to and from space. In turn, increased American military and commercial dependence on space will demand an increasingly robust space control posture to protect it.

Moreover, since the technology for developing and employing space launch vehicles is the same as for ballistic missiles, the commercialization of space can have severe threat implications. More than 20 nations, not all friendly to the United States, are expected to possess and depend on space-based intelligence and targeting capabilities in the first decade of the 21st century. It also is projected that by the year 2000 or shortly thereafter, some 20 countries will have roughly 12,000 short- and medium-range ballistic missiles.[19] In light of that, the proliferation of nuclear weapons to both state

---

[18] See Jonathan S. Landay, "Drawing Battle Lines in Space," *Christian Science Monitor*, December 17, 1997.

[19] General Thomas S. Moorman, Jr., "The Challenges of Space beyond 2000," in Alan Stephens, ed., *New Era Security: The RAAF in the Next Twenty-Five Years*, Proceedings of a Conference held by the RAAF, Air Power Studies Center, RAAF Fairbairn, Canberra, Australia, June 1996, p. 171.

and nonstate actors may well, as its first consequence of note, render the weapons in space issue moot.

As for the character of other possible threats to American space assets during the coming decade, opponents might seek to disrupt space-based information systems by applying information-based attack techniques. As former CINCSPACE General Ashy noted, it matters not whether threats to friendly space systems employ kinetic kill mechanisms or the ones and zeros of computer code.[20] Either way, the effect will be the same. One problem already at hand in this respect is attack characterization, including the determination of whether space-based information assets have in fact been attacked—as opposed to "hacked" by amateurs or subjected to natural disruptions.

Enemies also may seek, either by jamming or by physical interference, to disrupt the data stream transiting space. As just mentioned, the GPS constellation is especially vulnerable in this respect, since its signals are weak and easily blocked. In addition, unlike hardened or otherwise protected military systems, commercial space equities, particularly their uplinks and downlinks, could be highly prone to jamming or other countermeasures. This makes for a legitimate concern, since it is a reasonable projection that 70 to 80 percent of the military's space communications needs will eventually be handled by commercial satellites.[21] Commercial ground stations will also be more susceptible to physical attack than military systems, which typically will enjoy at least perimeter security.[22] Moreover, ground-based components of space systems will make for attractive targets because of their relative ease of access by garden-variety weapons readily available to all, as contrasted with satellites even in low orbit. Space platforms require extensive support from ground stations, some necessarily outside the United States.

Hostile exploitation of space, even if only by leveraging the capabilities of commercial remote sensing systems, could cause American forces to be imaged in a way and at a time that would seriously compromise their effectiveness—and even safety—at crucial moments during an impending showdown. Indeed, much of the high-end space reconnaissance technology that gave the coalition such a pronounced edge in Desert Storm is now becoming readily available on the commercial market for anyone willing and able to pay for it. Commercial satellites now nearing operation offer a resolution of as little as three feet, clearly within the range of militarily useful detail. Paced by the French in the mid-1980s and the Russians in 1992, who in turn made commercially available global imagery with a resolution of

---

[20] Conversation with General Joseph W. Ashy, USAF (Ret.), Las Vegas, Nev., April 18, 1997.
[21] Moorman, "The Challenges of Space beyond 2000," p. 168.
[22] Johnson, Pace, and Gabbard, *Space*, p. 23.

first 30 feet and then ten feet, the Clinton administration in 1994 finally faced
the inevitable and approved the commercial sale of selected U.S. overhead
reconnaissance technology so as to ensure a fair position for American industry in the emerging post–cold war competition in this sector.

The current prospect is for a dozen or more civilian satellites offering a
militarily usable fineness of resolution to be launched over the next decade,
thus ending the long-standing monopoly of the advanced powers in space-
based surveillance and reconnaissance. The net result will be to give rogue
states like Libya and North Korea access to reconnaissance capabilities analogous to those of the United States and the former Soviet Union, potentially
undermining the ability of U.S. air and space power to capitalize on its current advantage of strategic and tactical surprise.[23] Had Iraq been able to access real-time commercial satellite information, the shock effect achieved
by General H. Norman Schwarzkopf's left hook into Iraq and Kuwait most
likely would have been compromised. Fortunately, the Soviets, by all indications, elected not to apprise Saddam Hussein of that impending move,
even though they almost surely knew of it from their own overhead monitoring. U.S. commanders in Desert Storm were further concerned that Iraq
might benefit militarily from information available from Western commercial weather satellites. Since there was no way to deny downlink transmissions to Iraq without denying satellite weather data to allied forces in the
Gulf region as well, known Iraqi weather satellite downlinks, along with an
unauthorized Iraqi Landsat receiver, were targeted and destroyed in the air
campaign.[24]

Already, hostile forces can threaten vital ground-based satellite uplinks
and downlinks. In the not-too-distant future, they also may be able to deto-
nate a nuclear weapon in the Van Allen belt, causing a blanket disruption of
many of the West's most vital satellites. Concern over such a prospect was
pointedly raised in a series of high-level war games conducted by the U.S.
Army, U.S. Strategic Command, and other joint agencies. By one informed
account, they gave land, sea, and air commanders "a new appreciation for
how dependent on space resources their operations have become."[25] In one
Army-sponsored game, a scenario set in the year 2020 involving an invasion of Ukraine by "a neighboring state" featured the early neutralization of
many American satellites by detonations of nuclear weapons on orbit aimed
at disrupting intelligence and communications channels and inhibiting any
Western intervention. As one game participant later said of this gambit,

[23] For additional details, see William J. Broad, "Private Ventures Hope for Profits on Spy Satellites,"
New York Times, February 10, 1997.

[24] Ibid., p. 27.

[25] William B. Scott, "Wargames Underscore Value of Space Assets for Military Ops," *Aviation Week
and Space Technology*, April 28, 1997, p. 60.

"They took out most of our space-based capabilities. Our military forces just ground to a halt."[26]

In all, American space power will need to protect both military and commercial space systems, just as the United States has ensured freedom of passage on the high seas since its emergence as a naval power. The United States can be expected to lead the way with military operations in and through space for much the same reason that it created its land, sea, and air arms—to provide a shield for valued equities that only such forces could ensure. Antisatellite weapons with conventional warheads will probably be the first to see service, since these have already been tested successfully and first-generation technology is well in hand.[27] Later space weapons effects, both defensive and offensive, may include radiation, directed energy, electromagnetic beams, and kinetic kill mechanisms. The development of space weapons for use against terrestrial targets almost certainly lies farther downstream, since the demise of the Soviet threat has eliminated the main source of urgency in that respect. In the interim, it may make more sense economically to rely on space-based sensors to find, fix, and identify surface targets, as they did in Desert Storm, and then cue terrestrial kill mechanisms, instead of pursuing more expensive space weapons.

THE PROMISE OF SPACE POWER IN NEW-ERA WARFARE

Most notable about the evolution of space power is not the individual systems and technologies as much as it is the way in which their interaction has yielded increased leverage from terrestrial weapons by extending the accessible reaches of both the vertical and horizontal dimensions. In so doing, it has hastened the transformation of air power at the same time it has heightened the lethality of other force elements. Because of what space power has brought to the military equation, *all* force elements can now see farther than ever before, indeed to the point of being able to see both globally and in real time. As a result, commanders in the field can now know better what they are seeing and where to hit. More important, they can know how better to make astute force committal decisions, all the way from the strategic and operational levels down to tactical confines. The big difference is that air power enjoys a pronounced advantage over the more reach-limited surface force elements in standoff capability, along with the increased survivability and speed of movement in all directions that naturally goes with it.

---

[26] Ibid.
[27] For the pertinent details, see Peebles, *High Frontier,* pp. 59–69.

Although still in early adolescence compared to the now-mature U.S. air posture, space power has nevertheless become an enabler that largely makes routinely possible the new strategy of precision engagement. It works, moreover, at all levels of conflict. Not only did it permit the successful outcome of Operation Desert Storm, but also it has been instrumental in supporting every American "presence" mission around the world since the end of the cold war. It was pivotal in facilitating the location and rescue of U.S. Air Force Captain Scott O'Grady, whose F-16 was downed by a Serbian SA-6 surface-to-air missile (SAM) over Bosnia in June 1995.

What new options in particular does space bring to air and joint warfare? First, the global awareness it offers in principle can take "shaping the battle-field" a considerable step further by allowing the United States situation control even before the first shot is fired. By providing commanders and planners with a much-enhanced, if still highly imperfect, real-time knowledge of where enemy forces are concentrated, space-derived battlespace information can better inform joint-force decisionmakers as to where to commit friendly assets and where to avoid making contact with the enemy. Second, space brings a new quality to air power by providing *persistent* presence. This is far more than simply "virtual" presence. Although America's space assets may be out of sight and therefore out of mind to most observers, they constitute a continuous on-station capability. To would-be opponents who understand what this can do, it will make for an omnipresent factor in their planning by bringing an open-ended dwell time to military assets working in the vertical dimension.

We can expect a directed migration of many military missions from air to space over time, moreover, as space technologies and systems continue to mature. Missile warning, communications, weather reporting, intelligence, and navigation have already made the transition. Surveillance by airborne platforms such as the airborne warning and control system (AWACS), the joint surveillance target attack radar system (JSTARS), and unmanned air vehicles (UAVS) is now being augmented and, in time, may too be supplanted by space-based surveillance systems.[28] Ultimately, space, intelligence, precision air attack, and information warfare will blend into a seamless whole,

---

[28] Such migration, however, will not occur until it becomes cost-effective in addition to being technically feasible. In the case of supplanting AWACS with a space system, as General Moorman explained, "You must develop a global system to have sufficient revisit rates to be useful. Additionally, if you are putting a radar capability in space, it has to be at low altitude because of a power aperture problem. You can't get the resolution at geosynchronous [orbit] or something like that. As a consequence, the combination of having to have a global capability with a high revisit rate and power for resolution means that you have to buy a large number of satellites. Depending on the altitude, it could be between 25 and 40 satellites. That may be a very expensive way to do the AWACS job." Moorman, "The Challenges of Space beyond 2000," Stephens, ed., *New Era Security*, p. 174.

with space-based information, surveillance, and reconnaissance (ISR) capabilities providing operational sequencing in the form of fusing and transmitting information, in some cases directly from the sensor to the shooter.

Third, space offers the unique downstream promise of supporting direct action by combatants who themselves are not at risk. Threats to employ forces that are unburdened by the risk of return fire can be wielded more credibly and confidently than might otherwise be possible. Operations from space that cannot be readily countered by terrestrial forces promise a radical extension of what, in air-to-air combat, is now called first shot with impunity.

Fourth, operating from space offers the advantage of transcending— quite literally—certain geopolitical constraints that sometimes hinder air power, such as overflight restrictions and the need for forward basing. Unlike terrestrial forces deploying to a theater of operations, space assets do not become increasingly prone to attack as they approach employment. In effect, space-based assets are constantly "forward deployed" and engaged, whether in peacetime or during crises and war.

Finally, and perhaps most important for the changing relationship between air and land forces in imposing combat effects, the heightened awareness made possible by the military exploitation of space is creating new maneuver options. First and foremost, by virtue of the awareness of enemy troop locations it offers, it means that the placement of friendly land forces in harm's way may no longer be necessary when those enemy forces can be better engaged by precision standoff air attacks.

Of course, as with reliance on most new technologies, the routine use of space-based assets can have a boomerang effect on occasion. Such an effect may have been at work in the untimely death of the Chechen rebel leader Dzhokar Dudayev, who was finally taken out, apparently, in an uncharacteristically effective application of Russian air power on April 24, 1996. In an operation that most likely reflected a fortuitous blend of skill, technology, and luck, Russian intelligence zeroed in on Dudayev's location and transmitted coordinates to Russian ground-attack aircraft, which in turn reportedly fired radio-frequency homing missiles that targeted Dudayev while he was talking on a satellite field telephone.[29] According to later press accounts, two missiles were electronically guided by signals bouncing between the portable phone's antenna and a relay satellite. Understandably, the Russian Ministry of Defense refused to confirm or deny this account of events. If there is any truth to it, however, Dudayev may have been the first victim not

---

[29] See Richard Boudreaux, "Chechens Drop Russia Talks after Leader's Death," *Los Angeles Times*, April 25, 1996. Russian forces had been on the hunt for Dudayev, without success, ever since the beginning of the Chechen war in December 1994.

only of Russian "information warfare," but perhaps also of an emerging law of unintended consequences for military space exploitation that should concern us all.

GROWING THE INTEGRATION OF AIR AND SPACE

Aside from the windfall collapse of the Soviet threat in 1992, the unprecedented focus that has been placed on bringing together U.S. air and space capabilities since Desert Storm may have been the most pivotal development behind making American military power so preeminent in the world today. As General Moorman summarized where the nation is headed in this respect, "An integrated air and space program that combines total battlefield awareness and knowledge with rapid and dependable communications to get information to the decisionmaker or shooter, fully integrated with highly capable, survivable aircraft and a fleet of unmanned aerial vehicles, both with precision munitions, is the wave of the future."[30] Owing to this new focus, space has now been routinely integrated into joint training and exercise schedules, U.S. Space Command maintains a presence in support of every combatant commander, and a permanent space support cell has been provided for every JFACC around the world. These are but three of the many steps toward the closer integration of air and space that have been implemented by the defense establishment since Desert Storm.

That said, the Air Force has a considerable way to go before its transmutation into a true aerospace force will be fully consummated. Its vision statement promulgated in the immediate wake of its watershed 1996 Corona conference flatly announced that the service saw itself as transitioning from an "air force" into an "air and space force" on an evolutionary path toward becoming a "space and air force."[31] That announcement, according to General Moorman, was "incredibly significant" in that it reflected not just the thinking of "a subset of folks doing a focused study, but rather the consensus of the Air Force leadership."[32] Yet since then, both friends and critics have raised some troubling questions over the extent to which that leadership is genuinely committed to moving the Air Force into space and, indeed, as to whether the Air Force is even the appropriate service to inherit the mantle of space exploitation in the first place.

On both counts, echoing the concerns of many space promoters both in

[30] Moorman, "The Challenge of Space beyond 2000," p. 173.
[31] Quoted in Daniel Gouré and Stephen A. Cambone, "The Coming of Age of Air and Space Power," in Daniel Gouré and Christopher S. Szara, eds., *Air and Space Power in the New Millennium*, Washington, D.C., Center for Strategic and International Studies, 1997, p. 38.
[32] Letter to the author from General Thomas S. Moorman, Jr., USAF, July 8, 1997.

and out of uniform, General Horner offered his own view in 1997 that with respect to space exploitation, "the Air Force is kind of where the Army was in 1920" regarding the nation's embryonic air power, namely, "in a state of denial." In league with others who have wondered whether the Air Force's claim to being on an evolutionary path toward becoming a space force was genuinely motivated or merely reflected a clever ploy to buy off, while the time was ripe, any would-be separatists who might, at some point, seek a divorce from the Air Force to form an independent space service, Horner added that "it almost becomes, at its most cynical, a roles and missions grab on the part of the Air Force to do this air and space to space thing."[33]

In the face of such questioning of the Air Force's depth of commitment to space, the chairman of the Senate Armed Services Committee's Subcommittee on Strategic Forces, Senator Bob Smith, fired an unmistakable shot across the bow at a conference on aerospace power held in 1998 when he challenged the Air Force leadership, in effect, to show its commitment by sinking more of its resource share into space or else give up its claim to space and clear the way for the establishment of a separate space service. While freely acknowledging everything the Air Force has done thus far to grow a space infrastructure and to bring its contributions to the warfighter, he complained that even the cutting-edge activities of SWC as described in the preceding pages have been focused "primarily on figuring out how to use space systems to put information into the cockpit in order to more accurately drop *bombs* from *aircraft*." He added—correctly if also disapprovingly—that "this is not space warfare; it is using space to support air warfare." Charging that the Air Force viewed space essentially as little more than an information medium to be integrated into existing air, land, and sea forces rather than as a new arena for being developed as a mission area in its own right, Smith went on to note that he did not see the Air Force "building the material, cultural, and organizational foundations of a service dedicated to space power." As evidence, he cited its "paltry" investments in such areas as space-based missile defense and a spaceplane, its failure to advance more space officers into the most senior general-officer ranks, and its alleged slowness to nurture a cadre of younger officers dedicated exclusively to space warfare.[34]

Warming to his theme, Smith then charged that "the notion that the Air Force should have primary responsibility for space is not sacred," invoking as proof a gauntlet thrown down by Marine Corps commandant General

---

[33] Quoted in Brendan Sobie, "Former SPACECOM Chief Advocates Creation of Separate Space Force," *Inside Missile Defense*, November 19, 1997, p. 24.

[34] Senator Bob Smith (Republican, N.H.), "The Challenge of Space Power," speech to an annual conference on aerospace power held by the Fletcher School of Law and Diplomacy and the Institute for Foreign Policy Analysis, Cambridge, Mass., November 18, 1998, emphasis in the original.

Charles Krulak, who had declared at the same conference the year before that "between 2015 and 2025, we have an opportunity to put a fleet on another sea. And that sea is space. Now the Air Force [is] saying, 'Hey, that's mine!' And I'm saying, 'You're not taking it.'" While acknowledging that any interservice competition that might develop along these implied lines could quickly devolve into an undesirable "Balkanization of space power," the Senator nonetheless put the Air Force on notice that if it "cannot or will not embrace space power," then Congress would have no choice but to step into the breach and establish a new service.[35]

Most of the Air Force leadership today would probably respond to that charge by countering that it is not so much a question of *whether* to invest in space as one of when, how, and according to what schedule and plan. On the sensible premise that one must perfect walking before striving to run, they would also counter that the Air Force's next moves into space must necessarily ensure first the further integration of space with the needs of the terrestrial warfighter, however much that might appear to shortchange the career Air Force space officers who are ready *now* to make space the "fourth medium" of warfare.

In seeking a reasonable middle ground here, it seems fair to suggest that the development of military space applications by the United States must entail an orderly evolution over time and that the Air Force leadership, as well as space supporters in Congress, must endeavor to *enable* change toward that end rather than try to force it. Moreover, since the potential offerings of space promise to redound ultimately to the benefit of all terrestrial force elements, and not just to that of air power, it may be that solely "air and space" integration is an excessively narrow paradigm for the kind of evolutionary change that is really called for and that the real question, at least for the near term, should be what tomorrow's joint-force commanders will need in principle by way of ISR support and how best to meet those needs irrespective of the medium. As for the good news, all concerned players in this regard are working with a clean slate when it comes to doctrine and concepts of operations. Key directives have yet to be written, and a master plan for system development remains to be agreed upon. As a result, the sky is literally the limit for fresh thinking and new ideas.

Next Steps in the Move to an Air and Space Force

For the immediate years ahead, the most effective leveraging of space will come from seeking synergy through closer integration of existing forces, such as tying together in real time inputs from space systems and UAVs to cue a B-1, B-2, or F-15E loaded with accurate, through-the-weather conven-

[35] Ibid.

tional munitions. This is the sort of innovative option that a dedicated Air Force tactics, techniques, and procedures manual for air and space might usefully codify. Along the way toward refining a repertoire that makes the fullest use of the nation's space assets, it will be essential, as always, that airmen, space and information warriors, and intelligence professionals all train the way they plan to fight.

Beyond that, developing a more common language among those communities and breaking down the institutional walls that still keep them apart will be crucial for ensuring that such a transformation becomes complete. This will necessarily involve a two-way street. Senior fighter pilots who have made the transition to space have been among the first to acknowledge that resistance to change persists among aviators no less than among diehard space separatists.[36] On the plus side, those in the flying world who still characterize their nonrated space brethren as "space geeks" are, more and more, now doing so in a tone of accepting comradeship rather than in their once-dismissive way. This is as it should be, for the latter will have to be nurtured as fully equal fellow combatants, just as weapons systems operators in the fighter world have gradually come to be over time, if full air and space integration is to occur.

Toward that end, consciously directed cross-fertilization between the two communities should help greatly toward building and spreading space awareness throughout the armed forces. One such avenue might involve putting greater numbers of combat pilots into space billets, just as Air Force fighter pilots are now assigned as air liaison officers with Army field units, and bringing space operators with weapons schooling and swc experience into mainstream mission planning and training assignments not only throughout the combat air forces but also in the principal U.S. joint-force commands around the world. In tomorrow's air and space community, combat aviators will increasingly find themselves sharing the operator spotlight with UAV pilots, space controllers, and information warriors, all of whom will be bona fide trigger pullers with a common operational-level responsibility and outlook. It may not be for some time yet that information warriors and space combatants will displace line pilots in the topmost positions of Air Force leadership. However, there is no question that rated operators will have to become more fluent in the instruments of space and information warfare if they are to become truly adept in their use. There also is no question that the very conception of the term *operator* will have to be rethought from the ground up in the face of the space and information revolutions.

All of this suggests that any idea of gravitating toward a separate U.S. space service, at least today, would be more counterproductive than help-

---

[36] Conversation with General Howell M. Estes III, USAF, Headquarters U.S. Space Command, Colorado Springs, Col., April 4, 1997.

ful, considering that the synergy offered by recent developments in space exploitation has already worked wonders for joint-force commanders and, as such, warrants closer integration with air power rather than detachment from it. The Air Force's former deputy chief of staff for air and space operations struck the right tone in this connection when he stressed that "we want to make sure that as we evolve into the . . . era of air and space, we're all airmen at heart. . . . We shouldn't be arguing about the line of demarcation up there where the last molecule of air has departed and we enter the vacuum of space. We should be arguing about the effects."[37]

Worst of all would be the establishment of a separate and independent space service for the wrong reason. There is an entirely plausible argument why such an option might appear superficially attractive to some who knew better but might nevertheless feel driven toward it of necessity. As General Horner repeatedly insisted in this connection, "As long as each service is funded at an artificial rate almost equal to one-third of the defense budget, the Air Force will be hard-pressed to fill its core air responsibilities, while expanding its role in space. All of this means that our space force may indeed become a military entity in its own right." Horner was on target in cautioning that "at some point, the nation must ask itself whether our air and space capabilities should remain artificially limited with the present budgeting methodology, when both functions are becoming of greater importance to our defense strategy."[38] That point noted, however, it would seem a perversion of common sense were such a problem to be addressed, in the end, by organizational sleight of hand rather than by rational choice.

What the nation arguably needs most today from the military promise of space is more seamless air and space operations and making more of investments already made before spending additional funds in new directions. To split off a separate space service now would merely insert a new seam, and perhaps even a wedge, between air and space at just a time in history when the Air Force has made major gains in bringing operationally meaningful space support to the regional CINCs and to the subordinate force elements in all four armed services. Perhaps by 2020 or even before, the weaponization of space and the application of force through, from, and in space will have evolved to a point where U.S. Space Command will have earned all the rights and responsibilities of an independent service, and conceivably even the justification for being transformed into one. In the meantime, much progress remains to be made in bringing the operational community to a fuller understanding and appreciation of what *existing*

[37] Lieutenant General John Jumper, USAF, "Air Power Initiatives and Operations: Presentation for the European Air Attaché Conference," annotated USAF briefing, no date given.
[38] General Charles A. Horner, USAF (Ret.), "Air Power: Growing beyond Desert Storm," *Aviation Week and Space Technology*, April 16, 1997, p. 73.

space systems have to offer. On this count, the director of the National Re-connaissance Office, Keith Hall, complained with good reason after the con-clusion of NATO's Operation Allied Force in 1999 that although allied com-manders and planners turned in an effective performance in the end, they made some important aspects of the campaign harder on themselves than they needed to be as a result of their still-underdeveloped space literacy. Stressing that professional military education in the four services still does not offer enough needed training in space systems, he went on to say: "I im-press upon [the service chiefs] the need to organize, train, and equip to use this stuff if they're going to rely on it, and not just call up the NRO [which ac-quires and operates the nation's diverse intelligence collection satellites] and say, 'Can you do this for us?' when we're engaged in an operation. . . . We're dealing with a situation where people are not trained, it hasn't been practiced in peacetime, and you have to scramble. . . . If they're going to rely on it, they're going to have to do their part of it."[39]

Resource Considerations

As noted earlier, the combination of the many and still-growing U.S. space and information assets has become an enabler not just of air power, but of *all* military power. This, in turn, has paved the way for a potential quantum change in the outlines of the interservice debate over roles and missions. Until recently, airmen could claim fairly that only they enjoyed a complete and unrestricted view of the battlespace because of their exclusive command of the vertical dimension. Now, however, with the growing ac-cessibility of space-derived global information by all combatants, *all* play-ers—those on the surface no less than those associated with air and space—can claim to "see beyond the horizon" and will have every incentive to seek an expanded piece of the action as a result. Already there have been mani-festations of this in some of the positions that were taken by the Army and Navy in the U.S. Defense Department's Deep Attack Weapons Mix Study and Quadrennial Defense Review of 1996 and 1997. In developing joint space doctrine, it will be important for U.S. civilian defense leaders to en-sure that the new leverage afforded by space is not allowed to feed distract-ing bureaucratic trench warfare over budget shares among the services when the desired goal is a rational allocation of resources in the interest of greater force integration by all of them.

Today, the United States stands at a crossroads regarding next steps in leveraging its space opportunities to greatest effect. One pointed question raised by some senior space officials concerns whether the services should

[39] John Donnelly, "NRO Chief: Services Ill-prepared to Work with Spy Satellites," *Defense Week*, July 12, 1999, p. 2.

take the near-term gamble of minimizing, or even skipping altogether, sizable chunks of the next generation of platform procurement so as to free up the necessary resources for operationalizing the new high ground of space sooner rather than later. Of course, few among them would deny that the United States must maintain adequate levels of capability in the more developed elements of air power, such as combat aircraft, precision weapons, and data fusion systems that will make the most of what they have to offer in the near term. Yet with no peer competitor on the horizon for at least the next decade and perhaps longer, it has become entirely debatable what "adequate levels of capability" means in practice. A core choice among the many options from which any resource allocation trades with respect to space are likely to come may thus be between continuing as planned with next-generation platforms like the F-22 and joint strike fighter and proceeding more aggressively to jump-start the military-technological revolution as it relates to the possibilities offered by developed space power.

Whatever the outcome, only in the context of a well-conceived and agreed-upon national strategy can such choices be made intelligently and responsibly. Without question, as General Estes pointed out in 1997, the Air Force will never succeed in making good on its vision statement about becoming a "space and air force" if it does not begin to invest greater sums in space.[40] Yet of all the uncertainties that currently affect the Air Force's near-term prospects for making the next steps toward becoming a true aerospace force, none is more overarching than the most basic question of how, and at what opportunity cost, that transformation will be financed. General Estes acknowledged that in an era of unusually tight budgets, space priorities will have to be balanced against equally vital nearer-term acquisition needs, and few other Air Force leaders would suggest that the Air Force can afford to abandon its core missions simply to free up money for moving into space.

Perhaps the main challenge the Air Force faces in this respect will be to learn better how to divest itself of existing legacy programs in an orderly fashion so as to generate the funds needed for taking on tomorrow's challenges. That will require careful trade-off analyses to determine the most appropriate medium—air or space—toward which its resources should be directed for any mission at any given time. Just because a mission *can* be performed from space does not mean that it *should* be. Any transition to space should be paced by a prior determination that the mission or function in question can be performed more cost-effectively from space than from the air. That, in turn, will mean laying down a firm technology base first, and then identifying reasonable transition points at which a migration of effort can be rationally justified. However much some may deem the military

[40] William B. Scott, "'Space' Competing for USAF Funds," *Aviation Week and Space Technology*, December 1, 1997, p. 69.

exploitation of space to be a categorical imperative for the United States, not every investment need be a crash effort like the Manhattan Project, which developed the first American atomic bomb.

Finally, there is the hot-button issue of whose program interests across service lines will be forced to suffer when push comes to shove in order to finance an accelerated movement of American military power into space. For all his insistence on the need for a separate U.S. space service, General Horner also stressed that next-generation space investment opportunities and the F-22 "are too important to trade off against each other" and that the "fundamental problem" is to "expand air power *and* expand space power, obviously at the cost of the surface forces."[41] At best, it is debatable whether the establishment of a separate U.S. space force would generate the additional funds that would be needed to pay equal heed to the nation's air and space development needs without cutting into closely guarded Army, Navy, and Marine Corps accounts. What is not debatable is that the four services in the joint arena, let alone the Air Force by itself, are incapable of reapportioning the defense budget in favor of both air and space interests at the expense of U.S. surface forces. Trade-off decisions of that magnitude are what the most senior U.S. civilian defense leaders are paid to make, based on prior determinations of national priorities that lie well beyond the purview of the uniformed services.

In the meantime, as in the case of UAVs, perhaps the most well-advised development path for Air Force planners to follow will be to tackle the easy before taking on the more difficult. For example, despite the high likelihood of directed-energy weapons in space at some future point, it would seem to make sense for would-be space warriors first to understand and master ground- and air-based lasers, decide beforehand where the smartest investment areas lie, and then underwrite systems development selectively. One way of helping to ensure that the right choices get made will be to have a disciplined space roadmap that begins with clear concepts of operations and lets these drive requirements, rather than giving technology the lead. Here, America's past experience with air power theory (see Chapter 8) could be especially pertinent in counselling against repeating the mistake of the early pioneers of air power by promising too much too soon.

Toward a Dissolution of the Seams between Air and Space

Ideally, military space development should end up evolving much as air power did from its modest beginnings in World War I to its coming of age in Desert Storm. With their application limited solely to combat support through overhead reconnaissance and command and control enhancement,

---

[41] Sobie, "Former SPACECOM Chief Advocates Creation of Separate Space Force," p. 24.

U.S. space assets arguably contributed to joint operations in Desert Storm much in the same way that fledgling air power did when it was employed by the Italians against the Turks in Libya in 1911. Today, military space activities are a close analog of air power in its infancy during World War I, which generally has been accepted by historians as "the first air war."[42]

It follows that if one views space from an operational rather than an organizational or systems perspective, as this chapter has sought to do, one will naturally be driven to see it, at least for the near term, as simply an extension of the vertical dimension, which U.S. airmen should strive to exploit, to the extent of their resources, in pursuit of air power goals that have remained abiding since the first days of military aviation. After all, just as air power was the cradle of space exploration, so exploiting space as a part of the vertical dimension will be crucial to the continued transformation of air power.

Granted, Air Force planners would do well to reflect on Colin Gray's cautionary note that "a good case for Air Force preponderance in space . . . remains endangered by claims that no operational boundary exists . . . between air and space" and that while space assets indeed share with air assets the conduct of military activity in the "overhead flank" of terrestrial operations, it is essential to remember that "the space environment is geophysically and hence technologically, tactically, and operationally as distinctive from the air as it is from the land and the sea."[43] Yet while there is merit in Gray's stricture that any notion such as "aerospace" that "effects a linguistic fusion of physically and operationally distinctive elements needs to be treated with caution," it is no less true that physical differences between space and the atmosphere, such as those that distinguish astrodynamics from aerodynamics, will affect the *mode* of space operations but not their purpose. A functional or operational, as opposed to a systems, approach to thinking about space power application should make the differences between orbital and atmospheric operations irrelevant.

Those at the leading edge of military space exploitation over the past two decades have, to date, been much like modern-day equivalents of the early pioneers of the U.S. Army's Air Corps Tactical School during the 1920s and 1930s, who struggled hard to earn a place at the table for air power in the development of national military strategy and capability. Among the many indicators of this, one could include the emergence of "space" as an Air Force career field, the issuance of special "space" uniform insignia to symbolize it, efforts to formulate a military "space" doctrine, calling Desert Storm the first "space war," and ultimately the creation of AFSPC and U.S. Space Command. These and similar occurrences have been inevitable yet, in all likeli-

---

[42] See Lee Kennett, *The First Air War, 1914–1918*, New York, Free Press, 1991.
[43] Colin S. Gray, *Explorations in Strategy*, Westport, Conn., Praeger, 1996, pp. 64–65.

hood, also transitional milestones in today's still-embryonic process of making the leap from air power to air and space power. As such, they will probably become more and more vestigial over time as the seams between air and space ultimately dissolve.

Once that happens, U.S. airmen of the second decade of the 21st century should be as comfortable with operations in and around space as they are today with the lower reaches of the vertical dimension. Such a future also may see a gradual dissolution of the current organizational lines that separate space from the more familiar world of air-breathing aviation, much as TAC and SAC disappeared as separate entities with the dawning realization that distinctions between "strategic" and "tactical" had become artificial with the improved instruments of air warfare. There is every reason to expect a similar withering away of today's demarcations between "air" and "space," both conceptual and organizational, as working in the medium of space toward the application of air and space power toward terrestrial joint-force objectives becomes second nature to operators, whether or not they wear wings.

[8]

Untangling the Air Power Debate

Any attempt to understand the continuing controversy over air power and its proper place in American defense policy must begin with a retracing of the interservice dispute over which force elements did what in Operation Desert Storm and how that dispute moved into the larger arena of service roles and budget politics. As noted in Chapter 4, *no* one in the senior U.S. defense leadership knew at the outset of Desert Storm that the Gulf war would turn out the way it did. True enough, there were visionary airmen who, for reasons right or wrong, harbored confidence that air power would decide the outcome, perhaps even single-handedly. Yet what, in the end, largely predetermined the allied victory had never been tested before, least of all in the synergistic combination that proved so overwhelming against Iraq. The power of a few stealthy F-117s to operate with impunity and to substitute for mass by way of precision, the confident knowledge of the battlefield at any moment that air- and space-based information superiority gave the coalition's commanders, and the strategic effectiveness of round-the-clock bombing of Iraqi ground forces were all, to varying degrees, revelations whose extent of leverage became clear only as the war progressed. Indeed, the American airmen most closely involved in the planning and execution of the air campaign were pragmatic people keenly mindful of the limitations of air power. As the endgame neared and the actual accomplishments of the air campaign became clear, the coalition's air commander, Lieutenant General Charles Horner, frankly conceded that he had "underestimated the efficiency of air power."[1]

Once it was over, however, the impression that the air campaign's accomplishments left on virtually all observers was profound. Not only did they

---

[1] Walter V. Robinson and Peter G. Gosselin, "U.S. Officers Hope to Avoid a Ground War," *Boston Globe*, February 4, 1991.

finally seem to confirm some long-standing claims that had been put forward by air power proponents, but also they put America's land combatants on notice, at some level at least, that they were facing a new approach to theater warfare that called into question their most time-honored doctrinal beliefs. Indeed, in its worst manifestations, the latter dynamic may have been captured in Albert Einstein's observation on the Ptolomaic school of geocentric astronomy when confronted by the irrefutable power of the Copernican alternative: "It was as if the ground had been pulled out from under one, with no firm foundation to be seen anywhere upon which one could have built."[2]

Yet instead of facing the new day squarely and asking how this seeming transformation in the respective roles of air and land power in joint warfare against fielded enemy forces offered new combat possibilities across the board, the land warfare community appeared to read the results of the air campaign as a warning notice that its long-familiar conventions were in danger of being bowled over by the newly demonstrated capabilities of precision air-delivered weapons and improved combat information systems. Rather than stepping out proactively to seek alternative approaches toward making the most of the new information and firepower technologies in joint warfare, the most outspoken representatives of the other services instead assumed a defensive crouch to protect their existing preconceptions and program equities.

The dispute ignited almost spontaneously in the early aftermath of Desert Storm, as the four services began taking stock of what the war experience meant for their respective doctrines and strategies. Richard Hallion, an air power advocate who later was appointed the Air Force's chief historian, no doubt reflected the private thoughts of many Air Force officers when he wrote, less than a year after the war's end, that "simply . . . stated, air power won the Gulf war."[3] For their part, the most senior Air Force leaders stopped considerably short of endorsing that categorical claim, at least in public, although as noted in Chapter 1, the Air Force chief of staff at the time, General Merrill McPeak, came close enough in his comment during a press conference shortly after the cease-fire that Desert Storm, in his view, represented "the first time in history that a field army [had been] defeated by air power."[4]

Yet despite the widely acclaimed contribution of the air campaign toward enabling the prompt allied victory on the ground with such a low incidence of friendly casualties, many Army leaders countered that coalition

[2] Albert Einstein, "Autobiographical Note," in P. A. Schilpp, ed., *Albert Einstein: Philosopher-Scientist*, Evanston, Ill., Northwestern University Press, 1949, p. 45.
[3] Richard P. Hallion, *Storm over Iraq: Air Power and the Gulf War*, Washington, D.C., Smithsonian Institution Press, 1992, p. 1.
[4] General Merrill A. McPeak, USAF (Ret.), *Selected Works 1990–1994*, Maxwell AFB, Ala., Air University Press, August 1995, p. 47.

air power had *not* met their needs in Desert Storm. That view was most pointedly reflected in the official Army portrayal of the ground offensive by then–Brigadier General Robert H. Scales, Jr., and a team of eight deputies.[5] Scales's book offered a detailed, and even riveting, account of what took place during the four days of ground operations that preceded the Gulf war's end. It further acknowledged that the Army "recognizes its dependence on the other services."[6] That aside, however, it proceeded from the first pages onward to maintain that it was the U.S. Army, in the end, that "decisively defeated the fourth largest army in the world . . . at the lowest cost in human life ever recorded for a conflict of such magnitude."[7] The dominant perception of the air campaign in Scales's treatment of Desert Storm was that "despite 41 days of almost continuous aerial bombardment, the Republican Guard remained a cohesive and viable military force able to fight a vicious battle and survive to fight insurgents in northern and southern Iraq."[8]

Two parallel but separate arguments in fact make up the American air power debate today, even though they tend to get lumped together and confused in the eyes of most observers. The first centers on disagreements over classic air power theory and involves the twin questions of whether "strategic bombardment" (the meaning of which is more often assumed than carefully defined) can compel an adversary to capitulate and whether such air power employment can win wars independently of other force elements. The second, over service doctrine and prerogatives in joint operations, is more focused on such practical matters as which force employment concepts offer the greatest value for the money spent and how combat roles should be apportioned among forces fielded by the four services at a time of reduced outlays for procurement and operational support.

The latter argument is, first and foremost, about service program interests and budget shares. More fundamentally, however, it is also about competing force employment concepts and the proper relationship between air and surface forces in joint warfare. In it, there has been recurrent sparring between the Air Force and Navy over command and control issues raised by the Desert Storm air tasking experience and over the degree to which carrier-based aviation shoulders its fair share of the burden for the disproportionate cost and limited ability to sustain the concentrated application of force it represents. The main confrontation, however, has been between the Air Force and the Army over the more basic question of whether air power in *all* services has displaced the traditional role of heavy-maneuver ground

---

[5] Brigadier General Robert H. Scales, Jr., usa, *Certain Victory: The U.S. Army in the Gulf War*, Washington, D.C., Brassey's, 1994.

[6] Ibid., p. vii.

[7] Ibid., p. 5.

[8] Ibid., p. 358.

forces in contributing the preponderance of effort toward achieving joint-force objectives in war.

Because it affects not only service interests but also future force structure and national strategy, this second argument is by far the more important of the two. Yet an understanding of its stakes has been hampered by the interference of stray voltage emanating from the often heated, but now largely anachronistic, contretemps over air power theory. With a view toward sorting out the increasingly fractious interservice debate over the relative capabilities and contributions of U.S. air power compared to other force elements, the discussion that follows attempts to untangle these two arguments and clarify each. In the process, it explains why the first has been rendered largely moot by recent refinements in technology and concepts of operations. It then spotlights the second as constituting the principal hot spot in U.S. defense controversy and seeks to flesh out the underlying positions and schools of thought in contention.

The Dispute over Air Power Theory

The current argument over the validity of classic air power theory has its roots running back to the pioneering work of General Giulio Douhet, an early 20th-century Italian artillery officer who wrote the first serious treatise on air power and its significance, and the public activism of U.S. Army Brigadier General William "Billy" Mitchell, a passionate advocate of the preeminence of the air weapon over all other instruments of warfare. In the aftermath of World War I, these progenitors of modern air doctrine argued that the airplane embodied such advantages over other weapon types as to "possess the power of destroying all surface installations and instruments, ashore or afloat, while itself remaining comparatively safe from any effective reprisal from the ground." According to a landmark appraisal of these early air power advocates, the emergent standoff between "the most zealous adherents of the cult of air power and the most stubborn and extreme skeptics [was not] a difference about theories of strategic or tactical employment of the available instruments, but about the fundamental power of a particular weapon." The perceived institutional stakes were as high as they could get, for if the argument of the air power proponents were conceded by soldiers and sailors to be correct, it would all but guarantee "the predominance of the role of the air force in the military establishment."[9]

The essence of Douhet's theory was its insistence that civilian morale would be shattered by aerial bombardment of enemy population centers and that ensuring an adequate defense in the dawning age of military avia-

---

[9] Edward Warner, "Douhet, Mitchell, Seversky: Theories of Air Warfare," in Edward Mead Earle, ed., *Makers of Modern Strategy*, Princeton, Princeton University Press, 1943, p. 485.

tion made it "necessary—and sufficient—to be in a position in case of war to conquer the command of the air."[10] Douhet further argued that the primary objects of aerial attack should not be the enemy's military forces, but rather its industries and urban centers. The idea was that if these targets could be successfully brought under fire from the air, something that land and naval forces were incapable of doing, supplies to fielded enemy forces would be cut off and populations of enemy states would sue their leaders to capitulate.

Mitchell shared Douhet's conviction regarding the vulnerability of an enemy's economy and infrastructure and the fragility of civilian morale in the face of relentless aerial bombardment. However, he continued to believe in the importance of air power for destroying enemy surface forces, both ground and naval. As these ideas were assimilated and pondered by the U.S. Army's embryonic Air Corps Tactical School in the late 1920s and early 1930s, they soon led to the belief that it would be possible to identify and engage discrete targets whose destruction would bring an entire industry to a grinding halt. As David MacIsaac described the implications of this idea, "If a number of such 'bottleneck' targets could be identified and destroyed, it might be possible, with a relatively small force, to bring an enemy's war production to a halt with almost surgical precision."[11]

Persistent disagreement over the relative merits of these views has prompted an often-heated dispute among defense professionals over two questions. First, given its ability to reach and attack lucrative targets in an enemy's "vital center," might strategic bombardment produce results as advertised by its early advocates? And second, if it could, might air power then decide the outcome of wars independently of other force elements— and even without the need for their involvement at all? The air power theory debate has centered on these two questions for decades. Yet as the ensuing discussion seeks to show, these questions are less pertinent now than ever before because of the sweeping improvements in air and space technology over the past decade that have so altered the former complexion and capability of U.S. air power.

Does Strategic Bombing Work?

The first bone of contention in the air power debate concerns whether strategic bombing has been effective in past wars and whether it constitutes an appropriate focus for air campaign planning today. The framing of this

[10] Giulio Douhet, *The Command of the Air*, translated by Dino Ferrari, New York, Coward-McCann, 1942, p. 28.
[11] David MacIsaac, "Voices from the Central Blue: The Air Power Theorists," in Peter Paret, ed., *Makers of Modern Strategy from Machiavelli to the Nuclear Age*, Princeton, Princeton University Press, 1986, p. 634.

question has often had the effect of elevating strategic bombardment to the level of being the one and only purpose of air forces. In strong testimony to this, historian Caroline Ziemke contended not long after the Gulf war that "strategic bombing is not mere doctrine to the USAF; it is its lifeblood and provides its entire *raison d'etre*. Strategic bombing is as central to the identity of the Air Force as the New Testament is to the Catholic church."[12]

Later, toward the end of 1991, Jeffrey Record wrote that Saddam Hussein's persistence in power after the cease-fire had "irreparably tarnished claims still being made on air power's behalf by the Air Force and other air power zealots."[13] Record went on to assert that this alleged failure of air power "must be judged . . . an embarrassment to the Air Force's almost religious faith, despite decades of contrary experience, in the power of strategic bombardment." Considering that removing Hussein from the picture was never an express goal of U.S. policy or of U.S. Central Command's (CENTCOM's) war plan to begin with, Record's broadside took air power to task for failing to accomplish something it was never formally asked to do in the first place.[14] Apart from that, his indictment shared the view of many who have insisted, for decades if not generations, that proponents of strategic air power have been longer on promise than on delivery.

Air power's detractors like Record have not been the only ones to raise such questions. Robert Pape similarly concluded from his study of 33 strategic air campaigns dating back to 1944 that "strategic bombing cannot be decisive."[15] Whether or not this latter assertion is on point, however, depends crucially on how one understands "strategic bombardment." Much of the post–Gulf war debate over the contribution of air power to the allied victory has been over whether or not attacks against so-called center-of-gravity targets (defined, in this case, as leadership and infrastructure assets located in and around Baghdad) made a significant difference in shaping the war's outcome. This, however, has been a controversy over a side issue, in that it has overlooked air power's real contribution by falsely bifurcating the air campaign into "strategic" and "theater" dimensions. Pape succumbed to this mischaracterization repeatedly in his insistence that two-thirds or more of the precision munitions employed by the coalition against Iraq were delivered against "theater" rather than "strategic" targets. In so doing, he

---

[12] Carolyn Ziemke, "Foreword," in Earl H. Tilford, *Setup: What the Air Force Did in Vietnam and Why*, Maxwell AFB, Ala., Air University Press, 1991, p. ix.

[13] Jeffrey Record, "The Air War Missed Its Biggest Target," *Baltimore Sun*, November 21, 1991.

[14] As President Bush later recalled in his memoirs, "We discussed again whether to go after [Saddam Hussein]. None of us minded if he was killed in the course of an air attack. yet it was extremely difficult to target Saddam, who was known to move frequently and under tight security. . . . The best we could do was strike command and control points where he may have been." George Bush and Brent Scowcroft, *A World Transformed*, New York, Alfred A. Knopf, 1998, p. 463.

[15] Robert A. Pape, *Bombing to Win: Air Power and Coercion in War*, Ithaca, N.Y., Cornell University Press, 1995, p. 317.

overlooked the more important point that these ostensibly "theater" operations yielded clear-cut strategic results. Indeed, Republican Guard forces were expressly designated as "strategic" targets in CENTCOM's air campaign plan from the very outset.

Of course, Pape is absolutely correct to insist that those whom he categorizes as "strategic air power advocates" overestimated the likelihood that bombing a tiny target set inside the Baghdad ring would intimidate or overthrow the regime of Saddam Hussein. He needlessly weakened an otherwise compelling argument, however, in suggesting that the allegedly opposed "theater air power advocates" underestimated the coercive potential of large-scale bombing of Iraq's fielded forces because of their presumed sense that they were simply playing a supporting role in preparing the battlefield for a ground war that would ultimately ensure the coalition's win. The joint-force air component commander (JFACC) in Desert Storm, Lieutenant General Charles Horner, and his staff would have been perplexed at this characterization of their thinking and would have trouble figuring out exactly where they belonged in Pape's schema. On this point, Barry Watts observed that Pape's characterization of the Gulf war as an act of coercion rather than an allied quest for victory "not only fails the test of common sense, but would be a genuine surprise to those who oversaw the war's conduct."[16]

The narrow fixation of the debate over air power theory on whether attacks against enemy infrastructure targets are worth the effort has missed the real essence of American air power's new-found leverage, namely, its ability to seize prompt control of the air and then to proceed, using that dominance, to destroy, or at least neutralize, an enemy's diverse sources of military power and thus enable one's own ground forces to perform any remaining tasks in most circumstances of medium- and high-intensity combat with a minimum of difficulty and loss. Caroline Ziemke offered a thought-provoking reflection on the import of this when she observed, shortly after the Gulf war ended, that "by making strategic bombing synonymous with air power, strategic bombing theory effectively excluded some of the most potentially decisive aspects of air power from its own scale of effectiveness. . . . In the process, those who sought to prove that strategic bombardment alone was a war-winning capability did a grave disservice to the interests of broader air power concepts."[17]

In Desert Storm, there was a clear difference in intended outcome be-

[16] Barry D. Watts, "Ignoring Reality: Problems of Theory and Evidence in Security Studies," *Security Studies*, Winter 1997/98, p. 149.
[17] Caroline F. Ziemke, "Promises Fulfilled? The Prophets of Air Power and Desert Storm," paper presented at a seminar series titled "Air Power and the New Security Environment," sponsored by the Washington Strategy Seminar, Washington, D.C., January 1992, pp. 16–19.

tween the air campaign's effort to facilitate the earliest and least painful achievement of the coalition's battlefield objectives and its concurrent attempt to affect Iraq's ability to be a source of trouble in the post–Desert Storm world—or, less politely, to blunt the edges of the Iraq that the United States and its partners might have to contend with again some day. The first usage dealt with CENTCOM's here-and-now concern for meeting its proximate goal of ejecting Iraqi forces from Kuwait. The second, although no less concerned with achieving that goal, involved the extra value to be had by taking fullest advantage of an ongoing war to affect Iraq's political and military hereafter.

It is with respect to its less-than-resounding performance on the second count in Desert Storm that air power has come in for its greatest berating by its critics. Yet that is an inappropriate yardstick by which to measure its effectiveness. It was on the crucial but less appreciated first count, namely, in achieving prompt air dominance and then systematically destroying Iraq's fielded forces on the ground, where allied air power met the preconditions for winning the war by making the attainment of CENTCOM's core objectives relatively easy for all the other players. Aside from the controversial infrastructure attacks (which, as noted earlier, accounted for no more than 10 percent of the total number of allied strike sorties flown throughout the war), what mattered most were the uses of air power by the coalition that bore directly on CENTCOM's declared mission of liberating Kuwait from Iraqi military occupation. The successful defense-suppression and offensive counterair missions flown from opening night onward permitted the sustained intimidation and physical destruction of Iraqi ground formations that paved the way for, and made possible, the coalition's ultimate consolidation of military victory on the ground with only minuscule allied bloodshed.

In their account of Operation Desert Storm, Michael Gordon and Bernard Trainor certainly saw this as one of the chief inferences to be drawn from the Gulf experience. As they concluded, "In the final analysis, the air war had confirmed the Air Force's growing ability to destroy targets deep in the enemy heartland and on the battlefield. . . . While the air war commanders had not won the war in downtown Baghdad, they devastated the Iraqi army. By depriving it of any help from the Iraqi air force, forcing it to dig in, eliminating the prospect of a mobile defense, and knocking out much of the Iraqi armor and artillery, the air campaign had all but won the war."[18]

As attested by this example, what mostly accounts for the growing quaintness of the current debate over "strategic bombing," defined as air attacks on so-called center-of-gravity targets in urban settings, has been the

---

[18] Michael R. Gordon and Bernard E. Trainor, *The Generals' War: The Inside Story of the Conflict in the Gulf*, Boston, Little, Brown, 1995, p. 331.

dramatic growth in the lethality of American conventional air power compared to what it was capable of doing even a short decade or so ago. The early visionaries of Billy Mitchell's persuasion argued that air power could be the decisive force element in war by attacking a nation's will to fight and its ability to support fielded forces. Yet even today, the first objective has remained elusive. The Air Force's Gulf War Air Power Survey (GWAPS) found little evidence that the air campaign's infrastructure attacks against Baghdad and other targets north of the Euphrates River were pivotal in determining the coalition's ultimate victory. On the contrary, as noted earlier, GWAPS concluded that the destruction of nearly all of Iraq's petroleum capacity yielded "no significant military results," in large part because the Gulf war did not last long enough for fuel shortages to affect Iraq's military performance.[19]

The second objective, however, finally proved itself in Desert Storm to be attainable. What most undermined Iraqi military performance was the coalition's attacks on Iraq's deployed armor and infantry forces, even though the 23,000 sorties committed against those forces failed to achieve, in and of themselves, the 50-percent attrition level stipulated by General Schwarzkopf as a precondition for beginning the allied ground push. As borne out by that performance, American air power showed its ability to achieve strategic effects against fielded enemy ground forces through its enhanced survivability, precision, and lethality. Accordingly, it now has the wherewithal to proceed directly toward strategic goals, at least in many cases, that bypass any compelling need to attack an opponent's urban-industrial assets.

As in the case of Desert Storm, such goals now include attacking and destroying an enemy's ability to employ military force. They include quintessentially his fielded ground units. Insofar as they also include urban aim points such as electric power stations and transportation grids, their intent is to destroy an enemy's ability to operate militarily by neutralizing his air defense control centers and depriving his frontline units of needed resupply. Although the overarching goal of "strategic victory" remains unchanged, the intent of such attacks is not to erode "the will of the people" in vain expectation that this will eventually prompt a leadership surrender, but rather to deprive an enemy directly of his ability to continue fighting. Talking about the strategic effectiveness of American air power without reference to this changed capability is analogous to rendering judgments about the potential and limits of medicine based on technologies and techniques used three generations ago. True enough, there are abiding principles of air war that transcend technological changes, just as there are timeless prin-

---

[19] Rick Atkinson, *Crusade: The Untold Story of the Persian Gulf War*, Boston, Houghton Mifflin, 1993, p. 494.

ciples of medical practice. Yet like medicine, air power can do things today that could only be dreamed of even in the early aftermath of the Vietnam war, let alone in World War II.

In sum, air campaign strategies centering on the presumed debilitating power of counterindustrial targeting have now been overtaken by technological improvements and new concepts of operations. In generations past, the U.S. Air Force and other developed air arms around the world pursued such strategies because they were the only employment options that extant "strategic" weapons, at least nonnuclear ones, could underwrite with any hope of achieving the desired physical results. Today, however, no full-spectrum air service like the U.S. Air Force need contemplate employing air power for simply imposing pain any longer, because there is so much more one can do with it throughout an enemy's battlespace to produce outcomes that more directly affect his ability to continue resisting. For developed air arms, the kind of punishment-oriented strategies that dominated Douhet's thinking about air power and that underlay much of the allied bombing of Germany and Japan during World War II are now passé, unless all one wishes to do is to seek revenge for a transgression or retard an enemy's postwar economic and societal recovery.

If American air power can now do these things, we need to change the way we think about it. The debate over air power theory has been slow to move beyond its fixation on Douhet and Mitchell, in large part because of the continued absence of a clear understanding of the changed essence of strategic attack. The Air Force's basic doctrine manual rightly defines strategic attack, without qualification, as the application of air power "to achieve maximum destruction of the enemy's ability to wage war."[20] Yet the comparable Joint Staff document, Joint Publication 1-02, remains mired in the past in its portrayal of "strategic air warfare" in terms of target types rather than combat outcomes. It defines such warfare as the systematic application of "air combat and supporting operations" toward the progressive destruction of an enemy's ability or will to wage war. It does so, however, in terms of such now-archaic "vital targets" as "key manufacturing systems, sources of raw material, critical material, stockpiles, power systems, transportation systems, communications facilities, concentration of uncommitted elements of enemy armed forces, key agricultural areas, and other such target systems."[21] In so doing, it sets the pace for all other mistreatment of strategic air warfare in the current debate.

Properly applied, the term *strategic* refers not to any particular delivery

---

[20] *Air Force Basic Doctrine*, Air Force Manual 1-1, Vol. II, Washington, D.C., Department of the Air Force, March 1992, p. 147.
[21] Joint Publication 1-02, *Department of Defense Dictionary of Military and Associated Terms*, Washington, D.C., U.S. Government Printing Office, March 23, 1994, p. 363.

platform or target *type*, but rather to decisive operational *effects*. Carl Builder stated this well when he wrote in 1996 that the adjective should be taken to connote such things as "going for the jugular," focusing on ends, and being "transformatory" and "game-changing" in nature.[22] In this sense, there was indeed a "strategic" focus to the allied air campaign against Saddam Hussein. Yet it had nothing to do with leadership decapitation or infrastructure attacks. Rather, it had to do with destroying Iraq's situation awareness and capacity for collective action from the outset; attaining prompt control of the air as a sine qua non for everything else that followed; and then seeing to it that deployed Iraqi armor, artillery, and infantry were denied any ability to undertake coordinated counteroffensive action against attacking allied ground forces. As the Air Force Doctrine Center more recently defined it, strategic attack is now aimed at achieving combat outcomes at the highest level "without first having to engage the adversary's forces at the operational and tactical levels" in slow-motion and costly attrition warfare.[23] This is light-years removed from the still-widespread image of strategic bombardment that remains mired in remembrance of outdated visions of "hundreds of B-17s flying at 200 miles an hour through flak and fighters from one target one day to another the next" as the standard yardstick for measuring strategic success.[24]

Simply put, Giulio Douhet's conception of air power and its potential contribution to winning wars has been rendered obsolete by technological advance. As Pape noted, the Douhet model hinged on the belief that "the infliction of high costs can shatter civilian morale, unraveling the social basis of resistance, so that citizens pressure the government to abandon its territorial ambitions."[25] These are scarcely likely to be the goals of any present-day allied joint-force commander. Douhet was driven by that logic because at the time he wrote, air power had no capability to do anything *but* cause indiscriminate destruction of civilian targets, leaving aside the provision of interdiction and close support to friendly ground forces in direct contact with enemy troops on the battlefield. The Gulf war, however, was about something entirely different. As it plainly demonstrated, air power in modern war now permits the achievement of strategic goals of a supremely *military* nature from the outset of fighting.

In light of this, the time has come to end further argument over whether Douhet's model of aerial warfare has been vindicated. For all the other con-

---

[22] Carl H. Builder, "Keeping the Strategic Flame," *Joint Force Quarterly*, Winter 1996–97, p. 77.

[23] Draft Air Force Doctrine Document (AFDD) 2-1.2, *Strategic Attack*, Maxwell AFB, Ala., Air Force Doctrine Center, 1997, p. 3.

[24] Gene Myers, "Strategic Attack Is No Myth," *Proceedings*, U.S. Naval Institute, Annapolis, Md., August 1997, p. 37.

[25] Pape, *Bombing to Win*, p. 60.

ceptual problems that attend his characterization of modern air power, Pape convincingly showed that counterinfrastructure bombing alone entails both an insufficient exploitation of air power's capabilities and an inappropriate focus for today's air power debate. As Richard Hallion wrote three years after the Gulf war ended, air power professionals can no longer afford to continue drawing their "doctrinal and strategic sense from the great air power prophets of the past—the Douhets, and Trenchards, and Mitchells—men who wrote over 60 years ago."[26] There are now better ways of thinking about air power and its potential as a tool of strategy than by seeking guidance from the now-antiquarian writings of the early-20th-century air power classicists.

Can Air Power Do It Alone?

Critics of air power have further charged that the air weapon has never vindicated the promises of its visionaries that it can win wars single-handedly. In one of the more pointed renditions of this charge, Jeffrey Record commented shortly after the start of Desert Storm how "initial hopes that the war against Iraq would be relatively short and cheap, courtesy of overwhelming U.S. and allied air power, evaporated within days of its beginning."[27] Having thus demolished another straw man, this time the notion that General Horner and his target planners had envisaged an air campaign that would be "relatively short and cheap," Record took to task those who had allegedly concluded that the war "can be won by air power alone, or at least without any major, prolonged, and bloody offensive on the ground."[28] He dismissed that conclusion as a judgment revealing an underlying "ignorance of air power's history, as well as an underestimation of the resilience and determination of Iraq's leadership." He further declared that there was "little prospect for a conclusive victory over Iraq through air power alone."

Some senior officials in the Bush administration who were presiding over the Pentagon's preparations for war against Iraq gave voice to similar sentiments, albeit in a less overtly polemical tone. General Colin Powell, for example, had for years been a doubter of the more extravagant claims made by air power prophets. Not surprisingly, considering his background and upbringing, he was a firm believer in the Army's core conviction that it took

[26] Richard P. Hallion, "The Future of Air Power," in Alan B. Stephens, ed., *The War in the Air: 1914–1994*, Canberra, Australia, RAAF Air Power Studies Center, 1994, p. 357.

[27] Jeffrey Record, "The Seductive Charms of Air Power," *Baltimore Sun*, January 30, 1991.

[28] Ibid. In fact, Horner's air operations deputy, Brigadier General Glosson, had expressly cautioned that General Schwarzkopf "needed an air campaign that would last for fifteen rounds, not two or three." As Glosson described it, the air campaign "would be a marathon, not a dash." Gordon and Trainor, *The Generals' War*, p. 96.

"boots on the ground" to consummate any victory. Indeed, Powell commented in his memoirs how he had prevented a proposed air-attack option from being briefed to President Bush by the Air Force because the president was already being allegedly "oversold on air power."[29]

Powell himself declared in a private meeting with Bush before the start of Desert Storm that "history offered no encouragement that air power alone would succeed."[30] Echoing this same theme, he later told a group of American pilots in Saudi Arabia while on tour to inspect the Desert Shield buildup that although allied air power would be "overwhelming," the fact remained that "in every war, it's the infantryman who will have to raise the flag of victory on the battlefield."[31] Powell insisted to the end that "many experts, amateurs and others in this town [Washington] believe that . . . a sustained air strike" would run Iraq's forces out of Kuwait, but that "such strategies are designed to hope to win, they are not designed to win."[32]

Even after the war ended and the contributions of allied air power to its outcome had been widely accepted, Record repeated his charge that Air Force planners had "become persuaded that air power defeated Iraq almost singlehandedly," as though such Gulf war principals as Secretary Cheney and even President Bush were somehow misinformed when they themselves acknowledged as much in the wake of the allied victory. Record rejected out of hand the assumed convictions of airmen who allegedly believed that Desert Storm "proved that the kind of carefully phased air campaign conducted against Iraq is universally applicable" and that air power can be a "potentially complete substitute for ground forces."[33] No doubt in part, at least, prompted by such commentary, Pape suggested in his study on air power and coercion cited earlier that the "key question" of the Gulf experience was not just whether air power has become "extremely powerful," but indeed whether it has become *so* capable "that it can decide international disputes, not simply without costly ground campaigns but even without deployment of any credible ground threat."[34]

Undoubtedly, as Pape observed, there were indeed strategists in the Air Force who believed, as a matter of personal conviction, that the Gulf war could be won entirely from the air and that air power alone would prompt a withdrawal of Iraqi forces from Kuwait. Most notable among them, the principal drafter of the original Instant Thunder air campaign plan, Colonel John Warden, was, by every indication, convinced that the United States

[29] Colin Powell, *My American Journey*, New York, Random House, 1995, p. 499.
[30] Ibid., p. 489.
[31] Ibid., pp. 476–477.
[32] Ibid., p. 342.
[33] Jeffrey Record, "Gulf War's Misread Lessons," *Baltimore Sun*, July 9, 1991.
[34] Pape, *Bombing to Win*, p. 211.

would not have to go beyond that strategic attack plan to achieve its declared objectives against Saddam Hussein. However, it was never even remotely a claim of the corporate Air Force or a belief of any of its top generals that air power had the ability "to change governments" or would win the war "by destroying Iraq's governing infrastructure and causing Saddam Hussein's overthrow." It is simply unfounded to insist that "senior Air Force leaders" believed that the Instant Thunder air campaign would force Iraq out of Kuwait without a ground offensive "or even significant strikes against Iraqi ground forces." [35]

On the contrary, as noted in Chapter 4, General Horner had no patience whatever with such thinking and declined to retain Warden on his staff in Riyadh in part because of his disagreement with it. [36] Similarly, the commander of British forces in Desert Storm, RAF Air Chief Marshal Sir Patrick Hine, accepted without question the need for a strong and credible allied ground presence opposite Iraq in the Kuwaiti theater of operations (KTO). Although he personally believed that the coalition's air campaign might well defeat Iraq without any need for serious ground fighting, Hine asked himself, when pressed by Schwarzkopf, "Was it sensible to rely on that?" His answer: "Frankly, while I was confident that allied air power would prove very effective if not decisive, I felt that the risks of going to war with . . . an adverse ground force ratio were too high. . . . So I favored further reinforcement." [37] For his part, Schwarzkopf saw the planned "strategic" attacks against infrastructure targets in and around Baghdad as a precursor to an offensive plan aimed at reducing Iraq's military strength on the ground. So did Horner, not surprisingly, and that is how the air war ultimately played itself out.

Yet if no airman in a position of senior leadership was suggesting that air power could "do it alone," there were expectations aplenty that were air power properly employed, it would go far toward substituting for ground power in many cases and making life less dangerous for advancing ground forces in others once the time came to make the final push. Such expectations, moreover, were by no means limited to air power's most ardent enthusiasts. For example, the director of operations on the Joint Staff, Army Lieutenant General Thomas Kelley, commented that frontal tank warfare was a "big nasty thing" and added that for that reason, "we can't have a land war." [38] General Kelly further observed, "I think the whole purpose of our

[35] Ibid., p. 221.

[36] See Colonel Richard T. Reynolds, USAF, *Heart of the Storm: The Genesis of the Air Campaign against Iraq*, Maxwell AFB, Ala., Air University Press, January 1995, pp. 120–130.

[37] Air Chief Marshal Sir Patrick Hine, RAF (Ret.), "Air Operations in the Gulf War," in Stephens, ed., *The War in the Air*, p. 307.

[38] Bob Woodward, *The Commanders*, New York, Simon and Schuster, 1991, p. 232.

strategy . . . is to continue to pound that force, to attrit it to the point where either they'll decide to give up or they'll be weak enough for us to reasonably go in and get them."[39]

Granted, airmen have mainly themselves to blame for the enduring persistence of controversy over the question of whether air power can win wars independently of other forces. It was, after all, their own anointed fountainheads of wisdom, Douhet and Mitchell, whose early forecasts of what the airplane could do single-handedly in war have kept alive the debate over air power and its potential. Beyond that, there is no denying that the Air Force, along with other developed air arms around the world, continues to harbor its share of true believers in the gospel articulated by Douhet, Mitchell, and their later apostles. However, the Air Force as an institution has done little by way of studied effort to nurture a belief that air power can win wars by itself.

To conclude on this point, the debate over whether air power can "do it alone" involves a contretemps over a nonissue, just as the debate over the effectiveness of strategic bombing involves a dispute over an issue that has been largely overtaken by events. The charge levied by Record and others that air power "cannot take and hold territory" asserts a point with which few airman would disagree. Yet if holding enemy territory is deemed synonymous with winning wars, then that begs the important question of what it means to "win." On that question, to which we will return in the concluding chapter, one can fairly ask whether seizing and holding an opponent's terrain by way of friendly "boots on the ground" need invariably be a precondition for operational success. That aside, the most careful advocates of air power did not—and do not—claim that air power could have won the Gulf war single-handedly. Rather, they say something close, but with an important difference: that air power created the conditions for victory by making the endgame relatively painless for all other force components. In that, they have grasped the true meaning of American air power's coming-of-age. The question that matters is not whether air power can "do it alone," but rather how substantial the change has been in the *relative* capacity of the air weapon, compared to that of more traditional combat arms, to determine the course and outcome of wars.

THE BATTLE OVER RESOURCES AND DOCTRINE

If much of the recent debate over air power theory can be dismissed as no longer relevant to current concerns, the same cannot be said about the controversy over resource priorities and joint-force employment doctrine. On

[39] Bill Gertz, "Allied Air Strikes Put Chink in Iraq's Armor," *Washington Times*, February 6, 1991.

the contrary, the latter has grown more acrimonious and laden with policy import than ever, as it has become increasingly clear that even with a defense budget of $270 billion, it will be all but impossible for the U.S. services to have all they seek by way of new systems and support funding. This problem has become all the more acute in light of the fact that domestic pork-barrel politics have continued to hamper the Defense Department's expressed desire to make draconian cuts in unneeded facilities and personnel in the interest of reduced costs.

Much of the sharpness of this debate over roles and resources has been a natural consequence of the unprecedented defense drawdown that began in the early 1990s following the breakup of the Soviet Union. At stake are not just budget shares but also service roles and, ultimately, the direction and thrust of U.S. strategy.[40] At the center of the debate is the core question of whether new information and target attack capabilities largely aggregating in the air and space forces of the four services have attained enough leverage that they should supplant heavy-maneuver ground forces, primarily tank forces, as the instrument of choice for defeating enemy armies. The debate further involves the question of whether the United States is developing excessively redundant deep-attack capabilities and the extent to which each service needs to retain and nurture such autonomous capabilities — what Senator Sam Nunn in 1992 called the "four air force problem."[41] From both an organizational and a strategy viewpoint, it concerns how the United States should define and apportion joint-service warfighting responsibilities toward ensuring maximum effectiveness while preventing needlessly duplicative deep-attack capabilities.

An Attempt to Clarify Roles and Missions

In an effort to bring at least a semblance of closure to this controversy, congressional legislation in 1993 mandated a high-profile national review of service roles and missions. With competing plans on the books for billions of dollars worth of investment in deep-battle platforms and munitions, a key question posed for the Commission on Roles and Missions of the Armed Forces established by that legislation concerned how much overlapping investment by the four services was really necessary to ensure that the deep-attack mission was adequately covered. The ensuing review of roles

---

[40] See Tony Capaccio, "'Everything on the Table' in New Strategy Review," *Defense Week*, November 19, 1996, pp. 1–4.

[41] According to JCS Publication 1-02, "deep attack" means "the application of force in adversary space outside the area of close engagement." This generally means 15 miles or more behind the FSCL, or inside enemy-controlled battlespace. Weapons available for deep attack include fixed-wing and helicopter aircraft, air-delivered munitions, ballistic and cruise missiles, and special operations assets.

and missions took the debate over who did what in Desert Storm into the heart of the services' force planning. One issue that surfaced along the way concerned how much air power independence the United States can afford for each service at a time of unusually constrained funding for defense.

Each of the four services, in the interest of arriving at a sensible division of labor, is tasked to organize, train, and equip forces for a particular operational "role" as defined in Title X of the Official Code of the Laws of the United States (more commonly known as the U.S. Code). The secretary of defense, in turn, allocates specific operational tasks or "functions," such as close air support, to the services so that they might perform their assigned roles. For their part, the combatant commanders in chief (CINCs) of the U.S. unified commands around the world are responsible for carrying out assigned "missions" within their respective geographic areas of responsibility (AORs), using forces provided by the four services.

Viewed from this vantage point, there is little express duplication in service "roles" as outlined in Title X, since the most basic purposes of the four services are defined along broad and abiding lines that are well known to all. As the Marine Corps's then–assistant deputy chief of staff for plans, policies, and operations summed it up in early 1994, "The Army fights land wars, the Air Force fights in the air, the Navy fights at sea, and the Marine Corps projects power ashore from the sea. Any 'roles' issue that might exist concerns what is left out—such as space." [42] The real controversy, he pointed out, involves service "functions," particularly as they relate to seeming overlaps in expensive weapons such as aircraft. In some cases, he noted, the services "have similar functions to solve different tactical or operational problems in their assigned roles." He suggested that calls for redefining service *roles* were misplaced and risked unintentionally altering national strategy. The real issue in most cases, he said, has to do instead with the allocation of *resources*, which inevitably leads to the question, "Do the services still require the same proportion of resources to accomplish their assigned roles?" [43]

As the various service inputs for the Commission on Roles and Missions were being refined and aired in 1994, some levied charges that the Air Force chief of staff at the time, General McPeak, had launched an unseemly effort to garner a larger share of Air Force control over operational functions at the expense of other service prerogatives. Viewed in hindsight, it is not hard to understand why. Speaking for the Air Force, McPeak noted that the heart of the roles and mission controversy involved deciding "what each service's core business will be and how we [should] expect resulting service-

[42] Colonel James A. Lasswell, USMC, "Roles and Missions Myths: A Division of Labor or a Division of Resources?" *Armed Forces Journal International*, May 1994, p. 27.
[43] Ibid., p. 28.

provided capabilities to operate jointly on the modern battlefield."[44] He granted that the Army, Navy, and Marine Corps both possess and require "niche" aviation capabilities that should be owned and operated by them. The challenge, he suggested, was to eliminate overlapping rather than complementary capabilities. As he put it shortly after retiring from active duty, it entailed "the matter of how to divide up the work [the services] will do together on the battlefield."[45]

In his report to the Commission on Roles and Missions, McPeak tried to get around the stranglehold of traditional thinking on the allocation of service functions by dividing up a notional theater war into what he called the "rear, close, deep, and high battles" as a departure point for spotlighting potentially excessive cross-service duplication of effort. He defined the close battle, however "deep" it might be, as the one in which friendly ground forces are directly engaged. This battle, he stipulated, is rightly the responsibility of the land component commander, either an Army or Marine general, depending on the situation and nature of the deployed forces. Because the close battle necessarily includes close airspace, McPeak further stipulated that the air up to an agreed altitude above it was an integral part of that battle and that it accordingly was a rightful prerogative of the land component commander to integrate close air support and close air defense with ground combat operations.

As for the high and deep battles, McPeak saw these as the proper responsibility of the air component commander, either an Air Force general or possibly a naval-aviator admiral in situations involving a predominantly littoral contingency. McPeak was quick to add that he did not regard this proposed allocation of responsibility as a clever ploy for giving the Air Force "two out of three," as he put it, since there was also the rear battle, along with a possible amphibious battle and maritime battle, the command of which would be Army, Marine Corps, and Navy prerogatives, respectively. However, he portrayed it as the most efficient division of labor in portions of the battlespace in which the Air Force was likely to be the key player.

McPeak conceded after his retirement that the issue essentially involved a zero-sum game for the services, since "any meaningful revision of roles and missions would shift the workloads, creating at least the perception of winners and losers." He further acknowledged that the issue was so divisive that the services were naturally chary about debating it openly and instead had "silently conspired to keep it in the basement, like some crazy rel-

---

[44] General Merrill A. McPeak, USAF, *Presentation to the Commission on Roles and Missions of the Armed Forces*, Washington, D.C., Government Printing Office, September 14, 1994, p. iii.
[45] General Merrill A. McPeak, USAF (Ret.), "The Roles and Missions Opportunity," *Armed Forces Journal International*, March 1995, p. 32.

ative."[46] Yet he insisted that the services had no choice but to face up to the issue squarely, whatever pain that might cause for some, because of a gathering fiscal crunch that necessitated doing more with less and extracting greater combat leverage from the same cost.

McPeak maintained that just as it was the prerogative of the JFACC and joint-force land component commander (JFLCC) to manage the so-called interservice "seams" within their respective operating areas, it was the more overarching responsibility of the theater CINC, as the sole warfighter exempt from the specialization rule, to determine where such lines of responsibility should be drawn and to manage the seams separating the close, deep, and high battles.[47] Both how far in front of friendly ground forces the deep battle line should be drawn and how much airspace above the close battle should belong to the JFLCC were likewise, in McPeak's characterization, proper decisions for the CINC. Only he, McPeak argued, is sufficiently well placed to manage those seams because only he has authority over forces operating on *both* sides of the seam.

McPeak's statements that accompanied his presentation to the Commission on Roles and Missions reflected a studied absence of any special pleading for Air Force programs, as well as a frank acknowledgment of the important contributions made by the other services and an admission, on repeated occasion, that air power cannot win wars single-handedly. McPeak also repeatedly emphasized that air power will be decisive in some but not all conflicts and that in many cases, it will play only a supporting role to the other combat arms. Nevertheless, his attempted dissection of future joint battlespace, and especially the conclusions he drew from it, were read by the Army and Marine Corps as all but a declaration of interservice war. Although McPeak conceded that his approach argued for increased efforts by the Army to modernize its artillery and attack helicopter inventories to improve its fire support for the close battle, he also argued that the Army and Marine Corps should begin to "transition out of the airlift business and deep battle systems like ATACMS [Army tactical missile system] and the F/A-18," as well as give up any pretensions they might have to staking out a claim in the area of space operations.[48] In the face of such claims, regardless of how sensible they may have seemed from a purely operational viewpoint, the Army's point man on roles and missions at the time, Lieutenant General Jay Garner, charged that the Air Staff's pronouncements on anything having to do with roles and missions reduced, in the end, to "Air Force *uber alles*."[49]

---

[46] Ibid.
[47] Ibid., p. 33.
[48] Ibid., p. 34.
[49] Tony Capaccio, "New USAF Vision Could Trigger More Interservice Fighting," *Defense Week*, November 4, 1996, p. 6.

Retired Army General Glenn Otis took similar exception to McPeak's approach to dividing up the joint battlespace into what amounted, in effect, to carefully delineated service fiefdoms. Otis portrayed *deep* as a "relative" term and argued that the Army, in any case, no longer regarded modern air-land battlespace as a linear setting dominated by the sort of echeloned force arrays that characterized the NATO–Warsaw Pact confrontation—and, one might add, Operation Desert Storm. Instead, he described it as "nonlinear and characterized by using long-range, highly accurate fires to destroy enemy forces and break up their cohesion long before [Army] maneuver forces are triggered to engage in a short-range, direct-fire assault."

Otis's characterization had the effect of giving the JFLCC a claim to unlimited control of all air and land battlespace to the front of his maneuver forces. As he bluntly put it, presaging what has become a new Army catechism since Desert Storm, there is no longer any "concept of a Forward Line of Troops (FLOT) from which to visualize 'close' or 'deep' fires. Instead, long-range artillery, longer-range missiles (ATACMS), long-range helicopter attacks, and long-range fixed-wing air will attack enemy enclaves throughout the battlespace." Otis added that the success of this concept of operations required that the "land commander . . . employ not only large numbers of long-range fires, but also a variety of attack modes." These pointedly included "high-performance aircraft" dedicated to a "firm and steady land commander to orchestrate the campaign, *supported* by sea and air forces."[50]

As interservice disagreement continued to percolate over this and related issues, the chairman of the Roles and Missions Commission, John White, acknowledged that McPeak's conceptualization had played an important role in smoking out the various service positions and that the commission's members had found it both "thought-provoking and helpful" as a stimulus for debate, even if some in the other services had said, "Gee, we didn't need that." White further acknowledged that the question of where ownership and control lines should be drawn between the close and deep battles was "one of the most contentious issues that we have seen." He then stressed the importance of remembering that what mattered most was "making sure that the capabilities of the services are harmonized into an effective fighting force," not "spending a lot of time arguing with each other about who gets to do what."[51]

Ultimately, the final report of the Commission on Roles and Missions ducked the most prickly question of how the services' functions and force structure should be amended in light of the impact of recent technological

[50] General Glenn K. Otis, USA (Ret.), "Shuffling Assets Isn't the Answer: There Are No 'Deep Battles' and 'Close Battles,'" *Armed Forces Journal International*, May 1995, pp. 36–37, emphasis added.
[51] John G. Roos, "Roles and Missions Countdown: Chairman White Remains above the Intramural Fray," *Armed Forces Journal International*, May 1995, p. 34.

changes. Instead, it concluded that the proper focus of the defense debate should be on what capabilities were needed by the joint-force CINC in the field. That, predictably, drove contention over functions and force structure back into its prior domain of service doctrine and long-range planning and occasioned such subsequent internal Defense Department assessments as the Deep Attack Weapons Mix Study, the Quadrennial Defense Review, and the National Defense Review. Early on in this succession of high-profile studies, the Pentagon's director of Program Analysis and Evaluation, William Lynn, captured the high-stakes nature of the controversy when he observed that it "goes to the institutional identities of the services, the operational concepts of the commands, and even to the most hallowed part of the department—the budget shares of the individual components."[52]

Interservice Rivalry Escalates

In the continued absence of any clear adjudication of the most intractable interservice issues by the top civilian defense leadership, it was all but inevitable that the roles and resources debate would become ever more pointed in the wake of air power's signal accomplishment in Desert Storm. For its part, the Air Force lost little time in the early aftermath of the Gulf war in attempting to convert its successful performance in the air campaign into a new concept of joint operations that stressed the dominance of air and space power. Toward that end, it began marshalling an argument that precision air power, properly packaged and employed, offered the theater CINC the option of delaying, halting, and possibly defeating an enemy armored offensive well before U.S. ground forces would have time to arrive in any remote theater in fighting strength. The Air Force further argued that in light of the newly revealed capabilities of precision air attacks against fielded enemy land forces, any premature commitment of U.S. and allied ground troops to battle would risk incurring needless friendly casualties. Citing the Gulf experience as a case in point, air power advocates asserted that it was deep rather than close operations that now made the crucial difference, that the coalition could have achieved the same results in Desert Storm with far fewer deployed land forces, and that it was accordingly "inappropriate for the Army alone to be assigned the role of defeating enemy land forces."[53]

Lending support to that view, a RAND study commissioned by the Air Force shortly after Desert Storm concluded that although air power could scarcely be considered sufficient by itself to support the needs of U.S. joint-

---

[52] Tony Capaccio, "Army Readies for Defense Review Food Fight With Air Advocates," *Defense Week*, November 18, 1996, p. 15.

[53] Lieutenant Colonel Price T. Bingham, USAF (Ret.), "Let the Air Force Fight Future Land Battles," *Armed Forces Journal International*, August 1993, p. 42.

force commanders, rigorous analysis could be mobilized to show that "air power's ability to contribute to the joint battle [had] increased," owing to its ability to "destroy enemy ground forces either on the move or in defensive positions, at a high rate, while concurrently destroying vital elements of the enemy's warfighting infrastructure." That improvement in the capability of U.S. air power at the operational and strategic levels of war, the RAND study concluded, suggested that in order to underwrite adequately the development and deployment of needed air mobility assets, advanced munitions, combat aircraft, and information systems, "it may be necessary to 'trade' a portion of U.S. joint force structure for selective modernization." That, in turn, would inevitably "require a new approach to coping with spending cuts, which in the past have focused primarily on reducing procurement accounts and have tended to be apportioned more or less evenly across services and mission areas." [54]

As one might have expected, such expansive claims on behalf of air power, and especially the force structure implications that the Air Force and its supporters drew from them, were scarcely received with open arms by the land warfare community. On the contrary, the Army leadership, in particular, saw large parts of its existing and planned force structure being increasingly challenged by the new concepts of operations being propounded by airmen that sought to make the most of technologies to find, fix, and engage targets in near-real time from standoff distances. That, in turn, spurred the Army to compete ever more aggressively in the indirect-fire mission area, traditionally an acknowledged preserve of fixed-wing aviation, by seeking to supplement its primary reliance on such organic direct-fire weapons as heavy tanks with the equally accurate indirect fire now made possible by its own extended-range ATACMS and by prospective stealthy, deep-attack helicopters that promised to cost as much as an F-16. Under the aegis of its chief of staff, General Gordon Sullivan, the Army developed a long-range plan called Force XXI, which projected the institution out to 2020 with such a new look expressly in mind. Sullivan's successor as chief, General Dennis Reimer, then initiated the Army After Next project to look beyond 2020 along a similar vector. Through that process, Reimer envisaged the Army transforming itself into a new fighting force that would be "much more strategically and operationally mobile," in light of its increasingly apparent need to "move ground capabilities anywhere around the globe in a short period of time." [55]

---

[54] Christopher Bowie, Fred Frostic, Kevin Lewis, John Lund, David Ochmanek, and Philip Propper, *The New Calculus: Analyzing Air Power's Changing Role in Joint Theater Campaigns*, Santa Monica, Cal., RAND, MR-149-AF, 1993, pp. 84–85.
[55] Interview with General Dennis J. Reimer, USA, "The Army After Next," *Assembly*, January/ February 1998, p. 7.

In conjunction with this long-range planning, and almost surely prompted, at least in part, by the Air Force's perceived effort to monopolize what it had come to characterize as the potentially decisive "halt phase" of a future war, the Army's declaratory policy and program emphasis underwent a noticeable shift from armored vehicles toward attack helicopters and other deep-attack options, along with giving active consideration to reducing the size of the Army's ground maneuver units in the interest of gaining greater flexibility and deployability. This shift suggested that the Army's leadership had come to appreciate that the indirect-fire support now available or within reach, not only from fixed-wing aviation but also from organic Army assets, has become of sufficient prospective range and lethality that direct-fire engagements against enemy ground forces should rarely be necessary any more.[56]

Almost surely an important catalyst of this Army thinking was the role played by the allied air campaign in Desert Storm, which, not insignificantly, included the use of Army deep-attack helicopter and ATACMS fires in shaping the battlefield for the final four-day land offensive. For the most part, direct-fire engagements by coalition ground forces with Iraqi armored units were not required. On the contrary, as that experience showed, joint-force commanders now have the ability to locate, attack, and destroy enemy ground forces in large numbers, without having to engage them head-to-head with direct fires, by holding them off and beating them down from stand-off ranges while denying them the ability to inflict casualties on friendly ground forces through return direct fire.

Consistent with its apparent determination to reestablish itself as a co-equal of the Air Force in shaping future battlefields from the earliest moments of combat, the Army has announced plans to upgrade its 70-ton M1A2 Abrams main battle tank, while working toward a lighter successor-generation armored fighting vehicle in the interest of greater ease of deployability. It further has redoubled its efforts to acquire the RAH-66 Comanche attack helicopter, a planned successor to the AH-64 Apache that will incorporate stealth features to make it more difficult for enemy air defense radars to detect and track it. On a different level, the Army has also worked hard to advance the notion that the sort of operational arenas typified by the Iraqi desert, in which American air power performs best, are by no means the most likely ones that will challenge U.S. security interests in the post–cold war era.

In a telling reflection of Army concern to stanch what its leadership has come to portray as an unwise rush on the part of some to place technology over people in the ranking of America's military investment priorities, for-

---

[56] See Major General Jasper A. Welch, Jr., USAF (Ret.), "Notes on 21st Century Land Warfare," unpublished manuscript, June 1996, p. 4.

mer Army Chief of Staff General Sullivan warned in 1994 that ongoing trends in U.S. force modernization ran the danger of devolving into "a rationalization process based on the illusory notion that technological advances can be decisively applied to nearly all military and political affairs." Sullivan singled out for special criticism what he saw as "the seemingly insatiable desire to narrow our military capabilities and fight by 'remote control,'" a desire "fueled by the hope for victory without risking an American life." He further noted that the United States will be engaged in the future in operations "ranging from major regional conflicts such as Desert Storm to small groups of servicemen and women teaching their counterparts in fledgling democracies the appropriate role of the military in a democracy"—a situation which, in his view, meant that "we cannot pursue technologically sophisticated programs at the expense of other, less glamorous, aspects of the defense program."[57]

Two advocates of land power, Marine Lieutenant General Paul Van Riper and Army Major General Scales, expressed the same point even more bluntly when they asserted that their services were "troubled by recent claims that technological supremacy will allow the United States in the future to abjure the use of ground combat forces in favor of delivering advanced precision weaponry from platforms remote from conflict areas." They depicted this as a false promise of "high-tech, bloodless victory."[58] They then went on to castigate airmen for allegedly insisting that "emerging technologies will utterly transform the nature of war, permitting the defeat of future adversaries from a distance with no need to risk precious lives in the maelstrom of land combat."[59]

On this point, it bears noting that the Marine Corps, even though it possesses a well-endowed and highly respected strike aviation component of its own, has generally supported the Army's positions in the roles and resources debate. Indeed, the sort of new thinking on ways of fighting the land battle to which the the Army leadership has given such vocal note since Desert Storm was closely echoed in an observation by the Marine Corps commandant, since-retired General Charles Krulak, that "in the past, the goal was to use firepower to allow the infantry to close with and destroy the enemy with direct combat. . . . Now, we're thinking more of using maneuver not to close with an enemy, but to bring long-range fires on him. Maneuver will have more to do with staying away from the enemy than with closing with him."[60] In a reflection of this new thinking, the Marine Corps Combat

---

[57] General Gordon R. Sullivan, USA (Ret.), "Limited Options Will Lose Wars," *Los Angeles Times*, January 27, 1997.

[58] Lieutenant General Paul Van Riper, USMC, and Major General Robert Scales, USA, "Preparing for War in the 21st Century," *Strategic Review*, Summer 1997, p. 14.

[59] Ibid., pp. 16–17.

[60] Quoted in Jim Blaker, "The Owens Legacy," *Armed Forces Journal International*, July 1996, p. 21.

Development Command has pursued an experiment called Sea Dragon, which envisages inserting deeply into a combat zone small teams of Marine infantry personnel equipped with the latest generation of communications and sensor support that allows them "to direct long-range precision fire support while minimizing their own vulnerability."[61]

Even more than their Army compatriots, the marines insist that the current defense debate is, at bottom, less about force structure alternatives and which service should "own" what functions and more fundamentally about the very nature of future war. On the latter count, their spokesmen maintain that major theater wars of the kind typified by the 1991 Persian Gulf conflict are less likely than ever to occur in the post–cold war era, since the United States now lacks a credible peer competitor, and that military conflicts around the world, at least in the near future, will most likely be dominated by smaller-scale contingencies such as the American peacemaking interventions in Somalia and Bosnia and by urban combat and forcible-entry operations in the broad genre of what former Marine Corps commandant Krulak characterized as "three-block wars."[62] As Van Riper commented in this respect, he would endorse "absolutely" the Air Force's perspective on the primacy of its "halt-phase" approach to the allocation of missions and functions, yet only "so long as we refight Operation Desert Storm."[63] His successor at the Marine Corps Combat Development Command similarly noted, "Technology right now does a fantastic job in wide open spaces. It does not, however, do all we would like it to do in a cluttered environment."[64]

Some marines, notably including Van Riper, have, on absolutely solid ground, further admonished Air Force airmen and other proponents of "information dominance" and its putative virtues that despite admitted improvements in U.S. information, surveillance, and reconnaisance (ISR) capabilities since the mid-1980s, there can be no such thing as "total battlespace awareness" because of the omnipresent fog of war and that the idea of a bloodless and antiseptic war waged with standoff weapons from fighter cockpits and remote consoles is self-delusional. Sooner or later, they maintain, in close harmony with their Army brethren, U.S. ground forces will be

[61] General Charles C. Krulak, "The United States Marine Corps in the 21st Century," *RUSI Journal*, August 1996, p. 25.
[62] A concise overview of these opposing schools of thought is presented in Elaine M. Grossman, "Duel of Doctrines," *Air Force Magazine*, December 1998, pp. 30–34.
[63] *Clashes of Visions: Sizing and Shaping Our Forces in a Fiscally Constrained Environment*, A CSIS-VII Symposium, October 29, 1997, Washington, D.C., Center for Strategic and International Studies, 1998, p. 32.
[64] Interview with Lieutenant General John Rhodes, USMC, *Jane's Defense Weekly*, February 4, 1998, p. 32.

obliged to go in and root out the enemy, especially in combat settings other than open-desert wars.[65]

Yet at the same time that it has sought to portray urban combat and operations short of war as the wave of the future, the Army has opted to compete with Air Force air power in the deep battle against modern armored and mechanized forces. Not at all by accident, its new vision of land combat has quietly appropriated many of the long-acknowledged distinguishing features of air power, such as speed, range, flexibility, ubiquity, firepower, and rapidity of maneuver. Senior Army leaders now envisage tomorrow's Army as looking quite different from today's tank-heavy maneuver forces and evolving from its current manpower-intensive combat formations to a leaner force aimed at dominating air-land battlespace through increased mobility and reliance on digitization, new information technologies, and speed of maneuver to employ precision fires.

Air Force airmen might understandably be tempted to write off such Army ambitions toward controlling the deep and high battles in future warfare as nothing but a naked bureaucratic run on traditional Air Force combat functions. Yet the problem is not simply one of petty bickering over rice bowls, as interservice rivalry is so often portrayed as being, but rather one of honest disagreement among professionals who find themselves viewing the world through very different perceptual filters. As one historian observed on this score, "The airman tends to see himself as an independent operator who does not want the flexibility of his instrument shackled to the limitations of the surface. The soldier on the ground may intellectually comprehend the benefits to be derived from the independent application of air power, but he also has a very real desire for its effects to be useful to his immediate milieu of land warfare."[66] Another writer, amplifying on this theme several years before Desert Storm underscored its continued pertinence, added that "these problems stem from fundamentally different worldviews held by soldiers, sailors, and airmen, creating honest differences over how warfare should be conducted."[67]

In fact, what has happened in the roles and resources controversy since Desert Storm, as typified by the tug-of-war between the Air Force and Army over control of the deep battle and who should be "supported" and "supporting" in it, was foreseen several years earlier by Air Force doctrine expert Colonel Thomas Cardwell, who noted how "improvements to a system that

[65] For amplification on this perspective, see in particular the comments by Lieutenant General Paul Van Riper, USMC (Ret.), in *Clashes of Visions*, pp. 32–42.
[66] Harold R. Winton, "A Black Hole in the Wild Blue Yonder: The Need for a Comprehensive Theory of Air Power," *Air Power History*, Winter 1992, p. 33.
[67] Colonel Dennis M. Drew, USAF, "Joint Operations: The World Looks Different from 10,000 Feet," *Airpower Journal*, Fall 1988, p. 5.

is owned by one service may extend that service's employment capability into another service's primary function." Such issues, he said, have three possible outcomes: do nothing to resolve the issue, resolve the issue in favor of one position, or reach a compromise. Characteristically, as Cardwell observed, "The Joint Chiefs have usually chosen compromise."[68] In a related vein, Air Force Colonel Richard Szafranski more recently commented that any truly honest debate over American strategy and force requirements would put the spotlight squarely on "differing views of the utility of surface maneuver forces."[69] Yet what has happened instead throughout most of the 1990s has been a ducking of the most contentious issues by the most senior defense leadership in the interest of political expediency. That, in turn, has left the air and land warfare communities at a bitter and unproductive standoff. Nevertheless, the way the debate has unfolded has raised an important question regarding the extent to which the articulation of service interests has reflected underdeveloped or obsolescent notions of joint-service operations in the interest of winning tomorrow's theater wars.

Two Competing Visions of Warfare

Despite the best intentions of the 1986 Goldwater-Nichols Act described in Chapter 4, the four services today, more than a decade after that legislation's passage, have produced anything but a common conception of how to organize, train, and equip their respective forces for joint operations. The Air Force and Army, in particular, continue to speak fundamentally different languages when it comes to their respective images of modern war. Without question, the struggle over roles and resources has high budgetary stakes for all protagonists. Yet all of the service chiefs would probably agree that it ultimately involves a more principled clash over what seem to have become two divergent conceptions of warfighting.

For its part, the U.S. Army continues to operate within a frame of reference which holds that the proper role of air power is to support land combat. Its leadership appears more wedded than ever to the idea that "boots on the ground" constitute not only the definitive measure of military victory but also an indispensable precondition for achieving such victory. In his official account of U.S. Army combat operations in Desert Storm, General Scales neatly encapsulated the Army's position in this respect in his assertions that "wars are won by quality soldiers"; that it is an "enduring truth" that in joint operations, "land combat plays a decisive role in winning wars

[68] Colonel Thomas A. Cardwell III, USAF, "How Interservice Issues Arise," *Air University Review*, May 1986, pp. 79–80.
[69] Colonel Richard Szafranski, USAF, "Interservice Rivalry in Action: The Endless Roles and Missions Refrain?" *Airpower Journal*, Summer 1996, p. 49.

with minimum casualties"; and that "land combat is now, more than ever, the strategic core of joint warfighting."[70]

More to the point, Army spokesmen insist that the Army is the nation's "force of decision," in contrast to air and naval forces, which allegedly can only produce "transitory" advantages in joint warfare.[71] According to prevailing Army thinking, only an invading and occupying ground force can impose "decisive defeat" on an enemy and bring a conflict to a successful termination. It follows from this, Army spokesmen maintain, that all other force elements should remain subordinated to the overarching imperative of producing success for the Army in the land battle. It further follows, in the Army's view, that air operations should continue to be treated as supportive of the ground commander's needs, rather than as an independent mode of force employment. The Army's emphasis on the theme of "dominant maneuver," along with the hardware adjuncts it believes are necessary to underwrite it, envisages ground maneuver warfare and precision engagement by air and space forces as coequal in leverage and importance.

From an airman's perspective, it is easy enough to accept that CENTCOM needed its four corps of allied ground troops deployed and ready to move when the time came in Desert Storm so as to telegraph an unambiguous message of American seriousness to Baghdad. Fair-minded airmen will further concede that the four-day left hook and invasion of Kuwait were required to give Baghdad the added incentive it needed to withdraw its occupying forces, by providing a credible anvil to backstop the hammer of allied air power. On that score, the Army's *Vision 2010* statement is on solid ground in asserting that "no other single gesture so clearly demonstrates the ultimate commitment of the U.S. to a particular outcome as placing American soldiers in harm's way."[72] Most airmen would be among the first to agree that no other type of force deployment, including the deployment of naval or air assets, so clearly commits the prestige of the nation to a major operation.

It hardly follows, however, at least in the view of airmen, that the Desert Storm experience "demonstrated" that determined opponents can "only be defeated with certainty by decisive ground action." Or, as General Scales proffered as an overarching axiom, that "maintaining an immediately deployable capability for decisive land combat to end a conventional conflict successfully" was "the the single most enduring imperative of the Gulf war."[73] To air power professionals, insisting on full Army control of the

---

[70] Scales, *Certain Victory*, p. 358.
[71] Grossman, "Duel of Doctrines," p. 32.
[72] Patrick Pexton, "The Future Sees Operations Other Than War," *Army Times*, November 25, 1996, p. 8.
[73] Scales, *Certain Victory*, pp. 359–360.

"land battlespace" begs the question of where "land battlespace" should yield to deep operations beyond the Army's purview. The same can be said for the Army's claim to "shaping the battlespace" and achieving "simultaneity." In the view of airmen, by the time Army forces arrive in a remote theater in sufficient strength to make contact with the enemy in tomorrow's intelligently fought war, the needed "simultaneity" will already have been achieved by air and space forces in the high and deep battles.

The two-dimensional image of force employment that still largely predominates among land warriors, despite the recent transformation in American air power's ability to achieve strategic effects independently of ground operations, is most clearly telegraphed in the conclusion of Scales's book that in future wars, "the single most distinguishing characteristic of joint land combat [notice, "land" combat, not just combat] will be the presence of aerial vehicles from every service and *in support of* every battlefield function."[74] Characteristic of this outlook, Scales referred to "the new style of fighting" made possible by modern technology, yet treated it solely as something that occurs on a *land* battlefield, thus casting even tomorrow's air power in, at best, a supporting role.[75]

For their part, Air Force airmen approach the question of what offers the best promise for fighting and winning tomorrow's wars from a different point of departure. As former Air Force Chief of Staff General Ronald Fogleman repeatedly maintained, the transformation of air power's ability to shape combat outcomes has presaged a qualitative change in the American way of war. By the early 21st century, Fogleman predicted, air and space sensors will be able to find, fix, track, and target forces moving almost anywhere on the earth's surface. Reasonable airmen would not quarrel with the insistence of skeptics like Van Riper that such a prospective capability is neither perfect nor appropriate to all occasions that might concern a warfighting CINC. However, they would counter that for the most demanding circumstances of war against organized and mechanized opponents, it has revolutionized the leverage of the air weapon compared to that of land forces. It is this argument of a fundamental paradigm shift in the means of modern warfare, counterpoised against the Army's more traditional view of evolving surface operations, that has kept the larger American defense debate at a near-boiling point.

Airmen who have reflected on the meaning and potential of current trends in air and space systems maintain that what is going on here is less an evolution in joint operations than a technology-driven transformation in the relationship between maneuver and fire. With the E-8 joint surveillance target attack radar system (JSTARS) and associated deep-attack platforms

---

[74] Ibid., p. 370, emphasis added.
[75] Ibid., pp. 360–361.

like the F-117, F-15E, and B-2, U.S. strike aviation is now comfortably situated to handle ground threats from standoff ranges, thereby reducing the workload for the Army's organic close-in air attack systems, to say nothing of eliminating a dire threat to U.S. ground forces, who otherwise might have to engage enemy ground forces within lethal range of return fire. In light of this new capability, airmen insist that if there is any one principle that should guide the continued development of American air power, it is the principle that it can save lives and provide theater commanders with a more effective and responsible way of employing force than through head-to-head, manpower-intensive combat on the ground. Air power proponents argue that this transformation not only permits, but indeed dictates, fundamental trades in force structure that would not have been advisable until recently.[76]

The Unending Roles and Resources Controversy

As attested by the increasingly embittered clash of visions outlined in this chapter, the competition over roles and resources continues to pit airmen against soldiers and marines in what is shaping up to be a high-noon showdown over whether American planning for future war will be dominated by air and space forces or by land forces. Beyond the rhetoric of contention over unsettled Gulf war issues, the debate persists as the Air Force and Army, in particular, remain locked in a more fundamental struggle over the future ownership of roles and the control of deep-attack assets. The stakes, both programmatic and strategic, could not be higher for the defense establishment as a whole. As retired Air Force Colonel Szafranski summarized them in 1996, "If air power and space power win assent . . . , the size and investment in surface maneuver forces will diminish. If air power and space power continue to be viewed as useful adjuncts to surface maneuver forces, the Air Force likely will continue to shrink."[77]

The issue of greatest note here concerns the proper mix of air and land forces and the question of whether air power should operate independently or be configured and employed to support surface warfare. This issue is *not* one of which service is the "most important" or whether any single service or service arm can win wars alone. Rather, it concerns how most efficiently and affordably to underwrite America's military needs. Reduced to basics, it involves a choice between two fundamentally opposed images of how future war should be fought, images that increasingly have taken on a life of their own as all-but-ingrained worldviews of the concerned services.

---

[76] For a fuller development of this argument, see Zalmay Khalilzad and David Ochmanek, "Rethinking U.S. Defense Policy," *Survival*, Spring 1997, pp. 43–64.
[77] Capaccio, "New USAF Vision Could Trigger More Interservice Fighting," p. 6.

Unfortunately, the interservice debate as sketched out here has seen little serious intervention one way or the other from the most senior civilian leadership. The 1997 quadrennial defense review at least tacitly endorsed the Air Force's halt-phase planning when it concluded that "failure to halt an enemy invasion rapidly can make the subsequent campaign to evict enemy forces from captured territory much more difficult and costly."[78] However, the subsequent National Defense Panel did not even mention the halt phase, let alone acknowledge the Air Force's considerable work on it. In a statement afterward, the study's chairman, Philip A. Odeen, explained at a press conference that the panel "didn't feel [it] could endorse that particular approach because we don't think it has been demonstrated yet."[79] Instead, the long-awaited report of the $4.5 million National Defense Panel inquiry punted the ball back to the civilian defense leadership and to Congress when it came to making hard judgments. With exquisite equivocation, it concluded in December 1997 that "it is not clear whether the solution is to be found in Air Force long-range precision strikes; strikes from a Navy task force composed of a 'distributed' strike force—carriers, arsenal ships and Trident 'stealth battleships' fitted with hundreds of vertical launch systems for long-range precision-guided missiles; Army forces employing long-range missiles and weaponized unmanned aerial vehicles; [or] Marine 'infestation' teams calling in long-range precision fires."[80]

As the debate continues in the absence of unequivocal civilian leadership guidance from the top, one contentious issue posed by the Air Force's proposed approach to winning major theater wars concerns whether the initial halting of a surprise armored attack, the buildup of allied combat power in the affected region, and the counteroffensive must take place sequentially or whether they can be carried out simultaneously. General Reimer, during his tenure as Army chief of staff, insisted that the theater CINCs in the most threatened AORs require "the synergism of simultaneous dominant maneuver and precision engagement," the former being a code expression for an Army core competency and the latter a term used to describe the Air Force's principal stock in trade.[81] Typically, Army scenarios for future joint operations against armored attacks have U.S. air power working hard during the initial halt phase, then standing down during the so-called "build" phase while large numbers of U.S. ground forces are deployed to the involved theater. The Air Force counters that a more intelligent use of American and al-

---

[78] *Report of the Quadrennial Defense Review*, Washington, D.C., Department of Defense, May 1997, p. 13.
[79] Grossman, "Duel of Doctrines," p. 33.
[80] National Defense Panel, *Transforming Defense: National Security in the 21st Century*, Arlington, Va., National Defense Panel, 1997, p. 58.
[81] *Clashes of Visions*, p. 16.

lied air power can provide a more efficient and less costly alternative than committing heavy-maneuver land forces to the canonical buildup and counteroffensive phases of a halt campaign. More specifically, Air Force leaders insist, there should not be any need for a reduction or hiatus in the use of air power after the halt phase, certainly not to support a buildup of troops for a land counteroffensive that may, in the end, not be required.

What matters most here is that modern air and space assets can both deny freedom of action to enemy land forces and destroy or neutralize those forces faster than they can mass in pursuit of their operational goals. In effect, Air Force strategy posits that the counteroffensive really begins the moment allied air forces begin fighting. Indeed, some airmen now maintain in hindsight that the Desert Storm air campaign could have begun well before the allied ground buildup in Saudi Arabia had been completed, since it would have become clear to any reasonable observer at some point that a further buildup of allied ground forces would have been unnecessary to put down what remained of Iraqi ground resistance after the air campaign had achieved its goals. This point, they further argue, applies not only in the case of aggression in deserts and other open spaces, but also in mountain and jungle contingencies as well, since would-be aggressors cannot easily mass armored forces in such settings.

In all, the Air Force touts air power as the preferred instrument for halting and reversing a major armored attack not only because of its precision engagement and standoff capability, but also because it can deploy to a threatened region much more quickly than can heavy ground maneuver forces. For its part, as a result of the Desert Storm experience, the Army has witnessed the deep battle becoming progressively more decisive than the close battle in major wars. In a natural response to this development, which has called into question its most time-honored combat role, it has backpedalled away from its former emphasis on the proper placement of the fire support coordination line (FSCL) and is now endeavoring instead to claim more of the likely battlespace for the land component commander in the next war. That, in turn, has led to a renewed controversy between the Air Force and Army over which component commander should control joint firepower application in future theaters of operations.

The latest flare-up between the two services over this recurring issue was the slugfest that came to a head in early 1998 over Joint Publication 3-09, entitled *Doctrine for Joint Fire Support*. The conceptual groundwork for that document was laid a decade earlier, with the Army the designated lead agent for the project. Two years previously, the Goldwater-Nichols Act had assigned wide-ranging prerogatives to theater commanders in what were called AORs. A later amendment empowered the theater CINC to assign so-called areas of operation *within* an AOR to the land and maritime component commanders, with no express provision for a separate area of operation for the JFACC. At the same time, the traditional term "joint fire support," which had been understood to mean applications of firepower in direct support of land forces, was amended to "joint fires" and redefined to include *all* "lethal or nonlethal effects." [82]

As the debate over this arcane issue unfolded in the joint arena, the Army, backstopped by the Navy and Marine Corps, used this reformulation as a departure point for arguing that the land or maritime component commander was entitled to claim "primacy" over combat operations and the control of fires within their respective areas of operation. What made this a sticking point for the Air Force was that the Army wanted the land component commander to control *all* firepower application, including fixed-wing interdiction and strategic attacks, whether or not it directly supported ongoing or planned land operations. The Army was able to make this claim owing to a process through which the FSCL, originally assumed to be no more than some 20 miles in front of friendly land forces, was now extended hundreds of miles ahead, with the so-called forward boundary so far in front of friendly land units as to obviate any possibility of independent air activity whatever, other than airlift and surveillance.

This stratagem was more than a bit reminiscent of the Army's earlier attempt in the debate over AirLand Battle during the 1970s to empower its corps commanders to dictate targets, attack timing, and air power priorities in engagements over land battlespace that have no bearing on the immediate land battle. It also, as in the case of AirLand Battle, reflected a clear difference of view between the Army, which was mainly concerned for the needs of its corps commanders, and the Air Force, which was necessarily concerned with the CINC's needs extending above corps level to embrace missions and objectives of theater-wide significance. Above all, it reflected the Army's continuing insistence that air power, notwithstanding its substantial gains in effectiveness since the mid-1980s, must invariably remain subordinated to the land commander's "scheme of maneuver."

The issue of Joint Publication 3-09 was ostensibly resolved in a meeting of the JCS on May 12, 1998, in a manner that honored an Air Force stipulation that *any* component commander, so designated by the CINC, could execute operations of theater-wide significance within land and naval areas of operation. However, disagreement has persisted over the practical meaning of that resolution, with no interservice consensus on how such a stipulation might be implemented or on how theater battlespace control should actually be allocated. The Air Force demurred because of an explicit reference in the document that the theater CINC had the final say on determining which fires take priority in any area of operation, which presumably would ensure the proper servicing of his own and, by implication, the JFACC's operational

---

[82] John T. Correll, "Joint Fire Drill," *Air Force Magazine*, July 1998, p. 2.

needs.[83] However, in a widely discussed book on the future of land warfare published the previous year, Army Colonel Douglas Macgregor touched the heart of underlying Army thinking when he wrote that "control of the air in contemporary concepts of future warfare has become synonymous with centralization of control over all land-based and sea-based deep-strike assets in the hands of the JFACC." That approach, Macgregor complained, "does not admit the possibility that the success of future operations may depend on more than success in the preparatory phase . . . or that aircraft will 'not always get through.'"[84]

Air Force leaders have sought to counter such Army attempts to preempt the JFACC's prerogatives by insisting that the controlling role over deep-fire-power application should be played by the service or force element that is best able to see throughout the battlespace, destroy targets throughout the battlespace, and maintain effective command and control of operations throughout the battlespace. In the contretemps over Joint Publication 3-09, according to some Air Force generals, the Army was insisting on a dominant role for itself for which it lacked the requisite assets to perform effectively. Nevertheless, the Air Force concedes that it lost an important battle by failing to make its case that airmen should work exclusively for airmen in joint operations, with only the air component commander reporting to the theater CINC in the interest of achieving the greatest theater-wide efficiencies.

Viewed in hindsight, the core issue with respect to Joint Publication 3-09 had to do with Air Force concern that the draft document, as written, would allow surface commanders undue authority over air operations in a given AOR. More specifically, it concerned whether, during a joint-force operation, a JFACC would be free to exercise authority over air application theater-wide or would be obliged to gain approval for his attacks (or "fires," as they are called in Army parlance) from the surface commanders in their assigned areas of operation. The Air Force insisted that joint doctrine clearly specifies that the JFACC is empowered to exercise such authority on a theater-wide basis. The other services countered that the JFACC must support the operational needs of the surface commander, citing, of all things, the danger that JFACC-directed air attacks might threaten the lives and objectives of friendly surface combatants.[85]

On reflection, it should not be surprising that the Army would have

---

[83] "Military Chiefs Resolve Joint Fire Support Doctrine Issue—For Now," *Inside the Pentagon*, May 21, 1998, p. 3.

[84] Colonel Douglas A. Macgregor, USA, *Breaking the Phalanx: A New Design for Landpower in the 21st Century*, Westport, Conn., Praeger, 1997, p. 176.

[85] "Air Force Chief of Staff Plans to Appeal Army on Fire Support Doctrine," *Inside the Pentagon*, April 23, 1998, pp. 1–2, and "Military Chiefs Resolve Joint Fire Support Doctrine Issue—For Now," p. 3.

sought to pursue such a doctrinal counteroffensive in the joint arena. Between 1991 and 1997, it shrank to its smallest size since before World War II,
and the 1997 quadrennial defense review recommended still a further reduction in the size of the active Army force by 15,000 personnel, or around
3 percent of the Army's total residual strength. Moreover, after the end of
the cold war, the Army's forward presence abroad shrank some 60 percent
in 10 years, from 258,000 fielded troops in 1988 to 105,000 a decade later. Finally, the Army's annual percentage of total obligational authority in the
1998 U.S. defense budget was only 25 percent, compared to some 30 percent
each for the Air Force and Navy (with the remaining 15 percent going to
other defense agencies).[86] Of course, the other three services have suffered
comparably from the post–cold war budget drawdown. However, the
Army might have legitimate reason to argue that it has fared worst of all in
the final assessment.

Nevertheless, the Air Force views the Army's continued efforts to control
Air Force assets for deep interdiction beyond the FSCL as a serious threat to
air power's single greatest comparative advantage, namely, its flexibility to
meet the theater-wide needs of a joint-force commander as they may arise.
This doctrinal competition has apparently been fed by increasing fears on
the Army's part that its heavy-maneuver forces are becoming less and less
relevant to the needs of a theater CINC for future contingencies involving
massed armored assaults. In effect, the Army seems to be seeking to retain
a modern-day version of its land force–centric AirLand Battle doctrine,
even though that doctrine was designed to accommodate a problem that no
longer exists, namely, defending NATO against a surprise Warsaw Pact armored offensive by placing primary reliance on heavy in-place maneuver
forces, backed up by conventional air assets that lacked anything even remotely like the operational effectiveness they have today.

On balance, in the words of an Air Force doctrine expert, Army–Air Force
competition since Desert Storm over such issues as the definition of joint
fires and the demarcation and control of theater assets and areas of operations "are all manifestations of [larger] ecclesiastical battles." However, he
added, they are but "symptoms of the underlying problems of the Army's
fear of loss of strategic mission and the divergence of respective service doctrines."[87] In some respects, the opposed service stances on the relative merits of air and land power reflect genuine differences of view on the nature
of the challenges facing the United States and on the most appropriate concepts of operations for dealing with them. In other respects, they seem to
have the services talking past one another rather than engaged in produc-

[86] Jim Courter and Loren Thompson, "Army Vision and the Transformation of Land Power in the
Next Century," *Strategic Review*, Summer 1997, pp. 31–33.
[87] Gene Myers, "Army-Air Force Doctrinal Disputes: Symptoms or Causes," Arlington, Va., Eaker
Institute for Aerospace Concepts, 1998, p. 5.

tive dialogue aimed at working toward a solution that serves the best interests of the theater CINC. In all instances, with outlays for defense procurement at their lowest ebb in constant dollars since the eve of the Korean war in 1950, they entail arguments on behalf of competing force modernization options in a budget crisis in which one service's gain stands increasingly to be another's loss.

With such high programmatic stakes involved, it was perhaps only to be expected that the debate over roles and resources would have assumed such a take-no-prisoners attitude on all sides. Army partisans continue to seek headway by flogging the straw-man argument repeatedly ascribed to Air Force leaders that air power "can nearly singlehandedly win a future conflict without the assistance of ground combat or naval forces."[88] Critics of air power likewise persist in sustaining the bogus issue of which service "won" the Gulf war by claiming that "more Iraqi military equipment was captured or destroyed in the four-day ground offensive than in six weeks of air strikes," begging entirely the question of whether that equipment had already been abandoned or otherwise rendered ineffective as a result of the air campaign. In a thorough distortion of the Air Force's position in the roles and resources debate, air power detractors repeatedly fault "air power enthusiasts" for allegedly believing that "aerial bombardment has made more costly ground assaults obsolete."[89]

In self-defense against such charges, some Air Force spokesmen counter in kind that modern air and space capabilities and the Air Force's halt-phase strategy now obviate the need to commit large U.S. ground forces to combat, owing to the air weapon's putatively single-handed potential for "eliminating" enemy ground strength.[90] Other air power proponents feed the interservice fire by espousing a new paradigm for force employment that claims to be joint-minded but is unabashedly "aerospace-centric."[91] Finally, on *both* sides of the argument, there have been recurrent instances of the pot calling the kettle black, as exemplified by inveterate Air Force critic Earl Tilford, who charged that "the Air Force, more than any other service, traditionally has focused on the potential of its form of warfare to be decisive"—at a time when the very essence of the Army's own vision statement is that *land* power constitutes the "decisive" force.[92]

In an effort to get beyond such unhelpful confrontations of countervailing caricatures, one Air Force commentary pointed out how surface warriors

[88] Major Robert F. Larson, USA, "The Role of Air Power," *Army*, March 1998, p. 8.
[89] William R. Hawkins, "Back to Vietnam? Iraq and the Limits of Air Power," *Strategic Review*, Spring 1998, pp. 46–48.
[90] Major General Charles Link, USAF (Ret.), quoted in Patrick Kelly, "Will Technology Win the Next War?" *Defense Week*, June 15, 1998, p. 6.
[91] Richard Hallion, "Air Power: Not 'Limits of . . .' but 'Limits Imposed On,'" letter to the editor, *Strategic Review*, Summer 1998, p. 74.
[92] Ernest Blazar, "Inside the Ring," *Washington Times*, August 20, 1998.

tend to view war from the ground up. So oriented, they typically assume that maneuver warfare is something that naturally occurs solely on the earth's surface and to consider that other realms of operations, such as air and space, are significant only insofar as they relate to supporting surface actions. Conversely, airmen tend to take a top-down perspective which, in its worst manifestations, dismisses ground operations as insignificant and assumes that only "command of the air" will yield victory. This visceral reaction, the Air Force commentary concluded, "is usually interpreted as both arrogant and uninformed by those who hold the ground-up view. What the two sides have managed to achieve so far in this debate is to polarize the issue to such an extent that only these two very extreme viewpoints are recognized: Air power is a supporting arm for ground maneuver, or air power is the sole instrument of victory. As is usual with extremes, both views miss the mark."[93]

Encouragingly, senior principals in the two services have rued the impact of the post–cold war budget drawdown in forcing such unseemly competition for limited resources among mature professionals who should be focused on more important concerns. As the since-retired commander of Air Combat Command, General Richard Hawley, expressed it with pained honesty, the hard reality of a budget top line "that is too low to both sustain today's force and modernize for tomorrow . . . pits military leaders against one another for dollars—leaders who should be working arm in arm to find better ways to defeat the nation's adversaries."[94] Similarly, the Army's former chief of staff, General Sullivan, complained that the budget has become so tight that all of the services have been forced to weigh options "that shouldn't even have to be looked at in the United States."[95] Yet however much recent developments in air and space technology may have finally rendered irrelevant the once-simmering debate over whether strategic bombardment "works," the same cannot be said with respect to the higher-stakes issue of where air and space power properly falls in relation to land power in the evolving hierarchy of military forces. On the contrary, whatever Desert Storm may have done to create a mystique of American air power in the minds of potential opponents, the role of air and space power in U.S. defense strategy remains as unsettled and contested as ever.

[93] Air Power Research Institute rejoinder to Martin Van Creveld, with Steven L. Canby and Kenneth S. Brower, *Air Power and Maneuver Warfare*, Maxwell AFB, Ala., Air University Press, July 1994, pp. 222–223.
[94] Doyle Larson, "All Signs Point to Another Hollow Air Force," *Air Force Times*, July 27, 1998, p. 29.
[95] Pat Towell, "Modern Army Prepares for War on Two Fronts: Present, Future," *Congressional Quarterly Weekly*, August 8, 1998, p. 6.

[9]

Air Power Transformed

Operations Desert Storm and Deliberate Force, each in its own way, bore out what nearly two decades of improvement in the U.S. air posture had produced by way of increased combat leverage. The effective role played by American air power in both cases stemmed from a combination of technology advance, increased intensity and realism of training, and a steadily mounting leadership focus on the operational level of war. The earlier misapplication of air power in Vietnam and the manifold shortcomings in equipment, training, and strategy that that misuse spotlighted were pivotal in determining how the U.S. air posture finally evolved to a point where it could perform as successfully as it did over Iraq in 1991 and Bosnia in 1995.

Since then, continued improvements in sensors and munitions have further increased the effectiveness of U.S. air power, as was exemplified by the B-2's consistently accurate through-the-weather use of the global positioning system (GPS)–guided joint direct-attack munition (JDAM) against Serbian targets in NATO's Operation Allied Force in 1999. It would be a pointless exaggeration to suggest that air power can now win wars single-handedly as a result of such improvements. Short of that, however, recent developments have dramatically increased the *relative* combat potential of air power in comparison to that of other force elements. That, in turn, has made possible the application of new concepts of operations in joint warfare. Although success in major theater wars will continue, as before, to require the involvement of all force elements in appropriately integrated fashion, new air and space capabilities should enable joint-force commanders to conduct operations against enemy forces more quickly and efficiently than ever before.

To be sure, there remain differences even within the Air Force over what should be the prime focus of air power application with respect to target types and operational objectives. Some, in light of the Gulf experience, now insist that the main emphasis should be on battlefield aim points rather than on infrastructure targets. Those of this view hold that airmen should have recognized early on during the planning for Desert Storm that the Republican Guard was the main power base of Saddam Hussein's regime. The putative "strategic" targets that were given top priority in Colonel John Warden's Instant Thunder plan, in this view, did not embrace key Iraqi vulnerabilities and thus merely wasted valuable sorties and munitions. Others, more convinced of what they see as the growing promise of "nodal warfare," counter that air power performs best when used in a more sophisticated and asymmetric way. To them, killing tanks from the air entails a symmetric approach to warfare, in which aircraft are used merely as expensive surrogates for tanks and artillery. Such employment of air power, they say, is not as highly leveraged as approaching an enemy as a system and targeting such crucial nodes as command and control centers, communications links, and key logistics.

Perhaps the most enlightened view on this issue is the eclectic one that argues for avoiding formulaic, single-recipe solutions to the exclusion of all others, whether they entail attacks on fielded forces or infrastructure, and instead identifying the specific vulnerabilities that make up an enemy's center of gravity and building a campaign plan that expressly targets those vulnerabilities. According to this view, air campaign planners should look carefully at what makes an enemy capable of aggression and then concentrate systematically on taking that capability away. In Desert Storm, that capability was first and foremost Saddam Hussein's fielded forces, starting with the Republican Guard but also including Iraqi units in the Kuwaiti theater of operations. In the case of Kosovo, in contrast, the key center of gravity evidently entailed values more closely identified with Milosevic's own perceived prospects for political and personal survival. In all events, the challenge now facing U.S. defense planners is to consolidate the recent improvements in battlespace awareness and precision attack into a strategy that will render the oft-cited expression "the new American way of war" an established fact rather than merely a catchy slogan with great promise.[1]

THE CHANGED ESSENCE OF AMERICAN AIR POWER

The main argument of this book is that American air power has been transformed over the past two decades to a point where it has finally become truly strategic in its potential effects. That was not the case before the

---

[1] This expression, popularized by General Ronald Fogleman during his tenure as Air Force chief of staff, has its origins in the seminal study by Russell F. Weigley, *The American Way of War*, New York, Macmillan, 1973.

advent of stealth technology, highly accurate strike capability, and substantially improved availability of battlefield information. Earlier air campaigns were of limited effectiveness at the operational and strategic levels because they simply involved too many aircraft and too high a loss rate to achieve too few results. Today, in contrast, air power can make its presence felt quickly and can impose effects on an enemy from the outset of combat that can have a governing influence on the subsequent course and outcome of a joint campaign.

To begin with, there is no longer a need to amass force as there was even in the recent past. Such advances as low observability to enemy radars and the ability to destroy or neutralize both fixed and moving targets with a single munition have obviated the need for the sort of cumbersome formations of strike and support aircraft that were typically required in Vietnam. The large force packages that the Air Force and Navy routinely employed during the air war over North Vietnam offered the only way of ensuring that enough aircraft would make it to their assigned targets to deliver the number of bombs needed to achieve the desired result. Today, improved battlespace awareness, heightened aircraft survivability, and increased weapons accuracy have made possible the *effects* of massing without having to mass. Owing to this, air power can now produce effects that were previously unattainable. As we ultimately saw in the case of the Kosovo air campaign, the only question remaining, unlike in earlier eras, is *when* these effects will be registered, not whether.

To note an important qualification here, air power has by no means become a universally applicable tool providing an answer to every conceivable security challenge that might arise. On the contrary, the spectrum of possible circumstances that could test a joint-force commander is so diverse that one can never say for sure that any single force element will always dominate across the board. Moreover, air power is not without continued limitations in what it can do for a joint force commander. For example, for all the recent claims made on behalf of air power's potential for halting and repelling an enemy armored attack, Air Force leaders would be the first to concede that they cannot execute their "halt-phase" strategy solely by using bombers based in the continental United States. The Air Force simply lacks a sufficient number of intercontinental-range combat aircraft with the required munitions capability and must necessarily depend on forward-deployed projection forces to stop enemy invasions.

To make matters worse, the sharp decline in the number of permanent U.S. overseas bases since the cold war's end has made regional access more essential than ever to the effective use of American land-based air power worldwide. Yet assumptions of easy and ready access can be dangerous. For example, 10 years from now the two Koreas may have reunited, leaving open the question of whether the new Korean government will be more or less amenable to the continued presence of American combat aircraft on the Korean peninsula. On top of that, Japan may not be willing to take on any more U.S. aircraft. That spotlights the need for the United States to be working hard now to ensure future access wherever and whenever it may be needed.

To be sure, the United States will most likely retain for some time its most vital air bases in Europe and the Pacific that survived the initial post–cold war drawdown. Yet more and more operations against certain regions may have to be conducted from the continental United States because of inadequate or uncertain basing alternatives closer to the theater. As a stopgap, the Navy commands a natural advantage with its aircraft carriers for some plausible contingencies that could occur in littoral settings suitable for carrier air operations. However, neither the nation's bombers *nor* its carriers have the needed numerical strength and persistence to sustain an air operation of campaign proportions. Only land-based attack aircraft, including Navy and Marine Corps aircraft as necessary and feasible, can do that. Accordingly, partnerships to ensure regional access by American and allied forces when global challenges require such access will be essential to air power's successful application in the 21st century.

To note another limiting factor, one must never forget that the operational setting of the 1991 Gulf war was almost uniquely congenial to the effective employment of U.S. air power. The going will not always be that easy in future showdowns in which U.S. air power might be challenged, as attested by the very different case of Korea. There is where the Gulf war analogy breaks down quickly and where the Air Force and Army have a powerful need for mutual respect because of their mutual dependency. Although air power will almost surely be a key ingredient of success in any war that might erupt there, no such war would be fought with the comparative luxury of fewer than 200 U.S. combat fatalities, as was the case in Desert Storm. To begin with, North Korea would presumably be fighting for its survival and might well employ, or attempt to employ, weapons of mass destruction. On top of that, with more than 500,000 armed combatants on both sides poised for immediate action along the demilitarized zone, any such war would necessarily entail close ground combat from the very start.

True enough, air power would quickly establish U.S. ownership of the skies over North Korea following any outbreak of a full-fledged war on the peninsula and would help reduce the incidence of friendly combat fatalities by blunting an armored attack, drawing down enemy missiles and artillery, and gaining situational control by forcing the enemy to remain underground. It could further engage in systematic "bunker plinking," although many of North Korea's underground facilities are sufficiently secure from air attack that it could require allied ground forces to go in and dig them out. But without question, U.S. air power would not be able to halt a North Korean armored and mechanized infantry invasion alone. It would not just beat up on enemy ground troops for 40 days as it did in Desert Storm while the other side did nothing. On the contrary, there would be plenty of fight for *all* allied force elements in any such war.

Finally, strategic air attack cannot be routinely expected to break an enemy leadership's will or bring down a political regime, a point that has important doctrinal implications to which we will return shortly. However, those need no longer be the goals of air power employment when "strategic attack" can now strike directly at an enemy's instruments of power and, in effect, deny him the ability to do anything of operational consequence, irrespective of his will. The increased effectiveness of air power against those instruments means that a theater commander in chief (CINC) may no longer need to crush an enemy in every case, but merely to disrupt his capacity for collective action in the pursuit of declared goals. There may also be no need in all cases to obliterate a target or target system, but merely to render it ineffective by destroying its ability to function.

With all due acknowledgment of air power's continued limitations, what benefits does the air weapon now offer its ultimate consumer, the theater joint-force commander, whose use for it will be directly proportional to its ability to answer his bottom-line operational needs? The first, and by far most important, payoff of air power's transformation in capability since the mid-1980s entails increasing the situational awareness of friendly forces while denying it to the enemy. The various air- and space-based information, surveillance, and reconnaissance (ISR) capabilities outlined in the preceding chapters now offer greatly improved knowledge of a battlespace situation for all command echelons in a joint operation. They cannot, at least yet, address the legitimate concern voiced by such land combatants as retired Marine Lieutenant General Paul Van Riper over finding and identifying a notional "enemy company in the basement of [a] built-up area" or "the 12 terrorists mixed with that crowd in the village market"—a challenge, one might note, that is no less demanding for U.S. ground forces.[2] However, they are more than adequate for supporting informed and confident force committal decisions by a theater CINC against large enemy armored formations on the move in the open. For all its continued limitations, such an advantage entails a major breakthrough in targeting capability and one which, in conjunction with high-accuracy attack systems, has made for a uniquely powerful U.S. force multiplier.

There is nothing new about this in and of itself. In a sense, belligerents have practiced "information warfare" ever since the days of sticks and

---

[2] *Clashes of Visions: Sizing and Shaping Our Forces in a Fiscally Constrained Environment,* A CSIS-VII Symposium, October 29, 1997, Washington, D.C., Center for Strategic and International Studies, 1998, p. 38.

stones. The 17th-century English philosopher Thomas Hobbes captured its essence well in his dictum that in the land of the blind, the one-eyed man is king. The difference today, however, is that commanders and planners are now at the threshold of understanding its importance and mastering it. Indeed, the broad area of fusing inputs from multiple sensors into a single, coherent real-time picture of an operational situation is arguably more pivotal than any other area of current technology development, since it is the sine qua non for extracting the fullest value from the new options for imposing combat leverage that are continuing to become available to all U.S. forces. Owing to the enhanced awareness it now promises, this synergistic melding of information and precision attack capability will strengthen the hands of warfighters up and down the chain of command, from the highest level to individual shooters working within tactical confines.

A second payoff area worth emphasizing is the broadened ability of air power to do things it could not do before, as well as to accomplish more with less for a joint-force commander. On the first count, it has shown the ability to maintain air dominance over the heart of an enemy's territory, enforce no-fly and no-drive zones, and engage enemy armies effectively from relatively safe standoff ranges. On the second count, increased ease of information processing and routing has enabled reduced cycle time, yet another force multiplier that creates a larger apparent force from smaller numbers by permitting a higher operations tempo. Relatedly, the current generation of combat aircraft embodies significant improvements in reliability and maintainability, making possible greater leverage from fewer numbers. Such enhancements now allow both greater concentration of force and a reduction in the amount of time it takes to perform an operational task.

A third major payoff afforded by recent improvements in American air power is control of the situation from the outset of combat, such that the first blow can decide the subsequent course and outcome of a war. Properly applied, air power now permits the attainment of strategic results through simultaneity rather than through the classic sequence of methodical plodding from tactical goals through operational-level goals to strategic goals at an exorbitant cost in lives, forces, and national treasure. This is quite different from what Giulio Douhet and his followers envisaged. Air power now has the ability to cause the early destruction or neutralization of an enemy's warmaking potential. Yet the main objectives are no longer the familiar ones of leadership, economic potential, popular will, and so on invoked by past "strategic bombardment" proponents. Instead, they embrace key assets that make up an enemy's military forces, critical infrastructure, and capacity for organized action. Before long, the initial attack may even be surreptitious —for example, into computer systems, to pave the way for fire and steel to follow.

[302]

Finally, the transformation of American air power has enabled the maintenance of constant pressure on an enemy from a safe distance, increased kills per sortie, selective targeting with a minimum of unintended damage, substantially reduced reaction time, and at least potentially, the complete shutdown of an enemy's ability to control his forces. These and other payoffs in no way add up to all-purpose substitutes for ground forces. However, they now permit theater CINCs to rely on air power to conduct deep battle for the greater extent of a joint campaign, foreshadowing an end to any need for friendly armies to plan on conducting early close-maneuver ground combat as a standard practice.

In previous years, the dialectic between maneuver and fire cast indirect firepower—whether from air or ground weapons—mostly in a supporting role because it could offer the ground commander little more. That, however, has changed dramatically over the past decade and continues to do so to the benefit of air warfare capabilities. As Barry Watts observed, "Foreseeable improvements in wide-area surveillance, the ability to act upon the information provided by such surveillance in seconds or minutes, and the range and lethality of indirect, precision fires raise the possibility of air-land combat becoming increasingly dominated by them. Indeed, increased dominance of outcomes by indirect fires from the air was precisely the hallmark of the Desert Storm air campaign, although airmen seldom formulated the point this way."[3]

All in all, possibly the single greatest effect of the transformation of American air power has been its demonstrated capacity to save lives—enemy lives through the use of precision to minimize noncombatant fatalities, and friendly lives by the substitution of technology for manpower and the creation of battlefield conditions in which land elements, once unleashed, can do their jobs without significant resistance because of the degraded capabilities of enemy forces. Viewed another way, modern technology skillfully applied in conjunction with a clear concept of operations offers today's air and space forces a means of gaining their goals through cleverness rather than brute force, in a manner reminiscent of top-scoring Luftwaffe ace Eric Hartmann's frequent injunction that the good combat pilot flies with his head, not his muscles.

A STRUGGLE BETWEEN NEW AND OLD

If U.S. air power has indeed registered such gains in capability over the past decade compared to what it was able to contribute to joint warfare in

---

[3] Barry D. Watts, "Ignoring Reality: Problems of Theory and Evidence in Security Studies," *Security Studies*, Winter 1997/98, p. 166.

earlier years, then why has it become so beleaguered from so many sides in today's defense debate? In shedding light on this question, it may be helpful to approach the ongoing confrontation between air and surface warfare functions as the early stirrings of a nascent paradigm shift in the American approach to war. In essence, a paradigm is a recognized and accepted frame of reference that, in the portrayal of science historian Thomas Kuhn, "for a time provides model problems and solutions to a community of practitioners."[4] Kuhn was speaking of revolutionary changes in scientific outlooks, such as that perhaps most famously exemplified by the gradual transition from the concept of an earth-centered cosmos to that of a solar-centered milieu. Yet the intellectual and professional dynamics that he identified in that process describe almost perfectly what has been happening in the relationship between the American air and land warfare communities since Desert Storm. At bottom, that relationship has entailed an increasingly open and heated dispute over fundamentals in a struggle between one long-accepted frame of reference and another that purports to be better.

By implication, Kuhn revealed much about the selective images of combat held by the various services in his characterization of how scientists of different upbringing perceive a common phenomenon: "On the road to professional specialization, a few physical scientists encounter only the basic principles of quantum mechanics. Others study in detail the paradigm applications of these principles to chemistry, still others to the physics of the solid state, and so on. What quantum mechanics means to each of them depends on what courses he has had, what texts he has read, and which journals he studies."[5] With the necessary changes for context, the same can be said with respect to the various protagonists in the current American roles and resources debate. Among other things, it tends to bear out the now-famous proposition first propounded in the early 1960s by the dean of Harvard's School of Public Policy, Don Price, that where you stand depends on where you sit.

In military doctrine no less than in the natural sciences, as Kuhn showed, the triumph of new ideas must invariably contend along the way with "life-long resistance, particularly from those whose productive careers have committed them to an older tradition." Kuhn explained how "the source of resistance is the assurance that the older paradigm will ultimately solve all its problems. . . . Inevitably, at times of revolution, that assurance seems stubborn and pigheaded, as indeed it sometimes becomes. But it is also something more."[6] Up to a point, at least, this natural and healthy phe-

---

[4] Thomas S. Kuhn, *The Structure of Scientific Revolutions*, Chicago, University of Chicago Press, 1962, p. viii.

[5] Ibid., p. 50.

[6] Ibid., pp. 151–152.

nomenon helps ensure that the old paradigm "will not be too easily sur-
rendered" and that any ultimate shift in outlook will be both valid and
warranted.[7] Pending the completion of such a shift, the embattled and ob-
solescing paradigm also remains a necessary key to cognitive consistency
and to the ability of its holders to operate effectively within the existing
framework.

The problem with the case at hand here, however, is that the would-be
"new paradigm" of American combat style is anything but self-evidently
an air and space power paradigm. True enough, some air power proponents since Desert Storm have argued as though an imminent shift to an
aerospace-dominated U.S. strategy is all but a foregone conclusion, save
only for those benighted obstructionists in the land warfare world who
seem so consistently unable to see the light. Yet as the preceding chapter
pointed out, the land warfare community has made a no less determined
counterclaim to being the vanguard of the military-technological revolution. Land warriors are now professing no less vigorously than airmen that
it is *they* who are the keepers of any "new paradigm" of joint warfare.

A major part of the basis for this counterclaim by the land warfare community is that recent improvements in information fusion and precision target attack have enhanced the combat capability of *all* U.S. services and force
elements. By way of example, a former Air Force chief of staff, General Larry
Welch, noted that irrespective of the medium, the essence of the emerging
change in U.S. force capability includes high lethality on the first mission,
near-complete freedom of operations from the outset of combat, round-the-
clock operations enabling a constant high pace while giving the enemy no
sanctuary, and the dominance of combat operations by information.[8] However much these attributes may represent what air and space power do
uniquely best in joint warfare, they are not exclusive attributes of air and
space power by any means.

Two imperatives, however, have made the right choices in this contested
paradigm shift crucially important. First, reduced funds for procurement
and operational support across the board have placed an unprecedented
premium on making and faithfully executing astute decisions regarding
successor-generation U.S. forces. With a balanced federal budget and an
associated legal stipulation that any increment in defense spending must
now be taken from other federal accounts, U.S. defense planners are facing
a need as never before to discipline the apportionment of resources among
the complementary and sometimes duplicative procurement programs offered up by the four services and to make ruthless triage choices in the in-

[7] Ibid., p. 65.
[8] General Larry D. Welch, USAF (Ret.), "Dominating the Battlefield (Battlespace)," briefing charts,
no date given.

terest of eliminating costly redundancies, notably in the area of deep attack against enemy armored and mechanized forces.

Second, there has been a rising American public unwillingness to tolerate combat casualties in more than token numbers. In part, this post-Vietnam phenomenon has been bolstered by the almost bloodless victory achieved by the allied coalition in Desert Storm. Indeed, the single most powerful testament to the newly acquired leverage of air power provided by the Gulf war was the fact that the coalition lost fewer lives to hostile fire during the five weeks of actual fighting than it did to routine accidents during the previous five months of in-theater workups. Unfortunately, one of the less auspicious results of that experience was that a low likelihood of producing combat casualties has increasingly become the norm against which Americans have come to evaluate *all* military commitments and their worth.

To be sure, recent research suggested that the widespread assumption that the American public will no longer accept casualties from the nation's military commitments abroad has been greatly oversimplified and that the staying power of public support is, in fact, very much a function of public perceptions of the stakes of a commitment and the competence of U.S. leadership in handling it.[9] Revealingly in this regard, the chairman of the respected Louis Harris and Associates polling firm toward the end of NATO's air campaign for Kosovo flatly rejected easy suggestions that the American people would inevitably oppose the commitment of ground troops or any other determined use of force. "When the U.S. achieves victory in a just cause," he pointed out, "the public applauds the use of force. When it loses—worse still, when America is defeated or runs away (as in Somalia or Vietnam)—the public reasonably says the use of the military was a mistake." Citing the precedent of Desert Storm, he recalled how during the days immediately preceding the outbreak of hostilities, not one in seven polls found a majority of Americans in favor of immediate military action. Yet immediately after the air campaign had begun and was deemed to have gotten off to a good start, surveys found that between 68 and 84 percent of those polled approved.[10] That said, it cannot be denied that increased public

---

[9] For some well-grounded empirical amplification on this point, see Eric V. Larson, *Casualties and Consensus: The Historical Role of Casualties in Domestic Support for U.S. Military Operations*, Santa Monica, Cal., RAND, MR-726-RC, 1996, and James Burk, "Public Support for Peacekeeping in Lebanon and Somalia: Assessing the Casualties Hypothesis," *Political Science Quarterly*, Vol. 114, No. 1, 1999, pp. 53–78.

[10] Humphrey Taylor, "Win in Kosovo and the Public Will Approve," *Wall Street Journal*, June 3, 1999. Similarly, up to the day before the Desert Storm ground push commenced, a typical poll taken by the *New York Times* and CBS found that 79 percent of the public preferred a continuation of the air war, with only 11 percent favoring the start of ground operations. A few days after the ground campaign began, however, a full 75 percent of those polled believed it had been "right to start the ground war," as opposed to only 19 percent who opposed it.

awareness of, and sensitivity to, the issue of casualties across the board have forced an increasing demand for technology to substitute for human life wherever possible. Insofar as air and space technology has made it ever more possible to apply effective force with a minimum of both friendly *and* enemy losses, it bodes well, compared to the extant alternatives, for accommodating this sensitivity by means of the new leverage afforded by air power.

If, however, the promise of air and space power outlined in this book is to be realized in tomorrow's U.S. force posture, merely the strength of a compelling idea will not suffice to bring it about. The first challenge for those air power proponents who purport to be the keepers of the new paradigm is to engage their counterparts in other combat arms in candid awareness of what air power *cannot* do and with candid respect for the intellectual and historical origins of the differing views held by their fellow professionals in the surface forces. Equally important, it behooves airmen to acknowledge what their surface-warrior brethren continue to offer the joint-force commander by way of needed combat capability, even in the face of the quantum improvements that have recently occurred in the instruments of air warfare.

More to the point, airmen must argue convincingly to those of the putative "old school" that there is not only a better way through air and space power, but also one that promises to underwrite the mission needs of surface warriors no less than the needs and interests of those who fly. Toward that end, they could benefit enormously by heeding the observation of Harvard political scientist Richard Neustadt years ago that the essence of influence lies in persuading those of different opinions that one's own version of what needs to be done by them "is what their own appraisal of their own responsibilities requires them to do in their own interests."[11] Any such attempt by airmen at a reasoned approach to doubters in other services will likewise be aided greatly by resisting the natural urge to counter parochial challenges from other warfare communities with equally parochial knee-jerk reactions aimed at scoring instant-gratification debating points and, instead, by offering more tempered arguments on behalf of air power that might appeal to a more broadly based audience of defense professionals.

Indeed, since air power can be everything from totally decisive to totally irrelevant to a CINC's needs depending on the situation, attempting to argue for an aerospace-centric U.S. defense strategy for all occasions is possibly the single most self-destructive error that air power proponents can make. The greatest failing of Douhet and Mitchell was their audacity in espousing not simply a theory of *air* power, but an overarching and universalist theory

---

[11] Richard E. Neustadt, *Presidential Power*, New York, John Wiley, 1963, p. 49.

of *war* that hinged everything on the air weapon to the virtual exclusion of all other military means. Because real-world security challenges are not likely to be amenable to generic force employment solutions, irrespective of their focus, it may even be that the decades-long search by air power advocates for a single "grand theory" of air power that could apply across the entire spectrum of potential problems that might warrant U.S. intervention was destined to fail from the very start. In all events, since air power cannot win wars single-handedly or render land power obsolete, the United States needs an appropriately balanced military posture. Air power may indeed now be the principal enabler of most other forms of military action. Nonetheless, it will always be a part of a larger campaign involving integrated forces, with the relative balance among forces employed varying as necessary with the situation.

Second, airmen must own up to the fact that achieving and maintaining air superiority is only a part of the air power story, a necessary but insufficient condition for air power to lay convincing claim to having become the predominant force. Part and parcel of any such acknowledgment must be for airmen to repudiate, once and for all, Douhet's signature axiom that "to have command of the air is to have victory."[12] That statement was false when it was first made in 1921, and it is no less false today. Although control of the air is an indispensable precondition for joint-force success, air power must also be able to perform the job on the ground by attacking an enemy's war-waging capacity faster and more efficiently than ground forces, and at less cost in terms of friendly casualties, if its proponents are to justify their claim to its being the force of first choice. What has lately come to be called "air dominance" will always be important to the successful outcome of joint-force campaigns. However, it is not now and never was air power's principal stock in trade.

Third, and relatedly, the new capability and promise of U.S. air power require that airmen unburden themselves of past teachings with respect to the utility of urban-industrial bombing to undermine an enemy's will to fight to a point where it can determine war outcomes single-handedly. Not only have the core arguments of those teachings been shown repeatedly to be baseless in fact, technology and new force employment options now permit a conception of air warfare that is genuinely "strategic," yet focused more directly on an enemy's instruments of military power and social control. The improved and still-improving ability of U.S. air power to produce desired combat results on the ground rapidly has invalidated many of the often-voiced doubts prompted by a reading of classic air power theory. As the discussion here will argue more fully, this implies a need for U.S. air planners to change their measures of effectiveness by shifting their attention to

---

[12] Giulio Douhet, *Command of the Air*, Washington, D.C., Office of Air Force History, 1983, p. 25.

air power's newly acquired capability against an enemy's forces of all kinds, if they are to ensure that air power theory remains relevant to the needs of U.S. joint-force commanders.

More to the point, it is time for airmen to bid farewell to the now-outmoded arguments espoused by Douhet and subsequent air power advocates on behalf of massive urban-industrial bombardment and, instead, to play up the fact that air power, properly applied, can now quickly neutralize enemy armies and surface navies anywhere. Toward that end, Air Vice Marshal Mason suggested a need to review critically the image of strategic bombardment put forward by the early theorists of air power because of the extent to which it has become discredited over the years as a result of its focus on the targeting of innocents. The equating of strategic attack with urban destruction, Mason pointed out, not only gave it invidious associations with the firebombing of Dresden and Tokyo in World War II but, worse yet, "inhibited a wider realization of air power's complete potential."[13]

On this point, military historian Russell Weigley highlighted a larger problem with classic air power theory, reflected most vividly in the fact that both scholarly and popular writings on air power have tended to oscillate between what he called "adulatory celebrations" and "espressions of outraged disapproval," with little by way of more balanced assessments in between.[14] Weigley suggested that the centrality of urban-industrial bombing to the rise of U.S. air power has been a key reason for "the tendency toward histories that castigate, because the strategy, at the least, raises grave moral doubts." Weigley further noted how all too many air power proponents have felt driven toward adulation of the air weapon as a result of their "defensiveness in the face of those histories, the insecurities . . . of an armed service possessing so little past and so little traditions, [and] the ahistorical values that prevail anyway in a service so oriented toward technology and the future."[15]

Fourth, and directly derivative from the above, air power practitioners need to develop a theory of air power application in theater warfare on a scale of the classic theories of "strategic bombardment," yet one that focuses more directly on the prerequisites for attacking and destroying an enemy's fielded army. In contrast to the highly sophisticated planning assumptions that underlay the coalition's suppression of enemy air defenses (SEAD) campaign in Desert Storm, there was nothing comparable to inform allied plan-

[13] Air Vice Marshal Tony Mason, RAF (Ret.), "The Future of Air Power," address to the Royal Netherlands Air Force, Netherlands Defense College, April 19, 1996, p. 3.

[14] Russell F. Weigley, "Flying Men and Machines," *New York Times*, November 23, 1997.

[15] For a notable example of the genre of writing cited by Weigley (ibid.) as being distinguished by "a ceaseless underlying cry of dismay at a strategy of aerial bombardment that targets noncombatants," see Michael S. Sherry, *The Rise of American Air Power: The Creation of Armageddon*, New Haven, Yale University Press, 1987.

ning for air operations against the Iraqi army. The latter were guided by little more than classic thinking on attrition warfare.

Similarly, U.S. Central Command (CENTCOM) had a theory for attacking Iraq's "strategic" infrastructure that was imbedded at the center of Colonel Warden's Instant Thunder attack plan. Unfortunately, that theory did not deliver on its promise. Nevertheless, the Instant Thunder approach at least was built on an organizing concept of a sort that CENTCOM lacked for the part of the air war that fortuitously worked so well in the end, namely, the portions of the air campaign that were targeted against Iraq's ground forces. Had it possessed such a concept, allied air operations might have given General Schwarzkopf both greater going-in confidence and greater economy of force in the neutralization of Iraq's army. Instead, as Williamson Murray pointed out, planning for air attacks against Iraqi ground forces largely followed a reductionist approach in which the planners "simply racked up targets—so many tanks, so many artillery pieces, so many ammunition dumps, etcetera—and then worked their way down from the top of the list. Nowhere in the planning documents . . . was there an effort to use air power in an operational sense, as a lever to gain larger strategic effects by attacking certain portions of the enemy's ground structure, to cripple the whole."[16]

For that reason, air campaign planners must develop better measures of effectiveness against ground force targets and, beyond that, against enemy warfighting capacity across the board. A year after Desert Storm, one air power theorist charged that by having failed to develop a middle ground between strategic nuclear attack and the tactical use of conventional air power in direct support of ground troops, the Air Force had become "ideologically adrift, encumbered with a doctrinal gap that distorts both its self-image and the image it presents to others."[17] Although Air Force airmen have since embraced a greater implicit realization of the potentially decisive *functional* effects of conventional air attacks in destroying an enemy army or denying it the ability to maneuver, they have not yet proceeded from that realization to a better theory of air power employment against enemy land forces that might be useful to a theater CINC in actual campaign planning.

The problem here is that purely attrition-based analytic models that assign primary value to killing armor by the numbers are inherently incapable of reflecting the functional effects of air power that were demonstrated to such telling effect at Al Khafji and afterward. They thus give no value to what air power can do against ostensibly "tactical" targets to produce strategic results in joint warfare. A particular hindrance to the devel-

---

[16] Williamson Murray, "Ignoring the Sins of the Past," *National Interest,* Summer 1995, pp. 100–101.

[17] Lieutenant Colonel Phillip S. Meilinger, USAF, "The Problem with Our Air Power Doctrine," *Airpower Journal,* Spring 1992, pp. 28–29.

opment of a better tool for incorporating the strategic effects of conventional air power is that what worked to best effect by way of air operations against enemy ground forces in Desert Storm, namely, the impact of nonstop bombing on Iraqi troop morale, was as impossible to anticipate beforehand as it has remained difficult to quantify and measure after the fact. As it was, the allied air attacks against Iraqi ground forces lacked any conceptual basis other than simply listing targets and going after them seriatim.

Unfortunately, CENTCOM's use of attrition as a measure of air power's effectiveness against enemy ground forces in Desert Storm continues to afflict the analytic models used for force planning by the office of the secretary of defense and the Joint Staff. The Air Force's former chief of staff, General Ronald Fogleman, complained with good cause in a memorandum to the chairman of the Joint Chiefs of Staff in 1996 that "these legacy models are most relevant when considering linear battlespace, the FEBA [forward edge of the battle area], and an employment strategy of attrition and annihilation. Models assessing force-on-force engagements, based upon force ratios and territory gained or lost, lack the capability to fully and accurately portray the significant effects of operations involving nonlinear battlespace or an asymmetric strategy directly attacking the enemy's strategic and tactical centers of gravity."[18]

To cite a case in point, the standard campaign model now used by the Defense Department and Joint Staff, called TACWAR (for "tactical warfare"), does not model interconnectivity or anything approaching the application of air power to achieve decisive functional effects as was demonstrated in Desert Storm. By one informed account, "It does not allow planners to open a hole through a surface-to-air missile (SAM) net and punch a strike through. . . . Instead, it requires air power to kill all SAMs along the entire front to achieve the same modeling effects." Similarly, the attacks against Iraqi early-warning radars that inaugurated the Gulf war "would be wasted in TACWAR because destruction of GCI [ground-controlled intercept] sites—even all GCI sites—has no impact on air defense capability." Finally, "intelligent target assignment is not modeled, and weapons and targets can be totally mismatched. Thus an F-15E in the interdiction role is forced to attack a bunkered ammo depot with a half-load of cluster bombs on one day, and on the next use a half-load of laser-guided bombs against second-echelon troops in the open."[19]

Fifth, if air power proponents are to have any influence in helping to bring about a transformation in American force development that makes the most

---

[18] Quoted in Lieutenant Colonel Steve McNamara, USAF, "Assessing Air Power's Importance: Will the QDR Debate Falter for Lack of Proper Analytic Tools?" *Armed Forces Journal International*, March 1997, p. 37.
[19] Ibid.

of what recent improvements in air and space technology have to offer, as a first order of business they will need to stop talking in terms of "dominant air and space power," a proclivity that has needlessly put the other services on the defensive in the budget wars. Instead, they should focus on how air and space power can contribute toward making the job of U.S. ground forces easier. Toward that end, there surely must be more imaginative ways of thinking about the changing relationship between air and land power than simply in reductionist "either-or" terms. For instance, indirect-fire support from the air, if well directed, lethal, and timely, can enable ground commanders to do things differently, as well as to do different things with their forces. Among other options one might imagine, it can hold a forward line until ground troops arrive on scene to secure it. It also can deter or disrupt and delay large-scale invasions even if friendly ground forces have not yet deployed to a threatened theater in fighting strength. In all events, the first rule for air power proponents should be to refrain from heralding an imminent "air and space revolution" and instead focus on explaining what airmen and land warriors *together* can do to best exploit the emerging realities of U.S. air and space power.

Sixth, in making the most of the new opportunities offered by air and space technologies, airmen should strive to articulate a more contemporaneous sense of what it means to "win" in today's joint operations. Colin Gray touched the heart of this need in his injunction that "air power has to be guided in its development by a comprehensive theory of success in deterrence and war," on the reasonable premise that air power, perhaps more than any other single force element today, is ultimately "an instrument that generates strategic influence."[20] Must one invariably seize and hold enemy terrain to reap the desired benefits of such influence? There continues to be a dominant belief in some U.S. defense quarters which holds that the only way to show that the United States is "truly serious" about prevailing in a regional confrontation is through the commitment of ground forces. This canonical image of victory entails defeating an enemy's ground forces in detail, occupying his territory, and controlling his population on an open-ended basis. Yet the latter two of these three objectives are rarely likely to be goals of any U.S. joint operation, and the first may no longer require the presence of a large land force to complete the job. Put differently, while the credible *threat* of a U.S. ground invasion may often be indispensable for U.S. air power to realize its fullest potential against fielded enemy forces, actually introducing U.S. troops into combat to "clinch a win" may no longer be needed as a rule for achieving declared national goals, as was borne out most recently by the results of NATO's 1999 Kosovo campaign. The chief aim of U.S. intervention policy today is not typically to "win" in the classic

---

[20] Colin S. Gray, *Explorations in Strategy*, Westport, Conn., Praeger, 1996, p. 71.

military sense so much as to shape situations and thereby affect enemy behavior.

Finally, it bears repeating a point stressed at the outset of this study, that the future leverage of the American air weapon will continue to be a complex blend of equipment, operator proficiency, and concepts of operations. As in years past, weakness in any one of these categories can engender debilitating deficiencies in the effectiveness of the air posture as a whole. To cite but one example, gradualism and "proportionality" have long been familiar whipping boys for the failure of U.S. air power in Vietnam, as well as for other less-than-astute applications of air power in subsequent years, including most recently the often agonizingly slow-motion NATO air campaign against Slobodan Milosevic in 1999. Yet 58,000 U.S. military personnel lost their lives and $150 billion in national treasure were frittered away in Southeast Asia not only because of those strategy deficiencies but also because of a failure to apply good air doctrine throughout most of the war's duration and a woefully underdeveloped capability for conventional air warfare. As a testament to the fact that the U.S. loss of the Vietnam war stemmed from more than just gradualism and flawed strategy, the nation sent its airmen into combat in that war with a level of training that would not even qualify them to take part in the Air Force's Red Flag, the Navy's Strike Warfare Center, or the Marine Corps' MAWTS-1 (Marine Aviation Weapons and Tactics Squadron One) peacetime exercises today. Owing in large part to the improvements in equipment and training that marked the ensuing 25 years of American air power development, NATO's air campaign against Milosevic in 1999 saw the air weapon prevail *despite* the resurgent burdens of gradualism and proportionality.

EFFECTING A NEW AMERICAN WAY OF WAR

Mindful of the emerging fight over roles and resources that was foreshadowed by the Title V imbroglio in the wake of Desert Storm, Air Vice Marshal Mason warned of "a danger that sensible and necessary debates about air power may be threatened by a reemergence of zealotry on the one hand and obtuseness on the other as resources are reduced, threats diminished, and role responsibilities blurred." [21] To a dismaying extent, that is exactly what has occurred in American defense politics during the ensuing years. In a thoughtful contribution to the post–Gulf war U.S. defense debate, Mason called for a stern exorcism of the sort of air power excessiveness that was reflected in the exaggerated claims of Giulio Douhet, which not

---

[21] Air Vice Marshal Tony Mason, RAF (Ret.), *Air Power: A Centennial Appraisal*, London, Brassey's, 1994, p. xvi.

only needlessly polarized discussion of strategy alternatives among the services for decades, but were wrong both in overestimating the ability of aerial bombardment to break the will of an opponent and in denigrating the continued need for ground and naval forces alongside strategic air power.

As for the latter-day air power proponents who would exploit the success of the Gulf air campaign to rekindle the flame first lit by the early air power advocates, Mason retorted that insofar as air power could be said to have predetermined the outcome of Desert Storm, it was "a result of strategic, operational, and tactical simultaneous synergism, not from any reincarnation of Douhet." As an antidote to further controversy over false issues, he suggested that it was past time "to place air power into the continuum of military history, to emphasize not just its unique characteristics, but the features it shares, to a greater or lesser degree, with other forms of warfare." Mason added that the preeminence of air power "will stand or fall not by promises and abstract theories, but, like any other kind of military power, by its relevance to, and ability to secure, political objectives at a cost acceptable to the government of the day."[22]

No one in any position of senior leadership in the U.S. Air Force has proposed that the United States no longer needs a capable army and navy, that air power can invariably substitute for land power, or that land-based air can routinely supplant sea-based air. On the contrary, today's Air Force leaders would be among the first to agree that it remains essential for the United States to maintain a land force capable of engaging and defeating a powerful enemy, if only to prove that by threatening to do so, the nation is wholly committed to any regional intervention it might undertake. Indeed, some senior airmen have gone so far as to suggest that the best deterrent of regional aggression may well be forward-deployed U.S. ground troops, assuming a host country in the threatened region is willing to accept them. That said, recent developments in the combat capability of U.S. air power have made possible a new way of war for the United States entailing entirely new concepts of operations. Owing to precision, stealth, and expanded information availability, airmen are now paradoxically able to apply air power as first envisioned by the early advocates, but not in a way that they could even remotely have foreseen.

Ironically, technology has occasioned a coalescence of the most basic Air Force and Army functions, although neither service has been inclined to portray things that way, for understandable reasons. The abiding goal of the Army has always been to defeat enemy armies. For its part, the newly independent Air Force set for itself the very different goal in 1947 of conducting independent operations against an enemy's "vital center" to destroy his ability and will to continue fighting. Technology developments over the

[22] Ibid., pp. 273–274.

past two decades, however, have now enabled air power to bypass that typically elusive goal and proceed directly to an enemy's throat by destroying his instruments of power, first and foremost his military forces of all types.

This does not mean, though, that there is no longer a vital need for other force elements of equal prowess for performing their own service-specific functions. On the contrary, no matter how the debate over roles and resources ultimately shakes out during the coming decade, all four U.S. services will have to become more integrated functionally if they are to benefit to the fullest from the new promise of air and space power that was previewed in Desert Storm. That will require not just lip service to the principle of "jointness," but a true team spirit on a daily basis, with a minimum of jockeying for position and an implicit understanding that the four services are all in the same boat when it comes to supporting the national interest. Any such evolution, in turn, will require resisting the temptation to allow defense planning to devolve into a situation in which the real enemy is seen as down the hall in the Pentagon rather than across the ocean in some remote desert or jungle. Instead of such intramural squabbling, the various warfare communities, airmen included, must accept that only through greater integration can tomorrow's forces produce effective results. It behooves them as well to honor a crucial point offered by Richard Szafranski that "while one form of force may be better suited to a particular function than another, that fact in no way makes one superior and another inferior, one 'dominant and decisive' and another subordinate or irrelevant."[23]

This does not mean that individual services or force elements will no longer perform as primary or even unitary players in some cases as circumstances dictate, much as allied air power did during the first five weeks of Desert Storm. However, traditional service lines are more and more being forced to break down under the pressure of the continuing integration of systems and capabilities. In future wars in which air activity will most likely be a precursor to any land operation and in which naval weapons can engage an ever-wider spectrum of land targets, the overarching interests of mission effectiveness will require a breakdown of narrow and retrograde parochialism and greater professional cross-communication as a routine matter of peacetime business. As one retired naval officer described it, the U.S. armed forces are now approaching a point where "an Air Force sensor operator and coordinator might be directing a Navy platform to release an Army weapon in direct support of Marines."[24] A demanding challenge for civilian policymakers presented by this trend will involve making the right

[23] Colonel Richard Szafranski, USAF, *Twelve Principles of Air Power*, Paper No. 48, Fairbairn, Australia, RAAF Air Power Studies Center, September 1996, p. 14.
[24] Captain James H. Patton, Jr., USN (Ret.), "The New 'RMA': It's Only Begun," *Naval War College Review*, Spring 1996, pp. 23–32.

investment choices and avoiding needless duplication of effort just so each service can claim a piece of the action. That challenge may prove more daunting than developing and integrating the new technologies themselves.

More bluntly put, true "jointness," as opposed to what one might call politically correct jointness, does not mean that each service should be allowed to play in equal measure in all cases, as they did in 1981 in a way that led to the embarrassing Iranian hostage rescue debacle. As some air power proponents have rightly complained in this respect, "jointness" has tended to become "a plea for the inefficient distribution of scarce resources that can lead to operational paralysis," motivated by a misguided sense that *jointness* means "an excuse to demand 'fair share' distribution of weapon system funding, regardless of the system's relative value to national defense."[25] Instead, *jointness*, properly understood, should be taken to mean fielding and employing the most appropriate elements of the four services as common sense would suggest.

Since the various force components can be used wisely or foolishly depending on the way they are mixed and sequenced, an important concern for joint-force commanders will involve managing the trade-offs between and among them to best effect. Ultimately, because of that, it may well be the regional joint-force theater CINCs who will end up making the single greatest difference in shaping the way the United States configures itself for tomorrow's wars. Unlike the service chiefs, the CINCs are not concerned, first and foremost, about rice-bowl issues, but rather about their responsibility to do right by the demands of their operations plans. They are also, not to put too fine a point on it, understandably concerned about their own reputations should the day ever come when they may be called on to execute those plans. A CINC cannot afford to indulge in parochial pursuits at the same time he is preoccupied with the more pressing concern for ensuring that his war plans will work if put to the test. In light of that, one would naturally assume that a CINC would be open to the potential value of air power along with any and all other options that might best serve his contingency needs.

A second reason why the theater CINCs may turn out to be the most crucial players in determining the American way of war during the first decade of the 21st century and beyond is because they, rather than the service chiefs, are ultimately the most credible witnesses before the Joint Requirements Oversight Council. Of all the military planning forums inside the Washington Beltway, the Joint Requirements Oversight Council is the nerve center for adjudicating and deciding on future U.S. force requirements. Accordingly, that is where the argument for air and space power will ultimately succeed or fail. That argument may stand to be articulated more persua-

---

[25] Colonel Brian E. Wages, USAF (Ret.), "DoD's Free Thinkers: Is the Air Force Surrendering Its Visionary Role?" *Armed Forces Journal International*, November 1995, p. 39.

sively by the CINCs who will depend on the offerings of air power than it can ever be by an Air Force chief of staff who, however eloquent he might be, is ultimately perceived in the joint arena as just a hardware accumulator and thus an advocate of his own service's corporate interests.

If the theater CINCs, given their freedom to organize their operations in any way they desire, indeed now wield such influence over the complexion of the U.S. force structure, then it should follow that they constitute the audience in greatest need of a credible telling of the "air power story." To make the most of that audience, joint-minded airmen should be advising the theater CINCs that if they wish to win in the quickest, least painful, and least costly manner, they should plan on using air power in abundance against enemy forces and support systems before committing to engage those forces on the ground. Along the way, airmen should stress the unique characteristics of air and space power, such as speed, flexibility, mass effects, and low collateral damage, that will have the greatest pertinence for the likely demands of future warfare.

One potential obstacle to a credible telling of the air power story to the CINCs and others in high policy circles who can act on it is the persistent divide one senses within the Air Force between those who view the wave of the future as precision strikes for conducting strategic offensive operations and those who, in the words of one informed observer, still hew to the "prevailing view . . . that the long-range precision strike mission should be accorded a priority below that of air superiority and air mobility." According to this view, there is a real danger that current Air Force investment planning could lead eventually to "a surprising yet plausible alternative future in which the Air Force no longer exists as an independent service." Such a view reflects understandable concern that "engaged primarily in the supporting roles of air escort and transport and lacking the robust long-range strike capability that was the Air Force birthright, the offensive Air Force of 2025 may bring very little to a battle fought at long range" and thus could find "many of its present roles, missions, and resources once again subsumed by its Army ancestor."[26]

To be sure, there is little sign today that the survival of the Air Force as a separate service is in any imminent jeopardy. Moreover, it would overstate matters considerably to suggest that the Air Force is fundamentally riven when it comes to the proper focus of its investment strategy. Yet there is much merit to the proposition that consummating any air and space "revolution" that may be in the offing will be aided immensely by a narrowing of the rift described in Chapter 4 that saw Tactical Air Command (TAC) and Colonel Warden's Air Staff planners at such odds in August 1990 over a pre-

[26] Colonel Robert P. Haffa, Jr., USAF (Ret.), "Wake-up Call: What the Air Force Study on Long-Range Planning Should Conclude," *Armed Forces Journal International*, September 1996, pp. 54–55.

ferred air campaign strategy for Desert Storm. That rift persists in the divisions one can see in today's Air Force between those committed to exploiting air and space power to their fullest potential and those still wedded to the more traditional view that the abiding purpose of the Air Force is to achieve air superiority and meet the indirect fire support and lift needs of ground commanders. The persistence of the latter view can be seen in the evident unwillingness of the Air Force to invest further in the B-2 and other long-range strike options because of its perceived preference for such platforms as the F-22, joint strike fighter, and C-17 at a time of limited funds.

Although it would take another book to review the full menu of force development alternatives now facing the Air Force, it bears noting that although that institution most definitely has come of age as a result of the mature capability it has acquired over the past two decades, it has yet to embrace the future fully by way of making the really hard choices regarding which of its long-familiar investment areas it may be prepared to give up in order to make good on its declared vision of becoming a true "air and space" force. For example, it can continue doing business as usual by stressing fighters, short-range attack systems, and expeditionary operations, or it can seek ways of fulfilling its familiar tasks in different and arguably more promising ways by emphasizing instead improved ISR capabilities, longer-range attack systems, and unmanned platforms for the higher-risk demands likely to arise in the 21st century. By the same token, it can continue to view space primarily as a medium for enhancing the execution of traditional air power missions and functions, or it can reach out to develop a grander vision of military space exploitation, arguing along the way with both conviction and clout why the Air Force should be the institution to define and realize that vision. These are but two of the major branch points now confronting the Air Force leadership as it continues to ponder which steps to take next now that its operational repertoire has matured as a tool of U.S. power.[27]

In the end, the essential precondition for any U.S. air and space "revolution" that may be in the offing almost surely will be found to lie on the affordability front. During the late 1970s, Norman Augustine produced his famous chart predicting that if cost growth trends in capital weapons continued uninterrupted, by the year 2054 it would take the entire U.S. defense budget to procure a single aircraft.[28] Today, two decades later, Augustine

[27] For a penetrating, if also harshly judgmental, look at such choices now facing the Air Force and how the institution seems to be responding, see Williamson Murray, "Drifting into the Next Century: The USAF and Air Power," *Strategic Review*, Summer 1999, pp. 17–24. A rather more compassionate, if no less concerned, treatment of the same issues may be found in Wages, "DoD's Free Thinkers," pp. 38–39.
[28] Norman R. Augustine, *Augustine's Laws*, New York, Penguin, 1986, p. 143.

maintains that that prediction remains on track. If American defense managers both in and out of uniform cannot control seemingly exponential cost growth in the next generation of weapons, they could eventually price themselves out of the defense business altogether. A continuing dilemma will entail where to invest and what sacrifices to make in order to achieve reasonable economies of scale. As always, the most difficult trade-offs will involve adequately attending to the needs of the theater CINCs who may have to fight tomorrow's wars, without shortchanging investment in systems to satisfy more downstream requirements which, by definition, cannot be clearly anticipated. Analysis can illuminate alternatives, trade-offs, and opportunity costs within limits.[29] But ultimately, sound development and procurement decisions will be the result of good judgment calls. The latter will turn, first and foremost, on best guesses about the nature of the strategic environment and the key challenges that may confront decisionmakers once planned weapons have attained operational status.

In pursuing any improvement in the American way of war through the new options held out by information technology and precision firepower, decisionmakers will also need to be careful not to lapse into complacency just because the United States is now the world's sole surviving superpower and because today's information and conventional attack capabilities have given it, to all intents and purposes, what used to be called "strategic superiority" over potential opponents. The promise of new technology indeed offers a windfall by-product in enhanced deterrence, since potential enemies will naturally be loath to challenge such proven capability if the resulting disparities in combat prowess are well known and understood, as clearly they were by most onlookers in the early aftermath of Desert Storm. Yet this same technology edge can spur a race by have-nots to develop asymmetric countermeasures. Retired Indian army Brigadier V. K. Nair set the tone in this respect by describing what determined Third World countries might do on the cheap to negate the superior technology shown by the coalition in Desert Storm.[30] Near-term options along these lines could include dedicated attacks against high-value soft targets such as the E-8 joint surveillance target attack radar system (JSTARS), the E-3 airborne warning and control system (AWACS), and tanker aircraft. Attacks on Air Force airlifters moving war materiel into an embattled theater and special operations or theater missile strikes against forward-area terminals and other allied

---

[29] For a useful sampler on the possibilities and limitations in this respect, see Paul K. Davis, ed., *New Challenges for Defense: Rethinking How Much Is Enough*, Santa Monica, Cal., RAND, MR-400-RC, 1994. See also the still-instructive RAND classic by E. S. Quade, ed., *Analysis for Military Decisions*, Chicago, Rand McNally, 1964.

[30] V. K. Nair, *War in the Gulf: Lessons for the Third World*, New Delhi, India, Lancer International, 1991.

bases could make for additional options. And, of course, there is the ever-present possibility of a desperation resort to a counterdeterrent based on nuclear and other weapons of mass destruction.

In all, however effective and promising they may appear to be today, the new capabilities of American air and space power that were so impressively foreshadowed during the 1991 Gulf war portend no "end of history" with respect to the enduring dialectic between offense and defense. One of the most demanding imperatives facing U.S. force development across the board in the coming years will be to ensure that today's one-sided U.S. predominance over potential troublemakers remains in effect for the indefinite future. That will require not resting on the laurels of the gains achieved to date, but continuing to invest as necessary to stay ahead of potential countermeasures that might even the odds. Beyond that, one must remain careful not to become so mesmerized by the apparent leverage of newly emerging military technology as to lose sight of the fact that future wars will not invariably offer easy going for the wielders of such technology. If U.S. defense planners are to succeed in institutionalizing any revolution in air and space technology that may now lie within their grasp, they will be aided greatly by remembering General George S. Patton's warning about how easily people can fool themselves into believing that wars can be won by some wonderful invention rather than by hard fighting and superior leadership.

To repeat an important qualifier noted earlier, nothing in this book has been intended to suggest that air power can win wars without ground or surface naval involvement, often even significant involvement. Nor have any of the foregoing chapters sought to argue that air power will, in each and every situation, inevitably be more important than land or sea power. That said, one can argue that the air power assets of *all* the U.S. services now have the potential to carry the bulk of responsibility for beating down an enemy's military forces of all kinds, thus enabling other friendly force elements to achieve their goals with a minimum of pain, effort, and cost when and if the time comes for them to enter the fight. More than that, one can argue that air power in its broadest sense, including such vital adjuncts as surveillance and reconnaissance in addition to combat platforms, munitions, and the mobility assets needed to deploy them, has fundamentally altered the way the United States might best fight any major wars over the next two decades through its ability to carry out functions traditionally performed at greater cost and risk by other force elements. Most notable among these are its demonstrated capacity to neutralize an enemy's army with a minimum of casualties on both sides and its ability to establish the preconditions for achieving strategic goals from the very outset of fighting.

Owing to these new capabilities, air and space power now offers the promise of being the swing factor in an ever-widening variety of theater-war situations. That, in turn, suggests that the primary role of U.S. land power in future circumstances involving the defeat of large-scale aggression may now be increasingly to *secure* a win rather than to achieve it. Just to be clear on an important point, this in no way vitiates the recurrent insistence of land combatants that only U.S. ground forces can administer the final blow should an enemy refuse to knuckle under in the face of withering air attacks against his combat capability.[31] Nor does it challenge the equally valid point made by surface warriors that the object of future land warfare should be to make close-in killing "a coup de grace rather than a bloody battle of attrition."[32] The question, however, concerns what measures now make the most sense for doing the hard work needed to position those U.S. ground troops so they can deliver the coup de grace, should one be required, both rapidly and with minimal risk to their own survival.

In this respect, there is growing ground for maintaining that a fundamental change has begun to take place in the long-familiar relationship between air and land forces when it comes to defeating large-scale attacks by enemy armored and mechanized units. In and of itself, that nascent change may or may not add up to a full-fledged "revolution in military affairs." Without question, however, it attests to a quantum improvement in the strategic effectiveness of American air power in all services when compared to the leverage of more traditional surface force elements in modern war. That, perhaps more than anything, is the essence of the transformation that has taken place in the capability of the American air weapon since Vietnam.

[31] See, for example, the comment by since-retired Army Lieutenant General Jay Garner to this effect in Tony Capaccio, "Army Readies for Defense Review Food Fight with Air Advocates," *Defense Week*, November 18, 1996, p. 15.

[32] Brigadier General Robert H. Scales, Jr., USA, *Certain Victory: The U.S. Army in the Gulf War*, Washington, D.C., Brassey's, 1994, p. 367.

Acronyms

AAA	antiaircraft artillery
ACC	Air Combat Command
ACM	air combat maneuvering
ACMI	air combat maneuvering instrumentation
AEF	Air Expeditionary Force
AFB	Air Force Base
AFSPC	Air Force Space Command
AFV	armored fighting vehicle
ALB	AirLand Battle
ALCM	air-launched cruise missile
ALFA	Air-Land Forces Application
AMRAAM	advanced medium-range air-to-air missile
AOR	area of responsibility
APC	armored personnel carrier
ARM	antiradiation missile
ARVN	Army of the Republic of Vietnam
ATACMS	Army tactical missile system
ATO	Air Tasking Order
AWACS	airborne warning and control system
BAI	battlefield air interdiction
BDA	battle-damage assessment
BVR	beyond visual range
C4ISR	command, control, communications, computers and information, surveillance, and reconnaissance
CALCM	conventional air-launched cruise missile
CAOC	Combined Air Operations Center

CAP	combat air patrol
CAS	close air support
CBU	cluster bomb unit
CEA	circular error average
CENTAF	Central Command Air Forces
CENTCOM	U.S. Central Command
CIA	Central Intelligence Agency
CINC	commander in chief
CINCCENT	CINC U.S. Central Command
CINCPAC	CINC U.S. Pacific Command
CINCPACFLT	CINC U.S. Pacific Fleet
CINCSPACE	CINC U.S. Space Command
DACT	dissimilar air combat training
DMPI	desired mean point of impact
DMSP	Defense Meteorological Support Program
DMZ	demilitarized zone
DOC	Designed Operational Capability
DRV	Democratic Republic of Vietnam
DSCS	Defense Satellite Communications System
DSP	Defense Support Program
ECM	electronic countermeasures
ELINT	electronic intelligence
EPW	enemy prisoner of war
EUCOM	U.S. European Command
FAC	forward air controller
FLIR	forward-looking infrared
FLOT	Forward Line of Troops
FM	Field Manual
FOFA	Follow-On Forces Attack
FSCL	fire support coordination line
FSD	full-scale development
GAM	GPS-aided munition
GATS	GPS-aided targeting system
GCI	ground-controlled intercept
GPS	global positioning system
GWAPS	Gulf War Air Power Survey
HARM	high-speed antiradiation missile
HUD	head-up display
IADS	integrated air defense system
IAF	Israeli Air Force
ICBM	intercontinental ballistic missile
IDF	Israeli Defense Forces
IFF	identification, friend or foe

IQAF	Iraqi Air Force
IRSTS	infrared search and tracking system
ISR	information, surveillance, and reconnaissance
JCS	Joint Chiefs of Staff
JDAM	joint direct-attack munition
JFACC	joint-force air component commander
JFLCC	joint-force land component commander
JSOW	joint standoff weapon
JSTARS	joint surveillance target attack radar system
JTIDS	joint tactical information distribution system
KFOR	Kosovo peacekeeping force
KLA	Kosovo Liberation Army
KTO	Kuwaiti theater of operations
LANTIRN	low-altitude navigation and targeting infrared for night
LGB	laser-guided bomb
MACV	Military Assistance Command, Vietnam
MAGTF	Marine Air-Ground Task Force
MANPADS	man-portable air defense systems
MAWTS	Marine Aviation Weapons and Tactics Squadron
MCAS	Marine Corps Air Station
MCM	Multi-Command Manual
MLRS	multiple-launch rocket system
MRC	major regional contingency
MTI	moving target indicator
NAS	Naval Air Station
NATO	North Atlantic Treaty Organization
NBC	nuclear, biological, and chemical
NIMA	National Imagery and Mapping Agency
NSC	National Security Council
NVA	North Vietnamese Army
NVAF	North Vietnamese Air Force
OMG	Operational Maneuver Group
OPORD	operations order
PACAF	Pacific Air Forces
PGM	precision-guided munition
PLO	Palestine Liberation Organization
POL	petroleum, oil, and lubricants
PT	patrol torpedo (boat)
RAAF	Royal Australian Air Force
RAF	Royal Air Force
RDF	Rapid Deployment Force
RPV	remotely piloted vehicle
SAC	Strategic Air Command

SACEUR	Supreme Allied Commander Europe
SAM	surface-to-air missile
SAR	synthetic aperture radar
SEAD	suppression of enemy air defenses
SHAPE	Supreme Headquarters Allied Powers Europe
SIGINT	signals intelligence
SIPRNET	secret internet protocol routed network
SLAM	standoff land-attack missile
SPEAR	Strike Projection Evaluation and Anti-Air Warfare Research
SWC	Space Warfare Center
TAC	Tactical Air Command
TACC	Tactical Air Control Center
TAF	tactical air forces
TALD	tactical air-launched decoy
TF	Task Force
TISEO	Target Identification System, Electro-Optical
TLAM	Tomahawk land-attack missile
TOT	time on target
TOW	tube-launched, optically tracked, wire-guided
TRADOC	Training and Doctrine Command
UAV	unmanned air vehicle
UHF	ultra-high frequency
UN	United Nations
USA	U.S. Army
USAF	U.S. Air Force
USAFE	U.S. Air Forces in Europe
USMC	U.S. Marine Corps
USN	U.S. Navy
VID	visual identification
WCMD	wind-corrected munitions dispenser
WSEP	Weapons System Evaluation Program

Index

CORNELL STUDIES IN SECURITY AFFAIRS

A series edited by
Robert J. Art
Robert Jervis
Stephen M. Walt

Report to JFK: The Skybolt Crisis in Perspective, by Richard E. Neustadt

The Sacred Cause: Civil-Military Conflict over Soviet National Security, 1917–1992, by Thomas M. Nichols

Liberal Peace, Liberal War: American Politics and International Security, by John M. Owen IV

Bombing to Win: Air Power and Coercion in War, by Robert A. Pape

A Question of Loyalty: Military Manpower in Multiethnic States, by Alon Peled

Inadvertent Escalation: Conventional War and Nuclear Risks, by Barry R. Posen

The Sources of Military Doctrine: France, Britain, and Germany between the World Wars, by Barry R. Posen

Dilemmas of Appeasement: British Deterrence and Defense, 1934–1937, by Gaines Post, Jr.

Crucible of Beliefs: Learning, Alliances, and World Wars, by Dan Reiter

Eisenhower and the Missile Gap, by Peter J. Roman

The Domestic Bases of Grand Strategy, edited by Richard Rosecrance and Arthur Stein

Societies and Military Power: India and Its Armies, by Stephen Peter Rosen

Winning the Next War: Innovation and the Modern Military, by Stephen Peter Rosen

Fighting to a Finish: The Politics of War Termination in the United States and Japan, 1945, by Leon V. Sigal

Alliance Politics, by Glenn H. Snyder

The Ideology of the Offensive: Military Decision Making and the Disasters of 1914, by Jack Snyder

Myths of Empire: Domestic Politics and International Ambition, by Jack Snyder

The Militarization of Space: U.S. Policy, 1945–1984, by Paul B. Stares

The Nixon Administration and the Making of U.S. Nuclear Strategy, by Terry Terriff

Causes of War: Power and the Roots of Conflict, by Stephen Van Evera

Mortal Friends, Best Enemies: German-Russian Cooperation after the Cold War, by Celeste A. Wallander

The Origins of Alliances, by Stephen M. Walt

Revolution and War, by Stephen M. Walt

The Tet Offensive: Intelligence Failure in War, by James J. Wirtz

The Elusive Balance: Power and Perceptions during the Cold War, by William Curti Wohlforth

Deterrence and Strategic Culture: Chinese-American Confrontations, 1949–1958, by Shu Guang Zhang